ROGER JENNINGS'

Database
Workshop

Microsoft®
Transaction
Server 2.0

ROGER JENNINGS'

Database
Workshop

Microsoft® Transaction Server 2.0

Steven D. Gray

Rick A. Lievano

Roger Jennings, Series Editor

SAMS
PUBLISHING

201 West 103rd Street
Indianapolis, Indiana 46290

Copyright © 1997 by Sams Publishing

International Standard Book Number: 0-672-31130-5

Library of Congress Catalog Card Number: 97-66948

2000   99   98   97   4   3   2   1

Interpretation of the printing code: the rightmost double-digit number is the year of the book's printing; the rightmost single-digit, the number of the book's printing. For example, a printing code of 96-1 shows that the first printing of the book occurred in 1996.

Composed in Utopia and MCPdigital by Macmillan Computer Publishing

Printed in the United States of America

President, Sams Publishing:	*Richard K. Swadley*
Publishing Manager:	*Rosemarie Graham*
Director of Marketing:	*Kelli S. Spencer*
Product Marketing Manager:	*Wendy Gilbride*
Assistant Marketing Managers:	*Jennifer Pock*
	Rachel Wolfe

Acquisitions Editor
Elaine Brush

Development Editor
Kristi Asher

Software Development Specialist
John Warriner

Production Editor
June Waldman

Indexer
Tina Trettin

Technical Reviewer
Stephen Loy

Editorial Coordinators
Mandie Rowell
Katie Wise

Technical Edit Coordinator
Lorraine Schaffer

Resource Coordinators
Deborah Frisby
Charlotte Clapp

Editorial Assistants
Carol Ackerman
Andi Richter
Rhonda Tinch-Mize

Cover Designer
Aren Howell

Book Designer
Sandra Schroeder

Copy Writer
David Reichwein

Production Team Supervisors
Brad Chinn
Andrew Stone

Production
Betsy Deeter
Michael Dietsch
Marcia Deboy
Cynthia Fields
Tim Osborn
Carl Pierce
Maureen West

Dedication

To Emma.—S.G.

To Jennifer and Nicolas for your love, patience, and understanding. —R.L.

Overview

Contents

Part III   Microsoft Transaction Server Components   161

10   Understanding Microsoft Transaction Server Components **163**

Preparation: Understanding Stateless versus Stateful Components 164

Stateful Version of a Customer Component 165

The Disadvantages of Stateful Components in Client/Server
Applications 167

Stateless Version of a Customer Component 170

Advantages of Stateless Components in Client/Server Applications .. 171

Task: Working with Component Transactions 173

Understanding Context Objects 173

Communicating to Microsoft Transaction Server through Context
Objects 174

Obtaining a Reference to `IObjectContext` 175

Enabling Transactions in Transaction Server Explorer 176

Inheriting a Parent's Transactional Context 176

Making Components Microsoft Transaction Server Friendly 177

Implementing the `IObjectControl` Interface 178

Safe References 179

Programmatic Component Security 179

Sharing Data Between Component Instances 180

Understanding Threading Models 181

Task: Viewing Component-Threading Models from Transaction Server
Explorer 184

Workshop Wrap-Up 185

Next Steps 185

11   Implementing Components in Visual Basic **187**

Using Real-World Components 188

Preparation: Knowing When to Use Visual Basic 188

Task: Creating an ActiveX DLL Project 189

Task: Importing the Common Data Access Routines 191

Setting the Project's References 192

Task: Adding New Class Modules to the Project 193

Importing the Remaining Beckwith Components 194

Task: Adding Methods to Class Modules 195

Task: Adding MTS-Specific Code to Your Components 198

Implementing the `IObjectControl` Interface 198

Accessing an Object's Context with the `GetObjectContext()`
Method 200

Task: Implementing Data Retrieval in Components 200

Calling the Common Data Access Routines from the `Alumnus`
Component 201

Implementing Data Access for the `Enrollment` Component 203

Acknowledgments

First and foremost I'd like to thank my wife, Emma, for tolerating my seemingly endless hours typing away at the computer. I'd like to thank Sams Publishing, and in particular Elaine Brush, our acquisitions editor, for giving me the opportunity to write about Microsoft Transaction Server—something I have been wanting to do from the moment I started playing with the beta of this wonderful piece of software technology.

I must also acknowledge those who have helped me during my long relationship with personal computers. Thanks to my grandfather who brought home that Apple][the summer before second grade and started it all, and thanks to my other grandfather who helped me buy my own Apple computer when I was 12. I am also grateful to my two wonderful computer science professors at Pacific University, Doug Ryan and Shaw Zavoshy, who both so excellently prepared me for a great career in software. You have all helped me enormously, and I am in your debt.

And finally to my parents, thanks for all of your support and encouragement over the years.

—S.G.

I'd like to promise my understanding wife, Jennifer, that in the next few months I'll spend as much time with her and Nicolas as I did with this book during its development. A million thanks and my eternal gratitude are in order for her constant support. I'd also like to thank Steve for stepping up to the plate when Nicolas decided to make an early appearance. Finally, I'd like to thank my parents for putting up with my nagging and buying me that TI-99/4A years ago. The investment paid off.

—R.L.

We'd also like to thank our colleagues at RDA who helped with the shaping of this book, including Don Awalt and Mike Besso, and special thanks to Eric Layne for his help and for tolerantly listening to us talk about nothing other than Transaction Server and this book for the past three months during lunch.

About the Authors

Steven D. Gray began programming on personal computers at the age of seven, when he taught himself BASIC and machine language on an Apple][computer. Beginning at age 14, he developed database applications for clients of a small personal computer consulting company. After graduating with a bachelor of science degree from Pacific University in Forest Grove, Oregon, Steven began writing client/server applications full-time on Windows platforms, using the latest Microsoft tools and technologies. He currently works as a consultant for RDA Consultants, Ltd., in the Washington, D.C., area, architecting and implementing advanced, large-scale client/server applications. Steven is a Microsoft Certified Solution Developer. You can reach him at
`sgray@mnsinc.com`.

Rick A. Lievano has been developing client/server solutions for the past four years. Although most of his work has been on the Windows platform, Rick has recently introduced client/server development concepts into Internet/intranet applications. Before the Internet changed everyone's lives, Rick's primary focus was on building advanced client/server applications using Visual C++ and the Microsoft Foundation Classes. As a consultant for RDA Consultants, Ltd., Rick has helped his clients transition legacy processes to traditional client/server and Internet architectures. Rick is a Microsoft Certified Solution Developer. You can reach him at
`rick@lievano.com`.

Roger Jennings is a principal of Oakleaf Systems, a northern California consulting firm specializing in Windows client/server database and digital video applications. Roger is the best-selling author of Sams Publishing's *Access 2 Developer's Guide* and *Database Developer's Guide with Visual Basic 4*. He has contributed to the *Microsoft Developer Network* CD-ROM and *Microsoft Developer News*. Roger was a member of the beta-test team for Microsoft Windows 3.1 and 95; Windows NT 3.1, 3.5, 3.51, and 4.0 (Workstation and Server); Exchange Server; SQL Server 6.0 and 6.5; Proxy Server; ActiveMovie; Media Server; and every release of Access and Visual Basic. Roger is also a contributing editor for the *Visual Basic Programmer's Journal.*

Tell Us What You Think!

As a reader, you are the most important critic and commentator of our books. We value your opinion and want to know what we're doing right, what we could do better, what areas you'd like to see us publish in, and any other words of wisdom you're willing to pass our way. You can help us make strong books that meet your needs and give you the computer guidance you require.

If you prefer the World Wide Web, check out our site at `http://www.mcp.com`.

> **Note** If you have a technical question about this book, call the technical support line at 317-581-3833.

As the team leader of the group that created this book, I welcome your comments. You can fax, e-mail, or write me directly to let me know what you did or didn't like about this book—as well as what we can do to make our books stronger. Here's the information:

FAX: 317-581-4669

E-mail: `enterprise_mgr@sams.mcp.com`

Mail: Rosemarie Graham
           Sams Publishing
           201 W. 103rd Street
           Indianapolis, IN 46290

Introduction

About This Book

Microsoft Transaction Server (MTS) acts as the "plumbing" for building robust *n*-tier client/server database applications on Microsoft operating systems. MTS provides a host of features that developers have traditionally created from scratch for each system. These features include distributed transactions, security, thread management, and resource pooling. In recent pilot projects MTS reduced by more than 40 percent the development effort required to create an *n*-tier client/server application.

MTS's most important feature is the management of complex distributed transactions across multiple servers. Transaction management is a huge, $50 billion industry currently dominated by IBM and Tandem. MTS is Microsoft's first significant entry into this enterprise market.

As part of the *Roger Jennings' Database Workshop* series, this book helps you acquire the skills necessary for success as a database professional. This book supplements the MTS product documentation and fills the enormous information gaps created as a result of the developer community's minimal levels of support for MTS.

The book presents a granular approach to learning. Tasks in each chapter enable you to learn specific skills quickly and easily and to apply new concepts almost immediately. *Roger Jennings' Database Workshop: Microsoft Transaction Server* uses the comfortable and familiar task-driven "interface" that you experience throughout the series.

This book strives to isolate and highlight the truly necessary MTS technologies and to give more advanced readers the opportunity to explore additional topics in special chapters. This book contains significant discussions on major topics such as Microsoft's Component Object Model (COM) and Distributed Component Object Model (DCOM), the Internet, distributed transaction processing, Java, the C++ Active Template Library, and the Microsoft Active Platform.

Who Should Read This Book?

The primary audience for this book is the full-time programmer, although some chapters include topics that are applicable to IT administration. These topics include deployment of MTS applications, security, and administration.

The minimum skills you need to benefit from this book include basic database skills, two-tier client/server experience, and competency in at least one mainstream programming language (for example, C++, Visual Basic, or Java).

MTS 2.0 requires you to have Windows NT 4.0+ or Windows 95+. Client applications that run outside the MTS environment can also use Windows 95. MTS 2.0 also requires Microsoft SQL Server or Oracle database; however, future releases of MTS will support additional databases.

You also need a programming language that can create COM objects. Although several such languages are available, the most popular are Visual C++, Visual Basic, and Visual J++ (Java).

How to Read This Book

This book has seven parts, beginning with core concepts such as COM, simple transaction concepts, and the features of MTS. Subsequent parts move on to more complex concepts such as transactional components, remoting client applications, Web-based clients, and advanced administration.

➤ In Part I, "Setting Up Shop," you learn the MTS basics, including its features, the architectures of client/server applications, transactions, and Microsoft's COM technology.

➤ In Part II, "Installing and Using Microsoft Transaction Server," you begin to get your feet wet by installing MTS on a server, exploring its interfaces, installing sample COM components under its control, and setting up security.

➤ In Part III, "Microsoft Transaction Server Components," you first learn the requirements for building MTS-friendly components and then you build components in three languages: Visual Basic, C++, and Java. These components use the Beckwith College sample database, which is also used by the other books in this series.

➤ In Part IV, "Creating Microsoft Transaction Server Client Applications," you complete the sample client/server system by using Visual Basic to write a client application that drives the components from Part III. You also learn how to create remote clients using Microsoft's DCOM technology.

➤ In Part V, "Integrating Microsoft Transaction Server and the Internet," you leverage the components from Part III to create a Web-based thin client using Microsoft's Internet Information Server and its Active Server Pages scripting environment. You build a functionally equivalent front end to the fat client developed in Part IV.

➤ In Part VI, "Advanced Microsoft Transaction Server Administration," you take advantage of advanced MTS features such as support for multiple MTS servers and the monitoring and tuning capabilities. You use the tasks in these chapters to refine the client/server application you developed in the previous parts.

➤ In Part VII, "Working with the Software Development Kit," you take advantage of the MTS SDK to programmatically script MTS's configuration and use the SDK's sample applications to listen in on MTS events. Both of these features extend your control over the MTS runtime environment.

➤ The appendixes in Part VIII provide the details necessary to install and configure the sample database used throughout the book and the entire *Roger Jennings' Database Workshop* series. The component reference in Appendix C is a handy guide to the methods implemented by the components you create in Part III.

> **Tip**   You will benefit more from this book if you start with the appendixes, where you learn about the Beckwith College database system and how to install it into a SQL Server environment. The sample database is necessary for the coding of components that begins in Part III.

Although the parts are meant to be read in order, you can read many of the chapters within the parts out of order. The tasks in each chapter are self-contained. When the output of one chapter depends on the input of another, the book's companion CD-ROM contains full source code and binary executables, eliminating the need to completely finish one chapter before beginning another.

This book also contains many notes and tips, which provide helpful and interesting information as you develop the Beckwith College sample client/server system, and cautions, which advise you against dangerous actions.

Menu choices use the vertical bar separator; for example, File | Open. In addition, the bold, underlined characters you see throughout the text are accelerator keys for menu choices. Reserved words are set in `bold monospaced` type; names of objects, packages, methods, and other code-related terms appear in `standard monospaced` type; words that you type appear in **bold** type.

The Tools You Need

You need the following tools and products to develop the sample application and run it under MTS control:

➤ Windows NT Workstation 4.0+, Windows NT Server 4.0+, or Windows 95+

➤ One of the following:

    ➤ Microsoft Transaction Server version 2.0—This product is part of Windows NT Enterprise Edition, as well as Internet Information Server 4.0.

    ➤ Microsoft Transaction Server version 1.x—This product is available as part of the Visual Studio 97 Enterprise Edition product.

➤ Microsoft SQL Server version 6.5+—This product is available in a standalone version from Microsoft or as part of Visual Studio 97. A 120-day evaluation trial version is available for download from Microsoft's Web site.

➤ Microsoft Internet Information Server version 4.x—The core of this product is bundled with Windows NT.

➤ One or more of the following development tools; they are available separately or as part of Visual Studio 97 Enterprise Edition. (Note that most of the sample components are written in Visual Basic.)

  ➤ Visual Basic 5.0

  ➤ Visual C++ 5.0

  ➤ Visual J++ 1.1

PART I

Setting Up Shop

CHAPTER 1

Exploring Microsoft Transaction Server

Microsoft Transaction Server (MTS), formerly a $2,000 standalone Microsoft product, is now an integral part of the Windows NT operating system. But what exactly is MTS, and what does it do?

You can use MTS for building multitier, distributed client/server system on components that conform to the Component Object Model (COM). MTS provides all the client/server "plumbing" code that enables systems to operate efficiently. MTS eliminates the need for developers of client/server systems to build all this plumbing code from scratch. One of MTS's primary goals is to simplify the creation and deployment of large-scale client/server systems, which also saves time and money.

Chapter 1 explores the MTS features that contribute to this overall goal of simplicity and collectively define the MTS plumbing. Each section examines a feature from a general perspective and provides pointers to later chapters that discuss the feature in detail. The chapter closes with some forecasts for the future of MTS as Microsoft adds new features and integrates it with future versions of Windows NT and Internet Information Server 4.0.

What Is Microsoft Transaction Server?

At its simplest, MTS is a runtime environment executing under Windows NT. The latest version of MTS, version 2.0, also runs in a limited fashion under Windows 95. The MTS runtime environment exposes functionality that your client/server system code can use for its plumbing. Additionally, the MTS runtime also eases the administration of client/server applications.

MTS is best suited for creating multitier client/server and Web-based applications. The usual subsystems of a three-tier system appear in Figure 1.1.

Figure 1.1.

The traditional three-tier model.

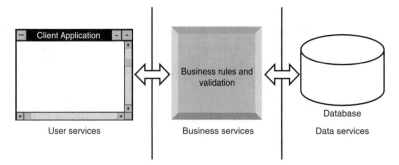

| User services | Business services | Data services |

➤ Data services—Routines that load and store data into databases. On most PC-based client/server systems, the databases are relational and use the Structured Query Language (SQL) for data manipulation. Data service code etreats data at this level as simple data types, devoid of business semantics.

> **Note** *Business semantics* are the logic and rules you apply to data.

➤ Business services—Modules in this subsystem are responsible for using the Data services code to manipulate data. The code in the Business services layer attaches business rules, data validation, and other business semantics to the data.

➤ User services—This subsystem is the end-user application that exposes the graphical interface to the data. User services code is a client of Business services— that is, Business services apply business semantics to the code before it reaches the end user through User services. This approach prevents the user from modifying the data beyond the constraints of the business, tightening the integrity of the system. For example, in a banking application, Business services code might process rules to prevent a user from transferring more money than is available from one account to another. The author of User services provides the GUI to transfer money, but doesn't worry about the limitations of that action.

> **Note** For more details on the partitioning and architectures of client/server systems, see Chapter 2, "Laying the Foundation: Client/Server Architectures."

Several tools are available to help developers rapidly construct user interfaces. Some of the more popular are Microsoft's Visual Basic and Visual C++, Borland's Delphi, and Powersoft's PowerBuilder. This user-interface code belongs in the User services subsystem domain.

In addition, several popular database systems (including Microsoft SQL Server, Oracle, and Informix) support the Data services layer. These databases expose a SQL interface to retrieve and store data persistently to a computer's disk.

Although developers have had the benefit of great tools for Data services (databases) and great tools for User services (for example, Visual Basic), before MTS no useful development tools were available for either Business services or communication among the three subsystems for PC-based client/server systems.

Before they had MTS, developers used tools like Visual C++ to implement Business services. But Business services is really more than just business rules and syntax checking; it also includes activities such as

➤ Coordinating concurrent transactions and data access among multiple simultaneous users

➤ Checking security permissions granted to different types of users

➤ Managing server resources such as database connections, processes, and threads

➤ Coordinating communication among all three subsystems from the database to the client application

Developers of client/server systems based on PC hardware had to implement these features from scratch; the entire infrastructure had to be in place before they could implement business-specific logic, such as rules and syntax validation. Consequently, development cycles for client/server systems were long, and the code in Business services was often complex and inflexible. MTS changed this picture.

MTS handles the plumbing code contained by Business services (see Figure 1.2). MTS enables developers to skip the step of writing basic services and to concentrate on business-specific logic. MTS generally reduces development times for client/server systems and encourages developers to spend more time on improving the business logic of the system.

Figure 1.2.

Development tools for each subsystem of a three-tier client/ server system.

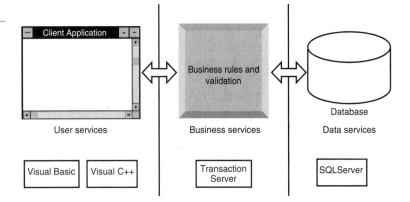

The Role of MTS in Client/Server Applications

So what role does MTS play in a client/server application? Typically, MTS runs silently on one or more server computers and provides the following services:

➤ Component transactions—MTS coordinates and monitors the transactional state of components running under its control as they interact with various transactional systems, such as databases.

➤ Object brokering—MTS acknowledges requests for object creation from remote clients. MTS coordinates the creation, maintenance, and destruction of COM component instances and the threads that execute inside them.

➤ Resource pooling—MTS optimally uses server resources by creating a pool of resources and sharing them with multiple clients. By creating a pool and sharing, more clients can effectively use a finite number of server resources. Examples of server resources include thread, objects, processes, and database connections.

➤ Security—MTS provides a flexible security model to control access to your components at runtime.

➤ Administration—MTS enables you to change the configuration of your client/ server system easily during and after its deployment, without the need to change the code of the system.

Later sections of this chapter examine these features in more detail, and the following chapters focus on how to implement code to take advantage of these features.

For the most part MTS lacks a user interface, but instead provides its services behind the scenes during the execution of your application. You write components—COM objects—that invoke the services exposed by the MTS runtime environment. This programming model is similar to interfacing with an operating system.

A single user-interface application—Transaction Server Explorer, which is now integrated as part of the new Microsoft Management Console—administers MTS configuration during both the development and deployment phases of construction. You can use Transaction Server Explorer to define and set up the system's configuration, as well as to monitor the system and make changes to the configuration while it is running.

Component-Based Architectures

To expose a common set of features, a system like MTS needs to expose a clean interface through which client applications can use its services. For example, Windows 95 and Windows NT use the DLL, C-based Win32 API. The Win32 API is a set of hundreds of well-defined methods that applications invoke to use the services of the Windows operating system. Any language capable of calling methods in a DLL can communicate with the operating system.

The interface mechanism in MTS—the COM—is more advanced than that in Win32. COM is a Microsoft binary standard for components and is the basis of several Microsoft technologies such as Object Linking and Embedding (OLE) and ActiveX. MTS exposes its functionality through COM objects, and for the most part MTS expects its clients to be COM objects as well.

Consequently, if you want the Business services layer of your client/server systems to take advantage of MTS, you must develop the layer with COM objects.

This restriction is actually advantageous because writing COM components yields many benefits, including

➤ Language independence—You can write COM objects in many languages, and you can mix and match components of several languages in the same system.

➤ Client flexibility—You can use COM objects for any client application that can conform to the COM standard. Therefore, client applications written in Visual C++ or Visual Basic, or Web-based clients written in Active Server Pages (ASP), can use exactly the same set of objects.

➤ Location independence—You can easily configure COM objects to run almost anywhere in the client/server system. Objects can run in the same process as the client application, in a separate process on the same machine, or on a remote machine with the help of Distributed COM (DCOM). COM takes care of the details of where the component lives, so client code doesn't have to change if you move the components to a different process.

The Role of Components in a Client/Server System

Components play many roles in the Business services subsystem. Here's a description of some of the roles:

➤ Business object model—Many business systems are analyzed and defined by an object-oriented business model. COM components are a convenient way to represent each object in the model. The COM component contains properties and methods that represent business objects. A typical business object is Customer, which represents name and address information about a particular customer.

➤ Data objects—Many designs of client/server systems require the tight encapsulation of the SQL code necessary to persist the application's data into the database. COM objects, especially those under MTS control, are particularly well suited for this task.

➤ Calculation objects—These objects are typically invisible to the user of the system, and possibly not even exposed to the User services subsystem. Calculation objects define very specific business rules and other business-specific code to perform on data. For example, financial institutions may have a set of COM components that calculate complex interest rates based on sets of loan data. Sales tax calculation is another common example.

Of course, components in the Business services layer can also play other roles and in some cases may not be appropriate at all. However, to take full advantage of the features of MTS, you should consider writing most of your Business services layer as COM components.

MTS Feature: Component Transactions

A *transaction* is a logical unit of work that is either performed in its entirety or not performed at all. Many steps or actions might take place within the scope of a transaction, but at the end of processing, the transaction must either be committed or aborted.

You are probably familiar with the concept of a database transaction in which a series of SQL statements is performed. Then either their entire effect is committed to the database or all the actions are rolled back. In the latter case the state of the database remains as it was before the transition was initiated.

> **Note** For more details on database transactions, see Chapter 3, "Working with Database Transactions."

Component transactions are similar to database transactions, but instead of a transaction encompassing SQL statements, a component transaction encompasses the work of one or more components. MTS provides support for component transactions by monitoring components as they interact with transactional resources such as databases. If the components are running under the context of a transaction and if the transaction is rolled back for some reason, MTS coordinates with the transactional resources to undo the changes made by the components.

Component transactions are particularly useful with databases, although other resources can be transacted as well. One important feature of component transactions is the capability to span a transaction across multiple databases. For example, consider the simple task of moving a record from one database to another (see Figure 1.3).

Figure 1.3.

Moving a record from the Human Resources database to the Sales database.

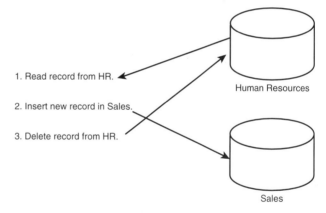

1. Read record from HR.

2. Insert new record in Sales.

3. Delete record from HR.

Human Resources

Sales

Moving a record from one database to another requires three steps:

1. Reading the record from the source database.
2. Inserting the new record into the destination database with the data read in step 1.
3. Deleting the original record from the source database.

You cannot execute these three steps independently. For example, if an error occurs during step 2, but step 3 executes successfully, the net result is that you lose the original record forever.

Another possible problem can occur if the system fails after the execution of step 2 but before the execution of step 3. This scenario leaves you with two records—one in the source database and one in the second, which is not likely to be a desirable condition.

Consider the classic case of transferring money from one account to another. The action might be implemented as moving a record from one database to the other. If an error occurs between steps 2 and 3, money is created—the original amount remains in the source account, and a duplicate amount appears in the destination account.

Most database systems allow the construction of transactions only within the same database. Because databases can reside on different server computers in a network, coordinating a transaction between remote databases is not a simple task. However, MTS provides this powerful service to your components for free with a very straightforward programming model.

> **Note** See Chapter 10, "Understanding Microsoft Transaction Server Components," for more details on transactional components.

> **Caution** MTS 1.1 supports component transactions only when they communicate with Microsoft's SQL Server database. MTS 2.0 also supports Oracle databases, and support for other databases is in development. With MTS, components can coordinate transactions among databases from different vendors.

MTS Feature: Transaction Monitoring

In a heavily used client/server system, many transactions—using transactional components—can be executing at the same time for different clients. Each transaction can succeed or fail. Most of the time transactions succeed, but sometimes they can fail.

MTS enables you to view currently executing transactions, as well as historical transaction statistics. This information is available using the only user-interface application for MTS—Transaction Server Explorer (see Figure 1.4).

Aborted transactions are a sign that something is not working properly in the system. By using MTS to monitor running transactions, you can determine the relative health of your client/server system and fix small problems before they become serious ones.

> **Note** For more details on using Transaction Server Explorer, see Chapter 7, "Using Transaction Server Explorer." For more information on monitoring components and their transactions, see Chapter 21, "Monitoring and Tuning Components."

Figure 1.4.

You can use Transaction Server Explorer to view current and historical transaction statistics.

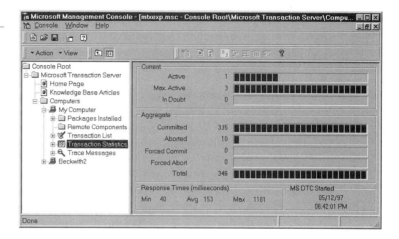

MTS Feature: Object Brokering

By acting as an object broker, the MTS runtime environment services requests made from various clients for instances of your components. When a request for a component instance comes in, MTS takes the following steps:

1. Prepares an environment in which to create the component instance. This environment contains context information related to the state in which the component is being created. A component's context includes transaction information, thread information, security information, and more.

2. Instantiates the object and returns a reference to the client.

3. Maintains the component's instance while the client uses the object. To minimize server resources, MTS may actually destroy the component's instance while the client isn't using it, even though the client still maintains a reference to the object. MTS creates a new component instance after the client resumes its use of the object.

4. Destroys or inactivates the object when the client is finished with it.

Along the way MTS manages the transaction state of the component, if any. If the component aborts the transaction under which it is running, MTS facilitates the rollback of any changes made by the component as well as any changes made by other components running under the same transaction context.

One of the primary advantages of being an object broker is the location independence of the component from its client. The client application doesn't care where the component is running. It is the job of MTS (along with COM) to locate the component and instantiate it and return a reference to the client application. This feature supports dynamic reconfiguration of a client/server system after the development phase. You can change the location from which the object executes without having to change the code of the client application.

Another advantage of object brokering is the capability to support object pooling. *Object pooling* is the concept of creating a finite number of component instances and sharing them among clients, rather than giving every client its own instance.

Object pooling is important, especially when you are trying to write highly scalable systems. Objects take memory, and a server that contains those objects has a finite amount of memory. Therefore, a server can support only a finite number of objects, which limits the number of clients the system can support.

Clients rarely require the services of their object all the time. Therefore, the potential exists for clients to share objects. This approach is known as *object recycling*. Rather than objects being created and destroyed for each client, MTS can create a pool of objects at startup and share the instances as clients need them. Hence object recycling enables many clients to use a relatively small number of objects.

> **Caution** MTS does not currently implement object pooling, but instead creates and destroys objects as needed. Object pooling will be implemented in a future version of MTS.

MTS Feature: Resource Pooling

Objects aside, MTS does provide pooling and automatic management of two critical server resources: threads and database connections. Additionally, the MTS Software Development Kit (SDK) provides the infrastructure for third parties to write interfaces for pooling resources that MTS does not natively support. For example, you can pool special connections to mainframe sessions under MTS control, enabling several clients to share a limited number of mainframe connections.

The MTS runtime environment handles threading for you. When you write components, you do not have to worry about the issues that arise when you allow multiple threads to execute inside your components. With MTS you write your components as if they are single threaded, and MTS takes care of the rest. MTS employs a pool of threads to make your components respond to client requests quickly.

> **Note** To learn more about threads and how they affect component development, see Chapter 10.

Database connection pooling is a significant feature of MTS. A database connection represents a communication link between a client application and a database. Many traditional client/server applications maintain a unique database connection for each client on the system (see Figure 1.5).

Figure 1.5.

A classic client/server system with a database connection for each client.

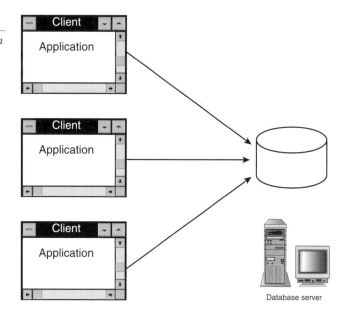

If you place all of your database code into Business services components (the preferred configuration in a three-tier client/server application), MTS coordinates the communication between the components and the database over a finite set of preestablished connections (see Figure 1.6). This type of connection pooling enables potentially hundreds of components (and hence hundreds of clients) to access the database with perhaps only a dozen database connections. The resulting reduction in demand for server resources such as database connections translates into a more scalable system.

Figure 1.6.

Using MTS to pool database connections.

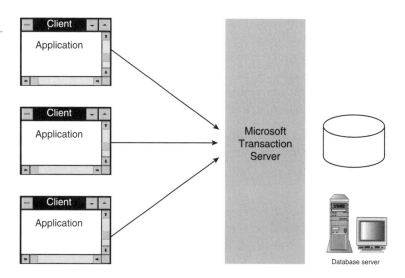

MTS Feature: Security

Another important feature of MTS is security. MTS provides a flexible but powerful security model that enables you to write very secure components for your system, protecting sensitive data from improper access.

The MTS security model is powerful enough to handle most, if not all, security requirements of a client/server system. MTS provides two modes of component security: declarative and programmatic.

Declarative Security

Declarative security enables you to grant or deny access to any of the components running under MTS control. Security access is granted at two levels:

➤ Component-level security—Users are either granted or denied access to the entire component.

➤ Interface-level security—Users are either granted or denied access to a component's interface. An *interface* is simply a collection of one or more methods. Taken to its extreme, a component can expose a separate interface for each method, so you can even set security at the method level.

The MTS declarative security model checks security only as a user crosses the "door" into the MTS runtime environment. The components under MTS control do not act with the identity and permissions of their client. Instead, the components take on the identity and permissions assigned to the MTS server process that contains them (see Figure 1.7).

Checking and verifying the security of the client's identity when it calls into MTS components simplifies system administration. In the MTS model, components running under MTS control are assigned their own identity, and this identity is then granted access to various server resources such as files and databases. Full access is usually acceptable. The code inside the components can then restrict the actions that the client can perform against the server's resources. Components expose only appropriate actions to clients through their methods.

During deployment of the system, an administrator uses Transaction Server Explorer to configure who has access to various components, thus defining who has access to the server's resources. The key is that only MTS has to be configured to grant access to the system's users. The database and other server resources do not need to be administered because all their clients are secure MTS components.

> **Note**   For more information about declarative security and how it is configured with the Transaction Server Explorer, see Chapter 9, "Configuring Component Security."

Figure 1.7.

The system checks client identity when it calls into a MTS component.

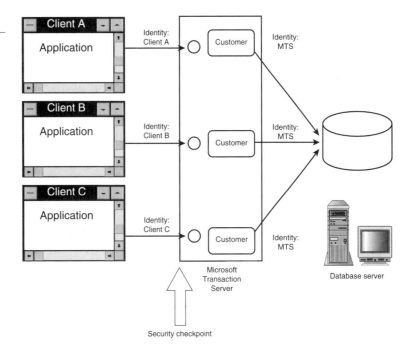

Security checkpoint

Programmatic Security

Sometimes simply preventing a user from accessing a component or one of its interfaces doesn't complete the security picture. Occasionally, you need the behavior of a component to change based on its client. For this situation, MTS includes programmatic security as part of its security model.

Programmatic security enables a component running under MTS control to ask the MTS runtime environment who its client is. A component can alter its behavior based on the response.

However, when a component asks MTS who its client is, MTS does not respond with the actual Windows user ID. To do so would tightly couple the code inside the component with the users of the system. And as users come and go over the lifetime of the system, the component would have to be modified and redeployed many times. This condition clearly is not acceptable for a robust client/server implementation.

MTS uses the concept of a Role to deal with this type of situation. A *Role* is simply a collection of Windows NT users and groups managed by Transaction Server Explorer (see Figure 1.8). A Role is identified by a label and is similar to a Windows NT group.

Roles are defined during the development of a client/server system. When a component asks for the identity of its caller, MTS responds with the Role under which the user is operating. The component then alters its behavior according to the caller's Role.

Figure 1.8.

Roles are collections of users and groups that are administered by Transaction Server Explorer.

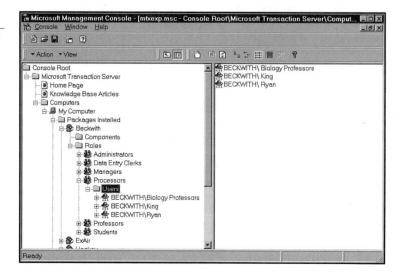

During deployment and maintenance of the system, users and groups are added and removed to the defined Roles of the system by an administrator. Because Roles do not change, you don't need to recode and redeploy the components.

Note Chapter 9 contains more detailed information on programmatic security, and Part III, "Microsoft Transaction Server Components," explains how to implement programmatic security in components written in C++, Visual Basic, and Java.

MTS Feature: Administration

Transaction Server Explorer handles the administration of the middle tier of a client/server system. Transaction Server Explorer is part of the new Microsoft Management Console (MMC), a graphical application that looks like Windows Explorer (see Figure 1.9).

With the MTS Explorer, you can administer the following:

- ➤ Installed components—Configure MTS-controlled components and their component properties
- ➤ Component locations—Specify where components run on the MTS server or other remote servers
- ➤ Transaction monitoring—Display currently active components and their transactions
- ➤ Diagnostic output—Capture and display the output strings that components and other services emit as they execute

➤ Role definition—Create and delete Roles; assign Windows NT users and groups to them

Figure 1.9.

Transaction Server Explorer.

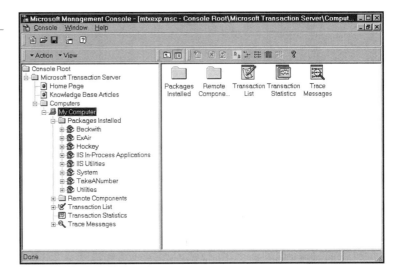

You can use Transaction Server Explorer during both stages of a client/server system: development and deployment. During development Transaction Server Explorer installs components under the MTS runtime environment's control and sets special properties associated with each component, such as whether the component participates in transactions.

During deployment and maintenance of a system Transaction Server Explorer associates users with roles and monitors the execution of the deployed system.

> **Note** For more details on what you can do with Transaction Server Explorer, see Chapter 7.

MTS Feature: Component Deployment and Client Setup

Another time-saving feature of MTS is the client configuration utility it uses to automate the DCOM-related configuration of remote client computers. Prior to MTS, developers had to set up client computers manually or through custom, scripted setup programs. Most of this manual setup requires less-than-obvious changes to each client's system Registry to tell the system where to create remote component instances.

With MTS, after you develop and configure your client/server system, you simply export its configuration into a standalone automatic client setup program. Then you take the setup program to each client and run it once; the client applications that rely on remote MTS components are automatically ready to run. This procedure means that you don't have to learn the internals of DCOM in order to configure your clients.

> **Note** For more details on the client configuration utility, see Chapter 15, "Setting Up Remote Windows Clients Using DCOM."

The Future of Microsoft Transaction Server

This book focuses on how you can immediately take advantage of the features supported by MTS up to and including version 2.0. However, MTS is a product with a long future (at least in terms of PC software lifetimes). MTS in its current state provides an environment from which client/server systems will be able to take advantage of future advancements, provided the systems are built on MTS today.

This section explores some of the directions Microsoft has publicly announced for MTS. Of course, Microsoft has not announced when it will implement these features, and some may never be implemented. However, understanding future features can help you design and implement systems that will live successfully into the next millennium with the help of Microsoft MTS.

> **Tip** For the latest news about MTS, check out its Web site at
> www.microsoft.com/transaction.

Tighter Integration with Internet Information Server

With MTS 2.0, the product is now tightly bundled with the Windows NT operating system as well as with another Microsoft product, Internet Information Server (IIS). The most significant integration aspect between MTS and IIS is the introduction of transactional scripts written with IIS Active Server Pages (ASP). See Chapter 17, "Creating Interactive Web Applications Using Microsoft Transaction Server and Active Server Pages," for tasks that illustrate this concept. Under this new scripting model, an ASP script can participate in a MTS-hosted transaction, right along with MTS components. If any part of the code contained in the script fails, the entire transaction is rolled back.

Dynamic Load Balancing

A large-scale client/server system can have hundreds or even thousands of users. Currently, MTS supports systems that scale to hundreds of users. To support thousands of users, more than one server computer is required. *Load balancing* is the concept of dispersing all active users among the available servers. The two types of load balancing are static and dynamic.

> ➤ Static—In static load balancing, each client computer is configured to communicate with a specific server. If a system has three servers, then a third of the clients are configured for each server.

> ➤ Dynamic—In dynamic load balancing, when client requests come in, MTS and the operating system determine which server is least busy and assign the client request to that server. Client computers do not realize (and do not care) that different servers may be servicing the requests.

MTS and Windows NT currently support static load balancing only. Future versions of these products will also support dynamic load balancing.

Another part of dynamic load balancing is the concept of *failover.* In addition to finding the least-busy server, if a given server goes down, MTS and Windows NT route client requests from the down server to an available up server. Failover support provides uninterrupted service to clients, increasing the stability of the system as a whole. This feature is extremely important for mission-critical applications in which down-server time can have extremely disastrous results. Failover is supported by Microsoft's Cluster Server 1.0 (formerly code-named "Wolfpack").

Code Downloading

Currently, configuring a client to instantiate components remotely under MTS control requires an administrator to visit each client computer and to modify its Registry, either directly or with a custom setup program.

MTS and Windows NT will introduce the concept of code downloading for MTS-controlled components—similar to the code downloading concept currently supported in Microsoft Internet Explorer 3.x. Extending code downloading to MTS components will enable administrators to configure client computers from a central location, which will certainly simplify the process of setting up client/server applications.

Hot Start and Hot Update

In the current version of MTS, when you start a MTS server process that hosts components, the components remain uninstantiated until clients request them. Future versions of MTS will support the notion of *hot start*, where objects are created as soon as a server process is created, making the objects immediately available to client requests. This approach helps to achieve the object-pooling feature discussed earlier in the chapter.

One of the drawbacks of MTS is that when you need to change the configuration of a component under its control, you must shut down the server process that contains the component before you modify its settings. After modification, you must restart the server process. During this time, that portion of the system is offline and unavailable to service client requests.

Future versions of MTS will provide a *hot update* feature, which enables you to modify a component's settings while the server process is running. The system can continue to service client requests while you make the necessary changes.

Workshop Wrap-Up

This chapter explains exactly what MTS is and describes what it does to speed up the development time of component-based client/server applications. You learned about some of the major time-saving plumbing features in MTS, including component transactions, object brokering, resource pooling, security, and administration. You also learned about some of the enhancements Microsoft expects to include in future versions of MTS, as well as how to make sure that the systems you build today can take advantage of these new features.

Next Steps

➤ Before beginning any coding, make sure you have installed and configured the sample database into an installation of Microsoft SQL Server. See the appendixes for more details on the Beckwith College sample database system.

➤ To learn more about component-based client/server architectures, read Chapter 2.

➤ MTS is built on components that follow the Microsoft component standard COM. If you aren't familiar with COM, turn to Chapter 4, "Getting Acquainted with COM."

➤ If you are familiar with client/server architectures and COM, skip to Part II, "Installing and Using Microsoft Transaction Server," to begin working with MTS right away.

CHAPTER 2

Laying the Foundation: Client/Server Architectures

From a software architecture view, client/server computing is the natural extension of modular and component-based software design. This software development approach reduces large and complex problems to manageable chunks (subsystems or components) that are relatively easy to design and implement. After you break a large system into logical subsystems, you can distribute the pieces among one or more computers. In the client/server equation, the client computers request services, and the server computers provide them (Figure 2.1).

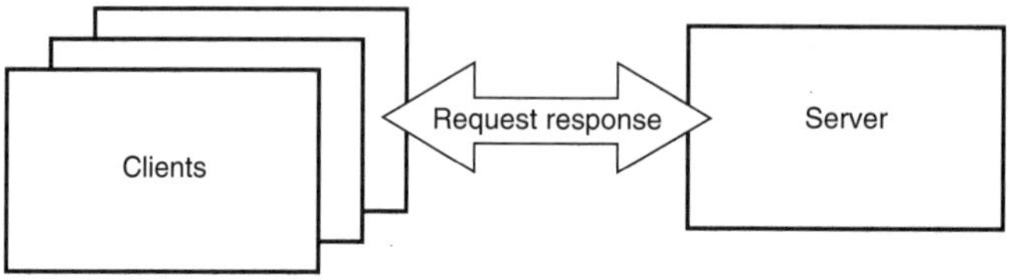

Figure 2.1.

High-level view of a client/server system.

Client/server systems contain at least two components. These components are usually distributed across computers (see Figure 2.2), although a single machine could act as both a client and server. The components are

➤ A front-end application that interacts with the system. This component usually contains a graphical user interface that enables end users to perform their work.

➤ A set of server applications that supply services such as access to data, HTML pages, printers, and files.

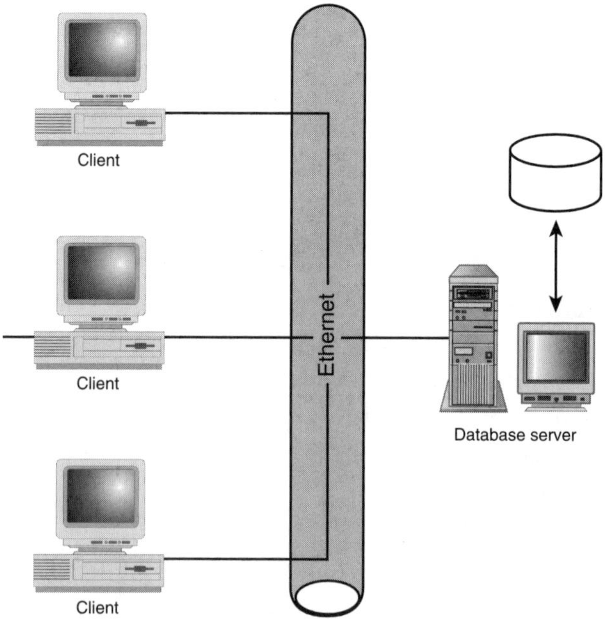

Figure 2.2.

Network view of a client/server system.

This chapter explores the foundations of client/server architectures, focusing on the benefits you can derive from a three-tier Microsoft Transaction Server (MTS) approach. If you already understand client/server architectures and are familiar with the MTS plumbing, you can continue with the remaining introductory chapters in this section or you can jump straight to Part II, "Installing and Using Microsoft Transaction Server."

Client/Server Fundamentals: Understanding Two-Tier Architectures

Developers use a two-tier architecture to implement most client/server systems. Clients communicate directly with the server; either the client or server process can host business rules, although they are usually on the client (Figure 2.3). Widely accepted development environments, such as Visual Basic, promoted this approach because of its simplicity and extensive industry support. For example, technologies such as data-bound controls are based on this architecture.

Figure 2.3.

Typical two-tier client/server configuration.

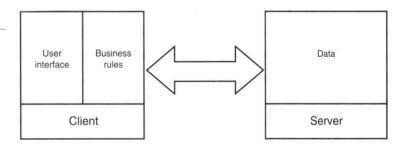

Applications that use a database server tend to rely heavily on the services provided by the database vendor. For example, vendor-provided client software (such as Oracle's SQL*Net) manages client-to-server connectivity.

Understanding Roles: Client

The primary responsibility of the client application is to expose an interface through which end users can send requests to the server. The server in turn may respond to this request with data that the client application can format and display. This type of interaction between computers is the basis of most common networking protocols. For example, when you surf the World Wide Web and request a Uniform Resource Locator (URL) through your browser (client), the specified server eventually responds by returning the requested page (shown in Figure 2.4).

Figure 2.4.

Processing an HTTP request on the Internet.

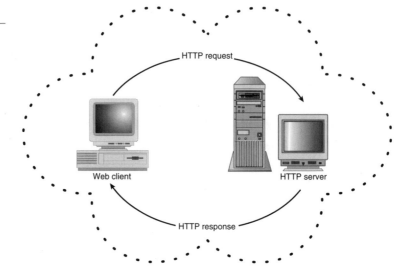

In addition to providing the application's user interface, two-tier clients typically perform validation of user-supplied data, execute the business rules of the system, and submit requests to the server applications. Clients may also need to manage local system resources such as memory, threads, and database connections.

As the complexity of a two-tier application increases, the demands on the client also increase. Clients responsible for executing business rules, performing complex calculations, or massaging result sets obtained from a database server, require substantial resources. To meet increased processing demands, the footprint of a client workstation can easily balloon to that of a small server.

Applications that fit this model are referred to as *fat clients*. These applications usually suffer from complicated or lengthy installations, are difficult to configure or upgrade, become expensive to maintain, and are troublesome to scale upwardly.

Understanding Roles: Server

Servers respond to requests initiated by the client applications. Servers may need to respond to many concurrent requests and to manage the resources required to fulfill them. Server-managed resources include databases, Web sites, files, and printers. The most common types of servers include

➤ Database servers—These servers manage client connections and requests to data. Database servers can also manage security, transaction processing, and backup/ recovery of critical business data. By using stored procedures and triggers, database servers can host a subset of the application's business rules (Figure 2.5).

Figure 2.5.

Two-tier client/server configuration using server-based business rules.

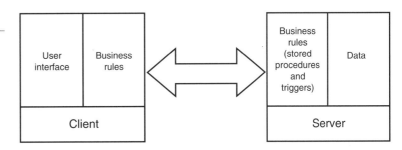

➤ Internet servers—These servers respond to client requests for Internet services such as the Web, FTP, Gopher, or Telnet. Due to the explosive growth of the Web, the most widely used Internet server is the HTTP server (or Web server). The primary responsibility of this server is to return the requested page to the calling client. The page can contain text, tables, images, and virtually any other element. Current versions of these servers, such as Microsoft's Internet Information Server (IIS) and Netscape Enterprise, include full-blown application frameworks that enable developers to build applications that can be hosted on the Internet/intranet.

Building a Conventional Three-Tier Application

Three tier applications are quickly displacing the traditional two-tier applications developers have been designing for years. In two-tier systems the client always handles data presentation, and the server manages the database system. The primary problem of the two-tier system is that the business rules must be implemented on either the server or the client.

When the server implements business rules (by using stored procedures), it can become overloaded by having to process both database requests and the business rules. However, if the client implements the business rules, the architecture can easily grow into the monolithic application reminiscent of the mainframe days. The three-tier client/server architecture provides an additional separation of the business logic from the database and the actual presentation.

Some applications that require gateways to legacy systems or that rely on additional servers are referred to as *three tier*. For example, many Internet/intranet applications are labeled as three tier because of the number of systems involved in a single transaction. In the case of an Internet application that employs a database, a request could involve three physical computers: client, HTTP server, and database server. This physical three-tier design (as shown in Figure 2.6), is not necessarily a logical three-tier system. The "Designing a Three-Tier System" section details the requirements for a logical three-tier architecture.

Figure 2.6.

Network view of a three-tier client/server system.

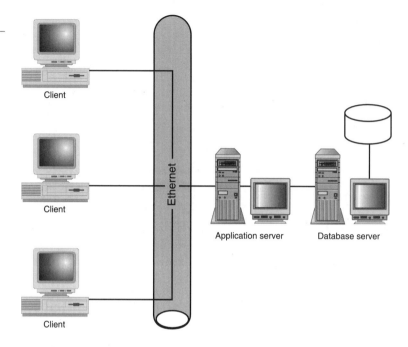

Middleware: The Glue of Three-Tier Architectures

The framework of services required to develop a logical three-tier system is collectively referred to as *middleware*. Although network protocols and data access standards (such as ODBC) are sometimes referred to as middleware, the term defines software that sits between the business applications and the hardware and operating systems. Middleware serves the following functions:

➤ Middleware insulates the applications from unique hardware and operating system interfaces. This approach improves the application's reusability and helps attain platform independence (at least on the server side).

➤ Middleware enables clients to access heterogeneous, distributed data stores. Through middleware, clients can potentially access data contained in legacy systems, desktops, and servers.

➤ Middleware controls and manages access to distributed data through distributed transactions. A single, atomic transaction can span multiple data stores from multiple vendors.

➤ Middleware coordinates concurrency between multiple simultaneous users.

➤ Middleware checks security permissions granted to different types of users.

➤ Middleware coordinates communication between all subsystems— from the database to the client application.

➤ Middleware coordinates object creation, maintenance, and destruction.

Most of these functions were described in Chapter 1, "Exploring Microsoft Transaction Server," as part of MTS. For this reason, MTS can be thought as the "glue," or middleware, of three-tier applications.

Designing a Three-Tier System

Conventional three-tier client/server applications are much more complex than their equivalent two-tier sibling. In general, three-tier applications require more subsystems and involve more issues that can cause the schedules to slip. Because the database server handles so much of the infrastructure of two-tier systems, developers are free to focus on the business logic of their applications. On the other hand, multitier solutions require programmers to develop much of this infrastructure before they write the first line of business-specific code.

The rest of the chapter explores the major infrastructure needs of a multitier system. This section defines the subsystems that make up a three-tier client/server solution (shown in Figure 2.7). The three tiers are

➤ Data services

➤ Business services

➤ User services

Figure 2.7.

The traditional three-tier model.

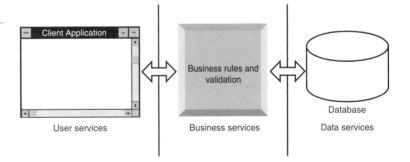

Data Services

The data services subsystem is the functional equivalent of the database subsystem in a two-tier client/server system. As with a two-tier solution, data services encapsulates functions, modules, and components that manipulate persistent data. These modules may consist of stored procedures, triggers, or external data access routines.

In the Windows NT platform, Open Database Connectivity (ODBC) manages most data access. Although developers can use proprietary call-level interfaces (CLI) to access a specific vendor's database, ODBC enables applications to support multiple database management systems (DBMS), or scale up or down to support a specific need. For example, an application can initially support a single user by using the Microsoft Jet database engine (Microsoft Access) and later be deployed to multiple users throughout the enterprise by using Microsoft SQL Server. By using ODBC, the application requires little or no change to the data access code in order to scale.

Business Services

The single biggest distinction between a two-tier and three-tier client/server system is the location of the business rules that govern the behavior of the system. Two-tier applications place these rules in either the client or database server, depending on the need; three-tier systems implement this logic in a subsystem of its own. The result is a highly scalable, robust system and a reduction in the client resource requirements.

Designers must deploy and maintain new applications to support this new subsystem. In reality, these servers could share resources with the database server or even with the clients. However, for optimum performance and manageability, you should use separate servers.

The application logic contained in the business services subsystem includes source code to use the data services subsystem and perform operations on its data. For example, this subsystem applies business rules, data validation, and other business semantics to the data.

When building conventional three-tier systems, the business services subsystem is also responsible for implementing the infrastructure services, or middleware. (Review the previous section for a description of these tasks.)

User Services

Every client/server application requires an interface to its business and data services subsystems. Most user services subsystems today are implemented as graphical front-end applications running under Windows. However, many user services are now being developed using newer Internet technologies. Regardless of how the user interface is exposed, user services code is a client of business services. As mentioned in Chapter 1, business semantics are applied to the data obtained from business services before the data reaches the end user. This approach prevents the user from modifying the data beyond the constraints of the business, thereby tightening the integrity of the system.

Establishing Connectivity

In a two-tier model, the database server and the client access software it provides manage connectivity. Connectivity and data access are performed by simply calling the appropriate CLI or ODBC functions.

By abstracting the data services subsystem away from user services, three-tier systems encounter a problem that doesn't develop in two-tier systems—communication. Many alternatives to using a database vendor communication framework exist, including implementing your own Socket interface, using a third-party comm (communication) library, or leveraging newer object technologies such as the Distributed Component Object Model (DCOM) or the Common Object Request Broker Architecture (CORBA). Neither solution is as simple as the two-tier approach, and each adds a layer of complexity.

Managing Transactions

The DBMS can manage transactions within the confines of a single database system. However, when transactions span multiple databases or components, the transaction management capabilities of a single DBMS no longer suffice. For example, an update operation to an Oracle database, a call to a CICS application, and a delete operation from a Sybase database can participate in a single distributed transaction. The transaction must still conform to the ACID properties (refer to Chapter 3, "Working with Database Transactions"), even though it spans multiple data stores (from different vendors). Transaction monitors have filled this gap by providing atomic transactions across heterogeneous data stores. However, integrating and managing another infrastructure support application can be a difficult task.

Application Performance, Scalability, and Reliability

Well-designed three-tier applications are usually more scalable and more reliable than their equally well-designed two-tier counterparts. With finite resources both on the client and server, three-tier applications scale superbly thanks to the autonomy of the business services subsystem and the resource management capabilities inherent in most middleware. However, the performance of a poorly designed three-tier application is generally no better than that of its two-tier equivalent.

Using Microsoft Transaction Server Plumbing for N-Tier Applications

Most of the infrastructure necessary for a great three-tier client/server application is not trivial to implement. Many functions involve highly complex, elaborate architectures that require system programming skills to implement. MTS does away with the complexities associated with three-tier client/server computing by providing the plumbing that makes this architecture possible. If you're unfamiliar with the benefits and features that make MTS a required component of your next three-tier system, go back to Chapter 1.

MTS provides much of the infrastructure covered in this chapter, as well as a runtime environment required to execute your business logic. MTS is the Microsoft design tool targeted at the "plumbing" code contained by business services. Developers who use MTS can avoid having to write multiple basic services before starting to work on business-specific logic. Consequently, MTS shortens development times for client/server systems and enables developers to spend more time on improving the business logic of the system.

MTS frees developers to concentrate on building the business rules that are specific to their product, rather than on developing infrastructure code. When they work on MTS applications, developers can devote most of their time to designing and implementing the components (objects) that model the business (Figure 2.8).

Figure 2.8.

A MTS application.

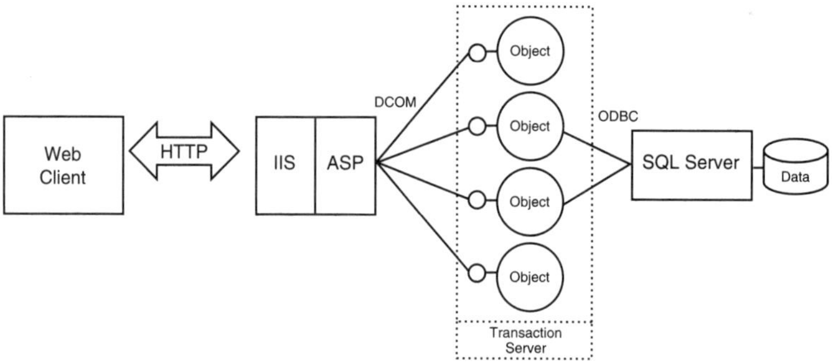

You can write MTS applications to be scalable and highly portable. For example, you can develop and deploy your MTS components along with a Visual Basic front end in a very short time. These components can scale to support a growing number of clients by simply increasing server resources (see Figure 2.9).

As time allows, you can port or Internet enable certain key areas of the application. Because most of your business logic and data access code is isolated from the presentation services layer, porting the application becomes a matter of simply reworking the necessary user-interface components. In many cases you can reuse source code from the Visual Basic version of the application in an Active Server Pages version of the same application. The Beckwith client applications presented in this book share some functionality and source code, although one version is written in Visual Basic and the other in Active Server Page scripts. See Appendix A, "Overview and Installation of the Beckwith College Sample Database," for details on installing the Beckwith applications.

Figure 2.9.

*Network view of a MTS tradi-
tional client application.*

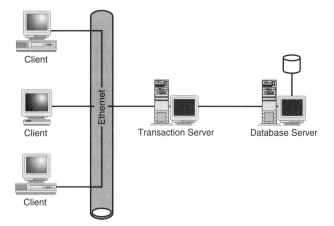

Figure 2.10.

*Network view of a MTS Internet
client application.*

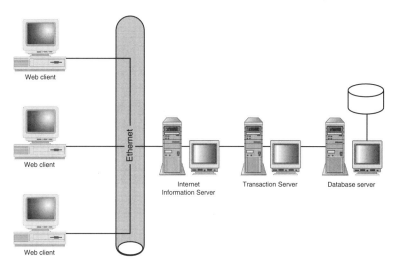

The Complexity Factor: Is N-Tier Worth It?

In most cases developing a conventional three-tier solution is a more difficult process
than developing an equivalent two-tier solution. However, the benefits of doing so
usually outweigh the negative side effects.

Because of the increased number of subsystems and the formal division of responsibili-
ties among them, a three-tier system requires you to develop more components than
you have to develop for a two-tier solution. And the additional development effort
translates directly into additional time. A large portion of the infrastructure also needs
to be developed—something taken for granted in a two-tier solution.

Using products such as MTS reduces these negative side effects and puts both architectures on a level (development) playing field. MTS helps you maximize your resources
while minimizing your effort.

Workshop Wrap-Up

This chapter introduced the basic concepts of client/server computing and added context to some of the MTS benefits. The role of middleware and the components of a three-tier application were also discussed. Although three-tier client/server development approaches are usually superior to their two-tier counterparts, the additional complexities they involve can be costly. Furthermore, the time required to develop much of the three-tier infrastructure from scratch is very likely to push any project over budget and out of schedule. By providing much of this infrastructure, MTS enables developers to focus on the business problems of their application.

MTS does away with the complexities associated with three-tier client/server computing by providing the plumbing that makes this architecture possible.

Next Steps

➤ To learn about transactions, refer to Chapter 3.

➤ MTS is built on components that follow the Microsoft component standard COM. If you aren't familiar with COM, turn to Chapter 4, "Getting Acquainted with COM."

➤ If you're ready to begin using MTS, skip to Part II.

Working with Database Transactions

Tasks in This Chapter

➤ *Explicitly Declaring a Transaction*

➤ *Committing a Transaction*

➤ *Aborting a Transaction*

➤ *Understanding Distributed Transactions*

Most client/server designs incorporate transaction-processing elements to manage atomic operations and concurrency. This chapter introduces the Microsoft Transaction Server (MTS) way of managing transactions, and how these methods relate to conventional RDBMS-based transaction management methods. The preparation section that follows briefly introduces the topic of transactions.

Some tasks in this chapter assume an understanding of SQL and are implemented using SQL Server's Transact-SQL language. Although you need SQL Server to perform the tasks as written in the chapter, you don't have to be familiar with Transact-SQL to understand them. You can easily modify the SQL source to execute on any ANSI SQL-compliant RDBMS.

The programming tasks serve as a brief introduction to MTS component transaction processing. The Visual Basic samples in the chapter illustrate concepts and do not require you to actually compile and build the components. For details on building MTS components, refer to Part III, "Microsoft Transaction Server Components."

> **Note** You must install the Beckwith database samples to complete this chapter's tasks. Refer to Appendix C, "Beckwith Component Reference," for instructions on installing the samples.

Preparation Understanding Database Transactions

A *transaction* is a collection of database operations grouped into a logical unit of work that is either completely executed or completely abandoned. In a sense, transactions are analogous to a contract between two or more parties. The contract is negotiated—the parties either come to a consensus and accept the contract, or they don't reach an agreement and reject the contract. A transaction is an all or nothing proposition—either it completes totally or it does not complete at all.

Most client/server systems of modest size rely exclusively on the RDBMS-provided transaction managers to implement transactions. RDBMS Application Programming Interfaces (APIs) enable applications to incorporate transaction semantics with limited scope. Typically, these transaction managers enable applications to issue transactions spanning only the current data context (usually the active database).

Transaction monitors (TMs) are a class of transaction-processing applications that were originally designed to manage very large numbers of simultaneous transactions against mainframe database management systems. Compared to conventional client/server RDBMSs, TMs are more robust and handle more simultaneous transactions. MTS brings this robustness and scalability to the client/server arena.

A transaction should function as a consistent and reliable unit of work for the database system and must guarantee the ACID properties when executing in a consistent database. (ACID stands for atomicity, consistency, isolation, and durability; see Table 3.1.) An *ACID transaction* guarantees that the transaction completely finished the actions on the database (atomicity), that the database was left in consistent form (consistency), that the transaction acted alone on the database (isolation), and that the changes made to the data were durable (durability).

Table 3.1. *ACID transaction attributes.*

Attribute	Description
Atomicity	A transaction can either commit or abort its changes. In a committed transaction all the changes remain, whereas in an aborted transaction all the changes are undone.
Consistency	After completing, a transaction guarantees the state of the information to be reliable and consistent.
Isolation	Concurrent transactions are isolated from modifications performed by other incomplete transactions.
Durability	When a transaction commits, its changes become permanent.

Task Explicitly Declaring a Transaction

Transactions can be classified as either implicit or explicit. *Implicit transactions* are single SQL statements that execute as an atomic unit. *Explicit transactions* are groupings of SQL statements surrounded by transaction delimiters: **BEGIN TRANSACTION, COMMIT TRANSACTION, ROLLBACK TRANSACTION**. The user defines explicit transactions.

Using SQL Statements to Begin a Transaction

The Transact-SQL statement **BEGIN TRANSACTION** denotes the beginning of an explicit transaction. To begin a transaction in a .sql file or when using the SQL Server SQL Query Tool (shown in Figure 3.1), use the following statement:

```
BEGIN TRANSACTION
```

For nested transactions, you can optionally assign a name to the outermost **BEGIN TRANSACTION** statement.

Figure 3.1.

Explicitly beginning a transaction.

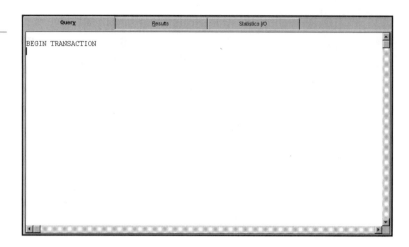

Managing Transactions in MTS Components

During certain actions, components may need to communicate with MTS. Most of this communication occurs through an object's companion context object; see Chapter 10, "Understanding Microsoft Transaction Server Components," for details. Every instance of a component under MTS control has an associated context object. This context object holds information about the requested object and serves as the object's communication link to MTS. MTS manages transactions through this context object.

To obtain a reference to this object within a Visual Basic MTS component, call the GetObjectContext method:

```
Dim objContext As ObjectContext
   Set objContext = GetObjectContext()
```

For details on using the context object in your Visual Basic components, see Chapter 11, "Implementing Components in Visual Basic."

Task Committing a Transaction

A COMMIT statement marks a successful completion of a transaction. The statement contains the processing to guarantee proper updating of the database and indicates the correct and atomic completion of a transaction. In this task you successfully complete transactions by using commit.

Using SQL Statements to Commit a Transaction

The Transact-SQL statement COMMIT TRANSACTION designates the successful end of a transaction. To commit a transaction in a .sql file or when using the SQL Server SQL Query Tool, use the following statement:

```
COMMIT TRANSACTION
```

For nested transactions, you can optionally assign a name to the outermost COMMIT TRANSACTION statement.

The Beckwith HumanResources database contains employee and department information. The Department table in Figure 3.2 consists of an identifier and description for each university department.

Figure 3.2.

The Beckwith HR Department table.

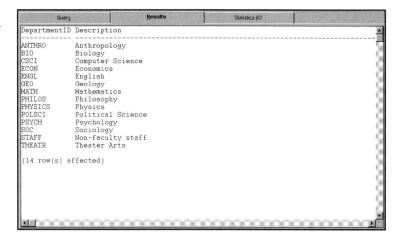

Use SQL Server ISQL to insert and commit a new department into the Department table:

1. Start the ISQL application.
2. Select the HumanResources database from the DB drop-list.
3. Type the following lines in the Query window:

```
BEGIN TRANSACTION
INSERT INTO Department VALUES ('MED','Medicine')
COMMIT TRANSACTION
```

4. Click the Execute Query button in the ISQL window.

The COMMIT TRANSACTION statement completes the transaction and permits the change to persist in the Human Resources database, as shown in Figure 3.3.

Programmatically Committing Transactions in MTS Components

When a transaction succeeds, the component's context object commits the work and makes the changes permanent. You must obtain a reference to the context object (refer to the previous section, "Managing Transactions in MTS Components") and then call the object's SetComplete method.

Figure 3.3.

*The Beckwith HR Department table after an **INSERT** transaction.*

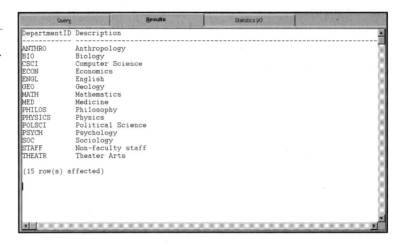

The code fragment in Listing 3.1 uses the SetComplete method to commit a transaction.

Listing 3.1. *Completing a transaction.*

```
Dim objContext As ObjectContext
Set objContext = GetObjectContext()

' Perform work

' success - complete the transaction
objContext.SetComplete
```

Task Aborting a Transaction

An abort marks the unsuccessful termination of a transaction. Commonly referred to as a "rollback," this action is necessary for transactions that fail for some reason. Reasons to abort transactions include invalid or erroneous operations, concurrency problems and data overwrites, and the failure to meet the ACID requirements. During an abort the RDBMS removes from the database any changes initiated by the transaction.

The two transaction-termination operations are mutually exclusive: You cannot roll back a transaction after it has been committed, and you cannot commit a transaction after it has been rolled back. This task demonstrates the effect of using abort to complete a transaction.

Using SQL Statements to Roll Back a Transaction

The Transact-SQL statement **ROLLBACK TRANSACTION** denotes the unsuccessful end of a transaction. To rollback a transaction in a .sql file or when using the SQL Server SQL Query Tool, use the following statement:

ROLLBACK TRANSACTION

For nested transactions, you can optionally assign a name to the outermost **ROLLBACK TRANSACTION** statement.

Use SQL Server ISQL to attempt to insert and rollback a new dentistry department into the Department table:

1. Start the ISQL application.

2. Select the HumanResources database from the DB drop-down list.

3. Type the following lines in the Query window:

```
BEGIN TRANSACTION
INSERT INTO Department VALUES ('DENT','Dentistry')
ROLLBACK TRANSACTION
```

4. Click the Execute Query button in the ISQL window.

The ROLLBACK TRANSACTION statement aborts the transaction and rolls back any changes made to the Human Resources database. Changes made to the database within the transaction do not persist. As Figure 3.4 shows, Beckwith College does not have a dentistry department.

Figure 3.4.

*The Beckwith HR Department table after an **INSERT** and **ROLLBACK** transaction.*

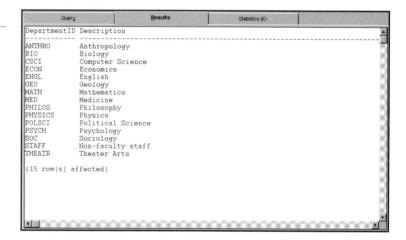

Programmatically Aborting Transactions in Your Application

When a transaction fails, the component's context object aborts the work and rolls back the changes. You must obtain a reference to the context object (see "Managing Transactions in MTS Components" earlier in the chapter) and then call the object's SetAbort method.

The code fragment in Listing 3.2 uses the SetAbort method to abort a transaction.

Listing 3.2. *Aborting a transaction.*

```
Dim objContext As ObjectContext
Set objContext = GetObjectContext()

' Perform work

' success - complete the transaction
objContext.SetComplete
Exit Sub

' failure - abort transaction
OnError:
objContext.SetAbort
```

Task Understanding Distributed Transactions

The advent of distributed applications has given rise to a new set of information technology problems. Because of their distributed nature, these types of applications are particularly vulnerable to hardware and software problems. Distributed applications depend on reliable servers, clients, and networks to perform optimally and without error—problems in any of these areas can easily cause the application to fail.

You can use transactions as a means of providing simple yet reliable transaction semantics to an application. The capability to perform transactions that can update data across multiple databases or objects is essential for building robust, scalable, and efficient distributed applications.

With MTS your applications and components can participate in transactions across databases, components, and servers. The Microsoft Distributed Transaction Coordinator (DTC) is the principal component for managing distributed transactions. In this task you learn how transactions can span beyond a database and how the DTC service manages and controls distributed applications.

Transactions Beyond the Database

MTS encapsulates the transaction semantics within the components that it hosts. If you declare components as transactional, MTS associates transactions with the component's objects. Multiple objects can perform actions that can be composed into a single atomic transaction.

The component's context object completes the transaction. Components can be distributed among servers, persist data to multiple databases, and still participate in a single atomic transaction.

The Beckwith database system must use distributed transactions to consistently promote prospect objects from the Admissions database to student objects in the

BusinessOffice database. Chapter 18, "Working with the Beckwith Online Sample Application," explains how to use transactions to accomplish this task.

The Microsoft Distributed Transaction Coordinator

MTS includes the Microsoft Distributed Transaction Coordinator (MS DTC), which provides a robust, high-performance, scalable, easy-to-use distributed transaction service. MS DTC is currently integrated with Microsoft SQL Server and will soon be part of most major RDBMS products. MS DTC enables remote stored procedure calls to participate in distributed transactions.

MS DTC uses a two-phase commit protocol to ensure that the outcome of a transaction is consistent across all components participating in a transaction. Consequently, changes on multiple servers can be committed as a single unit of work.

You can start the service automatically or start it manually from either the control panel or Transaction Server Explorer. Chapter 7, "Using Transaction Server Explorer," explains how to manage the MS DTC service using Transaction Server Explorer.

The MTS installation asks whether you want the MS DTC service to start automatically each time you restart the workstation. You can change this setting by using the control panel services applet:

1. Open the Control Panel.
2. Open the Services applet (Figure 3.5).

Figure 3.5.

The Control Panel Services spplet.

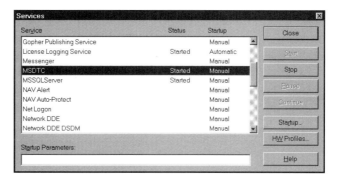

3. Find the MS DTC service in the list.
4. Click Startup to view the Service dialog (Figure 3.6).
5. Select the desired Startup Type (either Manual or Automatic). If hosting MTS is a primary role of the workstation, select Automatic.
6. Click OK to close the Service dialog.

   If MS DTC is not running, you can start the service by clicking Start. (You normally use Transaction Server Explorer to start this service.)

Figure 3.6.

The Control Panel Service dialog.

7. Click Close to close the Services applet.

> **Note** You can fully manage, configure, and monitor MS DTC through Transaction Server Explorer. See Chapter 7 for details.

Workshop Wrap-Up

A transaction is a collection of database operations grouped into a logical unit of work that is either completely executed or completely terminated. In this chapter you learned how to use simple transactions in Microsoft SQL Server's Transact-SQL and how these transactions relate to MTS components. You learned the basic principles of transaction processing and the ACID requirements for a successful transaction. Finally, you learned how to manage the MS DTC service from the Control Panel.

Next Steps

➤ See Chapter 4, "Getting Acquainted with COM," for a thorough discussion of the Component Object Model (COM)—the foundation of all ActiveX technologies. ActiveX and COM are the central technologies required to build and maintain MTS applications.

➤ In Part III you build MTS components that use the transactional concepts covered in this chapter.

➤ Chapter 18 includes tasks and samples that show you how to use distributed transactions in your applications.

CHAPTER 4

Getting Acquainted with COM

Tasks in This Chapter

➤ *Building a Simple COM Object*

As described in Chapter 1, "Exploring Microsoft Transaction Server," Microsoft Transaction Server (MTS) is designed to work as part of a component-based client/server architecture. These components are Component Object Model (COM) objects that are primarily responsible for data access and object encapsulation of business rules. COM defines a binary standard, which means objects can be built in virtually any language, provided their compiled output conforms to COM's standard. MTS provides a special runtime environment for these COM objects.

This chapter provides the information you need to design and build simple COM objects. (This chapter does not present a MTS-specific COM implementation; no previous knowledge of COM is necessary.) If you already know COM basics and how to build COM objects, refer to Part III, "Microsoft Transaction Server Components," for specifics on building MTS COM objects.

COM is an extremely broad subject, and a single chapter cannot possibly cover all aspects of the standard. This chapter covers the essentials you need to understand the material in this book.

What Is COM?

COM is a binary standard for objects. It defines how an object should present itself to the system after it has been compiled from its target language into machine code. Defining a standard enables objects to be compatible, regardless of their source language. For example, an object written in Visual Basic can communicate with an object written in Java as long as both objects are COM compatible.

The Origins of COM

COM arose out of the need for a decent interprocess communication (IPC) mechanism. Versions of Windows before 3.1 supported relatively primitive communication between applications through devices such as the Clipboard and Dynamic Data Exchange (DDE). These mechanisms enable applications to share data; for example, users could copy data from a Microsoft Excel spreadsheet and paste it into a Microsoft Word document.

The primary drawback to communication mechanisms like the Clipboard and DDE is that each application has to understand and handle the native data representation of each partner application it communicates with. In this scenario Microsoft Word has to have intimate knowledge of Excel's data format in order for Word to format and display the transferred information appropriately.

Under the old system, container applications typically support communication with only a few other applications, usually from the same vendor (for example, the Microsoft

Office suite). Workarounds to this limitation abound, however. Applications that are not explicitly coded to communicate with native data formats negotiate to a common data format when the user initiates a link. Examples of common data formats are

➤ Plain text

➤ Tab-delimited text

➤ Metafiles

Unfortunately, converting native data to a common data format usually results in a loss of information, and the copy passed from one application to the other is not as rich and expressive as the original data.

To solve this problem, Microsoft developed a technology known as *Object Linking and Embedding* (OLE). OLE allows applications to exchange and display information without explicitly knowing anything about the other application except that it is OLE compatible. Another benefit of OLE is that users can directly interact with data embedded in another application. With the Clipboard process, when data from Excel is pasted into Word, changes to the data in Word are local to its containing document only. In contrast, OLE automatically reflects changes to embedded Excel data in Word in the source Excel spreadsheet.

To develop OLE, the engineers at Microsoft designed and published the specification for COM. OLE version 2 is built on top of COM, and the introduction of OLE 2 was also the introduction of COM. Consequently, all OLE objects and all OLE-enabled applications speak COM to support the linking and embedding of objects between applications.

> **Note** Although Microsoft introduced OLE and COM together, they are no longer tightly coupled. OLE has transmogrified into ActiveX, and COM stands by itself. The objects you build for MTS are strictly COM objects and have little to do with OLE.

How Does COM Work?

In its simplest form, an object is a chunk of data, coupled with a set of methods that manipulate that data. Many languages, including Visual Basic, C++, and Java, can create objects. The trick in creating a system of these objects is to get them to communicate. If all the objects are written in the same language, communication isn't usually a big problem, but if the objects are written in different languages, object interaction is virtually impossible to achieve.

COM solves this problem by defining an object concept known as an interface. An *interface* is simply a collection of one or more methods. *COM-compliant objects* define, expose, and implement one or more interfaces. These interfaces are assembled and exposed to the system in exactly the same way, regardless of the language used to create the object. The commonality of this standard interface implementation is the feature that allows components built from different languages to communicate.

Interfaces are system entities that stand on their own, independent of objects. Interfaces merely define the number, name, and syntax of the methods they contain; interfaces are not associated with any code. Therefore, they can never be instantiated and used on their own. Instead, when developing COM objects, you define a set of interfaces and then assign those interfaces to individual objects. Each object is then responsible for implementing every method defined in all interfaces assigned to it.

An object exposing and implementing interfaces is only half the solution. When an object wants to communicate with another object (that is, invoke methods on the other object), it must somehow determine what methods it can invoke. Objects use a mechanism known as *interface navigation* to gain this information. The *initiating object* simply asks the *called object* whether it implements a specific interface, and the called object answers yes or no.

Interface navigation usually begins by asking an object for a pointer to its IUnknown interface. All COM objects guarantee that they implement IUnknown as mandated by the COM specification. IUnknown exposes three methods a client can invoke:

➤ QueryInterface()

➤ AddRef()

➤ Release()

QueryInterface() performs interface navigation. A client of a component invokes QueryInterface() to determine whether the object supports an interface the client knows how to use. The component provides an implementation for QueryInterface() that returns either yes if it implements the requested interface and no if it doesn't.

Interface navigation enables components to dynamically query at runtime the interfaces each supports. In other words, components and applications discover each other's functionality at runtime, instead of requiring developers to provide static hard code when they create an application. This design leads to a flexible system in which any component or application that speaks COM can communicate with any other existing or future COM-compliant component.

In COM, interfaces can be defined to inherit from another interface. *Interface inheritance* means that a derived interface automatically contains all methods defined by its parent and is also free to define additional methods. The COM specification states that all interfaces must ultimately inherit from IUnknown, which means that all interfaces expose the QueryInterface(), AddRef(), and Release() methods. Therefore, to navigate a component's interfaces, a client does not always have to invoke QueryInterface() off the component's IUnknown interface; instead, the client can invoke QueryInterface() on any interface the component exposes.

Reference Counting

The other two methods of IUnknown—AddRef() and Release()—manipulate a COM component's reference count. In its simplest form a reference count is an internal count of the number of clients using a particular COM component. A client calls AddRef() when it begins a conversation with a component and calls Release() when the conversation is over.

The purpose of a reference count is to tell an object when to destroy itself. Because COM objects are exposed to the system, several clients might invoke the services of the component at the same time. If the object's reference count is not zero, at least one client is using the component. When the reference count reaches zero, the component is free to delete itself because no clients hold references to it.

COM Servers

COM objects are compiled code and data. This code and data must persist on disk when the object is not in use and reside somewhere in memory (in one of the following types of COM servers) when it is in use:

➤ In-process servers

➤ Local servers

➤ Remote servers

In-process servers are dynamic link libraries (DLLs). Local and remote servers are executable files (EXEs); local servers run on the local computer, and remote servers run on a separate machine connected via a network.

Distributed component-based systems make heavy use of remote servers. Clients communicate with remote servers across a network using Distributed COM (DCOM), a communications protocol supported by Windows NT 4+ and Windows 95. For details on DCOM, see Chapter 15, "Setting Up Remote Windows Clients Using DCOM."

The coding of a COM component is similar for all types of servers, and the function of a COM component is the same in either a DLL or an EXE file. Each type of server has its own strengths and weaknesses.

An in-process server (DLL) enables the system to invoke methods on the COM object quickly. When a client instantiates or requests the services of a component contained in an in-process server, that DLL is loaded into the process space of client application. When the client invokes methods on the component, the calls involve little or no overhead. Because the component is in the caller's address space, invoking a method on the component requires the same amount of work as calling any other function defined in the base client application.

A local server (EXE), on the other hand, runs in its own address space because it is a standalone executable. When a client instantiates and uses a COM component contained by a local server, the operating system must pack any parameters passed into the method into a system buffer from the calling process and then unpack those parameters in the local server's process. This packaging of parameters is called *marshaling*. Marshaling must occur because the code of the client and server run in separate address spaces. Marshaling must also occur if any output parameter values are returned to the client, including a method return value. Although the system performs marshaling automatically (for the most part), the associated overhead makes the invocation of methods on a local server component slower than on its in-process counterpart.

Remote servers (also EXEs) function similarly to local servers except that the marshaling process occurs over the network. Network communication is much slower than interprocess communication on the same machine. As a result, remote servers perform more slowly than local servers do.

For MTS, all components must be built as in-process servers (DLLs) so that MTS can control which process the components run under. All DLLs must attach to a running process to be executed; that is, DLLs cannot stand on their own. MTS provides surrogate processes for components to run under. These surrogate processes then act as local or remote servers, allowing clients to run either on the local machine or on remote machines.

Identifying COM Objects

COM objects are identified to the system via two mechanisms: CLSIDs and ProgIDs. A CLSID is a unique 128-bit value, sometimes known as a globally unique identifier (GUID) or as a universally unique identifier (UUID). A CLSID uniquely identifies each type of exposed component, but not individual instances of that component.

The developer of the component can either assign a CLSID directly to the component or use the development environment to create the component automatically. Tools exist to automatically generate GUIDs that are statistically proven to not conflict with any other GUID created by any other developer in the world; hence the term *global* in GUID. This unique 128-bit integer is generated by reading a unique hard-coded value from the network card in a developer's machine (if one is installed) and the current system date and time. If the developer's machine does not have a network card, these tools use the system date, time, and a random number instead.

A GUID guarantees that any COM component you install on any machine anywhere will not have the ID as another type of component on the system. If two components were to share an ID, when a client attempted to create an instance of a component with the given ID, the system might instantiate the wrong component.

> **Note** The chances of developers ever creating identical GUIDs are extremely low. GUIDs are 128-bit integers, which represent the set of all integers from 0 to 2^128, or approximately 340,000,000,000,000,000,000,000,000,000,000,000,000. The likelihood of an asteroid colliding with and destroying the earth is greater than the chance that two GUIDs will collide!

CLSIDs are typically denoted as a string of hexadecimal digits, separated by hyphens to make the string slightly more readable. An example of a CLSID is

```
24053407-DF8F-11d0-BABE-00400520F095
```

Because CLSIDs are difficult for people to read, developers frequently use a second mechanism to identify their COM components; this mechanism is called a *programmatic identifier* (ProgID). A ProgID is simply a string that the system associates with a CLSID. Although a ProgID can be any string, developers typically use a string composed of the following three substrings, delimited by periods:

➤ Company name

➤ Component name

➤ Version

`Beckwith.Student.1` is an example of a ProgID.

The system doesn't strictly enforce the naming convention for programmatic identifiers, but you should try to make sure that the strings do not conflict.

Even though ProgIDs are optional for components, MTS uses ProgIDs for labeling components in the Transaction Server Explorer—its main user interface. Without ProgIDs, distinguishing components is much more difficult.

COM and the Windows Registry

Windows uses its Registry to maintain information about all the COM objects installed in the system. Each time an application creates an instance of a COM component, Windows consults the Registry to resolve either the CLSID or ProgID of the component into the pathname of the server DLL or EXE that contains it. For details on which Registry keys contain information about COM components and about tools you can use to modify the Registry, see Chapter 15.

After it determines the component's server from the Registry, Windows either loads the server into the process space of the client application (in the case of in-process components) or starts the server in its own process space (for local and remote servers). The server creates an instance of the component and returns to the client a reference to one of the component's interfaces.

Understanding Automation

Automation (formerly known as OLE Automation) is a technology built on top of COM; Automation allows one application to script another. Applications typically use Automation to expose an API to programming tools and macro languages.

Among the many commercial applications that expose Automation interfaces are Microsoft Office applications, Microsoft Visual Studio, and Microsoft Internet Explorer. Exposing these Automation interfaces enables developers to use a tool like Visual Basic to create custom applications that incorporate the functionality of these off-the-shelf applications.

COM components that support Automation do so by implementing an IDispatch interface. IDispatch is an interface defined by Microsoft and contains the following methods:

➤ GetIDsOfNames()

➤ GetTypeInfo()

➤ GetTypeInfoCount()

➤ Invoke()

GetTypeInfo() and GetTypeInfoCount() return type information about the component. Type information describes which properties, methods, and events the component exposes and responds to.

GetIDsOfNames() maps method and property labels from strings into integer identifiers. The developer assigns a dispatch identifier (an integer) to a component's methods and properties that uniquely distinguishes them from all other methods and properties. When the caller wants to execute the desired method, the component's client passes the dispatch identifier to the Invoke() method.

Invoke() is the primary method used to script the Automation component. The component's client never directly calls the actual methods exposed by the component. Instead, the client calls Invoke(), and the component's implementation of Invoke() dispatches execution to the appropriate method.

Dual-Interface Components

COM components that do not support Automation, but instead expose standard COM interfaces, are said to "implement custom interfaces." Components that support Automation are said to "support IDispatch-based interfaces." Components that support both custom and Automation interfaces are called *dual-interface components.*

Dual-interface components combine the advantages of both custom interfaces and Automation interfaces. A custom interface is faster than an Automation interface because each method of a custom interface can be invoked directly. On the other hand, an Automation interface is more flexible than a custom interface because the client's component does not have to know the details of the interface's composition up front. A dual-interface component supports both—clients can invoke methods directly or use Automation's IDispatch interface.

MTS supports all three types of interfaces—custom, IDispatch-based, and dual. You should base your choice of which type of interface to use on the potential clients for the components. Some clients, for example, Active Server Pages–based Web pages, must use components that support Automation. Others, such as C++ clients, can support all three types.

All the components developed later in this book for the Beckwith College sample database system are dual-interface components.

Task Building a Simple COM Object

This section describes the basic steps you follow to create a simple COM component in Visual Basic and Visual C++. Visual Basic is one of the simpler environments in which to build COM objects because Visual Basic hides the bulk of the COM "plumbing" code from the developer. Visual C++ lies on the opposite end of the spectrum, where COM support code is more exposed.

The component you create by following the steps in this section is called SimpleMath. It is a dual-interface component that exposes a single interface named ISimpleMath. ISimpleMath contains only two methods: ComputeMean() and ComputeMedian(). Both methods take three integer parameters. ComputeMean() returns the integer average of the three parameters; ComputeMedian() returns the middle parameter.

Building SimpleMath with Visual Basic

Follow these steps to build the SimpleMath component with Visual Basic:

1. Open Visual Basic.
2. Highlight the ActiveX DLL icon when the New Project dialog appears and click Open (see Figure 4.1).

   The ActiveX DLL icon allows you to create in-process COM servers. The ActiveX EXE icon allows you to create local and remote servers.

> **Note** Microsoft products often use the terms *ActiveX* and *COM* synonymously.

Figure 4.1.

The Visual Basic New Project dialog.

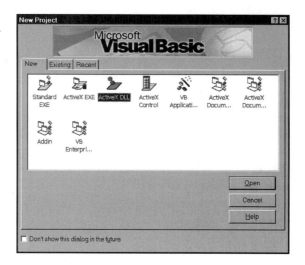

> **Tip** If the New Project dialog does not appear when you start Visual Basic, you previously checked the Don't Show This Dialog in the Future check box. Choose **F**ile I **N**ew Project from the main menu to display the New Project dialog.

Visual Basic automatically creates a new project named Project1 and adds a new class to the project labeled Class1.

3. Click the Project1 icon in the Project Explorer window and then click the Project1 edit box next to the (Name) property in the Properties window (see Figure 4.2) to change the (Name) property of the project from Project1 to SimpleMathProject.

4. Repeat step 3 to change the (Name) property of Class1 to SimpleMath.

5. Double-click the SimpleMath class icon in the Project Explorer window to make sure the code window for the SimpleMath class is displayed.

6. Add the following code to SimpleMath to implement both ComputeMean() and ComputeMedian().

```
Public Function ComputeMean(lngParam1 As Long, _
   lngParam2 As Long, lngParam3 As Long) As Long

   ComputeMean = (lngParam1 + lngParam2 + lngParam3) / 3

End Function

Public Function ComputeMedian(lngParam1 As Long, _
   lngParam2 As Long, lngParam3 As Long) As Long

   For i = 1 To 2
      If lngParam1 > lngParam2 Then
         lngTemp = lngParam1
         lngParam1 = lngParam2
         lngParam2 = lngTemp
```

```
            End If

        If lngParam2 > lngParam3 Then
            lngTemp = lngParam2
            lngParam2 = lngParam3
            lngParam3 = lngTemp
        End If
    Next

    ComputeMedian = lngParam2

End Function
```

Figure 4.2.

Changing the (Name) property of the current project.

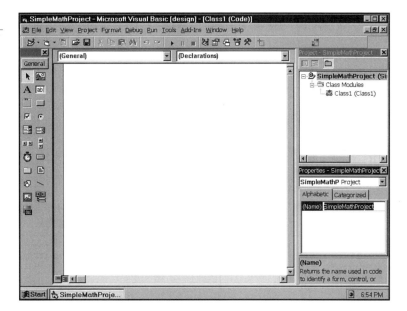

 Note Visual Basic implements COM objects as classes, as shown in the preceding code. You should always declare functions and subroutines inside these classes as `Public` to expose the methods to the rest of the system via the component's custom and Automation interfaces. Outside clients cannot call methods that are not `Public`.

7. Save the project and class source files by choosing File | Save Project from the main menu. Select an appropriate folder on your hard drive and save both the .cls and .vbp files.

   The next step is to compile the code you just added into a COM in-process server.

8. Select File | Make SimpleMathProject.dll to display the Make Project dialog. Click OK to accept the default server name of SimpleMathProject.dll and build the project.

Building the server performs several steps automatically. First, Visual Basic compiles your project, checking for syntax errors. Second, Visual Basic automatically generates CLSIDs for all classes in your project and creates type information to support the dual interface exposed by SimpleMath component. Third, Visual Basic registers the SimpleMathProject.dll server with the system and makes the server available for external clients to use.

Testing the SimpleMath COM Component with a VB Client

After you make the project and it successfully compiles, the COM component is ready for use by external clients. Follow these steps to build a simple VB client application that invokes the methods of the SimpleMath component.

1. Choose **F**ile | **N**ew Project from the Visual Basic main menu.

2. Select the Standard EXE icon from the New Project dialog and click OK.

   The newly created project contains a single form named Form1.

3. Add one button control to Form1 (see Figure 4.3). Command1 is the default name for the new button.

Figure 4.3.

The default form with one button added.

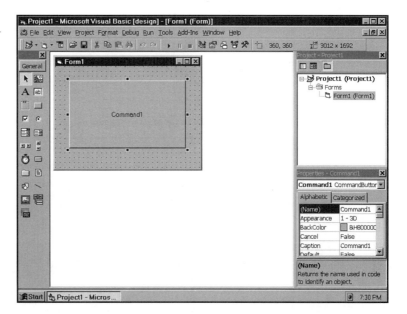

4. Double-click the Command1 button to create a handler for the button's Click event. The code editor window should appear with the cursor positioned just under the declaration of Command1_Click().

   One of the simplest ways to use a COM component from Visual Basic is to create a reference to it from the current project.

5. Choose **P**roject | Refere**n**ces from the main menu to display the References dialog (see Figure 4.4). This dialog displays a list of all COM servers publicly exposed on the system.

Figure 4.4.

The Project References dialog.

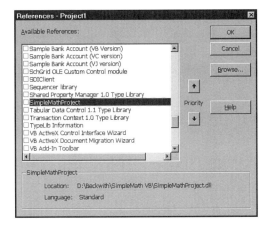

6. Scroll down the Available Reference list box until you find `SimpleMathProject`. Double-click this item or click the check box to the left of the label to add a reference to this component for the current project. Click OK to commit the selection.

7. Press the F2 key or choose **V**iew | **O**bject Browser from the main menu to make sure that the reference is valid. The Object Browser allows you to see all the methods, properties, and events exposed by all objects referenced by the current project.

8. Change the selection from <All Libraries> to `SimpleMathProject` in the top-left combo box. Your display should resemble Figure 4.5. Click the SimpleMath icon to display the methods exposed by this class.

9. Close the Object Browser window and return to the declaration of `Command1_Click()`. Add the following code to declare an instance of `SimpleMath` and use its services:

```
Private Sub Command1_Click()

    Dim objSimpleMath As New SimpleMath

    MsgBox objSimpleMath.ComputeMean(5, 17, 4)
    MsgBox objSimpleMath.ComputeMedian(5, 17, 4)

End Sub
```

The line

```
Dim objSimpleMath as New SimpleMath
```

declares and allocates an instance of the `SimpleMath` COM component. The instance is assigned to the variable `objSimpleMath`. The remaining two lines invoke the exposed methods of `SimpleMath`, providing three parameters and passing the method return values to a call to `MsgBox`, which displays the results.

Figure 4.5.

The Object Browser.

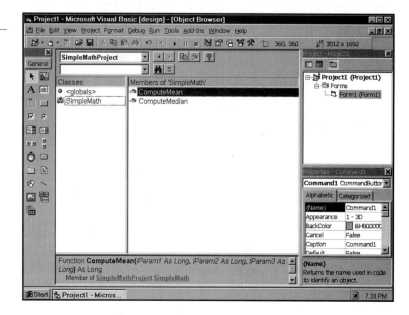

10. Run the test application by choosing **R**un | **S**tart from the main menu. Click the Command1 button. Two message boxes appear—the first message box displays a 9, and the second displays a 5. These values correspond to the integral mean and median of the set: 5, 17, and 4.

Building `SimpleMath` with Visual C++

Follow these steps to build the `SimpleMath` component with Visual C++. For more detailed information on building COM components, see Chapter 12, "Implementing Components in Visual C++ Using the Active Template Library."

1. Open Visual C++.

2. Create a new project by choosing **F**ile | **N**ew to display the New dialog. If the Projects tab isn't selected, click it to bring the Projects property page to the foreground (see Figure 4.6).

3. Click the ATL COM AppWizard icon from the list view to select it. The list view indicates what type of new project you want to create.

Figure 4.6.

The Visual Studio New dialog.

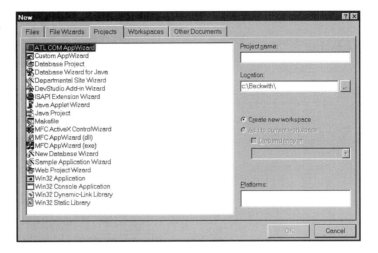

Note ATL stands for Active Template Library, which is a set of template-based C++ classes designed for creating lightweight COM components. There are other ways to create COM components in C++, the Microsoft Foundation Classes (MFC), for example, but ATL is one of the easiest ways because ATL was designed specifically for COM.

4. Type **SimpleMath VC** in the Project Name edit box. Click OK to create the new project and begin the ATL COM AppWizard.

   The ATL COM AppWizard is a one-step dialog that allows you to choose a type of server to create and set other options (see Figure 4.7).

Figure 4.7.

The ATL COM AppWizard dialog.

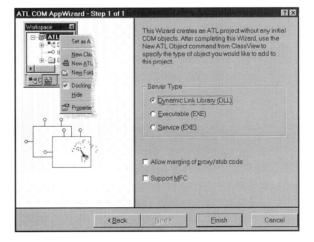

5. Click Finish to accept the defaults.

   The ATL COM AppWizard displays the New Project Information dialog that allows you to confirm the creation of your project (see Figure 4.8).

Figure 4.8.

The New Project Information dialog following the ATL COM AppWizard.

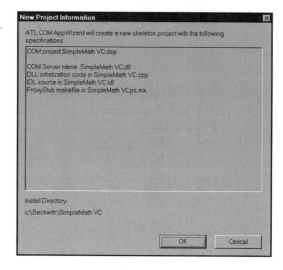

6. Click OK to proceed.

   New ATL projects begin without any COM components defined.

7. Add a new ATL object to the project by choosing **I**nsert | New **A**TL Object from the main menu. The ATL Object Wizard dialog—in which you can create a simple COM object—opens (see Figure 4.9).

Figure 4.9.

The ATL Object Wizard dialog.

8. Select the Simple Object icon from the list view on the right and click Next. The ATL Object Wizard Properties dialog opens (see Figure 4.10).

9. Type the name of the new COM object to create—in this case `SimpleMath`—in the Short Name edit control. As you type, all the other edit boxes change to reflect default values based on the Short Name you provide.

Figure 4.10.

The ATL Object Wizard Properties dialog.

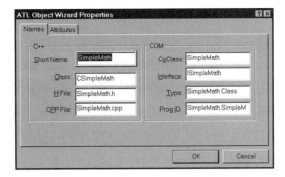

10. Click the Attributes tab to display the second property page of the dialog (see Figure 4.11). On this page you can change the threading model, interface type, aggregation mode, and other Boolean properties relating to COM objects. For the `SimpleMath` component, select the defaults by clicking OK.

Figure 4.11.

The ATL Object Wizard Properties dialog with the Attributes tab displayed.

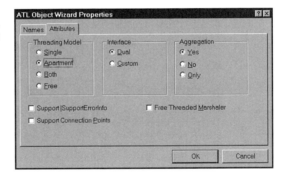

Clicking OK on the ATL Object Wizard adds the `SimpleMath` component to the current project. Find the `CSimpleMath` class and the `ISimpleMath` interface icons in the Workspace dockable dialog. If you can't see these icons, click the Plus icon to the left of the `SimpleMath VC classes` to expose the contained icons (see Figure 4.12).

The next step is to add the declaration of the `ComputeMean()` and `ComputeMedian()` methods to the `SimpleMath` component.

11. Right-click the ISimpleMath icon and choose Add **M**ethod from the context menu. The Add Method to Interface dialog opens (see Figure 4.13).

Figure 4.12.

The ISimpleMath interface highlighted in the Visual Studio Workspace dockable dialog.

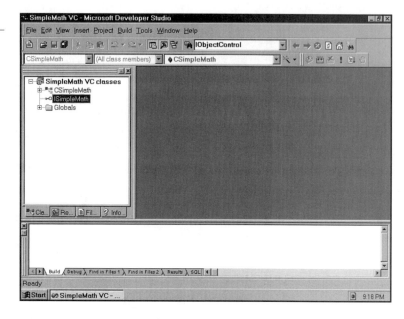

Figure 4.13.

The Add Method to Interface dialog.

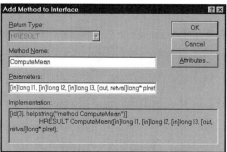

12. Type `ComputeMean` in the Method Name edit box. This value defines the new method's name. Type `[in]long l1, [in]long l2, [in]long l3, [out, retval]long* plret` in the Parameters edit box (see Figure 4.13). This string defines the parameters the `ComputeMean()` method takes as arguments and defines its return value.

> **Note** The `[in]` and `[out, retval]` tags that you entered in the Parameters edit box are obviously not part of standard C++ syntax. In fact, the string provided in the Parameters text box is not C++, but is part of the Interface Definition Language (IDL). IDL describes the methods and properties exposed by a COM object. Visual Basic hides the use of IDL, whereas Visual C++ enables you to work with IDL directly.

13. Repeat steps 11 and 12 but substitute `ComputeMedian` for `ComputeMean`.

> **Note** Adding methods to an interface performs two operations. First, it adds the
> definition of the methods to the project's IDL file. Second, it adds the declaration of
> those methods to the `CSimpleMath` C++ class, which implements the methods. To see
> the declaration of these methods in both places, expand the `CSimpleMath` icon in the
> Workspace dockable dialog and expand both `ISimpleMath` icons—the one contained by
> `CSimpleMath` and the `ISimpleMath` icon contained by the project (see Figure 4.14).

Figure 4.14.

*The declaration of
`ComputeMean()` and
`ComputeMedian()` exposed in the
Workspace dockable dialog.*

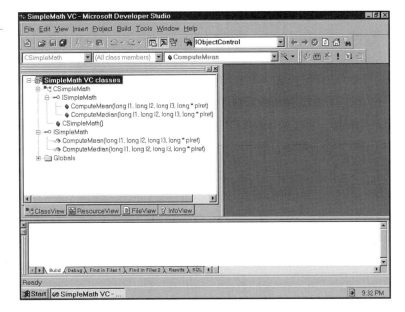

14. Double-click the first `ComputeMean` icon to open the source code window for
    `CSimpleMath`. This window is where you provide the implementation for
    `ComputeMean` in step 16.

15. Double-click the second `ComputeMean` icon to display the project's IDL file, which
    defines and exposes the method to the system. The bulk of this IDL file was
    automatically generated when the project was first created. It is not necessary to
    modify this file manually for the `SimpleMath` component.

16. Double-click the `ComputeMean` icon contained by `CSimpleMath` to return to the C++
    source code editor. Add the following code to `ComputeMean()` and `ComputeMedian()`
    to provide their implementations:

```
STDMETHODIMP CSimpleMath::ComputeMean(long l1, long l2,
   long l3, long * plret)
{
   *plret = (l1 + l2 + l3) / 3;
   return S_OK;
}
```

```
STDMETHODIMP CSimpleMath::ComputeMedian(long l1, long l2,
    long l3, long * plret)
{
    for(int i = 0; i < 2; i++)
    {
        if (l1 > l2)
        {
            long lTemp = l1;
            l1 = l2;
            l2 = lTemp;
        }
        if (l2 > l3)
        {
            long lTemp = l2;
            l2 = l3;
            l3 = lTemp;
        }
    }

    *plret = l2;
    return S_OK;
}
```

17. Build the project by choosing **B**uild | **R**ebuild All from the main menu. The
    compiler is executed. Visual C++ creates the COM server `SimpleMath VC.dll` and
    registers it with the system. The `SimpleMath` component is now ready for external
    clients to use.

Testing the `SimpleMath` COM Component with a C++ Client

Follow these steps to create a MFC-based Visual C++ client application that creates an
instance of the C++ version of `SimpleMath` and invokes its methods.

> **Note** The only reason that this test driver application is written in C++ is to
> demonstrate a test application written in a language other than Visual Basic. If you
> prefer, you can test the C++ version of `SimpleMath` from Visual Basic following the steps
> defined earlier in this chapter. The only difference is in setting the reference to the COM
> object to use: Instead of setting a reference to `SimpleMathProject`, set the reference to
> `SimpleMath VC 1.0 Type Library`. The VB code for testing the component remains
> exactly the same.

1. Create a new MFC AppWizard (exe) project by choosing **F**ile | **N**ew from the main
   menu to open the New dialog. Click the Projects tab and select the MFC
   AppWizard (exe) icon in the list view on the left.

2. Type **TestSimpleMath** in the Project Name edit box and click OK to display step 1 of
   the MFC AppWizard dialog.

3. Click Finish to accept the defaults in step 1 of the MFC AppWizard dialog.

4. Click OK when the New Project Information dialog appears to confirm all the default selections and create the project.

   To use a COM component from C++, you need to bring information about the component into the project. To do so, you use the new Visual C++ 5.0 keyword **#import**. **#import** is similar to **#include**, but instead of including an .h header file, you import a COM server. The following step imports the SimpleMath server.

5. Choose **F**ile | **O**pen from the main menu to open the project's StdAfx.h file. Add the following line to the bottom of StdAfx.h—*before* the **#endif** macro on the last line—to import the SimpleMath DLL server:

   ```
   #import "c:\Beckwith\SimpleMath VC\Debug\SimpleMath VC.dll"no_namespace
   ```

6. Replace the substring c:\Beckwith with the parent folder of the SimpleMath VC project on your local hard drive.

7. Build the project to make sure that it is error free. If you find any errors, make sure the **#import** statement you added in the previous step accurately points to the SimpleMath server DLL.

   The next step is to add code to instantiate and invoke the methods of SimpleMath.

8. Open the TestSimpleMath.cpp file and find the CTestSimpleMathApp::OnAppAbout() method at the end of the file. Remove this method's default implementation, which creates and displays the application's About dialog.

9. Add the following code in place of the default code:

   ```
   void CTestSimpleMathApp::OnAppAbout()
   {
       CoInitialize(NULL);

       ISimpleMathPtr pobjSimpleMath = new ISimpleMathPtr(__uuidof(SimpleMath));

       CString strMsg;
       strMsg.Format("Mean: %d", pobjSimpleMath->ComputeMean(5, 17, 4));
       AfxMessageBox(strMsg);

       strMsg.Format("Median: %d", pobjSimpleMath->ComputeMedian(5, 17, 4));
       AfxMessageBox(strMsg);
   }
   ```

   The call to CoInitialize() ensures that the COM libraries are loaded and initialized for the application.

   The next line creates an instance of the SimpleMath component and assigns a pointer to the object to a C++ smart pointer named pobjSimpleMath. The smart pointer is of type ISimpleMathPtr and is declared automatically by the compiler as a result of adding the #import keyword to the StdAfx.h file.

   The remaining lines of code use the pointer to the instance of SimpleMath to invoke its ComputeMean() and ComputeMedian() methods.

10. Rebuild the project. If the project is error free, run the test application by choosing **B**uild | E**x**ecute TestSimpleMath.exe from the main menu.

11. Choose <u>H</u>elp | <u>A</u>bout `TestSimpleMath` from the test application's main menu to invoke the code that instantiates `SimpleMath` and invokes its methods. If everything works correctly, you should see two messages boxes—the first displays the string `Mean: 8`, and the second displays the string `Median: 5`.

> **Note** You may have noticed that the implementation of `ComputeMean()` in Visual Basic generates a 9 from the inputs 5, 17, and 4. The C++ implementation of `ComputeMean()` returns an 8 from the same inputs. The reason for this discrepancy is that the decimal mean of 5, 17, and 4 is 8.67. Visual Basic handles integers by rounding results to the nearest integer; C++ does not round.

Workshop Wrap-Up

This chapter introduces the basics of the COM. It covers COM's origins, basic interfaces such as `IUnknown`, reference counting, Automation, CLSIDs, and dual-interface components. You created the simple COM component `SimpleMath` in both Visual Basic and Visual C++ and created applications in Visual Basic and Visual C++ to test it.

Next Steps

➤ For detailed information on building COM components with specific logic for supporting MTS, see Part III, "Microsoft Transaction Server Components." This part contains chapters for building MTS COM components in Visual Basic, Visual C++, and Visual J++ for Java.

➤ Before you build components, it's a good idea to install MTS and test pre-built components to ensure a successful installation. Continue to Chapter 5, "Configuring and Determining System Requirements," to begin the necessary steps of installing MTS.

PART II

Installing and Using Microsoft Transaction Server

CHAPTER 5

Configuring and Determining System Requirements

Tasks in This Chapter

As discussed in Chapter 2, "Laying the Foundation: Client/Server Architectures," client/server applications distribute the work between two or more computers (unless a single computer is acting as both the client and server). Most client architectures in the conventional client/server model contain rich user interfaces, database connections, and business-specific logic (often referred to as fat clients). This model relegates servers to returning the requested data from a common repository.

The Microsoft Transaction Server (MTS) model for building client/server applications uses the server (or servers) for much more than just processing database requests. Although this approach greatly simplifies client installation (for example, avoiding an open database connectivity [ODBC] data source installation in every client), it adds some complexities to the configuration and administration of the server side of the equation. Fortunately, the difference is a positive one. For instance, in the case of a large-scale intranet application, maintaining a handful of servers is much easier than maintaining thousands of clients.

This chapter examines the requirements for deploying MTS applications and explains how to determine which components they need.

Task Analyzing Your Hardware

You can install MTS on any Windows NT 4.0 (Intel or Alpha) compatible system. The hardware requirements for either version of Windows NT 4.0 are

➤ An Intel 486 or Pentium, or DEC Alpha computer

➤ A Windows NT–compatible display

➤ A hard disk with at least 125MB of available space

➤ At least 16MB of RAM

➤ A CD-ROM drive

➤ A mouse or other suitable pointing device

Install and configure either Windows NT 4.0 Server or Workstation before continuing. To determine which version is most suitable for your needs, see Chapter 6, "Installing Microsoft Transaction Server."

> **Tip** Visit the following site for the latest information on Windows NT server: www.microsoft.com/ntserver.

In addition to the Windows NT hardware requirements, your server must also include the following hardware to adequately run MTS:

➤ A minimum of 32MB of RAM

➤ An additional 30MB of hard disk space

Verify the amount of RAM available by starting Windows NT and performing the following steps:

1. Double-click the My Computer icon.
2. Choose **H**elp | **A**bout Windows NT from the menu bar.

   In the Windows NT About box, the Memory Available to Windows NT value should be at least 32,000KB.
3. Click OK to close the dialog.

Decide which hard disk you want to use to install MTS. Use these steps to validate the available space:

1. Double-click the My Computer icon.
2. Right-click the desired hard disk icon and choose Properties on the context menu.
3. Verify the Free Space attribute—it should be 30MB or greater (as shown in Figure 5.1).

Figure 5.1.

Verifying available disk space.

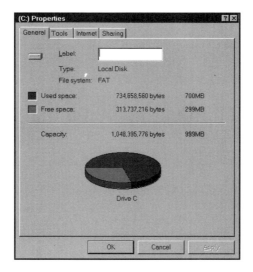

Some of the optional components you use to create MTS applications may require more powerful hardware. Review the product documentation prior to installing each component.

Meeting Software Requirements

The minimum software requirement for MTS is Windows NT 4.0. You should have already installed either the Intel or Alpha version of Windows NT 4.0.

Tip Windows NT 4.0 Service Packs correct various problems affecting MTS. Download the latest Windows NT Service Packs from `www.microsoft.com/ntserversupport/content/servicepacks/`.

You may need to install several other server components, depending on the types of applications you are deploying. You can install these server components on the same server as MTS, or you can distribute them across your network. The examples in this book assume you are using a single computer for all server components. This configuration is recommended during development of your applications because it greatly simplifies configuration and deployment of MTS applications. See Chapter 6 for possible network configurations.

To use Microsoft Windows 95 clients with MTS applications, you must install DCOM for Windows 95 on each client. Review Chapter 15, "Setting Up Remote Windows Clients Using DCOM," for details on configuring Windows 95 clients.

Tip For the latest information on DCOM for Windows 95, go to `www.microsoft.com/oledev`.

Task Selecting an Effective Component Development Environment

You can build MTS components using any development environment that supports building in-process ActiveX server components (previously known as OLE Automation servers). The latest versions of the following products possess this capability:

➤ Microsoft Visual C++

➤ Microsoft Visual Basic

➤ Microsoft Visual J++

➤ Borland Delphi

➤ Microfocus COBOL

➤ Powersoft Powerbuilder

Part III, "Microsoft Transaction Server Components," examines the details of the Visual C++, Visual Basic, and Visual J++ development environments. Because all MTS components are COM objects, you can easily integrate components created in various development environments. While you are learning the basics of MTS, use the development environment you are most comfortable with. In later chapters you can explore other environments and determine which best suits your needs.

Tip   If you are using Visual C++, you can also use the ActiveX Template Library (ATL) version 1.1 or later to build MTS components. This new framework is ideal for building light, fast, and efficient business objects suitable for MTS. See Chapter 12, "Implementing Components in Visual C++ Using the Active Template Library," for details.

Task Accessing Databases with Microsoft Transaction Server

Most client/server applications require a database management system (DBMS) to store and retrieve application-specific information. At the time of this writing, MTS provides full support for Microsoft SQL Server version 6.5 and recent releases of Oracle 7 and 8. Other DBMS vendors, such as Sybase and Informix, have committed to supporting MTS in the near future. For now, Microsoft SQL Server is the best alternative.

Tip   You should regularly update your SQL Server installation to the most current Service Pack. Download the latest SQL Server Service Pack at
`www.microsoft.com/sql`.

Both SQL Server and MTS install the Microsoft Distributed Transaction Coordinator (MS DTC). This service coordinates transactions that span multiple resource managers.

Caution   The SQL Server installation program overwrites MS DTC Registry settings and files. If you reinstall SQL Server after you install MTS, you must reinstall MTS.
Always install MTS after installing SQL Server.

To support distributed transactions, you must start the MS DTC service. Review Chapter 7, "Using Transaction Server Explorer," for information on starting and stopping the MS DTC service. No other configuration changes are required to use SQL Server in MTS applications.

Note   You can use other DBMSs in your MTS applications. However, only DBMSs that support the MS DTC service can participate in a transaction.

Task Configuring the Internet Server

Many applications execute within the confines of a Web browser. These "Web applications" look very much like conventional HTML pages, but they are interactive. In Part V, "Integrating Microsoft Transaction Server and the Internet," you learn how to create these applications using Internet Information Server (IIS), Active Server Pages (ASP), and MTS.

When creating a Web application, you must select and install an Internet server. This task assists you in making the appropriate selection.

Understanding the Microsoft Transaction Server Internet Application

The objects to the right of the Internet in Figure 5.2 represent the server architecture. You can install all server components in a single computer or distribute them across many. High-volume Web sites can have multiple servers for each service (for example, several Internet servers or several SQL Servers).

Figure 5.2.

MTS Internet application architecture.

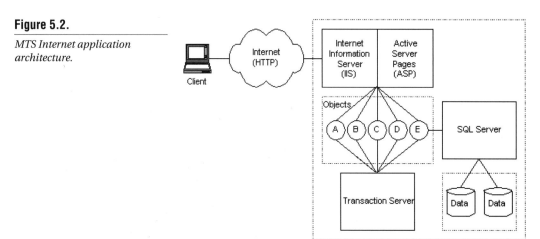

In this *n*-tier approach, the Internet server uses an application framework (such as Active Server Pages) to instantiate objects on behalf of a client. These objects can perform business-specific operations, such as retrieving data or executing some calculations. One of the many servers performs most of the work, so the clients have little overhead. The *n*-tier approach makes client installation and configuration a simple and efficient process.

Selecting the Internet Server

Many Internet servers are available for both Windows NT Server and Workstation. The version of Windows NT you are running usually influences which server you decide to use. Most MTS resources strongly recommend using Windows NT Server.

Select the appropriate Internet server, depending on the host operating system:

➤ If you are using Windows NT Server, install Internet Information Server (IIS). The IIS Internet Service Manager Snap-in appears in Figure 5.3. This combination gives you the most flexibility, performance, and scalability. You can get the latest information on IIS from

`www.microsoft.com/iis`.

Figure 5.3.

The Microsoft Management Console (MMC) Snap-in for IIS.

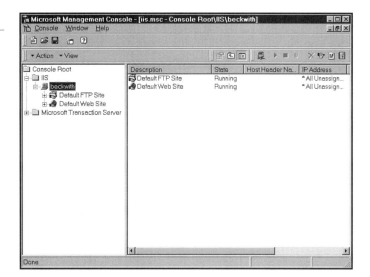

➤ If you are using Windows NT Workstation, you can use Personal Web Server (PWS) as your Internet server. Although this server limits you to 10 concurrent connections, you can use this configuration during your application development phase and for low-traffic applications. PWS is simply a stripped-down version of IIS. To install PWS, run the IIS setup program.

➤ Although not recommended, you can use PWS as your Internet server under Windows 95 (see Figure 5.4). As a desktop operating system, Windows 95 lacks many administration features; therefore, it is not a good application server. For the latest information on PWS, go to

`www.microsoft.com/frontpage`.

Regardless of the server you select, be sure to install the latest release. (See Table 5.1.) In some cases you may need to download a Service Pack or upgrade from the Microsoft

Web site. To integrate tightly with MTS, the server should support Microsoft's Active Server Pages (ASP).

Figure 5.4.

The Personal Web Server for Windows 95.

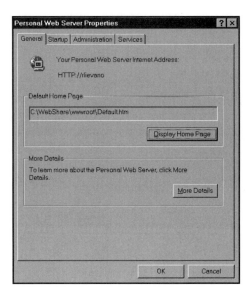

Table 5.1. *Internet servers.*

Operating System	Internet Server
Windows NT Server 4.0	Internet Information Server 4.0
Windows NT Workstation 4.0	Personal Web Server 4.0
Windows 95	Personal Web Server 3.0

> **Note** You can use other Internet servers to develop MTS Internet applications. However, most experts recommend IIS 4.0 and PWS 4.0 because of their tight integration with Windows NT, COM, and MTS.

Selecting the Internet Application Development Environment

After you select one of the servers outlined in the previous section, you must select an application development environment for your MTS Internet applications. Because of the flexibility of the MTS programming model, the choices can be diverse and confusing.

Most MTS Internet applications are built using the ASP application framework. ASP is an integral part of all current versions of the servers discussed in the previous section. For any Microsoft Internet server, you should use ASP to build applications unless you have an extremely valid and logical reason not to do so. See Chapter 16, "Building Dynamic Web Sites Using Active Server Pages," to learn how to build Internet applications using ASP.

Internet samples and tasks in this book use ASP. You can experiment with other programming environments, such as the Internet Server Application Programming Interface (ISAPI) or the Common Gateway Interface (CGI) to instantiate MTS components.

Installing Active Server Pages

If you don't have ASP support installed on your Internet server (IIS 4.0 and PWS 4.0 automatically support ASP), you must obtain the ASP upgrade provided by Microsoft. You can download this update from the Microsoft Web site at

`www.microsoft.com/iis`

or from the Site Builder Web site at

`www.microsoft.com/sitebuilder.`

To support ASP, the Internet server version should be 3.0 or higher. If you need to install the update, download or obtain the software from Microsoft and then follow these steps:

1. Execute the `asp.exe` update file. The Active Server Pages setup program starts.
2. Follow the Setup Wizard's instructions. After the initial information pages, the Select Options pages appear.

   The Active Server Pages Core option is a required component. You can optionally select to install ODBC 3.0 and the product documentation.
3. Select all items and click Next, as shown in Figure 5.5.

   If you opt to install the documentation (recommended), the setup program prompts you for the path for the documentation and sample files. You can modify this setting by clicking Browse.
4. Click Next after selecting and verifying the folder to use for documentation.

Note During installation, the setup program may prompt you to stop and restart the Internet server. Allow the setup program to perform these tasks.

Figure 5.5.

The Active Server Pages setup.

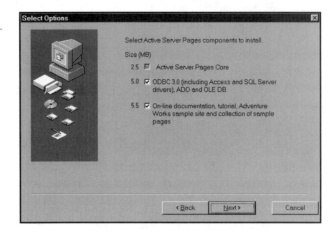

Task Using Open Database Connectivity (ODBC) Version 3.0

ODBC provides a generic interface for accessing information. The technology is based on the Structured Query Language (SQL) standard for accessing data. ODBC enables applications to connect to various databases without needing to rebuild or recompile their source.

ODBC applications are not tied to proprietary database APIs, do not need to concern themselves with the underlying data communication protocols, and can access data residing in any one of more than 50 DBMSs.

You should already be familiar with the benefits of using ODBC in your applications. This task discusses some of the new key features in ODBC 3.0 and explores the new ODBC Control Panel applet.

Exploring the New ODBC 3.0 Features

Many of the enhancements in this update of ODBC improve driver performance. In addition, developers and administrators should notice an improved driver manager, installer, and Control Panel applet.

ODBC 3.0:

➤ Adheres to, and is a superset of, the X/Open and ISO Call-Level Interface (CLI) standards. Many features support this integration, such as the use of descriptor and diagnostic areas.

➤ Contains many API enhancements, providing new data types, extended error reporting, and bookmarking.

> ➤ Includes support for saving connection information to a file, called a *File Data Source*. Multiple users can share these data sources, or they can be placed on a central server.

> ➤ Includes database connection pooling, a connection mechanism that maintains open database connections and manages shared connections to improve performance and reduce the number of idle connections.

The most visible new feature of ODBC 3.0 is connection pooling. The MTS ODBC Resource Dispenser is implemented in the ODBC 3.0 Driver Manager. This new version of the Driver Manager DLL is installed with MTS. Part III, "Microsoft Transaction Server Components," discusses resource dispensers in detail.

> **Tip** The latest information on ODBC 3.0 is available from
> `www.microsoft.com/odbc`.

Installing ODBC 3.0

Your version of Windows NT might not include the latest release of ODBC. If the ODBC Control Panel applet includes an About tab, you may be using ODBC 3.0 or higher. Verify the version numbers supplied by this applet—all file versions should be 3.0 or higher.

The ODBC 3.0 update is part of many other Microsoft software upgrades and sources, including

> ➤ Windows NT Service Pack 3

> ➤ Active Server Pages update (described in the "Installing Active Server Pages" section)

> ➤ The ODBC Web site at
> `www.microsoft.com/odbc`

If you are using ASP in your MTS applications, follow the steps in the "Installing Active Server Pages" section to install ODBC 3.0.

Using the ODBC Control Panel Applet

You can use the ODBC Data Source Administrator, shown in Figure 5.6, to configure data sources, obtain driver information, and enable or disable tracing. Data sources store configuration information used to connect to a specific database. You can configure different types of data sources, depending on your specific need. The ODBC data source types are listed in Table 5.2.

Figure 5.6.

The ODBC Data Source Administrator.

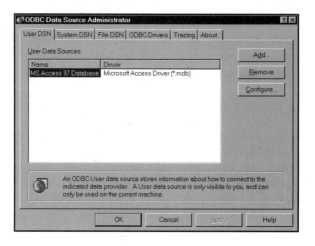

Table 5.2. *ODBC 3.0 data source types.*

Type	Description
User	These data sources are visible only to a specified user on the local machine.
System	These data sources are visible to all users on the local machine, including Windows NT services.
File	A file containing connection information. Users who have the correct ODBC drivers installed can share these files.

> **Note** Installing the sample applications also configures all required Beckwith data sources. If you installed the samples, the ODBC Data Source Administrator should display the five Beckwith data sources under the System DSN tab.

To simplify administration and development, Internet and MTS applications should use system data sources. To create a new system data source to use with the Beckwith Human Resources database:

1. Start the 32-bit ODBC applet from Control Panel.

2. Click the System DSN tab on the ODBC Data Source Administrator property sheet. The System DSN dialog (see Figure 5.7) opens.

3. Click Add.

4. Select SQL Server in the Create New Data Source dialog, shown in Figure 5.8, and click Finish. The ODBC SQL Server Setup dialog opens.

Figure 5.7.

Creating a system DSN using the ODBC Data Source Administrator.

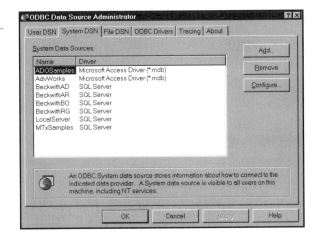

Figure 5.8.

Setting up an ODBC data source.

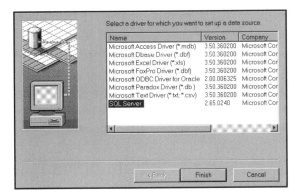

5. Type **BeckwithHR** in the Data Source Name edit text field. You can optionally include a description in the Description field.

6. Select (local) from the Server drop-down list if the local machine is hosting both SQL Server and MTS. Or type in the appropriate machine name if another server is hosting SQL Server.

7. Click Options to expand the dialog.

8. Specify the HR database under the Login group by typing **HumanResources** in the Database Name field (see Figure 5.9).

9. Click OK to close the ODBC SQL Server Setup dialog.

10. Click OK to close the ODBC Data Source Administrator.

By substituting the DSN and database names appropriately, you can apply the same technique to create data sources for use with your applications.

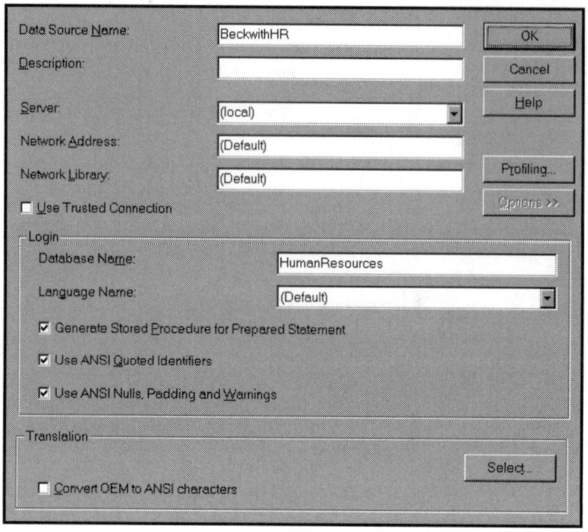

Figure 5.9.

Configuring a SQL Server data source.

Workshop Wrap-Up

MTS applications rely more heavily on servers than on clients. Database and Internet/intranet applications require server software in addition to MTS. This chapter guides you in installing and configuring the most common components required for deploying MTS applications. You learned about the tight relationship between MTS and SQL Server, the Distributed Transaction Coordinator (DTC), and Internet Information Server (IIS).

Next Steps

➤ Now you're ready to install MTS. Read Chapter 6 for detailed instructions and tips that can help you avoid common pitfalls.

➤ In Chapter 7 you learn how to administer MTS using the Explorer.

➤ This chapter provided a broad look at configuring the server components of a MTS application. To learn about configuring clients, read Chapter 15.

Installing Microsoft Transaction Server

Tasks in This Chapter

➤ *Running the Setup Application*

➤ *Verifying Correct Installation*

➤ *Uninstalling Microsoft Transaction Server*

Microsoft Transaction Server (MTS) is very easy to install. The process requires only a few steps, and you don't need any real configuration information at install time. The bulk of MTS configuration happens after installation, using MTS Explorer (see Chapter 7, "Using Transaction Server Explorer," for more information).

Starting with version 2.0, MTS is no longer installed as a standalone product. Instead, Microsoft products like Windows NT Server and Internet Information Server 4.0 include MTS as an installable component in their setup applications. MTS 2.0 is installed at the same time you install those applications. If you are using MTS 2.0, you can browse through this chapter for general installation guidelines.

This chapter walks you through the tasks necessary to install the standalone 1.1 version of MTS from start to finish. The entire process should take about 15 minutes. This chapter also shows you how to verify that the MTS setup is correct by installing and running one of the sample applications that ships with MTS.

Preparation Possible Network Configurations

You can configure systems developed with MTS in various ways. During prototyping and initial development, SQL Server, MTS, and client applications are likely to run on the same machine. MTS fully supports this configuration.

Later in the development cycle, the database server may get its own machine, leaving MTS and client applications on the same machine. MTS fully supports this configuration also.

Finally, when deployment of the client/server application occurs, the client applications are deployed on many separate machines, leaving MTS installed on a machine by itself between the clients and the database server. If scalability requirements mandate it, you can add multiple middle-tier servers to the network, each with its own installation of MTS and a different group of components.

MTS can handle any network definition. Also, don't worry if the machine on which you install MTS turns out to be inappropriate; MTS uninstalls itself just as easily as any Windows desktop application.

Choosing Between Windows NT Server and Windows NT Workstation

You can install MTS on either Windows NT Workstation or Windows NT Server. If you are deploying a production client/server application, you should plan to use a Windows NT Server machine to host MTS. Windows NT Workstation limits you to a maximum of 10 simultaneous network connections. With Windows NT Server the number of connections is unlimited.

> **Note** Unlike Microsoft's SQL Server, you do not need a Client Access License (CAL) for each user that accesses your installation of MTS. This policy is similar to Microsoft's policy for its Internet Information Server product. Because MTS is likely to be accessed in a high-volume enterprise environment in which the number of actual users may vary greatly—and perhaps be unknown—Microsoft decided to allow an unlimited number of clients to use the services of each installation of MTS. Of course, you need a CAL for each client of the Windows NT Server computer. For more details, see the End-User License Agreement (EULA) in the main MTS help file.

Task Running the Setup Application

MTS:installation begins just like the installation process of any other Microsoft product—locating and executing the `Setup.exe` application. However, you first have to acquire a copy of MTS, and unlike other Microsoft products, you probably won't find a shrink-wrapped unbundled copy of MTS on the shelf at your local software store. (MTS is a technical product and is not likely to be purchased by typical end users.)

Here are some ways to obtain a copy of MTS:

➤ Buy a new copy of Windows NT Server or Windows NT Server, Enterprise Edition. Microsoft believes that MTS is such a core technology that it now bundles MTS as part of Windows NT Server.

➤ Buy a copy of Visual Studio, Enterprise Edition. This product contains all Microsoft development tools, conveniently bundled into one package. MTS is part of this bundle.

➤ Order the MTS Evaluation Kit directly from Microsoft. This kit is a multimedia CD-ROM that contains all kinds of information about MTS, including white papers, testimonials, and NetShow presentations, as well as a copy of MTS.

➤ Subscribe to the Microsoft Developer's Network, Enterprise Level. This quarterly distribution of developer tools includes MTS.

➤ Download MTS from Microsoft's Web site. Check
   `www.microsoft.com/transaction`
   for details on how to download a copy of MTS.

> **Tip** Before you begin the MTS installation, make sure you close all applications (except for the Master Setup application if you install from Visual Studio 97). In particular, make sure to close the Windows NT Control Panel. During installation `Setup.exe` modifies the `Dtccfg.cpl` file in the Windows NT `System32` folder. If Control Panel is open, Setup may fail because Control Panel opens `Dtccfg.cpl`, preventing it from being updated.

> **Tip**　MTS 1.1 is designed to work with SQL Server 6.5. (MTS 2.0 now supports Oracle databases via Microsoft's ODBC driver.) If you are setting up a new Windows NT installation, you must install SQL Server before installing MTS. Even though you are not required to do so, always restart your machine after installing SQL Server but before installing MTS. If you attempt to install MTS immediately after a SQL Server installation, the MTS Setup program fails. Restarting between installations performs some cleanup chores that enable MTS to install successfully.

After you have obtained a copy of MTS and taken care of the preliminaries, follow these steps to install it:

1. Locate and open the MTS `Setup.exe` application.

   If you are installing from Visual Studio, select the Microsoft Transaction Server 1.0 option from the Master Setup dialog to start the MTS `Setup.exe` for you automatically (see Figure 6.1).

Figure 6.1.

The Visual Studio 97 Master Setup dialog with the Microsoft Transaction Server 1.0 option highlighted.

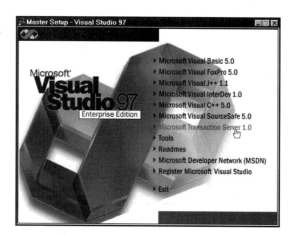

   The Setup program opens the Microsoft Transaction Server Welcome Dialog, which displays the end-user license agreement for MTS. You must accept the agreement to continue installation.

2. Click I Agree.

3. Enter your name and organization information at the prompts. Click OK to continue.

4. Examine the Microsoft Transaction Server Setup destination folder selection dialog (see Figure 6.2). This dialog prompts you for the MTS main installation directory. Unless you have special requirements, the default folder is usually appropriate. If it isn't, click Change Folder to select a different installation folder. Click OK to continue.

Tip   You can skip this dialog by clicking OK because a later dialog in `Setup.exe` gives you another opportunity to choose a destination folder for the installation.

Figure 6.2.

The Microsoft Transaction Server Setup destination folder selection dialog.

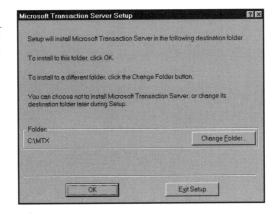

Note   MTS determines whether the MSDTC and MSSQLServer services are running on the system. If either service is running, MTS displays a message box requesting you to stop the service before continuing.

To stop the services, leave Setup running and open the Windows NT Control Panel. Choose the Services applet. In the Service list box, locate and select the MSDTC or MSSQLServer service. Click Stop to stop the service. If both services are running, stop them both.

Close the Services applet and make sure to close the Control Panel. Failure to close the Control Panel causes problems later in the installation.

Return to the MTS Setup program and click Retry to continue.

The Microsoft Transaction Server Setup dialog is shown in Figure 6.3. The current dialog again prompts you to choose the destination folder for the installation.

5. Click Change Folder to select a new destination if desired.

This dialog lets you pick the type of installation you prefer: Microsoft Transaction Server or Microsoft Transaction Server Development. Pick the development version if you want samples and the files necessary to develop MTS components. Choose the typical unattended version if all your components are already built and you don't need the samples.

The tasks later in this chapter require that you install the MTS samples so you can verify the correct installation and setup of MTS.

Figure 6.3.

The Microsoft Transaction Server Setup installation type dialog.

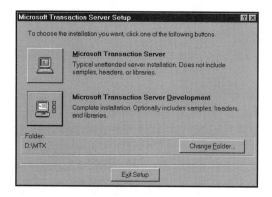

6. Click the Microsoft Transaction Server Development button to continue.

   When you select the development installation option, a list of components that you can selectively install appears. Table 6.1 details each option and its description.

Table 6.1. *Microsoft Transaction Server installation components.*

Name	Description
Transaction Server	This set of core MTS executables and utilities is necessary for a working copy of MTS.
SDK Files	These files create MTS components. Without these files you cannot create components on this machine, but you can still use components developed on other machines.
SDK Samples	MTS 1.0 ships with two samples: a bank application and a hockey game.
VB Addin	This utility installs itself as a Visual Basic add-in and refreshes components installed in MTS each time they are rebuilt. Not installing this add-in means that you must manually refresh the components using the MTS Explorer.

7. Click Select All to select all options and click Continue to proceed with the installation.

8. Click No when Setup asks whether you want to set the identity of the System Package. (You want to set the identity later.) For details on setting the System Package identity, see Chapter 9, "Configuring Component Security."

9. Click Yes when Setup asks whether you want the DTC service to start automatically. DTC is Microsoft's Distributed Transaction Coordinator and is a key MTS component. It is a good idea to automatically start DTC.

10. Wait while Setup copies the actual MTS files, along with all the support files, samples, and online help documents. It first installs the Java Virtual Machine. (MTS components can be written in Java and part of the bank sample is written in Java.)

> **Tip** During the installation of the Java Virtual Machine, Setup might ask whether to overwrite newer, existing Java files. If this confirmation dialog appears, you should click No to All to avoid overwriting your system's Java Virtual Machine with an older version.

11. Click Restart Windows to complete the installation of MTS.

Task Verifying Correct Installation

Follow these steps to ensure your MTS:installation is working properly. Although these steps are specific to MTS 1.1, you can also follow them to verify the correct installation of MTS 2.0.

1. Click the Windows NT Start button from the taskbar and choose <u>P</u>rograms | Microsoft Transaction Server | Transaction Server Explorer. This step opens MTS Explorer (see Figure 6.4).

Figure 6.4.

Microsoft Transaction Server Explorer.

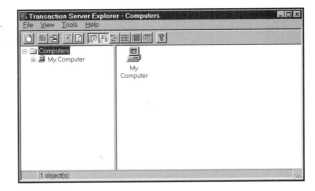

2. Double-click the My Computer icon in the right pane.
3. Double-click the Packages Installed icon.
4. Choose <u>F</u>ile | <u>N</u>ew from the main menu.
5. Click the large button next to the words Create an Empty Package (see Figure 6.5).
6. Provide a name for the new package. Type **Hockey** and click Next.
7. Click Finish.
8. Double-click the newly created Hockey icon.

Figure 6.5.

The Package Wizard dialog.

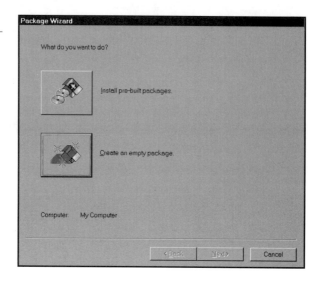

9. Double-click the Components folder.

10. Select File | New from the main menu to display the Component Wizard dialog (see Figure 6.6).

Figure 6.6.

The Component Wizard dialog.

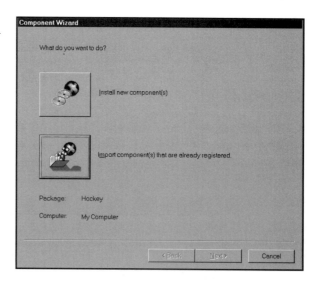

11. Select the Import Component(s) That Are Already Registered option by clicking the large button to the left of the label.

12. Scroll through the list box in the Choose Components to Import dialog until you find the item HOCKSVR.HocksvrObject.1; select it (see Figure 6.7). As a shortcut, press the H key until this item appears.

Figure 6.7.

Selecting the
HOCKSVR.HocksvrObject.1 *item*
from the Choose Components To
Import dialog.

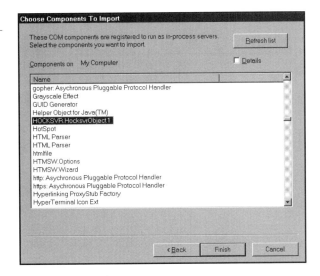

13. Click Finish. You return to MTS Explorer, and the new HOCKSVR.HocksvrObject.1 icon appears in its right panel (see Figure 6.8).

Figure 6.8.

MTS Explorer after importing the
HOCKSVR.HocksvrObject.1
component.

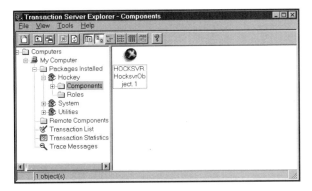

14. Run the Hockey sample application by choosing Start I **P**rograms I Microsoft Transaction Server I Samples I Hockey. Figure 6.9 shows the MTx Hockey opening dialog.

> **Note** If you are using MTS 2.0, you might not find the Hockey sample in the MTS program group on the Start menu. If this is the case, locate the Tpong32.exe application in the main MTS:installation folder (usually Mtx or Program Files\Mtx) and open it.

15. Type your name and click Continue.

16. Type **Game1** and click New.

Figure 6.9.

The MTx Hockey initial dialog.

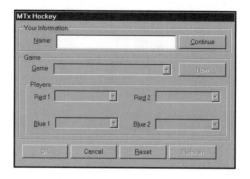

17. Change the Red 1 combo box by selecting the Computer item from its drop-down list.

18. Change the Blue 1 combo box by selecting the item with your name from its drop-down list.

19. Click OK. If MTS is installed correctly, you can start to play a simple game of hockey.

20. Choose **G**ame | E**x**it when you are finished.

Installing Service Packs

Following its tradition with Windows NT, Microsoft periodically releases service packs for MTS. These services packs are self-extracting executable files that patch MTS binaries to upgrade them by fixing bugs and add minor enhancements. After you have installed MTS from its CD, check the MTS support Web site at

`www.microsoft.com/support/transaction`

to see whether a current service pack is available. If you find a service pack, download it to your machine and install it. Each service pack contains the fixes and enhancements from the preceding service packs.

Task Uninstalling Microsoft Transaction Server

You may come across a situation that requires you to uninstall MTS. Follow these steps to remove MTS from your computer.

> **Note** Removing MTS also removes the correct operation of any components installed under its control.

1. Open MTS Explorer.

2. Delete all packages from MTS except the `System` and `Utilities` packages. To delete a package, highlight its icon in the Explorer's tree view and press the Delete key.

3. Open the Windows NT Control Panel and start the Services applet. Stop the MSDTC and MSSQLServer services. Close the Services applet and close the Control Panel.

4. Choose Start | **P**rograms | Microsoft Transaction Server | Setup.

5. Click Remove All when the Setup program displays its first dialog. Confirm your choice by clicking Yes in the confirmation message box.

   Setup removes all MTS files and cleans the registry.

6. Click Restart Windows when prompted. When your machine restarts, MTS is no longer on the system.

Workshop Wrap-Up

This chapter explains how to install MTS on your machine and how to verify the installation by configuring and running the hockey sample application. The chapter provides information on MTS service packs and tells you where to find the latest version. The final task in this chapter uninstalls MTS.

Next Steps

➤ Configuring the hockey sample included several steps that involved the MTS Explorer. For details about MTS Explorer, go on to Chapter 7.

➤ MTS is ready for components. To learn more about installing components, go to Chapter 8, "Installing Components."

➤ This chapter skipped the installation step on setting the System Package identity. For more information on how and why to set this package, see Chapter 9.

CHAPTER 7

Using Transaction Server Explorer

Transaction Server Explorer is the central administrative application for managing and deploying Microsoft Transaction Server (MTS) components. With MTS version 2.0, Transaction Server Explorer became part of Microsoft Management Console (MMC).

> **Note** Although the figures in this chapter show Transaction Server Explorer inside MMC, you can use the tasks in this chapter for the standalone version of Transaction Server Explorer that ships with MTS 1.0+.

Preparation **Understanding Transaction Server Explorer**

Transaction Server Explorer is the graphical front end that administers MTS components. Transaction Server Explorer uses the familiar Windows Explorer user interface found in most Windows 95-style applications (see Figure 7.1).

Figure 7.1.

Transaction Server Explorer window.

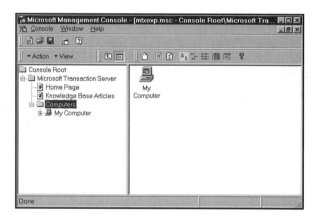

If you are an administrator, you perform most of your work with MTS through Transaction Server Explorer. You can use the application to deploy packages and components, monitor transactions, and manage security. If you are a component developer, you use Transaction Server Explorer to build packages that can then be distributed easily. In either case you should understand the basics behind this program and the runtime environment that it manages.

Transaction Server Explorer is the only application in the Microsoft Transaction Server group. Although other executables are installed in the Transaction Server folder \MTX (see Figure 7.2), you can accomplish most server management tasks with Transaction Server Explorer.

Figure 7.2.

Microsoft Transaction Server Start folder.

In general, you can use Transaction Server Explorer to perform the following tasks:

➤ Control and administer MTS servers

➤ Monitor and resolve transactions

➤ Manage packages and components

➤ Monitor performance

➤ Debug components and applications

This chapter takes a broad look at how you can use Transaction Server Explorer to manage the runtime environment. Future chapters discuss specific Transaction Server Explorer features in greater detail.

Understanding the Runtime Environment

The MTS runtime environment provides the services necessary for developing and administering highly robust and scalable applications. These services are frequently referred to as the MTS "plumbing" (see Chapter 1, "Exploring Microsoft Transaction Server").

Transaction Server Explorer enables you to administer and manipulate this infrastructure with ease. A tree control in the left pane of the Management Console houses a hierarchy of Transaction Server Explorer objects that represent items in the runtime environment. Through these objects you can add, modify, or delete items from the runtime environment.

Task Opening Transaction Server Explorer

To start Transaction Server Explorer, choose Programs | Microsoft Internet Information Server | Microsoft Transaction Server | Transaction Server Explorer from the Start menu (see Figure 7.3).

Figure 7.3.

Opening Transaction Server Explorer.

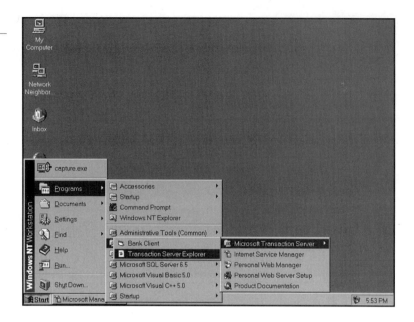

To start MMC with Transaction Server Explorer from the command line, open a command prompt window and type the command: `MMC \Mtx\Mtxexp.msc`. `Mtxexp.msc` is a configuration file that tells the Management Console to load Transaction Server Explorer.

> **Note** In MTS 1.*x* only one instance of Transaction Server Explorer process can be active at one time. Opening Transaction Server Explorer a second time only activates the application's window. Choose Transaction Server Explorer's **V**iew | **N**ew Window to create additional views.

Task Getting Around Transaction Server Explorer

Using Transaction Server Explorer is similar to using Windows NT Explorer (pictured in Figure 7.4). The similarity of the interfaces enables you to transfer your knowledge of Windows Explorer to Transaction Server Explorer.

As with most typical Windows applications, Transaction Server Explorer consists of a main window with a single menu bar, toolbars, and status bar. These objects contain functions that view and manipulate the MTS runtime environment. The sections that follow identify these user interface objects and describe how to use them.

Figure 7.4.

Windows NT Explorer.

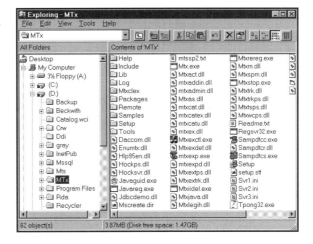

The Main Window

The main Transaction Server Explorer window, shown in Figure 7.5, contains the essential tools you need to administer servers and components. The Transaction Server Explorer is designed to be as basic as possible while allowing access to the underlying MTS framework, and as such it includes few bells and whistles. Transaction Server Explorer lacks the power and polish of more established administration components, such as Microsoft SQL Server's SQL Enterprise Manager.

> **Tip** You can compensate for the lack of advanced administrative features in Transaction Server Explorer by installing the Software Developer's Kit (SDK). This add-on enables you to program Transaction Server Explorer tasks, including modifying the Transaction Server Explorer hierarchy. Refer to Chapter 23, "Installing and Exploring the Software Development Kit," and Chapter 24, "Scripting Transaction Server Explorer with Automation," for details on using the SDK.

Figure 7.5.

Transaction Server Explorer - My Computer view.

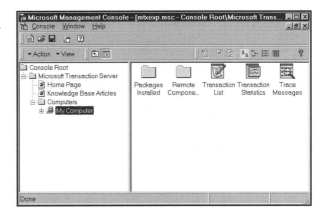

The most important elements of Transaction Server Explorer's interface are the hierarchy and view panes. You can use the splitter that separates these panes to resize the panes for optimal viewing. The left panel, or *hierarchy pane,* enables you to navigate easily through the runtime environment objects. The view pane to the right enables you to view the contents of a folder or obtain additional information on the selected object in the hierarchy pane.

The application's title bar identifies the application (Microsoft Management Console) and the highlighted hierarchy object. Clicking the various objects in the hierarchy changes the application's caption accordingly. This feature is particularly useful when the hierarchy pane is hidden from view.

> **Note** Certain functions animate Transaction Server Explorer icons when activated, showing you when work is being performed. For example, component icons spin in their corresponding view when they are being used.

The Management Console's menu bar is responsible for navigating between the snap-ins that MMC can display. To change Transaction Server Explorer, you need to use the Action drop-down menu on the second toolbar. All menu options from the standalone version of Transaction Server Explorer 1.1 now appear on the toolbar's drop-down menus. The Action drop-down menu enables you to access all Transaction Server Explorer features. The Action menu is context sensitive—its contents change based on your selection in the tree and list views.

> **Tip** Don't spend too much time customizing your Transaction Server Explorer view—Transaction Server Explorer and MMC contains do not preserve most changes you make to the user interface.

Navigating Through the Hierarchy

Transaction Server Explorer's hierarchy pane displays the MTS runtime environment items (Figure 7.6). You can show or hide this pane with the Show/Hide Scope button on the toolbar.

Selecting an item displays its contents in the right pane. Clicking the item's plus (+) symbol expands it; conversely, clicking the minus (–) symbol collapses it. Double-clicking an item selects and expands it.

In addition to using the mouse, you can use the arrow keys and the Enter key to navigate through the hierarchy. The arrow keys move the focus of the selected item, whereas the Enter key expands or collapses a node. You can also use the (+) or (–) keys on the keyboard's number pad to expand or collapse a node.

Figure 7.6.

Transaction Server Explorer hierarchy pane.

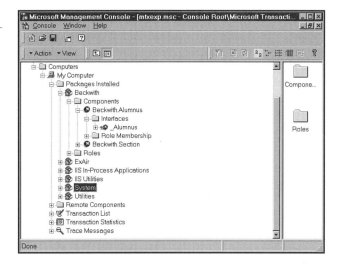

> **Tip**
>
> Many Windows Explorer–like applications support the use of the number pad's asterisk (*) key to expand all items under the currently selected node. If this node is the root, pressing the * key expands the entire tree. Although Transaction Server Explorer fails to expand the nodes under certain situations, the function still provides a quick way to get to some of the lower-level hierarchy objects.

The hierarchy pane does not support drag-and-drop operations, in-place editing, or customization. As mentioned in an earlier tip, you can use the SDK to script Transaction Server Explorer and modify the hierarchy.

You can add new items to the hierarchy and delete or modify existing items. Later tasks in this chapter show you how to perform operations on the hierarchy.

> **Tip**
>
> Context-sensitive menus are available for most of the hierarchy objects. These menus provide shortcuts for frequently used functions and can be accessed by right-clicking the desired object.

Managing the Views

You can use the right pane of Transaction Server Explorer to view the contents or details of a selected hierarchy item. You can switch between panes by clicking the desired pane.

The view pane acts as either a list view or a form view. When viewing lists of objects, such as a list of packages in the `Packages Installed` folder, the pane functions as a list control with from one to five possible views of its contents. These options appear in Table 7.1. Other hierarchy items, such as the `Transaction Statistics` object, display a form in this pane.

To change the view mode for all lists, choose the desired setting from the View toolbar drop-down menu (Figure 7.7) or click the appropriate toolbar button. View mode settings don't affect objects that display a form, rather than a list, in the right pane.

Figure 7.7.

Transaction Server Explorer View menu.

Table 7.1. *Available view modes for hierarchy lists.*

View Mode	Description
Large icons	Displays the items using large icons
Small icons	Displays the items using small icons
List	Displays the items in a list
Properties	Displays the property settings for the items
Status	Displays the current state of the items

The large icon, small icon, and list views simply provide various iconic views or layouts of the current item. The properties and status views provide additional details on the chosen item. Not all view modes are available for all lists. The available options for individual property and status views are discussed in later sections pertaining to specific views.

Task Starting/Stopping the Distributed Transaction Coordinator (MS DTC)

As discussed in Chapter 3, "Working with Database Transactions," most MTS components rely on the Distributed Transaction Coordinator (MS DTC) service.

You can start the service automatically, or you can start it manually either by using the Control Panel or Transaction Server Explorer. In any case Transaction Server Explorer reflects the current state of the MS DTC service by changing the color of the appropriate computer's icon in the hierarchy pane. The monitor piece of the computer icon appears:

➤ Dark green/gray indicates that MS DTC is not running.

➤ Yellow indicates that MS DTC is starting.

➤ Green indicates that MS DTC is running.

Automatically Starting the MS DTC Service

The MTS installation asks whether you want the MS DTC service to start automatically each time the workstation is restarted. You can change this setting by using the Control Panel services applet:

1. Open the Control Panel.
2. Open the Services applet (Figure 7.8).

Figure 7.8.

The Control Panel Services applet.

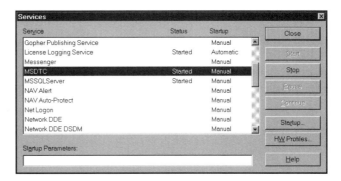

3. Find the MS DTC service in the list.
4. Click the Startup button to view the startup window (Figure 7.9).

Figure 7.9.

The Control Panel Services startup window.

5. Choose the desired Startup Type (either manual or automatic). If hosting MTS is a primary role of the workstation, choose Automatic.

6. Click OK to close the Service dialog.

> **Tip** If you need to start MS DTC, you can do so by clicking Start. You normally use Transaction Server Explorer to start this service.

7. Click Close to close the Services applet.

Starting and Stopping MS DTC Using Transaction Server Explorer

You can also toggle the state of the MS DTC service using Transaction Server Explorer. To start or stop MS DTC:

1. Move to the hierarchy pane. Choose the computer where you want to start or stop. Typically, you would select My Computer.

2. Choose Stop MSDTC from the Action drop-down menu to stop the DTC service.

3. Choose Start MSDTC from the Action drop-down menu to start the DTC service for the selected computer.

> **Tip** You can quickly toggle the start/stop state of the MS DTC service by right-clicking the desired computer object from the hierarchy pane.

Task Configuring My Computer

The Computers folder contains the MTS servers that you have chosen to administer. Chapter 20, "Managing Multiple Servers," explains how to add or remove objects from this folder. The My Computer icon represents the local system being administered. The following steps configure the settings for the local server.

Through Transaction Server Explorer you can configure a specific server's description, view refresh rates, and perform MS DTC logging. The three tabs on the computer property sheet enable you to configure these aspects of the server:

➤ General (Figure 7.10)—You use the General tab to enter a description for the server.

Figure 7.10.

My Computer properties— General tab.

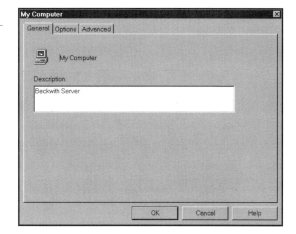

➤ Options (Figure 7.11)—You use the Options tab to set the server's transaction time-out property. This property is the maximum allowable time a transaction can remain active before the transaction manager terminates it. The transaction manager aborts transactions that remain active beyond this specified value.

> **Tip** You can disable transaction time-outs by specifying 0 as the value for the transaction time-out property. This setting is especially useful when debugging components and applications because during debugging you might set a breakpoint in the middle of a transaction.

Figure 7.11.

My Computer properties—Options tab.

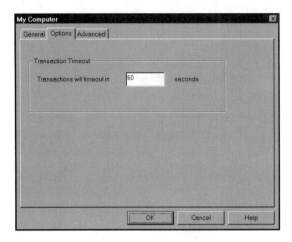

➤ Advanced (Figure 7.12)—You use the Advanced tab to configure the view refresh intervals and the MS DTC properties.

Figure 7.12.

My Computer properties—Advanced tab.

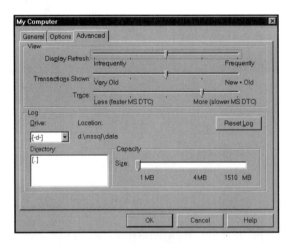

To view or change the properties for My Computer:

1. Select My Computer from the hierarchy pane.

2. Choose Action | Properties from the toolbar.

3. Select the appropriate tab from the property sheet.

Advanced Properties: Modifying the View Settings

The Advanced tab on the My Computer property sheet contains most of the user-configurable settings for the selected MTS server. The property page has two sections:

➤ View—You use this section to adjust how frequently the user interface objects are updated and to determine the level of tracing monitored by the trace messages view.

➤ Log—In this section you specify where to store the MS DTC log file, determine the maximum size of this file, and reset the log file when required.

The view section contains three options:

➤ Display Refresh specifies the refresh rate used to update the transaction windows. This value ranges from 20 seconds (infrequently) to 1 second (frequently).

➤ Transactions Shown indicates the minimum "age" of the transactions displayed in the transaction windows. This value ranges from 5 minutes (very old) to 1 second (new + old).

➤ Trace specifies the level of trace messages sent to the Trace Messages window. This value ranges from sending no trace information to sending all traces.

> **Tip** Setting these sliders to their maximum values (right-most setting) improves debugging. However, providing more frequent view updates incurs a significant performance penalty.

To change any of the view settings:

1. Click and hold the slider thumb for the desired option.
2. Slide thumb in either direction.

> **Tip** You can also move the slider's thumb control by using the left and right arrow keys when the control obtains focus or by clicking the desired tick mark.

Advanced Properties: Modifying the MS DTC Log File

In the Log section of the Advanced properties tab, you can change the drive and folder in which you store the MS DTC log file (MS DTC.LOG). Use the Drive drop-down list to select a drive and the Folder list box (directly below) to specify a folder name. The

Location label changes to reflect the new folder path. You can also reset the MS DTC log file and specify its size, from 1MB to the maximum available space in the selected drive.

To change the size or location of the log file:

1. Click Stop to stop the MS DTC service.
2. Wait for the Status indicator to show Stopped.
3. Use the Size slider to change the log file size.
4. Use the Drive and Directory controls to change the log file location.
5. Click Reset Log.
6. Click Start to restart the MS DTC service.

Task Creating New Hierarchy Objects

As you manage and configure MTS components and applications, you need to create new objects and add them to the MTS runtime environment. Transaction Server Explorer's Action | **N**ew menu option is a consistent way to add objects to this hierarchy. Later chapters examine the details of creating specific types of Transaction Server Explorer objects. In this task you learn how to determine which objects can be created and how to create new objects.

Determining Which Components Can Be Created

Selecting an object in the hierarchy pane displays or hides the Action | **N**ew menu option appropriately, depending on whether the object can have new child objects. Most objects represented by a folder icon can have new child objects. Specifically, you can create new

➤ Computers
➤ Packages
➤ Components
➤ Role memberships
➤ Roles
➤ Remote components

> **Tip** The state of the Create a new object toolbar button when you select a hierarchy object tells you whether you can create a component. The button is available only when a child object can be created.

Creating a New Object

To create a new hierarchy object:

1. Select the parent object of any of the objects listed in the previous section.
2. Choose Action | **N**ew from the toolbar.

Task Deleting Existing Hierarchy Objects

Administration and configuration of MTS applications require occasional removal of hierarchy objects. You can only delete administrator-created objects from the hierarchy—you cannot delete preinstalled objects, such as My Computer, and the System Package.

> **Caution** Transaction Server Explorer doesn't have an Undo option, so the only way to recover a deleted object is by reinstalling or recreating it. However, deleting a component or package does not delete the associated DLL that contained the object (only the reference to it is removed).

To delete a hierarchy object:

1. Select the object from the hierarchy pane.
2. Choose Action | **D**elete from the toolbar.
3. Click Yes in the Confirm Item Delete message box.

> **Tip** You can quickly delete multiple objects in the same folder by selecting all desired objects in the view pane and pressing the Delete key. (As with the Windows Explorer, multiple selection is available only in the view pane.)

Task Opening a New Window

Multiple Transaction Server Explorer windows can be open at the same time. Multiple windows enable you to monitor different views concurrently—you can view component activity within a package in one window while monitoring transaction statistics in another, as shown in Figure 7.13.

Figure 7.13.

Using multiple Transaction Server Explorer windows.

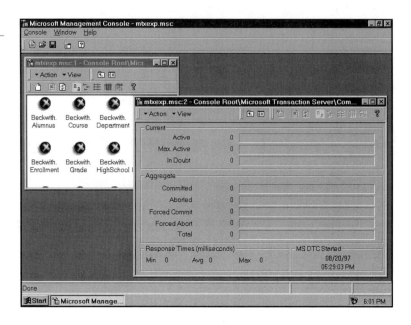

The transaction views (Transaction List, Transaction Statistics, and Trace Messages) can be active in only one Transaction Server Explorer window at one time. Other views can be opened multiple times.

To open a new Transaction Server Explorer window:

➤ Choose **W**indow | **N**ew Window from the menu bar.

Note All open windows immediately reflect the changes made to one Transaction Server Explorer window. For example, deleting a package in one window immediately deletes it from all other windows.

Task Exploring the Packages Installed Folder

The Packages Installed folder lists all packages that are installed on the selected server. Each package contains additional folders and objects that you can use to manage components and security. Chapter 8, "Installing Components," covers this folder in detail. This section explores the property view of the Packages Installed folder and reviews the folders and objects it contains.

The Packages Installed folder is the most extensive hierarchy object. The folder contains most configuration information for the packages and components installed on any MTS server. Figure 7.14 shows the objects in the Packages Installed folder. You can use Table 7.2 as a quick reference to this hierarchy.

Figure 7.14.

The packages installed view.

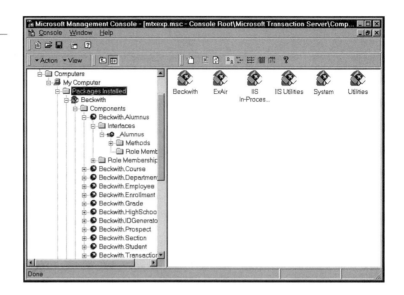

> **Note**   Review the applicable chapters for details on any specific object; see the "Next Steps" section at the end of this chapter.

Table 7.2.   *Package properties.*

Object	Description
Package Object	Collection of components
Components Folder	Lists components contained in this package
Component Object	An installed component
Interfaces Folder	Lists interfaces supported by this component
Interface Object	Supported interface
Methods Folder	Methods provided by this interface
Method Object	Specific method
Role Membership Folder	Lists roles supported at the interface level
Role Object	Specific role
Role Membership Folder	Lists roles supported at the component level
Role Object	Specific role
Roles Folder	Roles supported by this package
Role Object	Logical grouping of users
Users Folder	Users included in this role
User Object	Specific users

The Packages Installed **Property View**

The property view for the `Packages Installed` folder lists the current property settings for all packages installed on the selected server. To view the settings of the installed packages:

1. Click and expand the `My Computer` object in the hierarchy pane.
2. Click the `Packages Installed` folder in the hierarchy pane.
3. Choose View | Property view from the toolbar.

The property view (Figure 7.15) displays the most common properties for the packages installed. These properties, along with some brief descriptions, are listed in Table 7.3.

Figure 7.15.

Packages Installed property view.

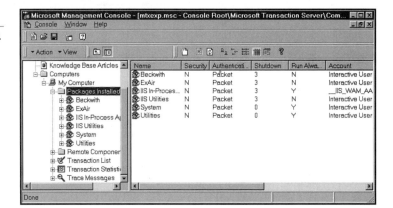

Table 7.3.   *Package properties.*

Property	Description
Name	The name of the installed package
Security	Displays whether authorization checking is enabled or disabled
Authentication	Displays the selected call authentication level
Shutdown	The period of inactivity after which the process shuts down
Run Always	Whether the process should always be available
Account	The user account under which the package runs
Package ID	Displays the package identification number

Understanding the Special Packages

In addition to user-installed packages, the `Packages Installed` folder also includes two special packages:

➤ `System`

➤ `Utilities`

These packages handle internal functions, and you cannot delete or modify them. The `System` package contains objects that classify and export packages, and the `Utilities` package contains the components that client applications use to begin and end transactions (the `ITransactionContext` interface).

Task Using the Remote Components View

The `Remote Components` folder (Figure 7.16) lists all the components that are registered on the selected computer to run remotely on another server. The property view for this folder displays the settings for these components. To learn how to add and manage remote components, read Chapter 20.

Figure 7.16.

Remote Components folder.

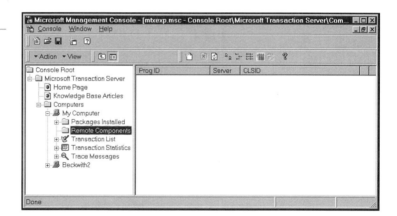

To view the properties for the contained remote components:

1. Click and expand the `My Computer` object in the hierarchy pane.

2. Choose the `Remote Components` folder in the hierarchy pane.

3. Choose View | Property view from the toolbar.

You must add a new computer to the runtime environment before you can add remote components (explained in Chapter 20). Then you use the new computer to remotely execute the desired components.

Task Monitoring Transactions with the Transaction List View

The transaction list view displays the transactions that are occurring on components installed in the selected server. The Advanced tab in the My Computer property sheet enables you to specify how frequently to update the transactions on the list. These settings were discussed in the "Configuring My Computer" task of this chapter. You can use the status icon to learn the state of the transactions on the list. The transaction pictured in Figure 7.17 has been aborted.

Figure 7.17.

The transaction list view.

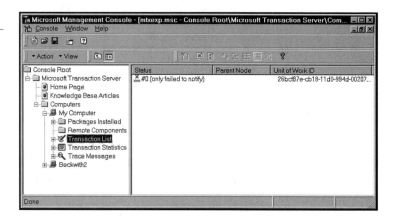

To view the transactions in which the current server is participating:

1. Click and expand the My Computer object in the hierarchy pane.
2. Select the Transaction List object in the hierarchy pane.

> **Tip** Although the view menu items are unavailable when the transaction list view is active, you can change the view mode with a context-sensitive menu.

To change the current view to provide details:

1. Right-click the Transaction List view.
2. Choose Details from the View pop-up menu.

In the details view, transactions are listed along their Status, Parent Node, and their Unit of Work Identifier. These attributes are defined in Table 7.4.

Table 7.4.   *Transaction attributes.*

Attribute	Description
Status	The current state of the transaction. This property is important when manually resolving transactions.
Parent Node	The originator of the transaction (the server where the transaction began).
Unit of Work ID	A unique identifier assigned by MS DTC.

For details on manually resolving transactions using the transaction list view, refer to Chapter 21, "Monitoring and Tuning Components."

Task Using the Transaction Statistics View

The transaction statistics view (Figure 7.18) displays current and cumulative information on transactions serviced by MS DTC. The view also presents some performance and status information regarding MS DTC.

Figure 7.18.

The transaction statistics view.

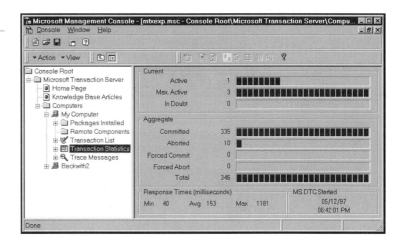

To view the statistics for the transactions in which the current server is participating:

1. Click and expand the My Computer object in the hierarchy pane.
2. Select the Transaction Statistics object in the hierarchy pane.

The view is divided into the four sections that are listed Table 7.5.

Table 7.5. *Transaction statistics groups.*

Group	Description
Current	The current number of active transactions, the maximum number of allowable transactions, and the failed number of transactions due to communication problems with the transaction coordinator and the database server
Aggregate	Cumulative statistics on committed and aborted transactions
Response Times	Statistics on transaction performance
MS DTC Started	The date and time when MS DTC was last started

Note Restarting MS DTC resets the aggregate transaction statistics.

Task Monitoring MS DTC Messages Using the Trace Messages View

The MS DTC service logs messages during certain activities, such as starting and stopping. The volume of trace messages issued depends on the setting of the Trace object in the Advanced tab of the My Computer property sheet. These messages are logged in the trace messages view shown in Figure 7.19.

Figure 7.19.

The trace messages view.

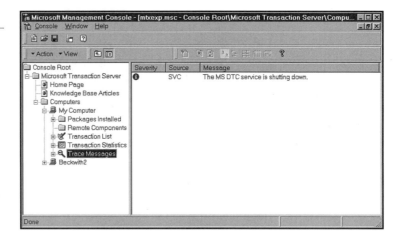

To view the MS DTC trace messages:

1. Click and expand the `My Computer` object in the hierarchy pane.
2. Select the `Trace Messages` object in the hierarchy pane.

The list displays any trace messages issued during the current MS DTC session, along with details regarding each message log. Table 7.6 describes the detailed information that is presented for each trace message.

Table 7.6. *Trace messages properties.*

Property	Description
Severity	This attribute describes the severity level of the trace message. The messages can be simply informative, warnings, or errors.
Source	Trace messages may originate from three sources: SVC (MS DTC service), LOG (MS DTC log), or CM (network connection manager).
Message	The message text.

Workshop Wrap-Up

Transaction Server Explorer is the single application that manages MTS. In this chapter you learned about the MTS runtime environment and how to use Transaction Server Explorer to manage and deploy applications within it. You navigated through Transaction Server Explorer's views and menus and learned the basic features of its user interface. The tasks that you mastered in this chapter help you learn the more complicated and detailed tasks presented in later chapters.

Next Steps

➤ In the chapters that follow, you use Transaction Server Explorer to create and install new packages, install new components, and manage application security.

➤ In Chapter 8 you explore the details of installing, configuring, and managing MTS components.

➤ System security is one of the most important aspects of a large client/server application. Find out how to integrate your MTS applications with Windows NT security in Chapter 9, "Configuring Component Security."

➤ The advanced chapters show you how to use Transaction Server Explorer to manage multiple servers, monitor performance, and troubleshoot difficult installations. Review Part VI, "Advanced Microsoft Transaction Server Administration," for important details on these features.

➤ To get the most out of Transaction Server Explorer, you learn how to script it with OLE Automation. See Chapter 25 to learn how.

CHAPTER 8

Installing Components

Tasks in This Chapter

- ➤ *Creating an Empty Package*
- ➤ *Importing Packages*
- ➤ *Deleting Packages*
- ➤ *Modifying Package Properties*
- ➤ *Adding Components to a Package*
- ➤ *Deleting Components from a Package*
- ➤ *Exporting Packages*
- ➤ *Refreshing Installed Components*

Preparation Understanding Packages

A *package* is a set of components that execute in the same server process. Although not required to do so, all components within a package usually perform similar or related functions. A *server process* is a system process capable of hosting application components. A single process can manage multiple components, and can provide services for hundreds of clients.

Microsoft Transaction Server (MTS) Explorer creates, manages, and deploys components. These components are encapsulated in packages and can be installed locally or remotely. Transaction Server Explorer enables you to configure the packages, components, and security attributes that constitute a MTS application.

Part III, "Microsoft Transaction Server Components," shows you how to create components. In this chapter you learn how to create packages to deploy these components. Many third-party components are also available for use in your applications. Tasks in this chapter guide you through importing commercially available packages and components.

> **Note** The tasks in this chapter require you to reinstall the Beckwith sample package. You may remove this package as necessary (see "Deleting Packages") and import it again after completing the chapter (see "Importing Packages"). Using this process to refresh the package ensures the correct operation of the sample application.

Task Creating an Empty Package

You can use Transaction Server Explorer to create empty packages. Follow these steps to create an empty package in the local server that can host the sample components:

1. Select and expand the My Computer icon from the hierarchy pane. You can expand the hierarchy item by clicking the (+) icon or by double-clicking the My Computer icon.

2. Select the Packages Installed folder (see Figure 8.1). Selecting this folder enables Transaction Server Explorer's Create New Object menu, enabling you to create new packages.

3. Choose Action | New from the Microsoft Management Console (MMC) toolbar. The Package Wizard helps you specify the package's general attributes.

> **Tip** You can use the toolbar's Create New Object button to quickly access the Package Wizard.

Figure 8.1.

Packages Installed folder.

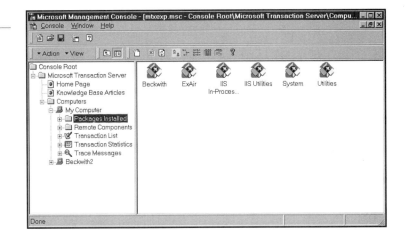

4. Click the Create an Empty Package button (see Figure 8.2).

Figure 8.2.

Creating a new package.

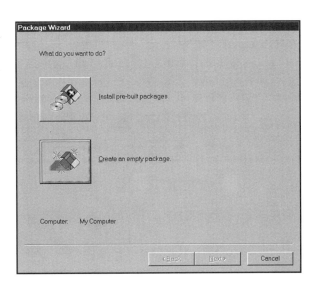

The Create Empty Package page opens (see Figure 8.3).

5. Type **Beckwith** in the text box to create a package that the sample applications can use.

> **Note** The New Package Wizard enables you to enter package names up to 500 characters long. Most symbol and punctuation characters are not valid characters for package names.

6. Click Next to continue creating an empty package.

Figure 8.3.

Naming a new package.

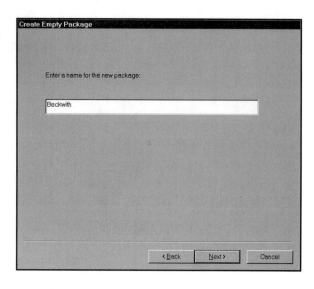

The Set Package Identity dialog, shown in Figure 8.4, prompts you to run the package under the account of the currently logged on user (Interactive User) or under a specific user account (This User).

7. Accept the default (Interactive User) and click Finish to create the empty package.

Figure 8.4.

Setting the package identity for an empty package.

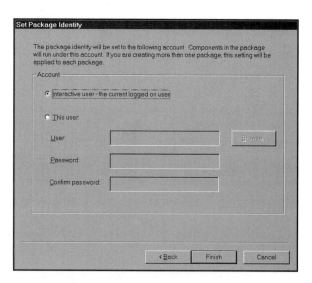

The new `Beckwith` package is added to the `Packages Installed` folder of My Computer. However, applications can't use this package until you install the necessary components and establish the user roles. Refer to the "Adding Components to a Package" task to learn how to add components to an empty package.

Task Importing Packages

To simplify installation across multiple servers, you can export packages. Exporting a package creates a package file containing the settings for each attribute. See the "Exporting Packages" task later in the chapter for details.

You can distribute your own components using exported packages, or you can purchase components that include a package file. Transaction Server Explorer installs these prebuilt packages. The import process creates and configures the package and installs and configures the necessary components. You don't have to add components manually to an imported package.

To import the Beckwith sample package into the local server:

1. Select and expand the My Computer icon from the hierarchy pane. You can expand the hierarchy item by clicking the (+) icon or by double-clicking the My Computer icon.

2. Select the Packages Installed folder. Selecting this folder enables the Explorer's Create New Object menu so that you can create or import packages.

3. Choose Action | **N**ew from the toolbar. The New Package Wizard helps you specify the Package's general attributes.

4. Click the Install Pre-Built Packages button (Figure 8.5) to open the Select Package Files dialog (Figure 8.6).

Figure 8.5.

Using the New Package Wizard to import a package.

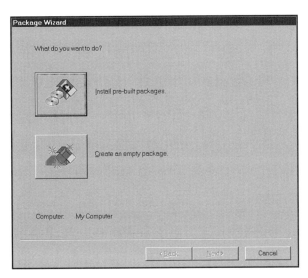

5. Click Add to open the Install from Package File dialog; then select the package files to install.

Figure 8.6.

Select Page Files dialog.

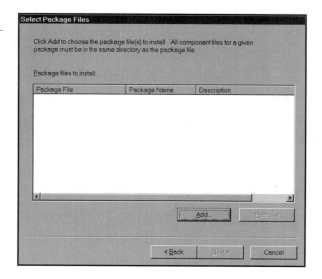

6. Look in the Install from Package File dialog and find the package file that you created in the "Exporting Packages" task or use the beckwith.pak file in the Beckwith/Components folder of the companion CD-ROM.

> **Note** The DLL containing the components for the specified package must be located in the same folder as the package file. An import error occurs if the import process does not find the DLL.

7. Select the appropriate package file and click Open. The package file is added to the Package Files to Install list in the Select Package Files dialog (see Figure 8.7).

> **Tip** Adding several package files to the Package Files to Install list in the Select Package Files dialog enables you to import multiple packages simultaneously. Importing multiple packages is a convenient way to deploy MTS applications that span multiple packages.

8. Click Next to continue installing the Beckwith package.

   The Set Package Identity dialog (see Figure 8.8) now prompts you to run the package under the account of the currently logged on user (Interactive User) or under a specific user account (This User).

9. Accept the default (Interactive User) and click Next to continue.

   You can install component container DLLs to a specific folder. As shown in Figure 8.9, MTS installs all DLLs in the \MTx\Packages folder by default.

10. Accept the default installation directory.

Figure 8.7.

Adding package files to the install list.

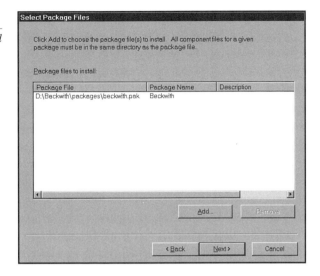

Figure 8.8.

Setting the package identity for a newly imported package.

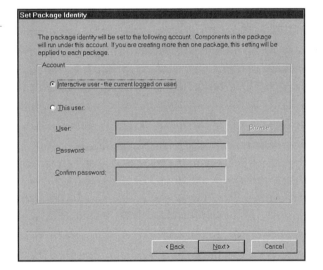

Note Exported packages can contain Windows NT user names associated with specific roles. A check in the Add NT Users check box tells the Package Wizard to automatically add the users that the package's components require. This option is available only if the package file contains any Windows NT user names. The sample package uses the Administrator and Everyone accounts. Windows NT initially installs these accounts, and they should already exist. Selecting the check box does not cause Windows NT User Manager to create duplicate accounts.

11. Click Finish to import the sample package.

Figure 8.9.

Setting the installation options.

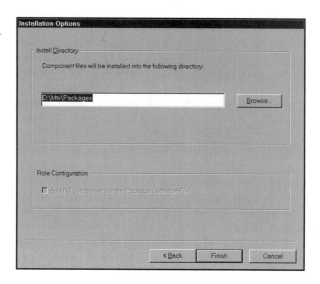

> **Note**   Throughout these tasks, you create and remove sample packages and components. The Overwrite Files warning may appear during package or component installation. You can safely allow the operations to overwrite the sample files because you can reinstall the sample package later to restore the samples to their original stable state.

After completing this task, Transaction Server Explorer includes the `Beckwith` package (see Figure 8.10). You can explore this package to find the sample components, some of which are developed in later chapters.

Figure 8.10.

The `Beckwith` *package and its components.*

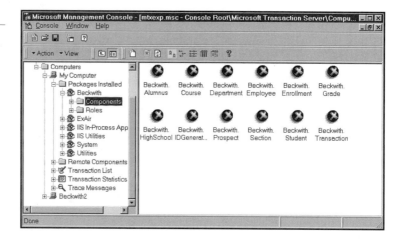

> You can import packages by dragging the package file from a Windows NT Explorer window into the view pane of Transaction Server Explorer while the `Packages Installed` folder is selected in the hierarchy pane.

Task Deleting Packages

As existing applications mature or are no longer used, you may need to remove packages. MTS Explorer does not directly support renaming of packages. Removing and re-creating a package is one way to rename a package.

You can use the Action | **D**elete menu or the Delete key to remove a package. To delete the sample package from My Computer:

1. Select and expand the My Computer icon from the hierarchy pane. You can expand the hierarchy item by clicking the (+) icon or by double-clicking the My Computer icon.

2. Select and expand the `Packages Installed` folder.

3. Select the `Beckwith` package from either the MTS hierarchy or the Packages Installed view.

> You can select multiple packages for deletion by using the Packages Installed view, instead of the hierarchy.

4. Choose File | Delete from the menu. The package is removed from the `Packages Installed` folder.

Task Modifying Package Properties

The properties of a package (see Table 8.1) control how MTS applications access the package. You can use the package property sheet to view or modify a package's attributes.

Table 8.1. *Package properties*

Property Page	Description
General	Displays the name, description, and identifier of the selected package
Security	Displays security information about the selected package

continues

Table 8.1. *continued*

Property Page	Description
Advanced	Enables you to specify how the server process hosts the package
Identity	Enables you to run the package under the account of the currently logged on user or under a specific user account
Activation	Enables you to specify the default location for instances of components in the current package

To view or modify the properties for the Beckwith package:

1. Select and expand the My Computer icon from the hierarchy pane. You can expand the hierarchy item by clicking the (+) icon or by double-clicking the My Computer icon.

2. Select and expand the Packages Installed folder.

3. Select the Beckwith package.

4. Choose Action | Properties from the toolbar.

> **Tip** Right-click the desired package to quickly delete, view properties, or export the package.

Modifying the General Information Attributes

The General tab contains the name, description, and package identifier of the selected package. You can alter both the package name and description through the object's properties.

> **Tip** Although you can't change the package's identifier, you can copy the information to the Clipboard by highlighting the text and right-clicking the selection.

To modify the package's description:

1. Activate the package's properties, as detailed in the "Modifying Package Properties" task.

2. Click the General tab to view the general attributes (shown in Figure 8.11) if necessary.

Figure 8.11.

The General tab displays the general attributes of a package.

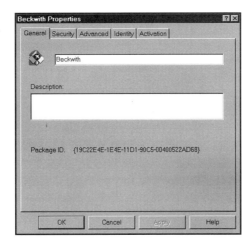

3. Type the desired new package name in the top text box and type a description in the Description text box. Descriptions can help users understand and identify packages.

> **Note** Like package names, descriptions can be up to 500 characters long. The user interface accepts of additional characters but displays an error when the count exceeds the expected number.

4. Click OK to accept the changes.

Packages are uniquely identified by their package identifiers. Much like the CLSIDs that identify components, package identifiers are a form of a globally unique identifier (GUID). MTS Explorer generates these unique identifiers when the package is created.

Modifying the Security Attributes

The Security page displays security information and settings for the package. Authorization checking enables MTS to validate the identity and security credentials of clients using the component. You can set authorization checking to various authentication levels that determine how often and how securely MTS checks a caller's identity.

For detailed information on MTS security, refer to Chapter 9, "Configuring Component Security."

To view or modify the package's security attributes:

1. Activate the package's properties, as detailed in the "Modifying Package Properties" task.

2. Click the Security tab to display the security settings (see Figure 8.12).

3. View or modify the desired settings and click OK to close the Security tab.

Figure 8.12.

The Security tab displays the package's security settings.

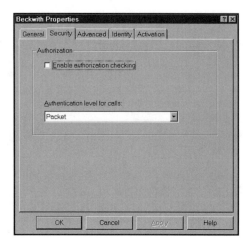

Modifying the Advanced Attributes

Components contained in a MTS package run inside a server process. This surrogate process can run on the local server or on a remote computer. Under certain conditions the components can also be loaded into a client's process space (in-process). (See the section "Modifying the Activation Attributes" later in this chapter for details on instantiating MTS components outside the server process.)

The package's Advanced properties enable you to specify whether the server process used to host the package's components should remain idle when not used or shut down after a predefined time interval.

To view or modify the package's Advanced attributes:

1. Activate the package's properties, as detailed in the "Modifying Package Properties" task.

2. Click the Advanced tab to display the advanced settings (see Figure 8.13).

Figure 8.13.

The Advanced tab displays server process shutdown options.

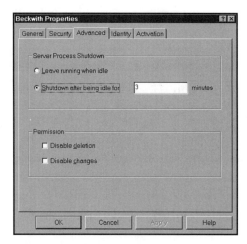

3. Select Leave Running When Idle to keep the server process running at all times.

4. Select Shutdown After Being Idle For to release the server process after a period of inactivity. Specify the number of minutes to use as the shutdown delay.

> **Note** The shutdown delay is the time-out period, in minutes, that determines when to shut down the process. The number must be between 0 and 1440.

5. Click OK to accept the changes.

> **Tip** To shutdown all the server processes running on a server, select the desired computer in MTS Explorer and choose Action | S**h**utdown Server Processes from the toolbar.

With MTS 2.0 the Advanced property tab includes two new permission-related check boxes:

➤ Disable deletion—Prevents any user from deleting the package from the MTS Explorer without first clearing this check box

➤ Disable changes—Prevents changes to the package's attributes and contained components unless the check box is clear

These two check boxes act as safeguards to prevent accidental changes and are most useful after you deploy a package into a production system.

Modifying the Identity Attributes

The identity properties for a package enable you to identify the users who have access to that package. The package can run using the account of the current user (interactive), or any specified user account.

For detailed information on MTS security, refer to Chapter 9.

To view or modify the package's identity attributes:

1. Activate the package's properties, as detailed in the "Modifying Package Properties" task.

2. Click the Identity tab to display the identity settings (see Figure 8.14).

3. View or modify the desired settings and click OK to close the Identity tab.

Figure 8.14.

The Identity tab specifies under which account the package should run.

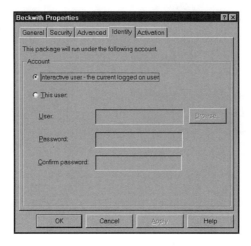

Modifying the Activation Attributes

The activation properties for a package enable you to control where the package's components are instantiated and to set this option at either a package or component level (see Figure 8.15).

You can select one of the following settings:

➤ In the creator's process—All components are created in the client process.

➤ In a dedicated server process—All components are created inside MTS processes. This location is the default.

➤ Allow component-level activation—This setting enables you to select activation at a component level versus the package level. If you select this option, you must modify the properties of each component to set its activation.

➤ By package startup only.

To view or modify the package's activation attributes:

1. Activate the package's properties, as detailed in the "Modifying Package Properties" task.

2. Click the Activation tab to display the activation settings (see Figure 8.15).

3. View or modify the desired settings and click OK to close the Activation tab.

Figure 8.15.

The Activation tab specifies where instances of the package's components should run.

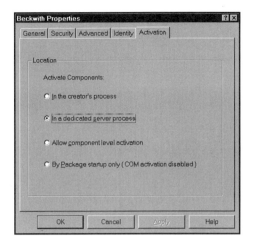

Task Adding Components to a Package

Packages are sets of components that perform similar or related tasks. Components within the same package execute in the same server process and have an implicit trust boundary. You add components to your packages by using Transaction Server Explorer.

Components can be installed either as new or imported. Although you can import components that have already been installed on the server, you should install components as new whenever possible. Imported components are subject to various limitations (described in "Importing Components").

Installing New Components

When using MTS to install a new component, the MTS hierarchy is updated to reflect the new object, the component is added to the specified package, and the Windows NT system Registry is modified with the component's information. Installing components as new is the preferred method for adding components to packages.

To install the sample components into an empty Beckwith package:

1. Select and expand the My Computer icon from the hierarchy pane. You can expand the hierarchy item by clicking the (+) icon or by double-clicking the My Computer icon.
2. Select and expand the Packages Installed folder.
3. Select and expand the Beckwith package. If components already exist, delete them as specified in the "Deleting Components from a Package Task." If the package does not exist, create the package (see the "Creating an Empty Package Task").
4. Select the Components folder.

5. Choose Action | <u>N</u>ew from the toolbar. The Component Wizard (see Figure 8.16) helps you add the new components.

6. Click Install New Component(s).

Figure 8.16.

The Component Wizard.

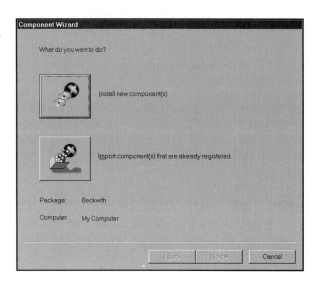

7. Click the Add Files button (see Figure 8.17) to select the component files to install.

Figure 8.17.

Installing components.

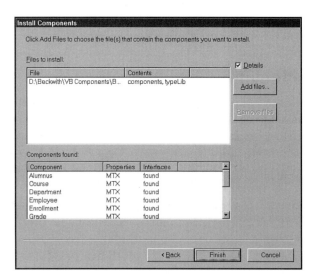

8. Find the sample component file (`beckwith.dll`) in the Install Components dialog. The default location for the file is the `\Beckwith` folder.

9. Select the appropriate component file and click Open.

> **Note** After you select a component file, the Files to Install list reflects the change. The Components Found list at the bottom of Figure 8.17 contains all components found in the DLL files you specified.

8. Click Next to continue installing the `Beckwith` package components.
9. Click Finish to install the sample components.

> **Tip** You can install components by dragging the component file (DLL) from a Windows NT Explorer window into the view pane of Transaction Server Explorer while the desired Components folder is selected in the hierarchy pane.

> **Note** All the components contained within the specified DLL are installed. You can remove individual components by deleting them from the package.

Importing Components

Your server already contains many registered components that you can use in MTS applications. In some cases you can even share components across many desktop applications. You can add these components to MTS by importing their existing Windows NT system Registry information.

Unlike the process of installing new components, you can select individual components to install (rather than all within a specified DLL). However, the interfaces and methods for the imported components are not accessible through Transaction Server Explorer.

> **Caution** You cannot view or set the attributes for interfaces or methods of imported components. Therefore, install your components as new whenever possible.

> **Note** To perform the following task using the sample components, you need to delete the installed components and register them by using `Regsvr32.exe`.

To manually register the components found in the `Beckwith.dll` file:

1. Choose Start | **R**un from the taskbar.
2. Use the `regsrv32` application to register the DLL by running:

    regsvr32 c:\beckwith\beckwith.dll

    `c:\beckwith\` is the folder containing the sample application DLL.

To import the sample components into an empty `Beckwith` package:

1. Select and expand the My Computer icon from the hierarchy pane. You can expand the hierarchy item by clicking the (+) icon or by double-clicking the My Computer icon.

2. Select and expand the `Packages Installed` folder.

3. Select and expand the `Beckwith` package. If components already exist, delete them as specified in the "Deleting Components from a Package" task. If the package does not exist, create the package (see "Creating an Empty Package").

4. Select the `Components` folder.

5. Choose Action | **N**ew from the toolbar. The Component Wizard that appears to help you add the new components.

6. Click Import Component(s) That Are Already Registered; you can select the components you want to import from the Choose Components To Import dialog (see Figure 8.18).

Figure 8.18.

Importing components.

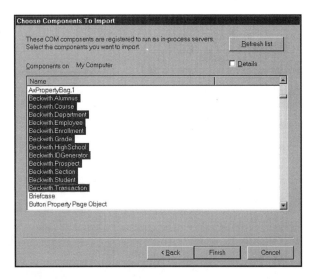

7. Find the sample components in the Components in My Computer list. By default, the ProgIDs for the components begin with `Beckwith`.

8. Select the appropriate components.

9. Click Finish to import the sample components.

Caution   Imported components are not available for remote access. Install the component as new if you need to access or install it as a remote component.

Task Deleting Components from a Package

As indicated in the "Deleting Packages" task, you can remove entire packages from the MTS Explorer hierarchy. You can also remove individual components within packages.

You can choose Action | **D**elete from the toolbar or use the Delete key to remove a component. To delete the sample components from the Beckwith package in My Computer:

1. Select and expand the My Computer icon from the hierarchy pane. You can expand the hierarchy item by clicking the (+) icon or by double-clicking the My Computer icon.
2. Select and expand the Packages Installed folder.
3. Select and expand the Beckwith package.
4. Select and expand the Components folder.
5. Select the component(s) to remove from the MTS hierarchy or from the Packages Installed view.
6. Choose Action | **D**elete from the toolbar. The components are removed from the Components folder of the Beckwith package.

Task Exporting Packages

You can also export MTS packages into prebuilt packages. Prebuilt packages consist of a package file (.pak) and the associated component files.

The package file contains information about the package and its components, as well as the settings for the object attributes.

Component files can contain DLLs, proxy/stub DLLs, or type libraries. If present, these files are copied to the same folder as the package file. The files must exist in the specified folder during import of the prebuilt package.

To export the Beckwith package along with its components:

1. Select and expand the My Computer icon from the hierarchy pane. You can expand the hierarchy item by clicking the (+) icon or by double-clicking the My Computer icon.
2. Select and expand the Packages Installed folder.
3. Select the Beckwith package.
4. Choose Action | **E**xport to open the Export Package dialog (see Figure 8.19).
5. Type the full path for the package file, including the filename, in the text box. Any required component files are copied to the same folder.

Figure 8.19.

Exporting packages.

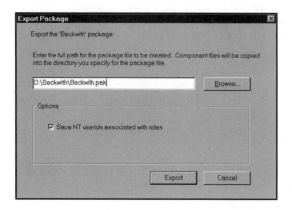

6. Check the Save NT Userids Associated with Roles box to include roles that you have configured for the package.

7. Click Export. If successful, a "success" message box appears. Click OK to dismiss the message box.

Task Refreshing Installed Components

The Windows NT system Registry stores information about the components installed in MTS. Other applications may also use these components; in some cases the applications may even modify the Registry settings of the components. If the Registry setting for any MTS component is modified, you need to refresh your components in order for MTS to resynchronize with the modified component.

To refresh the component and interface settings for all installed packages:

1. Select the My Computer icon from the hierarchy pane.

2. Choose Action | **R**efresh All Components from the main menu.

Workshop Wrap-Up

Packages are sets of components that execute in the same server process. You use Transaction Server Explorer to create, manage, and deploy packages. Managing and monitoring components are the primary roles of Transaction Server Explorer. This chapter explains how to use Transaction Server Explorer to manage MTS applications—a key component to mastering MTS.

Next Steps

➤ In the chapters that follow, you continue to use Transaction Server Explorer to manage and monitor components.

➤ In Chapter 9 you explore roles in detail and learn how to create, manage, and assign roles to components and interfaces.

➤ In Part III you create components using popular development tools such as Visual Basic, Visual C++, and Visual J++. You can deploy the components you create in later chapters by using the tasks outlined in this chapter.

CHAPTER 9

Configuring Component Security

Tasks in This Chapter

➤ *Creating Roles*

➤ *Assigning Windows NT Domain Users to Roles*

➤ *Assigning Roles to Components and Component Interfaces*

➤ *Enabling Package Authorization Checking*

➤ *Enabling DCOM Security*

➤ *Assigning Administrative Permissions*

One of the major features of Microsoft Transaction Server (MTS) is its support for security. This feature alone might be compelling enough for companies to put some of their corporate databases under MTS control. The key to taking advantage of MTS security is to place all access to your database in the hands of components and to put those components under MTS. Transaction Server Explorer securely controls access to each component, and even to each interface exposed by a component, with an easy-to-use graphical interface.

Understanding Package Identity versus Client Identity

The example in Figure 9.1 creates a user with the ID of Fred, most likely on a Windows NT domain. An administrator grants Fred certain rights on the database server and then grants him certain rights on each database housed on the server. When users add new databases, an administrator must grant Fred permission to use the new database. But what happens if Fred leaves the company? An administrator must remove Fred's permissions from each resource. What if thousands of users need to access the re-source? Administrators would spend all their time just managing user accounts and permissions. A potential maintenance nightmare exists with this security model when the number of users is large. Of course, creating Windows NT groups and assigning users to groups would mitigate much of the administrative hassle, especially in the worst-case scenario.

Figure 9.1.

A traditional client-identity-based security model.

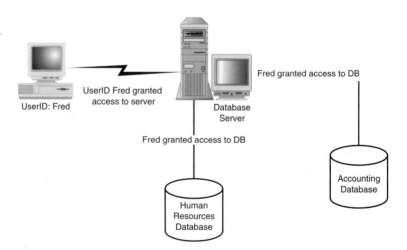

UserID Fred granted access to server

UserID: Fred

Database Server

Fred granted access to DB

Fred granted access to DB

Human Resources Database

Accounting Database

Nevertheless, a problem still remains with the client-identity-based model. When Fred connects to a database, part of the information contained in that connection is Fred's security identifier, which makes the database connection unique to Fred. If 1,000 unique users are attaching to a single database, then the database must maintain 1,000 unique connections. A separate connection for each user isn't very scalable.

The MTS security model eliminates this problem by introducing the concept of package identity. MTS hides client users and groups from server resources and instead exposes package identities to each server resource. Recall from Chapter 8, "Installing Components," that a *package* is a collection of components running in a single server process. MTS assigns a unique user account to each package and configures each server resource to grant privileges to the package user accounts, rather than to the client user accounts. In essence, each package is a virtual user. Figure 9.2 shows the behavior of an application under the MTS package-identity security model.

Figure 9.2.

MTS package-identity security model.

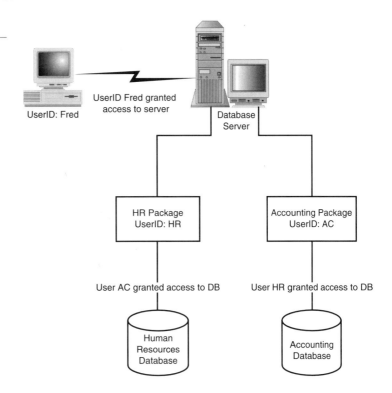

In the MTS model, components govern all access to server resources. MTS places the components inside a containing package; this technique limits access control to each resource to package identities. Consequently, an administrator does not need to configure permissions for specific users or groups on a server resource—in other words, components housed within packages control all access to that resource.

> **Note** Nothing in MTS forces this specific security model. Nothing stops you from configuring a database to accept logins from specific, actual users. The package-identity model that MTS supports is not mutually exclusive with any other security model. However, the package-identity security model for MTS applications leads to a cleaner implementation of security.

The package-identity security model offers numerous advantages.

➤ It simplifies the administration of server resources.

After a developer identifies packages during the development stage, he or she defines access to server resources only once, also during development. A developer does not need to change server resources as users and groups come and go over the lifetime of the application.

➤ The additional layer of packages between users and server resources supports more flexibility than the traditional model in the relocation of those users and resources.

For example, you can move a database from one server to another within the same domain without creating a problem for the traditional security model. However, if you move the database outside the domain, administrative hassles result. Package identity enables you to simply grant access on the other domain to the package's user account, instead of to potentially hundreds of groups and thousands of users in the traditional security model.

➤ The package-identity security model simplifies the permission settings of server resources.

Because a developer, rather than an end-user, controls the components, a database administrator can reasonably assume (hope) that carefully constructed components won't trash a database. Therefore, the database administrator grants full access to the database and all its tables to the package's user account. The components inside the package are responsible for varying the degrees of access to the database and its tables to the actual users, which lightens the burden of security administration for database administrators.

Understanding Declarative Security

An administrator uses declarative security when he or she deploys a client/server application. The administrator applies declarative security after all the components of a system are built prior to system delivery. *Declarative security* is the process of granting users permission to use the components that make up the system.

Figure 9.3 shows an example of declarative security. User Bob is granted access to a component in the Accounting package, but none in the Human Resources package. User Mary is granted access to components in both packages. This figure shows that you can grant permissions at the component level with MTS.

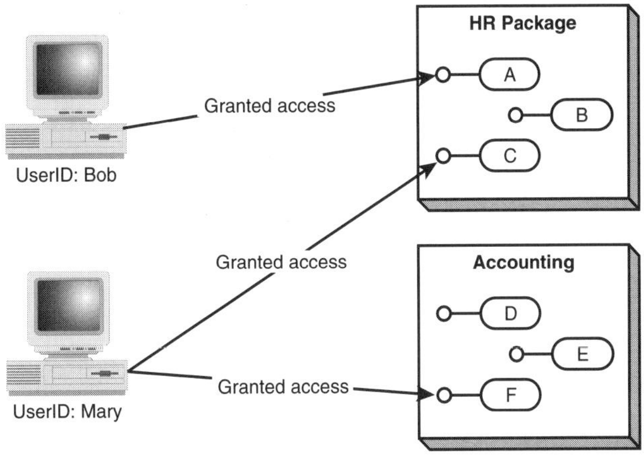

Figure 9.3.

Granting permissions to components.

Some situations require a finer grain of control over the access permissions on a component; for example, different permissions must be granted to multiple users of a single component. To accommodate this requirement, MTS permits you to set permissions at the interface level. Consequently, if one component exposes multiple interfaces, you can grant a user permission to use one interface but not another.

The example in Figure 9.4 shows a standard Account component, which represents the state of some account in a business. This Account component exposes two interfaces: IAccountRead and IAccountPost. The IAccountRead interface exposes a read-only mechanism to retrieve information about the account. The IAccountPost interface exposes a read-write mechanism to post transaction entries against the account. In Figure 9.4, user Jane has permission to read account information, whereas user Joe has permission to read and write to the Account component.

MTS checks declarative security only when a caller outside the package makes a request on a component. If components inside a package make calls to other components, MTS makes no additional security checks. MTS checks the identity of the outside caller and the caller's access permissions only when code outside the package calls code inside the package. Figure 9.5 illustrates this scenario.

Figure 9.4.

Declarative security at the interface level.

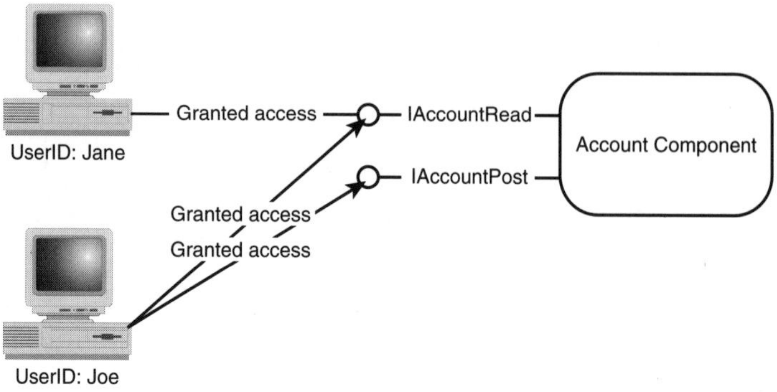

Figure 9.5.

MTS checks declarative security only for out-of-package calls.

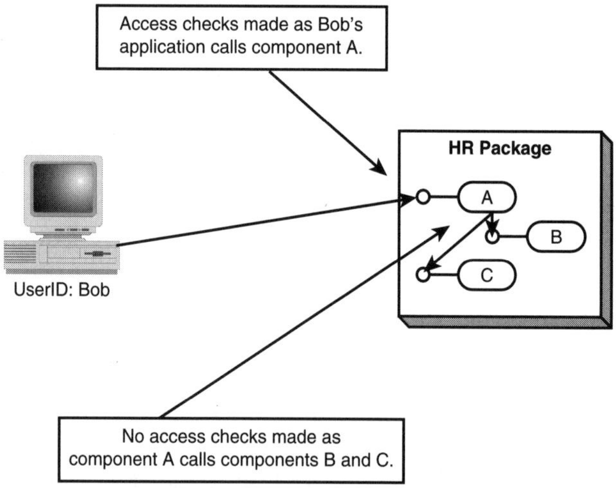

In a complex application, components in one package might call components in another package. In this case MTS performs another security check at the time of the call into the second package. However, MTS checks the identity of the calling package, not the identity of the user. Consequently, you must configure the called package to grant permissions to the identity assigned to the calling package. Figure 9.6 illustrates this situation.

Figure 9.6.

Package identity is checked in package-to-package calls.

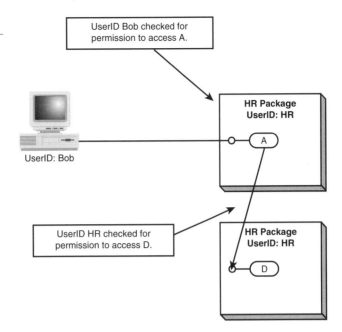

Understanding Programmatic Security

Simply granting or denying access to a component might not always provide adequate security. Many security requirements state that a component should behave according to the type of user accessing it. In this case two users are granted access, but the behavior of the component is different for each user.

For example, the Account component in the preceding section allows transactions to be posted against an account. A transaction can be either a debit or a credit—that is, money is either posted to or taken from the account. Suppose that two types of users can post transactions to the account: Clerks and Managers. The security model for the application states that Clerks can post transactions limited to $200, whereas Managers can post transactions of any amount (see Figure 9.7).

Programmatic security is a means of checking the identity of the caller inside the implementation of components. The component programmatically branches based on the caller's identity. In a client/server system, the analysis and description of the system's business rules captures the dynamic behavior of the components. Programmatic security can implement many business rules.

Figure 9.7.

A component's behavior depends on the user.

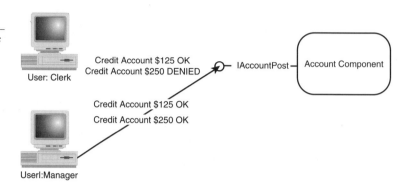

Chapter 10, "Understanding Microsoft Transaction Server Components," describes the steps necessary to implement programmatic security within components. Language-specific implementation of programmatic security can be found in Chapter 11, "Implementing Components in Visual Basic," Chapter 12, "Implementing Components in Visual C++ Using the Active Template Library," and Chapter 13, "Implementing Components in Java Using J++," for Visual Basic, C++, and Java, respectively.

Understanding Roles

MTS implements declarative and programmatic security with a feature called roles. *Roles* are an abstraction of a particular type of users and groups, defined at development time. Examples of roles include Clerks, Managers, Data Entry Personnel, Students, and Professors.

Simply defined, a *role* is a collection of Windows NT users and groups. The behavior of a role is similar to the behavior of a Windows NT group, but instead of existing at the operating system level, a role operates at the MTS package level. In most environments an administrator defines the actual users and groups that belong to a role at deployment time. The administrator is free to change those users and groups at will over the lifetime of the application. (If the roles aren't likely to change after deployment, either a developer or an administrator can define the roles while the system is being built.)

Roles were introduced in Chapter 7, "Using Transaction Server Explorer," because an administrator creates and maintains roles entirely within Transaction Server Explorer. The administrator performs the following functions:

➤ Adds users and groups to the various roles

➤ Removes users and groups from the various roles

➤ Grants access permissions to components and their interfaces to the roles

Rather than binding actual users and groups to components, which can frequently change, roles are bound to components and their interfaces. Roles act as a layer between users and components, isolating the components from change as users come and go.

The extra layer of isolation is useful for declarative security, but it is essential for programmatic security. If a component is programmed to behave a specific way for a specific user, and if the user goes away and a new one takes its place, then someone has to rewrite the code in the component. Writing a component's code to a specific role eliminates the need to recode the component when users change. An administrator removes the old user from the role and adds the new user; the component's code does not change.

Task Creating Roles

You should now have a solid understanding of roles and the MTS security models. This section explains how to create roles within MTS for the Beckwith sample database.

1. Start Transaction Server Explorer.

   If you haven't already done so, import `Beckwith.pak` (the `Beckwith` package) from the `Beckwith/Components` folder on the companion CD-ROM. (See Chapter 8 for detailed instructions.)

2. Expand the Beckwith package icon to expose the `Components` and `Roles` folders. Click the `Roles` folder contained by the `Beckwith` package. No roles are currently defined, so the list view portion of Explorer should be blank. Your display should match the one shown in Figure 9.8.

Figure 9.8.

`Roles` folders contained by packages in the Transaction Server hierarchy.

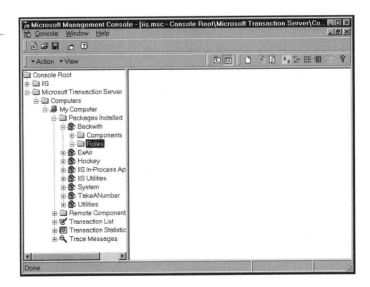

3. Create a new role by choosing Action | **N**ew from the Microsoft Management Console (MMC) toolbar, or by clicking the Create a New Object toolbar button.

   The New Role dialog (see Figure 9.9) is where you enter a name for the new role.

4. Type **Administrator** to create a new role and click OK.

5. Repeat steps 3 and 4 to create the following new roles: Data Entry Clerks, Managers, Processors, Professors, and Students. Figure 9.10 shows the Transaction Server Explorer window with all the roles for the Beckwith College sample application.

Figure 9.9.

The New Role dialog.

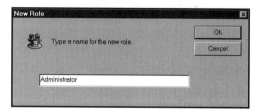

> **Caution** Role names can be of any length and include spaces, but cannot include most punctuation marks. (The dash and the underscore are valid punctuation marks.) The New Role dialog contains a free-form edit control, but you must remove all illegal punctuation from the Role name before you can edit text.

> **Note** Roles are unique to each package; therefore, it is safe to create roles with the same name in separate packages.

> **Caution** MTS identifies each Role by a role ID, a unique 128-bit globally unique identifier (GUID), in addition to a text label. Therefore, MTS allows you to create roles with the same label inside the same package. However, this practice is not recommended; because components use the text caption of a role to implement programmatic security, the duplication of role names may not be properly resolved.

Figure 9.10.

The Beckwith application's roles.

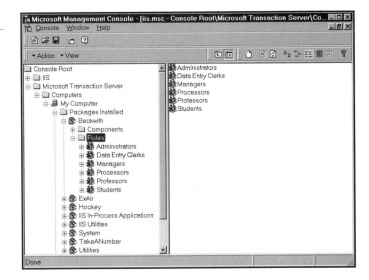

Task Assigning Windows NT Domain Users to Roles

After you define roles, you need to assign users and groups to the roles by adding them to the Users folder, which is contained by the newly created roles in the Transaction Server Explorer hierarchy. The tree view of Explorer in Figure 9.11 shows the Users folder of the Professors role.

Figure 9.11.

The Users folder contained by a role.

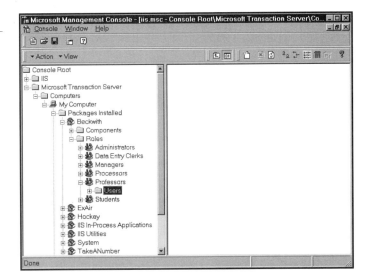

The following steps show you how to add users and groups to a role:

1. Open Windows NT User Manager and create some dummy users and groups. If your machine already has plenty of users and groups defined, you can skip this step.

2. Return to Transaction Server Explorer. Select the Users folder contained by the Professors role in the tree view as shown in Figure 9.11.

3. Choose Action | New, or click the Create a New Object toolbar button, to invoke the Add Users and Groups to Role dialog (see Figure 9.12). This dialog is common to many Windows NT applications and is responsible for enumerating all the users and groups on various machines and domains.

Figure 9.12.

The Add Users and Groups to Role common dialog.

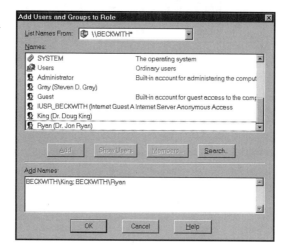

4. Select all the users and groups you want to add to the Professors role. Click Add and OK to commit the selection.

5. Verify your results with the screen shown in Figure 9.13. This figure shows Explorer with two users, Dr. King and Dr. Ryan, and one group, Biology Professors, added to the Professors role.

> **Note** One way to simplify administration is to create a single Windows NT group for each role defined in a package. Add this group to the role, and use the Windows NT User Manager to administer the security portion of the system. You can add/remove users to/from the Windows NT group and avoid the need to use Transaction Server Explorer at all for security administration after initial setup.

Figure 9.13.

Transaction Server Explorer after adding users and groups to a role.

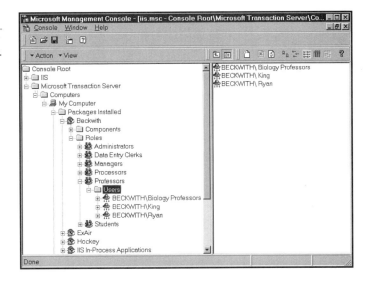

Task Assigning Roles to Components and Component Interfaces

In addition to creating roles and assigning users to them, Transaction Server Explorer is the place to implement declarative security. You accomplish this task by mapping roles to components within the package and to component interfaces.

Each component in the MTS hierarchy contains a `Role Membership` and an `Interfaces` folder. You can use the `Role Membership` folder to grant a role access to that particular component. A list of the interfaces that a component exposes appears under the `Interfaces` folder. Each interface contains another `Role Membership` folder through which you grant access to roles to that particular interface. Figure 9.14 shows the component and component interface `Role Membership` folders and their location in the hierarchy for the sample `Beckwith.Student` component.

The following tasks grant roles permission to access the `Student` component. You follow the same steps to grant access to a specific component interface, using the `Role Membership` folder of the interface, rather than the `Role Membership` folder of the component.

1. Click the `Role Membership` folder contained by the `Beckwith.Student` component.

2. Choose Action | **N**ew or click the Create a New Object button. Invoking this option displays the Select Roles dialog (see Figure 9.15).

Figure 9.14.

The Role Membership folders in Explorer hierarchy.

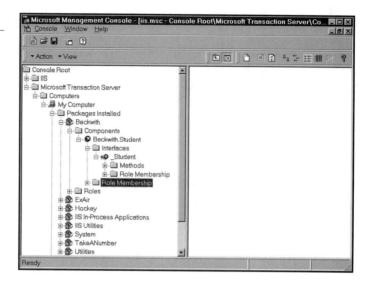

Figure 9.15.

The Select Roles dialog.

This dialog shows all roles defined for the current package.

3. Select roles from the list by clicking each one and then clicking OK.

Your Transaction Server Explorer should look like the one shown in Figure 9.16. You have successfully granted permission to all roles to use the Student component.

Figure 9.16.

Results of adding roles to the
Beckwith.Student component.

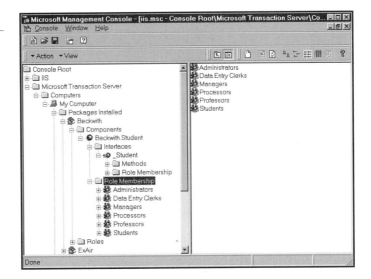

Task Enabling Package Authorization Checking

The final step to enabling security in MTS is to activate authorization checking and set an authentication level for calls to components inside a package. *Authorization checking* is the process that MTS uses to determine who is calling components inside its packages. This security is enabled at the package level, and by default it is disabled for newly created packages.

After you enable authorization checking for a package, each component inside the package can elect whether to participate in the checking. By default, each component participates in authorization checking if its package does.

You can set authorization checking to several different authentication levels. These levels determine how often, and how securely, a caller's identity is checked. Table 9.1 orders the authentication levels from weakest to strongest security.

Table 9.1.   *Windows NT authentication levels.*

Level	Description
None	Does not perform any checking or verification of the caller's identity.
Default	Uses the Windows NT default authentication level, which is Connect.
Connect	Checks and verifies the caller's identity one time only— on the first call into the package.

continues

Table 9.1. *continued*

Level	Description
Call	Checks security on every call into the package.
Packet	Encrypts the caller's identity to guarantee its authenticity. Encryption prevents a user from successfully impersonating another.
Packet Integrity	Similar to Packet, but checks the network packets for tampering during transit.
Packet Privacy	Similar to Packet Integrity, but encrypts the network packets to provide the highest possible level of security.

Follow these steps to enable authorization checking on the Beckwith sample package:

1. Select the Beckwith package from the Transaction Server Explorer tree view.
2. Choose Action | Properties to display the Beckwith property page dialog.
3. Click the Security tab (see Figure 9.17).
4. Check the Enable Authorization Checking check box.
5. Select an authentication level by using the Authentication Level for Calls combo box.
6. Click OK to dismiss the dialog and commit the changes to the package.

Figure 9.17.

The package Security property page.

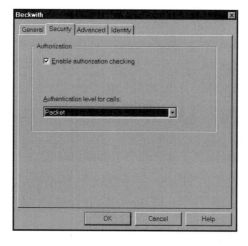

By default, all components in the package participate in authorization checking, but you can change this behavior for each component in the package. To disable authorization checking for a particular component, follow these steps:

1. Select any Beckwith component and open its property sheet dialog.

2. Click the Security tab to display the Security property page.

3. Clear the check mark from the Enable Authorization Checking check box.

Task Enabling DCOM Security

DCOM stands for Distributed COM and is Microsoft's mechanism to allow components running on separate machines to communicate. Although DCOM is not the only communication mechanism, it is the primary method used for MTS distributed applications.

Before DCOM can work, you need to enable it on each machine that participates as part of a client/server application. You also need to set two security attributes, authentication level and impersonation level, to work with MTS. Follow these steps to enable DCOM security properly:

1. Run the DCOM configuration utility Dcomcnfg.exe. This tool ships as part of Windows NT; you can find Dcomcnfg.exe in the Windows NT installation's System32 folder.

2. Select the Default Properties tab (see Figure 9.18).

3. Check the Enable Distributed COM on This Computer check box.

4. Set the Default Authentication Level combo box to a level that is equal to or higher than the authentication level set on the packages installed in MTS.

5. Set the Default Impersonation Level combo box to Impersonate. MTS requires this setting. For more information on impersonation levels, click the Default Impersonation Level combo box and press F1.

6. Click OK to close the Dcomcnfg utility and commit the security changes.

Figure 9.18.

The Default Properties tab of Dcomcnfg.exe.

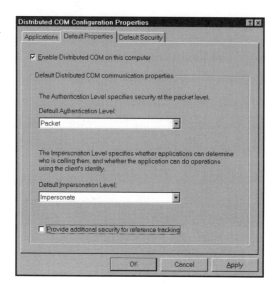

Task Assigning Administrative Permissions

All the tasks detailed earlier in this chapter enable you to wield ultimate power over who can access various components of your application. However, the security picture would not be complete if you could not also decide who gets to wield that configuration power. This section describes the steps necessary to secure Transaction Server Explorer to prevent unauthorized users from changing component security settings.

> **Caution** By default, MTS allows any user who can log into the machine in which MTS is running to modify its configuration. You can control this situation by following the steps outlined in this section.

The System Package

When MTS is installed, it automatically adds a special System package to the Explorer hierarchy. The System package controls who has access to Explorer's administrative functions.

By default, the System package has two predefined roles: Administrator and Reader. All users in the Administrator role have full access to the Explorer's features, whereas users in the Reader role have read-only access. Readers can inspect objects in the Explorer hierarchy but cannot add, delete, or modify them.

Steps Required to Enable Administrative Security

Enabling administrative security with the System package is a two-step process. The first step is to add users to the predefined Administrator and Reader roles. The second is to assign an identity to the System package.

> **Caution** Make sure you assign your login ID as a member of the Administrator role. Otherwise, you must log in to Windows NT under a separate account that has been assigned to the Administrator role. If you enable administrative security without first assigning any users to the Administrative role, you must reinstall MTS because no users have permission to configure MTS.

Follow these steps to enable administrative security under MTS:

1. Select the Users folder of the Administrator role of the System package from the tree view hierarchy (see Figure 9.19).

Figure 9.19.

The Users folder of the Administrator role of the System package.

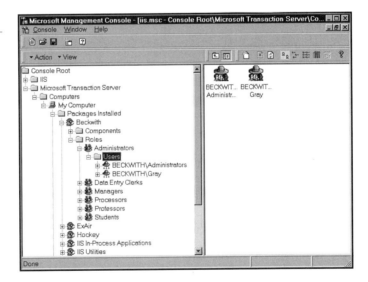

2. Add users to the Administrator role by choosing Action | New from the toolbar or by clicking Create a New Object. When the Add Users and Groups to Role dialog appears, select the users to whom you want to grant administrative privileges and click OK. This step completes the first half of enabling security—assigning users to the Administrator role.

3. Click the System package from the Explorer tree hierarchy.

4. Choose Action | Properties from the toolbar, or right-click the System package icon and choose Properties from the context menu. This step opens the System property sheet dialog.

5. Click the Identity tab to open the Identity property page (see Figure 9.20).

Figure 9.20.

The Identity page of the System package properties dialog.

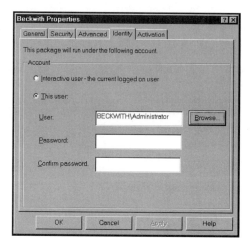

The Identity property page is where you elect to have the System package run either under the account of the currently logged on user or under a specific user account. Two radio button options control this selection: Interactive user and This user. Click the This user radio button to select it.

7. Assign a user ID to the System package by filling in the three edit boxes: User, Password, and Confirm Password. Type a name in the User field or click Browse to search for a user. (The user must have administrative permissions on the local Windows NT machine because MTS writes information to the local system Registry.)

8. Type the user account password in the Password and Confirm Password edit controls and click OK.

Tip Create a Windows NT user account for each package defined in MTS, including the System package. You should also use Windows NT domain user accounts rather than machine accounts. When distributing components and packages, you might have to grant permissions to various package identities on different machines. If the package identities are machine accounts, you must also set up a trust relationship between the remote machines, but you can skip this step if the package identities are domain user accounts.

9. Restart the process in which the `System` package executes to effect the security changes. To do so, either restart the computer or select the My Computer icon from the Explorer hierarchy and then choose Action | S**h**utdown Server Processes from the toolbar.

The System process restarts with the new security information.

Workshop Wrap-Up

This chapter explains how MTS implements security for its packages and components. You should now understand the difference between declarative and programmatic security and how to use Transaction Server Explorer to implement declarative security using roles. You assigned roles to various sample components and assigned users to those roles. You set authorization checking on the `Beckwith` package and set up DCOM to enable that checking. Finally, you learned how to enable security on MTS itself, preventing everyone from being able to modify security on its packages and components.

Next Steps

➤ So far, you have worked with the sample components on the companion CD-ROM. In Chapter 10 you begin to write your own components.

➤ For more information on DCOM and its security model, go to Chapter 15, "Setting Up Remote Windows Clients Using DCOM."

➤ For details on implementing programmatic security, see the following component-implementation chapters: Chapter 11 for Visual Basic, Chapter 12 for C++ and the Active Template Library, and Chapter 13 for Java.

PART III

Microsoft Transaction Server Components

Understanding Microsoft Transaction Server Components

Tasks in This Chapter

➤ *Working with Component Transactions*

➤ *Viewing Component-Threading Models from Transaction Server Explorer*

Microsoft Transaction Server (MTS) enables you to create large-scale, yet flexible, component-based client/server applications. You achieve this flexibility by partitioning business logic and data access into COM components and placing those components under MTS control.

Under MTS control you configure the components to run inside a large-scale enterprise-type scenario. However, you can design and implement your components as single-user components, which means that you can create them as if only a single user will use them at any one time. You can work this way in MTS because it has already implemented most of the multiuser code and logic.

As you might expect, this simplified programming model is not free. This chapter focuses on the "costs" of MTS at the general component level. The issues addressed here are common to all languages.

Preparation Understanding Stateless versus Stateful Components

The most significant design change required to achieve highly scalable component-based systems with MTS is the elimination of state from your components. *Stateless components* do not retain any information from one method call to the next. Each method invocation on a stateless object can stand on its own—the caller of a method passes all needed information to the object as parameters to the method.

More traditional components follow a *stateful paradigm* in which an object retains its data and method invocations read and manipulate that data. These stateful components follow the classical object-oriented definition of an object: An object is a collection of data and methods that act upon that data. The data is the object's state, and it is shared between the separate methods and the invocation of those methods on the object.

The following two sections illustrate the differences between a stateful and stateless version of the same object, which in this case is the classic Customer component. Client/server applications often use a Customer component to represent the name, address, and other demographic information about a business's customers. The following attributes are typically associated with a Customer component:

➤ First name
➤ Last name
➤ Street address
➤ City
➤ State
➤ Zip code

Stateful Version of a Customer Component

A traditional stateful object stores each attribute as an internal variable and exposes methods to enable clients of the object to read and set the value of each attribute. Often these attributes are exposed as properties—an attribute that has both `get` and `set` methods. Stateful objects can also expose methods, which when invoked perform some sort of action on the attributes or other aspects of the internal state of the object.

> **Note** Component properties do not always need both a `get` and a `set` method. Read-only properties implement only a `get` method, and write-only properties implement only a `set` method. Write-only properties are most commonly used for storing passwords.

Listing 10.1 shows a sample implementation of a Customer component implemented as a Visual Basic class. The first part of Listing 10.1 shows the declaration of the internal property values that store the state of the object. Following the variables is the declaration of two methods, `Save()` and `Retrieve()`, which load and store the component from a database, thus affecting the state of the component. Following `Save()` and `Retrieve()` are `Property Let` and `Property Get` methods that enable clients to read and alter each attribute of the component.

Listing 10.1.   *A sample implementation of a Customer component.*

```
'local variable(s) to hold property value(s)
Private mvarLastName As String 'local copy
Private mvarFirstName As String 'local copy
Private mvarAddress As String 'local copy
Private mvarCity As String 'local copy
Private mvarState As String 'local copy
Private mvarZipCode As String 'local copy

'methods to persist object in database
Public Sub Save()
   'perform database commit processing
End Sub
Public Sub Retrieve(CustomerID As Long)
   'perform database commit processing
End Sub

'property get and let methods
Public Property Let FirstName(ByVal vData As String)
   mvarFirstName = vData
End Property
Public Property Get FirstName() As String
   FirstName = mvarFirstName
End Property
Public Property Let LastName(ByVal vData As String)
   mvarLastName = vData
```

continues

Listing 10.1. *continued*

```
End Property
Public Property Get LastName() As String
    LastName = mvarLastName
End Property
Public Property Let Address(ByVal vData As String)
    mvarAddress = vData
End Property
Public Property Get Address() As String
    Address = mvarAddress
End Property
Public Property Let City(ByVal vData As String)
    mvarCity = vData
End Property
Public Property Get City() As String
    City = mvarCity
End Property
Public Property Let State(ByVal vData As String)
    mvarState = vData
End Property
Public Property Get State() As String
    State = mvarState
End Property
Public Property Let ZipCode(ByVal vData As String)
    mvarZipCode = vData
End Property
Public Property Get ZipCode() As String
    ZipCode = mvarZipCode
End Property
```

This component keeps its state in private variables (for example, `mvarLastName` and `mvarCity`). Clients modify this state whenever it invokes `Retrieve()` or any of the `Property Let` methods.

Listing 10.2 shows how a traditional client written in Visual Basic uses a stateful component.

Listing 10.2. *A typical Customer client implementation in Visual Basic.*

```
' Declare instance of component
Dim objCustomer as New Customer

' Fetch specific Customer information from database
objCustomer.Retrieve 12345

' Populate form with Customer attributes
txtFirstName.Text = objCustomer.FirstName
txtLastName.Text = objCustomer.LastName
txtAddress.Text = objCustomer.Address
txtCity.Text = objCustomer.City
txtState.Text = objCustomer.State
txtZipCode.Text = objCustomer.ZipCode

' We're done, so release object
Set objCustomer = Nothing
```

Client applications typically perform the following tasks when using a stateful object:

1. Create an instance of a component.
2. Populate the component with information from somewhere—typically a database.
3. Read and modify the component's state as you use it in your client code.
4. Save the modified state.
5. Destroy the object instance.

> **Caution**   The biggest problem with the preceding code is the number of server round-trips it makes to use a component. Each property `get`/`set` and method call results in a network round-trip; for example, Listing 10.2 needs seven trips to read the state of the Customer component. If this server runs in-process, no problem; but if it is invoked remotely over a network, performance suffers and limits scalability of the system.

The Disadvantages of Stateful Components in Client/ Server Applications

Stateful components are very object oriented. However, they don't work well in large-scale client/server applications for the following reasons: component lifetime, component ownership, and component performance.

Component Lifetime

As you may have noticed in the preceding steps, stateful components are created early, kept around for the entire duration of processing, and released only when everything else is complete. The problem with this long life is that each instance of a component takes up resources—in particular, memory. Lengthy object instantiation results in more memory collectively consumed on the server at any given time.

Component Ownership

Because a component contains state unique to the client that created it, that component cannot be shared with other clients. The reason is that only the creating client knows what steps it took to put the component into its current state. The result is a tight bind between each component instance and its original client. In small systems tight binding between component and client is not much of a problem because the number of component instances per client is likely to be small. However, as the number of clients using the system increases, the number of component instances increases in direct proportion.

For example, suppose the Customer component illustrated earlier is configured to execute on one server computer and that each client application requires at most n instances of the Customer component to do its processing. If you have m simultaneous clients, the server machine must support at least $n * m$ component instances (see Figures 10.1 and 10.2).

Figure 10.1.

A single client using many components using many database connections.

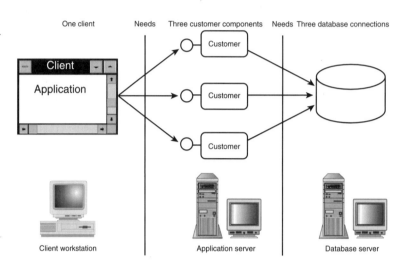

Figure 10.2.

Many clients using even more components using even more database connections.

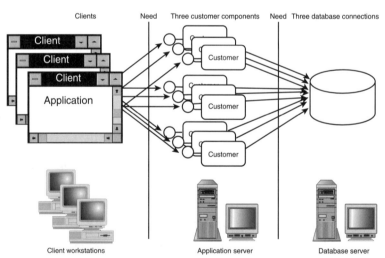

Figure 10.2 illustrates a second resource problem for database-specific stateful components. If each instance of a component creates a connection to a database server to retrieve and persist information, then the number of simultaneous database connections also increases as the number of users of the system goes up.

Database connections are another server resource that is rapidly consumed by stateful objects. Database connections are a much scarcer commodity than memory and much more expensive to create and maintain. For example, creating a connection to a Microsoft SQL Server database may take up to a second or two, and each connection takes about 50K of memory on the database server. If your application has only 10 users, this requirement isn't much of a problem. However, if your application has 1,000 concurrent users, it would take 50 megabytes of RAM just to maintain the connections—let alone handle requests from all of those connections.

> **Note** Of course, you can work around the requirement for each component to have its own connection to the database in several ways. For example, you can construct a connection pooling mechanism that enables all components to share a finite number of connections. However, as shown in Chapter 1, "Exploring Microsoft Transaction Server," MTS already does this work for you.

Component Performance

Stateful, property-based components do not perform well in a large-scale client/server system when run on a remote server. The reason is that each read or write of a component's property results in an expensive remote procedure call (RPC) across the network. If a component has 10 properties, you need 10 RPC calls to read the state of the component and 10 RPC calls to completely change the state of the component (see Figure 10.3).

Figure 10.3.

A property-based component needs many network trips.

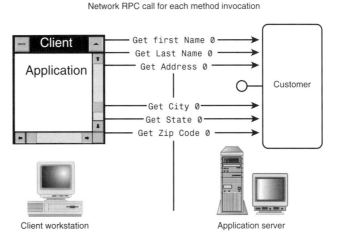

One possible solution to this performance problem is to instantiate your objects on each client workstation, instead of on a remote server. Although this model improves performance by eliminating the network RPC calls, it limits the flexibility of your system by transforming it from a powerful three-tier system to a more traditional two-tier client/server application. This model limits the scalability of your application.

Stateless Version of a Customer Component

To illustrate the advantages of a stateless component, consider the following version of the Customer component. In Listing 10.3, the component is written as a stateless Visual Basic class.

Listing 10.3.   *A stateless version of Customer written in Visual Basic.*

```
Public Sub Retrieve(CustomerID As Long, _
    strLastName As String, strFirstName As String, _
    strAddress As String, strCity As String, _
    strState As String, strZipCode As String)

    'Step 1: Create new database connection

    'Step 2: Perform SQL SELECT to retrieve attributes

    'Step 3: Set returned data into output parameters

    'Step 4: Close database connection

End Sub

Public Sub Save(CustomerID As Long, _
    strLastName As String, strFirstName As String, _
    strAddress As String, strCity As String, _
    strState As String, strZipCode As String)

    'Step 1: Create new database connection

    'Step 2: Prepare SQL INSERT or UPDATE statement

    'Step 3: Execute SQL statement

    'Step 4: Close database connection

End Sub
```

> **Note**   For a more detailed example of methods like `Retrieve()` and `Save()` in Listing 10.3, see Chapter 11, "Implementing Components in Visual Basic."

Listing 10.4 shows how a typical Visual Basic client uses the services of a stateless object:

Listing 10.4.   *A typical stateless Customer client implementation in Visual Basic.*

```
'Declare all output parameters
dim strLastName as String
dim strFirstName as String
```

```
dim strAddress as String
dim strCity as String
dim strState as String
dim strZipCode as String

'Instantiate, use, and delete Customer component
dim objCustomer as New Customer
objCustomer.Retrieve 12345, strLastName, strFirstName, _
   strAddress, strCity, strState, strZipCode
Set objCustomer = Nothing

' Populate form with Customer attributes
edtFirstName.Text = strFirstName
edtLastName.Text = strLastName
edtAddress.Text = strAddress
edtCity.Text = strCity
edtState.Text = strState
edtZipCode.Text = strZipCode
```

3 lines of Code

Clients of stateless components typically perform the following steps:

1. Allocate memory in the client application to receive the component's properties.
2. Create an instance of the component.
3. Invoke one or more of its methods in quick succession, capturing data as a result of invoking those methods.
4. Release the reference to the object as quickly as possible.
5. Use the captured data to populate forms or perform calculations.

> **Note** MTS does not require you to release a stateless, server component so quickly. Behind the scenes, MTS worries about swapping instances of the component in and out, so your client can hold references as long as it likes. For details, see Chapter 14, "Creating Windows Clients Using Visual Basic."

Advantages of Stateless Components in Client/Server Applications

Stateless components are particularly well suited for large-scale client/server applications for the following reasons:

➤ Component lifetime—As Listing 10.4 shows, the lifetime of the component is minimized to only three lines of code. The component is created, its `Retrieve()` method is invoked, and then it is released. Minimizing the object's lifetime reduces the load on the server that contains the object. This decreased load allows the server to scale to more clients.

➤ Component ownership—Because a stateless component contains no state information, you can recycle a single instance among several client applications. This concept is known as *object pooling*.

Object pooling breaks the n instances times m clients rules for objects. MTS helps to create a finite pool of object instances to service any arbitrary number of clients (see Figure 10.4). The capacity of the server—not the number of clients—mandates the number of objects in the pool.

Figure 10.4.

Many clients sharing component instances that share database connections.

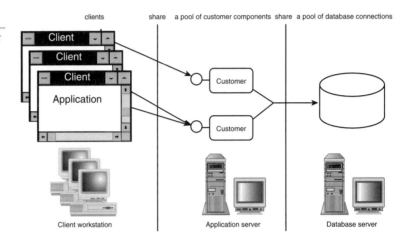

Notice also from Figure 10.4 that stateless components facilitate connection pooling to the database. Recall from Chapter 1 that MTS provides database connection pooling for free. This feature dramatically reduces the load on a database server because many clients (in this case, components) can share a finite number of connections. Because the components are stateless, they do not need to hold on to their database connections for their entire lifetime, but instead use connections only when needed.

➤ Component performance—All the attributes of a component are typically retrieved or saved in a single method call. This technique results in much improved performance by stateless components over stateful ones (see Figure 10.5).

Because stateless components are so conservative in the number of network RPC calls used to access them, you can deploy them on network servers, instead of on each client workstation. This approach returns the flexibility of a three-tier architecture to your application and enables the system to scale to many more clients.

Figure 10.5.

Method-based components require fewer network calls than property-based components require.

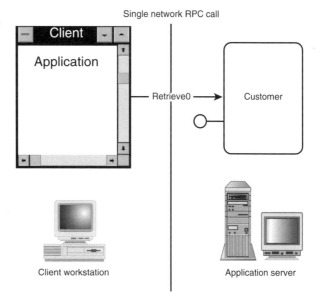

Task **Working with Component Transactions**

As discussed in Chapter 1, one of the most significant features of MTS is the support for component-based transactions. Component transactions are similar to database transactions; that is, either all operations performed in the transaction are successfully executed or all changes are rolled back when a failure occurs. Therefore, the state of the system is always reliably altered.

The immediate benefit of MTS transactional components is that a transaction can span across database boundaries. For instance, you can create an object that moves a record from one database to another by deleting from the first database and inserting it into the second. If an error occurs in either step, the entire transaction is reversed and both databases remain in their original condition.

The following sections describe how MTS accomplishes component transactions and what your components need to implement to participate in those transactions.

Understanding Context Objects

Recall from Chapter 4, "Getting Acquainted with COM," that you must build MTS components as in-process servers (DLLs). This approach enables MTS to control where to allocate the code and data for each component instance. Typically, the components execute within a MTS-hosted server process (see Figure 10.6).

Figure 10.6.

Components run inside MTS-hosted server processes.

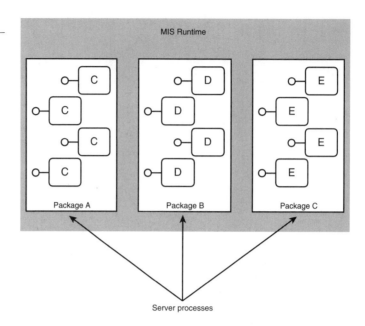

To provide component-based transactions, MTS must manage state information about every single instance of all components installed under its control. It does so by intercepting the instantiation of a component and creating a sibling object at the creation time of the original object. This second object is known as a *context object,* and its job is to maintain information about the context of the newly created object.

Some of the information contained in a context object includes

➤ Transaction participation

➤ Thread of execution information

➤ Security information, such as the component's creator

You do not need to know the details of a context object's implementation to create transactional components. Most of this information is useful only to the MTS runtime environment. Simply realize that a context object is created by MTS for all instances of your components that are installed under MTS control.

Communicating to Microsoft Transaction Server through Context Objects

In addition to containing state information, a context object is the primary mechanism through which your components communicate with MTS. Every context object exposes the COM interface IObjectContext, which defines several methods that your components can invoke. IObjectContext represents the primary API to MTS for your components.

The methods of IObjectContext perform the following main functions:

➤ Committing or aborting a component's transaction

➤ Enabling or disabling transactions

➤ Checking the security of a component's caller

Component security is discussed later in this chapter.

The two most important IObjectContext methods tell MTS whether a component's work succeeds or fails. These are SetComplete() and SetAbort(). Your component invokes IObjectContext::SetComplete() when its work executes without errors. You should invoke IObjectContext::SetAbort()when a work component fails. Either way, MTS knows about the outcome of a component's processing.

When should you invoke SetComplete() or SetAbort()? If your component is stateless (as it should be for highly scalable systems), it should invoke SetComplete() or SetAbort() at the end of every method. Invoking these methods tells MTS that a component has finished performing the work it started as a result of a client invoking one of the component's methods.

> **Note** For more details on SetComplete() and SetAbort(), see the remaining chapters in Part III.

Obtaining a Reference to IObjectContext

Given that IObjectContext is an interface, a component must request a reference to the interface from the MTS runtime environment to invoke IObjectContext's methods. To do so, the component uses the global API method GetObjectContext().

The code of a component calls GetObjectContext(). GetObjectContext() returns the IObjectContext interface pointer implemented by the component's sibling context object. After the code obtains the pointer to IObjectContext, the component can invoke IObjectContext's methods.

> **Note** GetObjectContext() is exposed to your components in various ways, depending on the language in which you implement your components. The next three chapters show you how to obtain an IObjectContext interface pointer in Visual Basic, C++, and Java, respectively.

Enabling Transactions in Transaction Server Explorer

After you install a component, you must tell MTS which transactional level the component supports. Table 10.1 describes the four possible levels of transaction support.

Table 10.1. *Component transaction support levels.*

Level	Description
Requires a transaction	Indicates the component always executes under a transaction. If the component's creator is running under a transaction, that transaction is used for the new object; otherwise, a new transaction is started.
Requires a new transaction	Requires MTS to start a new transaction for the object regardless of the transactional state of the component's creator.
Supports transactions	Runs the object under a transaction if its creator is running under one; otherwise, does not run the object under a transaction.
Does not support transactions	Instructs MTS not to run the object under the context of a transaction. Note that a sibling context object is still created for the component, even though the component does not support transactions.

You can specify a component's transaction support level by modifying the component's attributes in Transaction Server Explorer. Follow these simple steps to set the transaction attribute:

1. Install the component into the desired package.
2. Locate the component in the Explorer hierarchy and select it.
3. Choose Action | Properties and click the Transaction tab on the Beckwith Alumnus Properties page (see Figure 10.7).
4. Select the desired transaction support level and click OK to commit the change.

Inheriting a Parent's Transactional Context

Three of the four transaction support levels use the transaction context of the component's creator to determine the context of the new object. This situation occurs most frequently when a component creates and maintains a reference to a second component. If you select a transaction support level other than Does Not Support Transactions, MTS first checks the transaction context of the parent component to determine the context for the child component.

Figure 10.7.

*A component's Transaction
property page.*

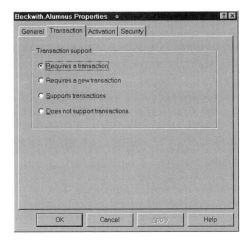

> **Note**   A client application, such as an application written in Visual Basic, can create its own transaction context, even though it is not a component under MTS control. Creating this client transactional context enables you to create a primary transaction for multiple components. The client application can then commit or abort the primary transaction, committing or aborting all changes made by each component participating in the transaction. For specific steps on implementing a transactional client application, see Chapter 14.

Selecting the Requires a New Transaction support level causes MTS to create a new transaction context for each instance of the component. Therefore, MTS creates a nested transaction if the object's creator is running under its own transaction. You should select Requires a New Transaction when you do not want the success or failure of child components to affect the success or failure of the containing transaction.

Making Components Microsoft Transaction Server Friendly

Stateless components instead of more traditional stateful components help achieve the scalability needed for large-scale applications. In addition to simply redesigning the interfaces of your objects, MTS provides other mechanisms to make your components more scalable. The following sections describe some of the things you can do to make your components more MTS-friendly. For details on how to implement these improvements, see the remaining chapters in Part III.

Implementing the `IObjectControl` Interface

Recall from Chapter 4 that all COM components expose their functionality to external clients through one or more interfaces. An interface is merely a collection of methods that the component guarantees to implement; interfaces are defined independently of any object. Therefore, many types of objects can implement the same interface.

When you install MTS, several new COM interfaces are defined and available for your components to implement. One of primary importance is `IObjectControl`. This interface contains the following methods:

➤ `Activate()`

➤ `Deactivate()`

➤ `CanBePooled()`

The `IObjectControl` guarantees to the MTS runtime environment that your component implements the preceding three methods, which MTS invokes as part of its object pooling feature. (See Chapter 1 for details on object pooling.)

The following sequence of events occurs when MTS tests your object for object pooling compatibility:

1. MTS instantiates your component and queries for its `IObjectControl` interface.

2. If your component supports `IObjectControl`, MTS invokes `IObjectControl::Activate()`. `Activate()` is like a C++ constructor but for COM components. You place any code necessary to initialize your component inside `Activate()`.

    If your component does not support `IObjectControl`, no big deal. MTS just won't invoke the `IObjectControl` related methods.

3. The normal processing of your component takes place as clients invoke its methods. Processing continues until the last client releases its final reference to your component.

4. MTS invokes `IObjectControl::CanBePooled()` to determine whether your component supports object pooling. You are free to accept or decline the invitation to join the pool by returning `True` or `False` upon the invocation of this method.

Note The current version of MTS (version 2.0) does not support object pooling. However, the method exists for forward compatibility—a future release of MTS will support full object pooling.

5. Just before your object instance is destroyed, the MTS runtime environment invokes `IObjectControl::Deactivate()` on your component. This method is a convenient place to implement cleanup code.

Note For language-specific instructions on implementing IObjectControl, see the remaining chapters in Part III.

Implementing IObjectControl is completely optional. If the MTS runtime environment queries your component for IObjectControl and the result is NULL because your component does not implement that interface, no adverse effects occur. MTS simply won't notify your component through Activate() and Deactivate() when its instance is being created and destroyed.

Safe References

Occasionally in a component-based architecture, an object must pass a reference to itself to satisfy a client's request. This situation occurs when a collection object maintains a list of many single-object instances and the collection's client requires a reference to a particular object. For example, in Figure 10.8 the client application asks for a reference to the second Object component by invoking ObjectCollection::GetObject(2). The ObjectCollection component complies by invoking Object::GetReference(). The implementation of GetReference() returns a reference to the specific Object instance.

Figure 10.8.

A component uses SageRef() *to return a reference to itself to an outside caller.*

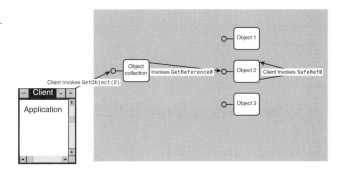

When this situation occurs, the implementation of Object::GetReference() must use a special MTS global API method. The SafeRef() method guarantees that references to the called object are safe. Because MTS keeps context information about the object in its sibling context object, MTS needs to know about every reference made to the object by its clients. SafeRef() tells MTS that a client is making a new reference to the object.

Programmatic Component Security

The programmatic security feature of MTS enables a component to identify the role under which the component's user is operating. (A role is collection of Windows NT users and groups; see Chapter 9, "Configuring Component Security.")

The key to implementing programmatic security is again through the component context object's IObjectContext interface. IObjectContext defines two methods that components use for programmatic security:

➤ IsSecurityEnabled()

➤ IsCallerInRole()

IsSecurityEnabled() returns a Boolean value that indicates whether security is enabled for the component. IsCallerInRole() accepts a single string parameter that identifies the role to check. IsCallerInRole() returns a Boolean parameter that indicates the caller's membership in the desired role.

You can invoke both IsSecurityEnabled() and IsCallerInRole() any time a component has a value interface pointer to the context object's IObjectContext interface.

Sharing Data Between Component Instances

Complex client/server applications often require you to transfer data between objects. You occasionally need to implement data sharing between independent instances of a component, even if those instance lifetimes aren't concurrent. For example, you might need to keep track of the number of instances created and destroyed of a particular object. (This type of information can be useful for a Web page counter or for performance analysis of the system.) MTS enables you to share data through its Shared Property Manager.

MTS implements the Shared Property Manager with a small object model consisting of three COM components:

➤ SharedPropertyGroupManager

➤ SharedPropertyGroup

➤ SharedProperty

MTS automatically allocates a single SharedPropertyGroupManager object instance in each server process that it manages. Recall that MTS manages a separate process for each package installed in it.

The SharedPropertyGroupManager simply manages a collection of SharedPropertyGroup objects. To gain access to the single instance of SharedPropertyGroupManager in the current server process, use the standard creation mechanisms of the target language. MTS ensures that a reference to the single instance is returned no matter how many times you try to instantiate the object.

A SharedPropertyGroup is a named collection of SharedProperty objects. SharedPropertyGroup objects can collect one or more properties under a single containing group object. This feature enables you to have multiple properties with identical names, provided the properties exist under different groups.

`SharedPropertyGroup` objects also control concurrent access to the properties they contain. Because many component instances can run simultaneously in different threads in the same process, you need controlled access to eliminate contention for the same property between two or more objects. The `SharedPropertyGroup` serializes property access so that only a single component can modify or read a property's value at any given moment.

The `SharedProperty` object is a data element that stores a single value. Essentially, a `SharedProperty` is a COM wrapper around a single `Variant`, which is a union of many basic data types (for example, `integer`, `double`, `string`, `array`). A `SharedProperty` component exposes no methods and only a single property, `Value`, from which you set or retrieve the property's value.

Understanding Threading Models

Designers use multiple threads per process to achieve high levels of scalability. This approach enables a single server to satisfy several simultaneous client requests. Without multiple threads, every client request must wait in a queue until the preceding request completes. This system does not lend itself to scalablility.

Three dominant and one proposed threading models currently exist for COM-based servers under Windows:

➤ Single threaded

➤ Apartment threaded

➤ Free threaded

➤ Worker threaded

Single-threaded COM servers are the least scalable because a single thread of execution services all component instances contained in the server (see Figure 10.9).

Apartment-threaded servers use more than one thread for individual component instances and are therefore more scalable than single-threaded servers. However, a single thread must still service all requests for an object. In Figure 10.10 the same thread services multiple objects.

Free-threaded servers are the most scalable because any number of threads can execute any object's methods at any time in any order. Multiple threads can execute within the same method at the same time. Although they are scalable, MTS does not directly support free-threaded servers. In addition, they are difficult to write given the concurrency issues of having multiple threads executing inside each object (see Figure 10.11).

Figure 10.9.

A single-threaded server.

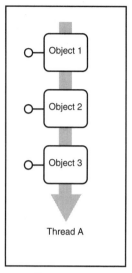

Server process

Figure 10.10.

An apartment-threaded server.

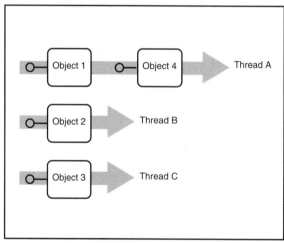

Server process

Worker-threaded servers are a new threading model that neither MTS nor component-creation tools such as Visual C++ yet support. Worker-threaded servers enable multiple threads to run within a single component instance, but only one thread executes within any given method. This threading model is less flexible than the free-threaded server model, but much simpler to implement. Worker threading is appropriate for stateless components that satisfy client requests in single method calls (see Figure 10.12).

Figure 10.11.

A free-threaded server.

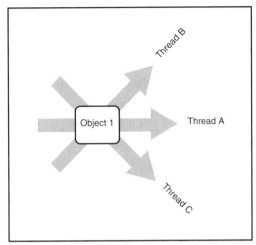

Server process

Figure 10.12.

A worker-threaded server.

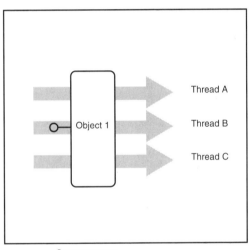

Server process

Note The worker-threading model is new, so its name might change before you read this book. MTS probably won't support this new model directly until advanced COM tools like Visual C++ and ATL integrate the appropriate support. This model is also called "rental" and "hotel" threading.

You do not need to have a thorough understanding of different threading models to write MTS systems. One of the goals of MTS is to simplify the building of highly scalable systems by hiding the details of multiple-threaded servers. You should not create and manage multiple threads in your COM servers—instead let MTS take care of the work. In other words, write your components as if they were single-threaded and simply enable multithreading support when you build your COM servers. MTS takes care of the rest.

Task **Viewing Component-Threading Models from Transaction Server Explorer**

You can use Transaction Server Explorer to determine a component's threading model. MTS directly supports single-threaded and apartment-threaded components, although Explorer labels apartment-threaded components as supporting Both in its list view.

To see the threading model of each installed component in a package, follow these steps:

1. Select the Components folder of the desired package in the Transaction Server Explorer hierarchy.

2. Choose View | Property view to display each component in a column-based list (see Figure 10.13).

Figure 10.13.

Transaction Server Explorer showing component properties.

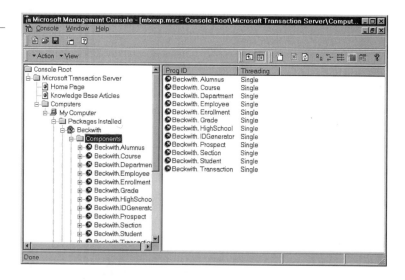

3. Scroll the list to the right to reveal the Threading column, which lists the threading model of each component in the package.

Workshop Wrap-Up

In this chapter you learned about MTS components. You learned the difference between stateful and stateless components, a key point to understand when developing components for your MTS system. You learned how MTS implements component transactions and how to write objects to participate in those transactions. You also learned how to use `IObjectControl` to take advantage of object pooling and how to use the MTS Shared Property Manager to share data between objects. Finally, you learned how MTS supports the major component-threading models.

Next Steps

➤ To write MTS components in Visual Basic, turn to Chapter 11.

➤ To learn how to write MTS components in C++ using Visual C++, skip to Chapter 12, "Implementing Components in Visual C++ Using the Active Template Library."

➤ To write components in Java using Visual J++, move on to Chapter 13, "Implementing Components in Java Using Visual J++."

CHAPTER 11

Implementing Components in Visual Basic

Using Visual Basic on a client/server project often provokes criticism from developers on the project. Previous versions of Visual Basic, although easy to use, do not perform well under most critical circumstances. However, Visual Basic 5.0 eliminates the problem of sluggish performance. Visual Basic 5.0 now includes a compiler that makes its code run almost as fast as compiled C++ code.

This chapter shows you every step necessary to create Microsoft Transaction Server (MTS) components with Visual Basic 5.0. To understand this material, you should have at least a working knowledge of BASIC, although you don't have to know Visual Basic. Even though MTS components are Component Object Model (COM) objects, Visual Basic shields you from almost every aspect of COM, so if you aren't that familiar with COM, don't worry about it.

The Beckwith College database system on the companion CD-ROM implements most of its MTS components in Visual Basic 5.0 because of its simplicity. (In later chapters several components are replicated in C++ and Java.)

Using Real-World Components

The MTS components you develop in this chapter are specific to a college's information system (for example, Grade, Student, and Enrollment). These components also perform only basic database manipulation. In real projects your components are likely to be more complex, as well as specific to your business domain. The MTS-related code in the Beckwith components is small—a testament to the architecture of MTS. MTS does not bog you down with plumbing code, but instead frees you to concentrate on business-specific logic.

Preparation Knowing When to Use Visual Basic

Put simply, developing MTS components is easier in Visual Basic 5.0 than in any other current language or development environment. Visual Basic 5.0 completely hides all the COM plumbing necessary for components. Visual Basic 5.0 takes care of all housekeeping details such as Interface Definition Language (IDL) files, reference counting, and creating in-process or local servers.

Two other features make Visual Basic 5.0 a good match for MTS. First, this version of Visual Basic is compiled, which means it runs faster than previous versions of Visual Basic, which were interpreted p-code. Second, Visual Basic 5.0 supports apartment-threaded servers. In contrast, version 4 created only single-threaded servers, which are not adequate in an enterprise-scale application.

Nevertheless, creating MTS components in Visual Basic 5.0 does have some drawbacks. Although Visual Basic 5.0 enables you to create apartment-threaded servers, it does not support worker-threaded (sometimes referred to as rental-threaded) or free-threaded servers. For complete scalability under MTS, a component should support the worker-threaded model. This model allows multiple threads to run inside a single instance of a component, but no more than one thread is executing inside each method of the component. In contrast, apartment threading allows only one thread per component. Worker threading enables multiple clients to access the same instance of a component, which increases the scalability of the system.

> **Tip** Visual Basic is easy to use and has a rapid development cycle; you should consider creating most, if not all, of a client/server application's business objects in Visual Basic 5.0—at least at first. After implementing end-to-end functionality, stress test the system and analyze its performance. Determine which objects are handling the large load and consider rewriting those objects in C++ for the best possible performance.

Task Creating an ActiveX DLL Project

You must build all MTS components as in-process COM DLLs, also called ActiveX DLLs. The first steps in creating the Beckwith sample components with Visual Basic are to create a new, empty ActiveX DLL project and to add class modules to it. *Class modules* are the construct Visual Basic uses to create components. Each class module in a project is a separate component.

Follow these steps to create a new, empty ActiveX DLL:

1. Create a new folder on your hard drive for the new Visual Basic project. You should create a folder named Beckwith in the root of your drive, with a Visual Basic Components subfolder.

2. Start Visual Basic 5.0. The Visual Basic development environment opens the New Project dialog (see Figure 11.1).

3. Double-click the ActiveX DLL project icon to create the new project.

   Visual Basic 5.0 creates a skeleton project named Project1 and an empty class named Class1 (see Figure 11.2). You can see the project and the class module it contains in the dockable Project Explorer window. By default this window is in the upper-right corner of the development environment's main frame window.

4. Change the project's (Name) property to Beckwith and change Class1's (Name) property to Alumnus. The properties for the project and class are modified in the Properties window, directly below the Project Explorer window. Click the Project1 icon in Explorer to display and modify the project's properties in the Properties window. Click the Class1 icon in Explorer to modify the class properties. Figure 11.3 shows what Project Explorer should look like after the name changes.

Figure 11.1.

The New Project dialog.

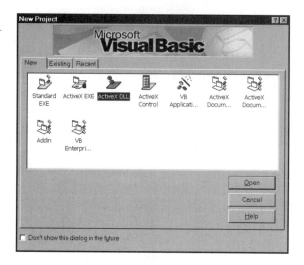

Figure 11.2.

The Visual Basic development environment with a new project and a new class.

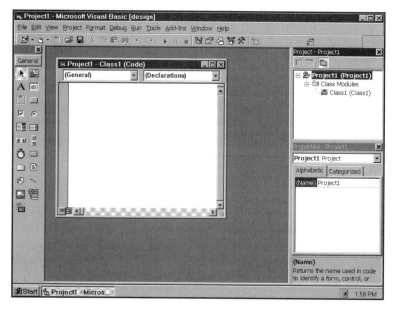

5. Save the project by choosing **File** | Sa**v**e Project or by clicking the Save button on the toolbar. Navigate to the folder you created for the project in step 1. Accept the default filenames for the `Beckwith` project and `Alumnus` class.

Figure 11.3.

Project Explorer after changing the project name.

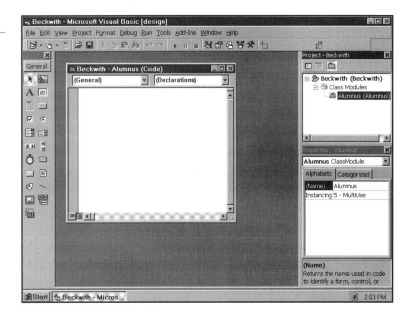

Task Importing the Common Data Access Routines

In the previous section you created an empty, do-nothing component. To provide some functionality, you need to add some data access code to the project to access the Beckwith database. The Visual Basic Beckwith project you are creating implements multiple objects, so all the database access code is implemented as a set of functions in a single code module. The details of the data access code appear later in this chapter; for now, follow these steps to import these routines from the book's CD-ROM into your newly created project:

1. Use Windows NT Explorer to copy the modDataAccess.bas file from the book's CD-ROM into the main project folder on your local hard drive. This file resides in the CD's Beckwith\VB Components folder.

2. Choose **P**roject | **A**dd File from the main menu to display the Add File dialog (see Figure 11.4).

3. Navigate to the project's folder on your local hard drive. This folder should contain the modDataAccess.bas file you copied in step 1.

4. Double-click the file modDataAccess.bas. This step makes the file a part of your project.

Figure 11.4.

The Add File dialog.

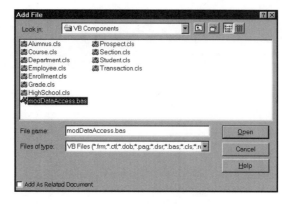

Setting the Project's References

The common data access routines you imported in the preceding section use Microsoft's Remote Data Objects (RDO). The class modules imported in the next task use MTS-defined interfaces as well as RDO, so now is a good time to set references to these two libraries. *Setting a reference* brings in all the type information for a library so that the Visual Basic 5.0 code can use the library in the project. Follow these steps to add references to RDO and MTS:

1. Choose **P**roject | Refere**n**ces from the main menu to display the References dialog (see Figure 11.5).

Figure 11.5.

The Project References dialog.

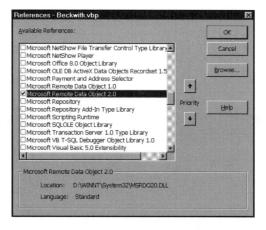

2. Navigate the Available References list box until you find the Microsoft Remote Data Object 2.0 item. Add this reference to the project by clicking the check box to the left of the item label.

> **Tip** Press the first letter of the item you are searching for in the Available References list box. The current selection jumps to the first reference that begins with the letter you typed. Pressing the same letter again advances to the next item beginning with that letter. This shortcut is useful because the list box can contain dozens of references, making it difficult to find a specific item using the mouse and the scrollbar.

3. Navigate to the Microsoft Transaction Server 1.0 Type Library item and click its check box.

> **Tip** The latest version of the MTS type library may not be 1.0 for your installation. Select whichever version number is highest.

4. Click OK to close the References dialog and commit your changes to the project.

5. Compile your project to check for errors. Choose <u>F</u>ile | Ma<u>k</u>e Beckwith.dll from the main menu to open the Make Project dialog. Accept the default project filename and click OK to compile the project. Visual Basic attempts to build the project and notifies you of any errors.

Task Adding New Class Modules to the Project

An ActiveX DLL project can contain more than one class module. The Beckwith project you have built so far contains only a single empty class module, Alumnus. Follow these steps to create a second new class module and add it to the project:

1. Choose <u>P</u>roject | Add <u>C</u>lass Module from the main menu to display the Add Class Module dialog (see Figure 11.6).

2. Select the Class Module icon and click Open to create a new class module and add it to the project.

3. Change the class's (Name) property to Enrollment. This class is the second MTS component you implement by following the remaining tasks of this chapter.

4. Save the Beckwith project and the new Enrollment class module by choosing <u>F</u>ile | Sa<u>v</u>e Project from the main menu or by clicking the Save button on the main toolbar.

Figure 11.6.

The Add Class Module dialog.

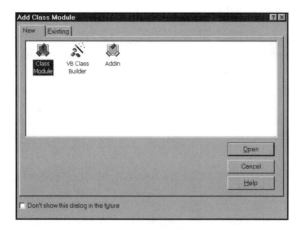

Importing the Remaining Beckwith Components

The Beckwith database system has 11 components. See Appendix B, "Sample Database Schema and Entity-Relationship Diagram," and Appendix C, "Beckwith Component Reference," for a complete description of all the Beckwith business objects. This chapter develops the `Alumnus` and `Enrollment` components from beginning to end, but rather than define and enter the code for the remaining nine objects, follow these steps to import them into your project:

1. Copy the .cls files from the `Beckwith\VB Components\Import` folder on the CD-ROM to your project's working directory.

2. Add each of the following .cls files to your project by choosing **P**roject | **A**dd File from the main menu: `Course.cls`, `Department.cls`, `Employee.cls`, `Grade.cls`, `HighSchool.cls`, `Prospect.cls`, `Section.cls`, `Student.cls`, and `Transaction.cls`.

Note You must choose **P**roject | **A**dd File from the main menu for each class.

3. Save the project by choosing **F**ile | Sa**v**e Project from the main menu or by clicking the Save button on the toolbar.

4. Compile the project by choosing **F**ile | Ma**k**e `Beckwith.dll` from the main menu. In the Make Project dialog, click OK to build the ActiveX DLL. Overwrite the existing DLL if prompted.

Tip If you come across errors when building the project, chances are the project reference to RDO or to MTS is missing. Verify that these references are present by following the task "Setting the Project's References" in the previous section. Return to the preceding step when the references are in place.

Task Adding Methods to Class Modules

The Alumnus and Enrollment classes in the current project are empty. Double-clicking either class in the Project Explorer window opens an empty source code window. To make these components useful, you need to declare methods for each class.

Listing 11.1 shows the definition of the Alumnus class, and Listing 11.2 contains the definition of the Enrollment class. The comments inside each declaration explain the purpose of the method and its parameters.

Listing 11.1.   *Declaring Alumnus's methods.*

```
Public Sub Create(rgPropNames As Variant, rgPropValues As Variant)

    'Creates a new Alumnus object by inserting a new row in the
    'Alumnus table.

    'rgPropNames and rgPropValues together define a Property Bag.
    'This Property Bag is merely a list of property-value pairs.

    'rgPropNames is an array of strings. Each element in the array
    'is a column in the Alumnus table.

    'rgPropValues is an array of values. For each element in
    'rgPropNames, there is a corresponding value element in
    'rgPropValues.

End Sub

Public Sub Read(strID As String, rgPropNames As Variant, _
    rgPropValues As Variant)

    'Reads an existing Alumnus record from the database.

    'strID is the identifier of the Alumnus to retrieve.

    'rgPropNames and rgPropValues is the Property Bag
    'which gets populated with the results of the read.

End Sub

Public Sub Update(strID As String, rgPropNames As Variant, _
    rgPropValues As Variant)

    'Updates an existing Alumnus record.

    'strID is the identifier of the Alumnus to update.

    'rgPropNames and rgPropValues is the Property Bag
    'to use for the update.

End Sub

Public Sub Delete(strID As String)
```

continues

Listing 11.1. *continued*

```
    'Deletes an existing Alumnus record from the database.

    'strID is the identifier of the Alumnus to delete.

End Sub

Public Sub Query(strWhere As String, rgIDs As Variant)

    'Queries the database for all Alumni who meet the
    'given WHERE clause

    'strWhere is the SQL WHERE clause used for the query

    'rgIDs receives an array of AlumnusIDs that meet
    'the query's WHERE clause.

End Sub
```

Listing 11.2. *Declaring Enrollment's methods.*

```
Public Sub QueryByStudent(strID As String, rgCourseIDs As Variant, _
    rgSections As Variant, rgCourseNames As Variant)

    'Queries the Enrollment table to see which classes a particular
    'student is enrolled in.

    'strID is the identifier of the student being checked

    'rgCourseIDs receives an array of course IDs that the student is
    'enrolled in.

    'rgSections receives an array of section numbers for each course
    'the student is enrolled in.

    'rgCourseNames receives an array of course names that the student
    'is enrolled in.

End Sub

Public Sub EnrollStudent(strStudentID As String, strCourseID As String, _
    nSection As Long)

    'Enrolls a student in a particular class

    'strStudentID is the identifier of the student to enroll.

    'strCourseID is the course identifier to enroll the student into.

    'nSection is the section to enroll the student into. A class can
    'be offered in more than one section.

End Sub

Public Sub DropStudent(strStudentID As String, strCourseID As String, _
    nSection As Long)
```

```
    'Drops a student from a currently enrolled course.

'strStudentID is the identifier of the student to enroll.

    'strCourseID is the course identifier to enroll the student into.

    'nSection is the section to enroll the student into. A class can
    'be offered in more than one section.

EndSub
```

Follow these steps to add the methods in Listings 11.1 and 11.2 to the Alumnus and Enrollment components:

1. Double-click the Alumnus class module icon from the Project Explorer window to open the Alumnus source code window.

2. Choose **T**ools | Add **P**rocedure from the main menu to display the Add Procedure dialog (see Figure 11.7).

Figure 11.7.

The Add Procedure dialog.

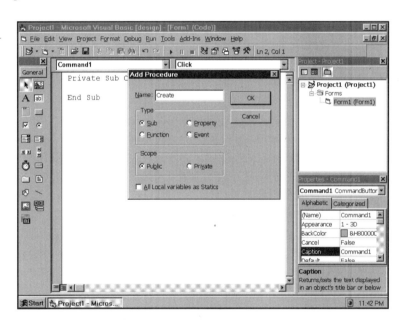

3. Type the word **Create** in the Name edit box of the Add Procedure dialog and accept the default settings by clicking OK. Visual Basic adds a skeleton method declaration for Create() when you close this dialog.

4. Repeat steps 2 and 3 for the remaining Alumnus methods: Read(), Update(), Delete(), and Query().

5. Repeat steps 1 through 4 for the Enrollment component; however, add the following methods Enrollment: QueryByStudent(), EnrollStudent(), and DropStudent().

6. Return to the `Alumnus` source code window and fill in the parameters for each method, using Listing 11.1. You don't need to add the comments inside the method definitions.

7. Repeat step 6 for the `Enrollment` component, using Listing 11.2 for its method parameters.

8. Rebuild the project to check for syntax errors. A successful build of the project means it has no errors.

> **Tip** If you don't like to use the Add Procedure dialog, simply type the method declarations as they appear in Listings 11.1 and 11.2. Using the Add Procedure dialog simply eliminates the need for you to type the `Public Sub` keywords. Note that when you type the first line of the method declaration beginning with `Public Sub` and press Enter, the Visual Basic code editor automatically adds the corresponding `End Sub` keywords for you.

Task Adding MTS-Specific Code to Your Components

At this point you have defined all the components of the `Beckwith` project, and all the data access code is in place. The next step is to make the `Alumnus` and `Enrollment` objects more scalable by implementing the `IObjectControl` interface. For more information on `IObjectControl`, see Chapter 10, "Understanding Microsoft Transaction Server Components."

Implementing the `IObjectControl` Interface

MTS uses the `IObjectControl` interface as part of its object-pooling feature. *Object pooling* enables many clients to reuse a component. `IObjectControl` gives your component a mechanism with which to communicate with MTS to coordinate object pooling.

`IObjectControl` defines three methods: `CanBePooled()`, `Activate()`, and `Deactivate()`. Perform the following steps to implement these three methods in the `Alumnus` and `Enrollment` components:

1. Open the `Alumnus` source code window by double-clicking its icon from the Project Explorer window.

2. Position the edit cursor on a blank line at the top of the source file—before the declaration of the `Create()` method. You may have to press Enter to insert a blank line before `Create()`.

3. Add the following line of code to the source file where you positioned your cursor in step 2:

```
Implements ObjectControl
```

The `Implements` keyword tells Visual Basic that your component implements a specific interface. The preceding code indicates that the `Alumnus` component implements the `IObjectControl` interface.

> **Note** Visual Basic 5.0 uses the `ObjectControl` class provided by the MTS type library as the prototype for the `IObjectControl` interface. That's why the code above uses `ObjectControl` instead of `IObjectControl`.

The next step is to provide implementation for each of the three methods in `IObjectControl`.

4. Select the `ObjectControl` item from the combo box at the upper-left corner of the code window. This combo box, known as the *Object Box*, displays a list of objects associated with the component.

   Selecting `ObjectControl` from the Object Box should automatically select Activate in the upper-right corner combo box of the code window. This combo box is the Procedures/Events Box. Additionally, Visual Basic automatically inserts the declaration of the `Activate()` method in the `Alumnus` source file.

   If you need to execute initialization code when an object is created or activated, you should put code in the `Activate()` method. MTS calls this method after an object is created or recycled from the object pool. The `Alumnus` object has no initialization code, so this method declaration can remain empty.

5. Select `CanBePooled` from the Procedures/Events Box to generate the declaration of the `CanBePooled()` method.

6. Add the following line of code to the `CanBePooled()` method to inform MTS that the `Alumnus` component can participate in object pooling:

```
ObjectControl_CanBePooled = True
```

   MTS calls this method immediately after deactivating the object to see whether the component supports object pooling. The value `True` tells MTS that the `Alumnus` component can be recycled. `False` prevents the object from being recycled, and instead the object is destroyed.

7. Select `Deactivate` from the Procedures/Events Box to generate the declaration of the `Deactivate()` method. `Alumnus` has no deactivation code, so leave this declaration blank.

8. Repeat steps 1 through 7 for the `Enrollment` component.

9. Rebuild the project to check for errors.

Accessing an Object's Context with the `GetObjectContext()` Method

A component needs to communicate with MTS under several conditions. As detailed in Chapter 10, most of this communication occurs through an object's companion context object. For every component under MTS control, when a client creates an instance of that component, MTS creates a context object in addition to the requested object. This context object holds information about the requested object and is also the object's communication link to MTS.

A component communicates with MTS by invoking methods on the object's context object. Before a component can invoke any methods, however, a reference to the object context must be obtained. Add the following code in each method in the Alumnus and Enrollment components to obtain a reference to the context object:

```
Dim objContext as ObjectContext
    Set objContext = GetObjectContext()
```

`GetObjectContext()` is a method defined in the MTS Type Library, so make sure your project still has a reference to this library. Choose **P**roject | Refere**n**ces from the main menu to check.

Task Implementing Data Retrieval in Components

All the components in the Beckwith project use RDO as their data access mechanism. All the RDO code is implemented in four global methods in the modDataAccess.bas file. Table 11.1 describes each method and its purpose.

Table 11.1. *The common data access methods.*

Name	Description
CommonCreate()	Composes a SQL INSERT statement and uses RDO to process the statement.
CommonRead()	Composes a SQL SELECT statement and returns its results. You can use this method to return a single row from a database table.
CommonUpdate()	Updates a row in a database table by using RDO and a SQL UPDATE statement.
CommonDelete()	Deletes a row from a database table by constructing a SQL DELETE statement.
CommonQuery()	Composes a SQL SELECT statement and returns its results. You should use this method when you expect more than one row from the query's result set.

Listing 11.3 shows the declaration of the common data access methods. Open the project's `modDataAccess.bas` for details of the implementation of these methods.

> **Note** This chapter does not give a detailed description of the RDO code in the common data access methods for the `Alumnus` component. However, the RDO code in the `Enrollment` object is unique to that component, so the next section presents more details of RDO's objects and methods.

Listing 11.3. *Declaring Beckwith's common data access methods.*

```
Public Sub CommonCreate(strDSN As String, strTable As String, _
    rgPropNames As Variant, rgPropValues As Variant)

Public Sub CommonRead(strDSN As String, strTable As String, _
    strTableCols As String, strWhereClause As String, _
    rgPropNames As Variant, rgPropValues As Variant)

Public Sub CommonUpdate(strDSN As String, strTable As String, _
    strWhereClause As String, rgPropNames As Variant, _
    rgPropValues As Variant)

Public Sub CommonDelete(strDSN As String, strTable As String, _
    strWhereClause As String)

Public Sub CommonQuery(strDSN As String, strTable As String, _
    strIDCol As String, strWhereClause As String, rgIDs As Variant)
```

Calling the Common Data Access Routines from the Alumnus **Component**

To provide functionality to the `Alumnus` component's methods, copy the code shown in Listing 11.4 to the `Alumnus` class module in your `Beckwith` project.

> **Tip** If you prefer not to type, open the `Alumnus.txt` file from the `Beckwith\VB Components\Import` folder on the CD-ROM with any simple text editor. Copy the code from this text file into the `Alumnus` source code module.

Listing 11.4. *Implementing the Alumnus component's methods.*

```
Public Sub Create(rgPropNames As Variant, rgPropValues As Variant)
    Dim objContext As ObjectContext
    Set objContext = GetObjectContext()

    On Error GoTo CreateError
```

continues

Listing 11.4. *continued*

```
    CommonCreate "DSN=BeckwithAR;UID=sa;PWD=;", "Alumnus", _
        rgPropNames, rgPropValues

    Exit Sub

CreateError:
    ' failure

End Sub

Public Sub Read(strID As String, rgPropNames As Variant, _
    rgPropValues As Variant)
    Dim objContext As ObjectContext
    Set objContext = GetObjectContext()

    On Error GoTo ReadError

    CommonRead "DSN=BeckwithAR;UID=sa;PWD=;", "Alumnus", "*", _
        "AlumnusID = '" & strID & "'", rgPropNames, rgPropValues

    Exit Sub

ReadError:
    ' failure

End Sub

Public Sub Update(strID As String, rgPropNames As Variant, _
    rgPropValues As Variant)
    Dim objContext As ObjectContext
    Set objContext = GetObjectContext()

    On Error GoTo UpdateError

    CommonUpdate "DSN=BeckwithAR;UID=sa;PWD=;", "Alumnus", _
        "AlumnusID = '" & strID & "'", rgPropNames, rgPropValues

    Exit Sub

UpdateError:
    ' failure

End Sub

Public Sub Delete(strID As String)
    Dim objContext As ObjectContext
    Set objContext = GetObjectContext()

    On Error GoTo DeleteError

    CommonDelete "DSN=BeckwithAR;UID=sa;PWD=;", "Alumnus", _
        "AlumnusID = '" & strID & "'"

    Exit Sub

DeleteError:
    ' failure

End Sub
```

```
Public Sub Query(strWhere As String, rgIDs As Variant)
   Dim objContext As ObjectContext
   Set objContext = GetObjectContext()

   On Error GoTo QueryError

   CommonQuery "DSN=BeckwithAR;UID=sa;PWD=;", "Alumnus", _
      "AlumnusID", strWhere, rgIDs

   Exit Sub

QueryError:
   ' failure

End Sub
```

Note The error handlers in Listing 11.4 are intentionally incomplete. You add complete error handling to your components later in this chapter in the "Implementing Component Transactions" section.

Implementing Data Access for the Enrollment Component

The Enrollment component implements three methods: QueryByStudent(), EnrollStudent(), and DropStudent(). The following steps walk through the coding of the EnrollStudent() method and show you how to import the code for the remaining two methods:

1. Double-click the Enrollment icon from the Project Explorer window to open the Enrollment source code window.

2. Add the following error-handling code immediately after the call to GetObjectContext():

   ```
   On Error Goto EnrollError
   ```

   The first step to using RDO to retrieve data from a database is to create a connection.

3. Add the following code to create an RDO connection to the Beckwith Registrar database:

   ```
   Dim rdoConn As rdoConnection
   Set rdoConn = rdoEngine.rdoEnvironments(0).OpenConnection("", _
      rdDriverNoPrompt, False, "DSN=BeckwithRG;UID=sa;PWD=;")
   ```

   The process of enrolling a student in a class requires inserting a row in the Registrar's Enrollment table.

4. Add the following code to build the SQL INSERT statement using parameters passed to the EnrollStudent() method:

   ```
   Dim strSQL As String
   strSQL = "INSERT Enrollment(CourseID, Section, StudentID)"
   ```

```
strSQL = strSQL & " VALUES ('" & strCourseID & "', " & _
    nSection & ", '" & strStudentID & "')"
```

5. Execute the SQL statement by invoking the RDO connection's `Execute()` method. Add this code:

```
rdoConn.Execute strSQL, Options:=rdExecDirect
```

One line of code is all that RDO requires for this method.

6. Close the RDO connection with this line of code:

```
rdoConn.Close
```

The student is now enrolled in the desired class. However, Beckwith College is not in the habit of letting students take classes for free, so to complete the implementation of `EnrollStudent()`, you need to implement code that debits the student's Business Office account for the cost of the class.

In the following code a component creates and uses the services of other components. In this case the `Course` component determines the cost of the class, and the `Transaction` component posts a debit to the student's account.

1. Add the code that obtains the course's cost:

```
' get course cost
Dim objCourse As Course
Set objCourse = GetObjectContext.CreateInstance("Beckwith.Course")
Dim rgPropNames As Variant
Dim rgPropValues As Variant
Dim colPropBag As New Collection

objCourse.Read strCourseID, rgPropNames, rgPropValues
PropBagToCol rgPropNames, rgPropValues, colPropBag

Dim nAmount As Double
nAmount = colPropBag("Cost")
```

This code performs several important functions:

➤ It declares several variables: `objCourse`, `rgPropNames`, `rgPropValues`, and `colPropBag`. `objCourse` is an instance of the `Course` component. `rgPropNames` and `rgPropValues` are arrays that receive the values of a particular course when the `Course` component's `Read()` method is invoked. `colPropBag` is a Visual Basic collection that stores values of `rgPropNames` and `rgPropValues` and provides a more user-friendly way for code to access the values of the returned property bag.

➤ It creates `objCourse`. Instead of using Visual Basic 5.0's `New` keyword to create an instance of the `Course` component, this code uses the `IObjectContext::CreateInstance()` method. This MTS method allows the context of the current object, `Enrollment`, to be carried forward to the new object, `Course`. This mechanism enables a transaction to span multiple components—MTS uses the transaction state of the parent to create the child. Based on the transactional property of the child component, it decides whether to participate in its parent's transaction, in its own transaction, or no transaction at all. The parent object doesn't care, but by using `CreateInstance()` MTS takes care of all the housekeeping involved in setting up the context for the child.

➤ After the variable declarations and instantiation of the `objCourse` variable, its `Read()` method retrieves information about the course in which the student just enrolled. The arrays `rgPropNames` and `rgPropValues` return the course information, and after the call to `Read()`, a call to `PropBagToCol()` converts the arrays into a collection.

➤ It retrieves the Cost attribute of the course and stores the attribute in the variable `nAmount`. (The next step uses this variable.)

After retrieving the price of the course, the code creates a `Transaction` object to post a transaction to the student's account.

2. Append the following code to post the transaction to the student's account:

```
Dim obj1 As Transaction
Set obj1 = GetObjectContext.CreateInstance("Beckwith.Transaction")
obj1.PostTransaction "Student", strStudentID, nAmount, _
    "Enrollment in " & strCourseID
```

This code simply declares and allocates an instance of the `Transaction` object and invokes its `PostTransaction()` method, passing in the parameters necessary to debit the student's account, including the cost of the course, `nAmount`, calculated in step 1 above. This process is similar to the instantiation of the `Course` component; both procedures use the `IObjectContext::CreateInstance()` method, instead of `New`. The single parameter to `CreateInstance()` is the component's programmatic ID.

The final step is to finish the error-handling code that you started in step 2 at the very beginning of this section.

3. Add the following code:

```
    Exit Sub

EnrollError:
    'failure

End Sub
```

4. Open the file `Enrollment.txt` from the CD-ROM `Beckwith\VB Components\Import` folder in a text editor. Copy the implementation of `QueryByStudent()` and `DropStudent()` from this file and paste into the `Enrollment.cls` source file.

5. Rebuild the project to check for errors.

Listing 11.5 shows the entire implementation of `EnrollStudent()`.

Listing 11.5. *Implementing the EnrollStudent() method.*

```
Public Sub EnrollStudent(strStudentID As String, strCourseID As String, nSection As Long)
    Dim objContext As ObjectContext
    Set objContext = GetObjectContext()

    On Error GoTo EnrollError

    Dim rdoConn As rdoConnection
    Set rdoConn = rdoEngine.rdoEnvironments(0).OpenConnection("", rdDriverNoPrompt, False, _
"DSN=BeckwithRG;UID=sa;PWD=;")

    Dim strSQL As String
    strSQL = "INSERT Enrollment(CourseID, Section, StudentID)"

    strSQL = strSQL & " VALUES ('" & strCourseID & "', " & _
        nSection & ", '" & strStudentID & "')"

    ' perform the insert
    rdoConn.Execute strSQL, Options:=rdExecDirect
    rdoConn.Close

    ' perform debit to student's business office account
    ' get course cost
    Dim objCourse As Course
    Set objCourse = GetObjectContext.CreateInstance("Beckwith.Course")
    Dim rgPropNames As Variant
    Dim rgPropValues As Variant
    Dim colPropBag As New Collection

    objCourse.Read strCourseID, rgPropNames, rgPropValues
    PropBagToCol rgPropNames, rgPropValues, colPropBag

    Dim nAmount As Double
    nAmount = colPropBag("Cost")

    Dim obj1 As Transaction
    Set obj1 = GetObjectContext.CreateInstance("Beckwith.Transaction")
    obj1.PostTransaction "Student", strStudentID, nAmount, "Enrollment in " & strCourseID

    'Success

    Exit Sub

EnrollError:

    'failure

End Sub
```

> **Note** None of the code implemented in this section does anything when an error occurs. The tasks in the following section show you how to remedy the situation by implementing component transactions.

Task Implementing Component Transactions

The components in the Beckwith sample are ready for transactions. Specifically, each component should call SetComplete() when its RDO statements execute successfully or call SetAbort() when an error occurs. Follow these steps to implement component transactions in the Alumnus and Enrollment components:

1. Open the Alumnus class module.

2. Add the following line to each Alumnus method, immediately following the call to the common data access method, but before the Exit Sub keywords:

   ```
   objContext.SetComplete
   ```

   If an error occurs in the RDO code performed by the common data access routines, the preceding line of code is never executed. Instead, execution skips to the label at the end of the method if an error occurs.

3. Add the following line after the error label at the end of each method on the line with the 'failure comment:

   ```
   objContext.SetAbort
   ```

   This line tells MTS that an error occurred, to abort the current transaction, and to roll back any changes.

4. Open the Enrollment class module.

5. Add the following line in the implementation of EnrollStudent(), after the call to PostTransaction() and before the Exit Sub keywords:

   ```
   objContext.SetComplete
   ```

6. Add the following line of code after the EnrollError: label:

   ```
   objContext.SetAbort
   ```

   As you can see, the Enrollment component implements transactions the same way as the other Beckwith components do, even though it invoked the services of other components. Each component worries about its own calls to SetComplete() and SetAbort(). The Enrollment component does not need to concern itself with transactions for the Course and Transaction components.

Task Sharing Data among Components

This task shows you how to use the Shared Property Manager to enable components and their instances to share data between themselves. Chapter 10 covers the Shared Property Manager in detail. The tasks below show you the Visual Basic syntax for accessing this feature of MTS.

The following tasks add a new class to this chapter's Beckwith project. The new class is IDGenerator, and its sole purpose is to return consecutive numbers each time its GetNextID() method is called. Many instances of IDGenerator can be created and destroyed, but consecutive numbers are always dispensed. You do not need to create a single instance and keep it forever. The Shared Property Manager enables you to create IDGenerator as a scalable, stateless MTS component.

Follow these steps to build the IDGenerator component:

1. Create a new class module and add it to the Beckwith project. Set its (Name) property to IDGenerator.

2. Add a public function called GetNextID() that returns a Long and takes no parameters to the IDGenerator.cls source code file.

3. Add the code in Listing 11.6 to implement the GetNextID() method. This code accesses the Shared Property Manager, obtains a reference to a Shared Property Group called Beckwith, and then increments the property IDGenerator. Finally, the newly incremented identifier is returned to the caller.

> **Tip** If you prefer not to type in the code, copy the IDGenerator.cls file from the Beckwith\VB Components\Import folder on the CD-ROM into your project's working directory. Choose **P**roject | **A**dd Files to add the IDGenerator.cls file to your project.

4. Add a reference to the MTS Shared Property Manager 1.0 Type Library with the Visual Basic 5.0 References dialog.

5. Save the project and rebuild the ActiveX DLL, fixing any errors that occur.

Listing 11.6. *Accessing the Shared Property Manager.*

```
Public Function GetNextID() As Long
   Dim objContext As ObjectContext
   Set objContext = GetObjectContext()

   On Error GoTo GetNextIDError

   Dim bResult As Boolean

   ' get SharedPropertyGroupManager
   Dim objSPGM As New SharedPropertyGroupManager

   ' get SharedPropertyGroup "Beckwith"
   Dim objGroup As SharedPropertyGroup
   Set objGroup = objSPGM.CreatePropertyGroup("Beckwith", _
      LockSetGet, Process, bResult)

   ' get SharedProperty "IDGenerator"
   Dim objProp As SharedProperty
   Set objProp = objGroup.CreateProperty("NextID", bResult)
```

```
    ' increment property
    objProp.Value = objProp.Value + 1

    ' we're done
    objContext.SetComplete

    GetNextID = objProp.Value

    Exit Function

GetNextIDError:

    objContext.SetAbort

End Function
```

Task Implementing Programmatic Security

As discussed in Chapter 9, "Configuring Component Security," MTS supports two types of security: declarative and programmatic. Transaction Server Explorer (see Chapter 9) handles declarative security. This task describes the steps necessary to implement programmatic security in the `Transaction` object used in the `Beckwith` project. *Programmatic security* is the process of adding security checks directly into the source code of your components.

This example adds code to the `PostTransaction()` method of the `Transaction` component to prevent users in the `Student` role from posting transactions of more than $1,000. Follow these steps to implement programmatic security in the `Transaction` object:

1. Open the `Transaction` class module.
2. Add the following code after the call to `GetObjectContext()` but before the `On Error` handler:

```
If objContext.IsSecurityEnabled And _
    objContext.IsCallerInRole("Students") And _
    nAmount < -1000 Then
    objContext.SetAbort
    Err.Raise vbObjectError + 1234
  End If
```

This code first determines whether security is enabled for the component. If it is, the code uses the context object's `IsCallerInRole()` method to check the role of the user calling this component. If the caller is a Student and the transaction is a credit of more than $1,000 (credits in this case are negative values; debits are positive), then the component's current transaction is aborted and the function throws an error, which the caller will catch.

3. Save and rebuild the project.

Task Testing the Visual Basic Components

All the development tasks for the Beckwith sample ActiveX DLL project are complete. This final task installs the component DLL under MTS and tests its functionality. You need to perform two tasks to test your components: install them under MTS control and then run the sample demo application to invoke the components.

Installing Components under Microsoft Transaction Server

Follow these steps to install your components:

1. Rebuild the entire DLL to make sure everything is up to date.
2. Start Transaction Server Explorer via the Microsoft Management Console (MMC).
3. Create a new, empty package labeled Beckwith. If one already exists, delete it. For details on creating new packages, see Chapter 8, "Installing Components."
4. Select the Beckwith package and choose Action | New from the toolbar to install new components.
5. Select the large Install new component(s) button from the Component Wizard dialog (see Figure 11.8).

Figure 11.8.

The Component Wizard dialog.

6. Click Add Files in the Install Components dialog.
7. Use the Select Files to Install dialog to navigate to the working directory of the Beckwith project you just finished.
8. Double-click the Beckwith.dll file.

MTS opens the `Beckwith.dll` file and registers each component that the server contains. The Install Components dialog returns and should resemble the dialog in Figure 11.9.

Figure 11.9.

The Install Components dialog after selecting an ActiveX DLL.

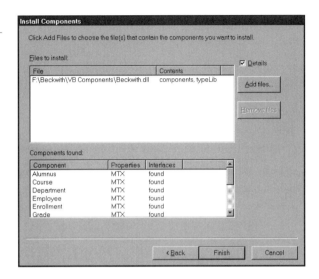

9. Click Finish to complete installation of the components under MTS.

Running the Sample Application

The book's companion CD-ROM contains a sample application that uses the `Beckwith` component you just built. This application is written in Visual Basic. To run the application and test your components, follow these steps:

1. Copy the `Beckwith\VB Client Apps\Bcds` folder from the CD-ROM to the `Beckwith` folder on your local hard drive.

2. Start Visual Basic 5.0 and load the `bcds.vbp` Visual Basic project file from the `Bcds` folder on your hard drive. The BCDS application is the Beckwith College Database System application that's described in Chapter 14, "Creating Windows Clients Using Visual Basic."

3. Make a reference to your Beckwith components by choosing **P**roject | Refere**n**ces from the main menu. Select the Beckwith item from the Available References list box.

4. Run the `bcds` application to open the Beckwith College Database System login dialog.

5. Click Login to accept the default Student ID and Personal Identification Number.

If everything works correctly, you should see the BCDS Main Menu dialog, from which you exercise various parts of the Beckwith database system. For details on what you can do with this application, see Chapter 14.

The process of logging in creates an instance of the Beckwith Student component and checks for a valid Student ID. If you make it to the BCDS Main Menu dialog, you know that your components are working correctly.

If you don't get to the BCDS Main Menu dialog, try some of the following solutions:

➤ Make sure you are running a local version of the BCDS sample application from your hard drive and not the CD-ROM.

➤ Make sure your ODBC data source names are set up correctly. See Chapter 5, "Configuring and Determining System Requirements," for details.

➤ Make sure the SQL Server service is started and working properly. Use the Services Control Panel applet to verify SQL Server is running. Use the SQL Enterprise Manager to perform some ad hoc queries against the database to make sure it is set up properly.

Workshop Wrap-Up

This chapter explains how to build the Beckwith College sample database business objects using Visual Basic. You implemented the IObjectControl interface to make your components participate in object pooling. You used a common set of RDO data access methods to enable database connections in your components. You implemented component transactions with SetComplete() and SetAbort(), and you created the Enrollment component, which illustrates a component calling other components. You also implemented programmatic security in your components and accessed the Shared Property Manager. Finally, you tested your components by installing them under MTS and running the sample client application.

Next Steps

➤ If you know that performance is an issue, check out Chapter 12, "Implementing Components in Visual C++ Using the Active Template Library." It explains how to create the lightest, fastest MTS components.

➤ To learn more about how client applications use your components, go to Chapter 14.

➤ To remotely install and instantiate your components with DCOM, skip to Chapter 15, "Setting Up Remote Windows Clients Using DCOM."

CHAPTER 12

Implementing Components in Visual C++ Using the Active Template Library

Tasks in This Chapter

➤ *Creating Simple Objects in C++ with ATL*

➤ *Retrieving Data from Databases*

➤ *Testing the ATL Component*

C++ is one of the most natural languages in which to create Microsoft Transaction Server (MTS) components. The binary representation of COM objects is very similar to that of compiled C++ classes. As a result, a simple one-to-one relationship exists between C++ classes and COM objects. This relationship makes implementing COM objects very straightforward in C++.

This chapter shows you how to create MTS components in C++ with Microsoft Visual C++ 5.0. This version of Visual C++ includes version 2.1 of the Active Template Library (ATL)—a set of C++ classes used to create lightweight COM objects. The tasks in this chapter use ATL and its associated wizards to create a transactional MTS component for use with the Beckwith sample database system.

> **Tip** Microsoft may release newer versions of Visual C++ or ATL after the printing of this book. The best place to look for updates to the compiler or class libraries is Microsoft's Visual C++ Web site:
> `www.microsoft.com/visualc`.

Preparation Deciding When to Use Visual C++

Of the various languages you can use to build COM objects, C++ is the most complex in terms of its syntax and amount of COM knowledge needed to successfully build COM-compliant objects. However, C++ produces the smallest code footprint of all COM-compliant languages and the fastest executing code. These features are important to consider when creating large-scale client/server applications.

You can use several approaches to create COM objects with Visual C++. Some of the more popular techniques are

> ➤ Straight C with hand-constructed function tables
> ➤ C++ with no class libraries
> ➤ C++ with the Microsoft Foundation Classes (MFC)
> ➤ C++ with the Active Template Library (ATL)

You can create and use COM objects in straight C source files. Using C imposes an additional level of difficulty because you have to hand craft the interfaces exposed by components—usually as structures containing function pointers. These structures of function pointers are very similar to virtual function tables (v-tables). The C++ compiler automatically supports v-tables, so using C++ is simpler than using C because you don't have to manually construct v-tables.

Another way to create COM components is to use standalone C++ without the aid of any third-party class libraries. This approach produces extremely compact COM executables, but all the COM support code has to be crafted by hand just as it does if you use straight C. The amount of C++ code necessary for a simple COM component is not trivial, so using straight C++ may result in lengthy development cycles.

Prior to the development of ATL, one of the primary mechanisms in which to create C++ COM objects was the Microsoft Foundation Class (MFC) library. MFC does a reasonably good job at providing a default implementation for much of the COM "plumbing" code, freeing developers to concentrate on component-specific logic instead of COM-specific code.

However, because MFC was designed before the invention of COM, the implementation of COM support in MFC is not as clean as it could be. One of the primary drawbacks is the amount of overhead code MFC COM object servers contain. MFC-based COM object servers must either link in the static MFC library or dynamically attach to the MFC runtime DLLs. Either way, MFC-based COM servers use a great deal of memory, especially compared to component-specific code. In addition, the component doesn't even use most of the MFC code dragged into the server.

To solve this problem, Microsoft introduced the ATL. Version 1.0 of ATL shipped in 1996 as a handful of C++ header files downloadable from the Visual C++ Web site. With Visual C++ 5.0, ATL 2.1 is a first-class citizen in the Visual C++ product, with plenty of wizards to make creating COM objects with ATL a very easy task.

ATL's primary benefit over MFC is that it produces extremely small, standalone COM servers. A standalone in-process ATL COM DLL with a single "do nothing" COM object takes only about 18KB of memory. This memory is the necessary COM support code for all objects defined in the server—the amount of memory each instance of a COM object uses depends on the size of its specific code and data allocations.

Small and lightweight COM objects are ideal for MTS components. One of the keys to scalability is to minimize resource usage on the servers of the system. The less memory a component uses, the more concurrent instances of the component the server can support.

So C++ and ATL provide an ideal environment in which to build MTS components when you know the number of instances of your object will be large. If only a handful of objects will ever be instantiated at any given time, you are probably better off writing the components in a simpler language like Visual Basic or Java.

The other reason to choose C++ is when speed is a primary concern. Under almost all circumstances, C++ COM objects perform better than those written in any other language. The C++ compiler also gives you the most optimization possibilities, from changing a few compiler switches to the extreme of writing your business logic in hand-coded in-line assembly language. This level of control is just not possible in other languages like Visual Basic.

> **Tip** Writing an object in C++ versus a language such as Visual Basic may not always result in a dramatically faster component. For example, components that contain mostly data-access functions using ODBC (or one of its derivatives) written in C++ will probably execute at relatively the same speed as a Visual Basic version of the same component. The reason is that the ODBC data-access latency is the same for both components, and this processing is the bulk of the component's total execution time. In the case of data-access objects, C++ is a better choice than Visual Basic only when component code size is an important consideration.

▌**Task**▌ Creating Simple Objects in C++ with ATL

The tasks in this chapter show you how to build the `Promote` object in C++ using ATL. The `Promote` object is part of the sample Beckwith College database system provided on the companion CD-ROM. Refer to Appendix C, "Beckwith Component Reference," for more details.

The role of the `Promote` object is moving records from one database to another. Specifically, the `Promote` component moves `Prospect` records from the Admissions database to `Student` records in the Business Office database. This promotion simulates the event of a prospective student deciding to enroll at Beckwith College. The `Promote` object is also responsible for moving `Student` records from the Business Office database to `Alumnus` records in the Alumni Relations database. This change occurs when a student graduates from Beckwith and becomes a part of the school's alumni (see Figure 12.1).

Figure 12.1.

The promotion of prospects and students with the Promote object.

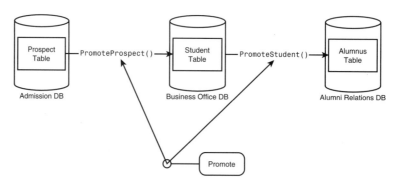

The `Promote` component accomplishes these tasks by exposing two methods: `PromoteProspect()` and `PromoteStudent()`. Each method takes two parameters. The first method identifies the prospect or student to promote, and the second is the Boolean flag `bForceFail`. `bForceFail` forces the failure of the invoked operation by passing `True` as its value. You use `bForceFail` later in the chapter to implement a MTS-facilitated rollback across two databases when a transaction failure occurs.

Creating an Empty ATL Project

The first step to creating ATL components for MTS is to build an in-process server to contain them. Follow these steps to build an ATL DLL:

1. Start Visual C++. Visual C++ is part of Visual Studio 97, and the development environment for Visual C++ is also known as the Microsoft Developer Studio.

2. Choose File | New from the main menu. Make sure the Projects tab is selected (see Figure 12.2).

Figure 12.2.

The Developer Studio New dialog with the Projects tab selected.

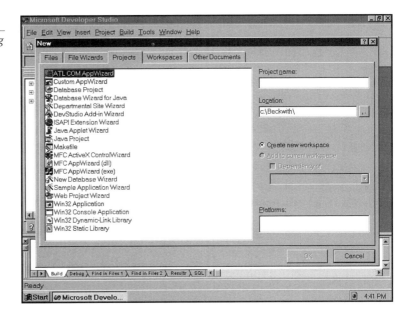

3. Select the ATL COM AppWizard item from the list control by clicking it. This step informs Developer Studio that you want to create a new ATL project and invoke the wizard to guide you through the initial steps.

> **Note** If you do not see the ATL COM AppWizard icon in your New dialog, it is because you have not installed or purchased the Visual C++ portion of Visual Studio 97. Install Visual C++ before continuing.

4. Enter the value `BeckwithATL` or any other suitable project name in the Project Name edit box.

5. Verify that the Location edit box contains an appropriate destination folder for your project.

6. Click OK to dismiss the New dialog and begin the ATL COM AppWizard (see Figure 12.3).

Figure 12.3.

The ATL COM AppWizard dialog with its one and only step.

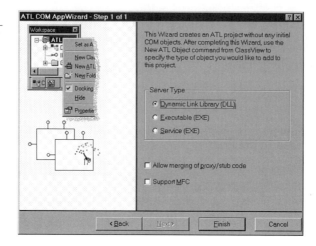

7. Make the appropriate choices in the ATL COM AppWizard dialog; you have three options:

   ➤ Server Type

   ➤ Allow merging of proxy/stub code

   ➤ Support MFC

   The Server Type option asks for the type of COM server to create: Dynamic Link Library (in-process), Executable (local), or Service. For MTS components, the only allowable choice is an in-process DLL server. This option is selected by default.

   Merging of proxy/stub code is a Boolean property that builds generated proxy/stub code as part of your server. If the check box is clear, the proxy/stub code is generated as a separate DLL. The `Promote` object you build in this chapter uses Automation types, so you do not need custom proxy/stub code. Leave this check box clear.

   The Support MFC option enables you to take advantage of some of the services implemented by MFC, for example, the `CString` class. Checking this option has the disadvantage that the MFC DLLs are bound to your server, taking up additional resources. For now, leave this checkbox clear.

8. Click Finish to commit your selections. A New Project Information dialog opens in which you can confirm your selections.

9. Click **OK** to commit and create a skeleton COM in-process server.

Adding Components to the Project

The ATL COM AppWizard initially creates an in-process COM server without any components in it. To add components to your project, you need to use the ATL Object Wizard.

1. Choose **I**nsert | New **A**TL Object from the main menu to display the ATL Object Wizard dialog (see Figure 12.4).

Figure 12.4.

The ATL Object Wizard dialog.

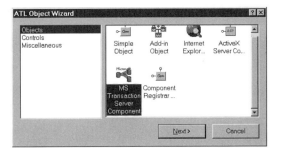

2. Select the type of ATL object to create and add to your project. The options include

   ➤ Simple Objects

   ➤ MS Transaction Server Components

   ➤ ActiveX Server Components

   ➤ ActiveX Controls

   Each type of object the ATL Object Wizard creates is a full-fledged COM object. However, the wizard places unique additional code and constraints on each object according to the context in which it is going to be used. (`Promote` is destined for MTS.)

3. Select the MS Transaction Server Component icon and click Next. The ATL Object Wizard Properties dialog opens (see Figure 12.5).

Figure 12.5.

The ATL Object Wizard Properties dialog.

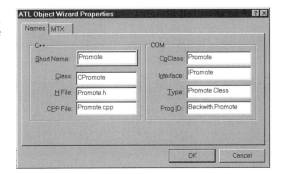

The ATL Object Wizard declares the name and other identifiers of the new COM object.

4. Type **Promote** in the Short Name edit box.

Notice that, as you type, the other edit boxes mimic your characters with slight modifications. This method provides reasonable defaults for the identifiers of your object.

> **Tip** The only edit box that does not provide a reasonable initial default is the ProgID edit box. The ProgID specifies the component's programmatic identifier. Recall from Chapter 4, "Getting Acquainted with COM," that programmatic identifiers usually follow the convention Company.Component.Version. In this case the ATL Object Wizard simply repeats the object's short name twice, delimited by a period. Change the first half of ProgID from Promote to **Beckwith** to more closely follow the standard. ATL automatically appends the version number to the ProgID.

5. Click the MTX property page tab to display properties unique to creating a MTS-compliant COM object (see Figure 12.6).

Figure 12.6.

The ATL Object Wizard Properties dialog with the MTX page displayed.

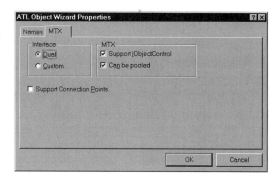

6. Make the appropriate selections. From this property page you can set the following properties:

➤ Interface type: Dual or Custom

➤ Support for the MTS IObjectControl interface

➤ Support for object pooling

➤ Support for connection points

MTS components can have either dual or custom interfaces. For the Promote component, use Dual. If desired, the ATL Object Wizard can automatically generate code to support the IObjectControl interface. This interface enables an object to decide if it wants to participate in object pooling and to receive notifications of activation and deactivation. IObjectControl is described in detail in Chapter 10, "Understanding Microsoft Transaction Server Components."

For the `Promote` component, check both the Support IObjectControl and Can Be Pooled check boxes. There is no need to support connection points for `Promote`, so make sure that check box is clear.

7. Click OK to close the ATL Object Wizard and add the new `Promote` component to your project.

8. Compile the project by choosing **B**uild | **R**ebuild All from the main menu. Compiling the project creates the COM in-process server and registers the DLL with the system, making it available to external COM clients.

> **Note** Your project should be free of compiler errors. All the code added to the project is automatically generated by Visual C++. If you do encounter compiler errors, check to make sure the path, include, and library environment variables are correct.

Defining Object Properties and Methods

As noted earlier, the `Promote` object exposes two methods: `PromoteProspect()` and `PromoteStudent()`. These methods are declared as follows:

```
HRESULT PromoteProspect(BSTR bstrProspectID,
   VARIANT_BOOL bForceFail);
HRESULT PromoteStudent(BSTR bstrStudentID,
   VARIANT_BOOL bForceFail);
```

You can use either of two techniques to add these two methods to `Promote`:

➤ You can manually add the function declarations in `Promote`'s .h, .cpp, and .idl files.

➤ You can let Visual C++ automatically modify `Promote`'s source files by using Visual Editing.

Visual Editing is a feature of Visual C++ that enables you to automatically add new properties and methods to an ATL COM object, simply by filling in some values on a single dialog.

Follow these steps to add `PromoteProspect()` and `PromoteStudent()` to `Promote`:

1. Right-click `Promote`'s main interface icon `IPromote` in the Workspace dockable dialog to display its context menu (see Figure 12.7).

2. Choose Add Method from the context menu to display the Add Method to Interface dialog (see Figure 12.8).

   The Add Method to Interface dialog is where you specify the name and syntax of the new method to add to the COM component.

3. Type `PromoteProspect` in the Method Name edit box. Type `[in]BSTR bstrProspectID, [in]VARIANT_BOOL bForceFail` in the Parameters edit box.

Figure 12.7.

Right-clicking the IPromote icon to add new methods.

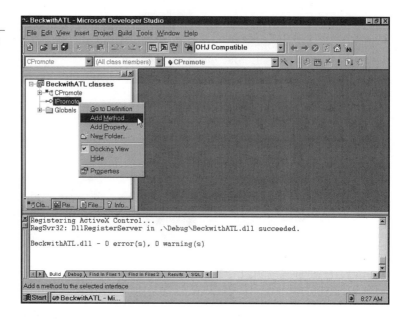

Figure 12.8.

The Add Method to Interface dialog with PromoteProspect() defined.

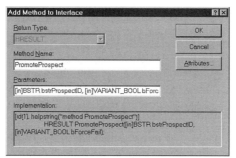

> **Note** The [in] tags in the Parameters edit box are interface definition language (IDL) attributes indicating that the parameters are passed in from the calling application. If the parameters pass information back to the caller, they are marked with the attribute [out] or [in, out] for parameters that pass both in and out of the method.

4. Click OK. Visual C++ automatically adds the declaration of PromoteProspect() to the Promote files with the following extensions: .h, .cpp, and .idl.

To see the changes made to the .idl file, double-click the IPromote icon in the Workspace dialog to view the BeckwithATL.idl file with the newly added PromoteProspect() method to the declaration of interface IPromote.

To see the declaration of PromoteProspect() in the .h header file, double-click the CPromote class icon in the Workspace dialog. This step displays the Promote.h header file that contains the declaration of Promote's C++ class CPromote. Scroll to the bottom CPromote's declaration until you reach the comment //IPromote. Beneath that comment Visual C++ inserts methods added to the component via Visual Editing.

To see the implementation of PromoteProspect(), navigate to the PromoteProspect icon in the Workspace tree view. Look under the CPromote class icon and then under the IPromote icon. Double-click the PromoteProspect icon to see the boilerplate stub implementation. This stub holds the implementation of PromoteProspect() that is executed whenever clients of the Promote component invoke its exposed PromoteProspect() method.

5. Repeat steps 3 and 4 to add the PromoteStudent() method to the Promote() component. Rename the first parameter from bstrProspectID to bstrStudentID.

6. Build your project by choosing **B**uild | **B**uild BeckwithATL.dll from the main menu. Again, because you have not added code manually, the project should build without errors.

With the completion of the preceding steps, you have successfully built a lightweight, compact COM object exposing the interface IPromote. IPromote defines two methods: PromoteProspect() and PromoteStudent(). The C++ class CPromote provides implementation for your component, including default implementation for PromoteProspect() and PromoteStudent().

Exploring Automatically Generated Microsoft Transaction Server–Specific Code

When you use the ATL Object Wizard to create MTS ATL components, the wizard makes several minor changes to the automatically generated source code for your component. The following is a list of differences between an MTS ATL component and a simple ATL component:

➤ In Promote.h, the wizard adds #include <mtx.h> is added near the top of the file. #include <mtx.h> brings in all the necessary MTS C++ declarations.

➤ The following code declares a simple ATL COM object C++ class:

```
class ATL_NO_VTABLE CPromote :
    public CComObjectRootEx<CComSingleThreadModel>,
    public CComCoClass<CPromote, &CLSID_Promote>,
    public IDispatchImpl<IPromote, &IID_IPromote, &LIBID_JUNKOLib>
{
};
```

ATL uses multiple inheritance of template classes to provide implementation of default COM code. In the preceding code, CComObjectRootEx, and CComCoClass provide the base COM plumbing code. IDispatchImpl provides default implementation of Promote's IDispatch-based interface for Automation support. CPromote automatically inherits all their functionality via multiple inheritance.

When you select the Support IObjectControl check box from the MTX property sheet of the ATL Object Wizard Properties dialog (refer to Figure 12.6), the declaration of CPromote is modified to inherit from IObjectControl, an interface declared in mtx.h. The following shows the modified declaration of CPromote:

```
class ATL_NO_VTABLE CPromote :
    public CComObjectRootEx<CComSingleThreadModel>,
    public CComCoClass<CPromote, &CLSID_Promote>,
    public IObjectControl,
    public IDispatchImpl<IPromote, &IID_IPromote, &LIBID_BECKWITHATLLib>
{
};
```

ATL, unlike MFC, uses multiple inheritance as its mechanism for supporting the multiple interfaces of a COM object. CPromote exposes two COM interfaces: IObjectControl and IPromote. Each one of these interfaces is parent of the C++ implementation class CPromote.

➤ You can't aggregate MTS components, whereas for simple ATL components, you can decide whether or not to aggregate a component. Creating a MTS component with the ATL Object Wizard automatically marks the C++ implementation class as a class you cannot aggregate. It does this by adding the following macro to the declaration of CPromote:

```
DECLARE_NOT_AGGREGATABLE(CPromote)
```

➤ Each interface exposed by a component is recorded in the C++ implementation class as an entry in its COM map. A COM map in ATL is a set of macros declared in the C++ class declaration that enumerates each interface. A default, simple component contains the following map:

```
BEGIN_COM_MAP(CPromote)
    COM_INTERFACE_ENTRY(IPromote)
    COM_INTERFACE_ENTRY(IDispatch)
END_COM_MAP()
```

MTS components that expose IObjectControl (for example, the Promote component) have an additional entry in their COM map for IObjectControl. The COM map for Promote looks like:

```
BEGIN_COM_MAP(CPromote)
    COM_INTERFACE_ENTRY(IPromote)
    COM_INTERFACE_ENTRY(IObjectControl)
    COM_INTERFACE_ENTRY(IDispatch)
END_COM_MAP()
```

➤ Because `Promote` exposes the `IObjectControl` interface, it pledges to provide all of its clients with an implementation of every method declared in the `IObjectControl` interface. Recall from Chapter 10 that `IObjectControl` declares the following functions:

➤ `Activate()`

➤ `CanBePooled()`

➤ `Deactivate()`

The ATL COM Object Wizard automatically provides the declaration and implementation of these three methods. The implementation is provided in `Promote`'s main source file `Promote.cpp`. Listing 12.1 shows the default source code generated by the ATL Object Wizard.

Listing 12.1. *The default implementation of* `IObjectControl`'s *methods.*

```
HRESULT CPromote::Activate()
{
    HRESULT hr = GetObjectContext(&m_spObjectContext);
    if (SUCCEEDED(hr))
        return S_OK;
    return hr;
}
BOOL CPromote::CanBePooled()
{
    return TRUE;
}
void CPromote::Deactivate()
{
    m_spObjectContext->Release();
}
```

Notice that in the default implementation of `CPromote::Activate()` a reference to `Promote`'s context object is retrieved via the call to the global MTS method `GetObjectContext()`. Recall from Chapter 10 that MTS creates a sibling context object for every instance of a component under MTS control. This context object is the primary means of communication between a component and the MTS runtime environment.

In `CPromote::Activate()` the COM smart pointer `m_spObjectContext` is set to point to the context object. This pointer is stored as a member variable so that you can use it elsewhere. The pointer to the object context is released when MTS invokes `Promote`'s `Deactivate()` method. At this point the context object is no longer valid, so it doesn't make sense to maintain a pointer to it anymore. If MTS uses the same instance of `Promote` again, MTS first invokes `Activate()`, which reestablishes `m_spObjectContext` to point to a valid context object.

> **Note** m_spObjectContext used in the default implementation of CPromote::Activate() is a COM smart pointer—a C++ class written to behave like a regular C++ pointer, but instead of pointing to arbitrary memory, a COM smart pointer points to COM objects. COM smart pointers automatically manage reference counts to COM object via AddRef() and Release() calls and override operators like -> to appear as pointers. ATL implements COM smart pointers with the CComPtr class. See the ATL documentation for more information.

Accessing an Object's Context via GetObjectContext()

As mentioned in the previous section, an object's context is the primary means for components to communicate with MTS at runtime. In ATL projects you can implement communication with MTS in two ways:

➤ Use m_spObjectContext if your object supports IObjectControl

➤ Call the global API method GetObjectContext() for all other cases

m_spObjectContext is available only if you elect to support IObjectControl from the MTX property page of the ATL Object Wizard or you write something similar yourself (refer to Figure 12.6).

The following code snippet illustrates an example of the second form of retrieving a pointer to a context object via GetObjectContext():

```
IObjectContext* pObjectContext = NULL;
HRESULT hr = GetObjectContext(&pObjectContext);
if (!SUCCEEDED(hr) || !pObjectContext)
{
    // do error processing
}
```

In the example, GetObjectContext() actually retrieves a pointer to the COM interface IObjectContext. Recall from Chapter 10 that IObjectContext comprises the following methods:

➤ CreateInstance()

➤ DisableCommit()

➤ EnableCommit()

➤ IsCallerInRole()

➤ IsInTransaction()

➤ IsSecurityEnabled()

➤ SetAbort()

➤ SetComplete()

These eight methods make up the primary API that MTS exposes to components. MTS controls its most important features—object brokering, component transactions, and security—by components with only these few methods.

You may wonder where GetObjectContext() is defined and implemented so that your component can invoke it. The answer is that when you include the Mtx.h file, your project automatically links to the MTS import library Mtx.lib. Mtx.h contains the following preprocessor command:

```
#pragma comment(lib, "mtx.lib")
```

This directive instructs the linker to search Mtx.lib when resolving external methods, in particular GetObjectContext(). By linking to Mtx.lib, calls to GetObjectContext() in code compile and link without unresolved external errors. MTS then provides the necessary implementation of GetObjectContext() at runtime when your component invokes it.

Caution Do not call GetObjectContext() from your component's C++ class constructor. The code in an object's constructor is executed before MTS has a chance to set up the sibling context object.

Task Retrieving Data from Databases

So far in this chapter, Promote has all the necessary code COM infrastructure in place, but nothing happens when a client invokes PromoteProspect() and PromoteStudent(). This section describes the steps necessary to implement these two methods and complete the construction of Promote.

Using ADO to Retrieve Data

ActiveX Data Objects (ADO) is a relatively new way for client applications to communicate with databases. ADO is a set of COM components that collectively define a data-access object model. A client application creates the necessary ADO objects and invokes their methods to perform queries or issue commands to the database.

ADO differs from other data-access mechanisms—for example, RDO and DAO—in many ways. Some of the primary differences between ADO and other data-access mechanisms follow.

➤ ADO uses OLE DB. OLE DB is a Microsoft technology that provides a standard interface on top of a variety of data storage mediums including databases, repositories, and email information stores like Microsoft Exchange.

➤ ADO exposes a disconnected object model. Unlike RDO and other data access object models that require you to navigate from a `Connection` object to a `Command` object to a `Recordset` object, with ADO you can simply create a single `Recordset` object and perform a query.

➤ ADO contains optimizations for Web-based applications. ADO is lightweight and fast, which makes it ideal for Active Server Pages (ASP) intranet- and Internet-based applications.

> **Note** This chapter serves as an introduction to the basics of ADO. For the latest information, check the Microsoft ADO and OLE DB Web pages at
> `www.microsoft.com/ado`
> and
> `www.microsoft.com/oledb`, respectively.

The following ADO objects are responsible for executing most of ADO's functionality:

➤ `Connection`

➤ `Command`

➤ `Recordset`

`Connection` represents a connection to the destination data source. You can use a single instance of a `Connection` object repeatedly. `Command` issues commands to a data source, such as SQL `DELETE` and `UPDATE` commands. `Recordset` objects represent a collection of rows returned as a result of issuing a query against a data source.

The `Promote` component only uses the `Connection` and `Recordset` objects to perform its functionality.

Implementing `Promote`'s `PromoteProspect()` Method

Follow these steps to implement `PromoteProspect()` using ADO:

1. Make sure ADO is installed on your computer. ADO ships as part of Internet Information Server 4.0. To see whether ADO is installed, search your hard drive for `Msado15.dll`—the primary implementation file for ADO.

   `Msado15.dll` is typically installed on your hard drive's `Program Files\Common Files\System\ADO` folder. If your installation of ADO resides in a different folder, note the different folder now because you need the complete pathname of `Msado15.dll` later to complete this task.

> **Tip** ADO also ships as part of the OLE DB SDK, which is available for download from www.microsoft.com/oledb.

To use ADO the BeckwithATL project needs to import ADO COM objects and their methods into its namespace, using Visual C++'s new COM compiler support. COM compiler support means that Visual C++ has direct support for COM objects via extensions to the C++ language.

2. Add the following line of code to its StdAfx.h header file to import the ADO object model into BeckwithATL:

```
#import "\Program files\Common files\System\ADO\MSADO15.dll"\
    no_namespace
```

The new **#import** directive tells the compiler to read the COM type information stored in the selected file and automatically generate C++ wrapper code for the COM objects and their methods. The pathname supplied to **#import** can be any file that contains COM type information, including DLLs, EXEs, and type library TLB files.

You use the **no_namespace** keyword to instruct the compiler not to create a namespace when automatically generating C++ wrappers for the COM objects it finds in the supplied type library. The compiler instead includes them in the current namespace. For more information on the syntax and behavior of **#import**, see the online documentation that ships with Visual C++.

> **Note** The preceding **#import** code illustrates the new C++ compiler support for COM. The traditional mechanism of creating instances of COM objects in C++ is to invoke the global API method CoCreateInstance(). COM smart pointers automatically invoke this method for you.

3. Rebuild the BeckwithATL project. You must rebuild now because the following step examines files that the C++ compiler automatically generates as a result of adding the **#import** directive (see step 2).

   If you encounter any errors while rebuilding the project, make sure the **#import** directive correctly points to the instance of Msado15.dll on your hard drive.

   As a result of rebuilding the BeckwithATL project, the C++ compiler creates two new files and places them in the project's Debug folder: Msado15.tlh and Msado15.tli. Msado15.tlh is a C++ header file that defines C++ wrapper classes for all the ADO objects contained in Msado15.dll. Msado15.tli is a C++ implementation file for those wrapper classes.

4. Open `Msado15.tlh` from the `Debug` folder used by `BeckwithATL`. `Msado15.tlh` contains the following:

   ➤ Declarations of ADO objects and interfaces with their associated GUIDs

   ➤ COM smart pointer declarations for ADO interfaces

   ➤ Enumeration declarations for all ADO constants

   ➤ Declarations of C++ wrapper classes for each ADO component

   For information on the details of these declarations, refer to the Visual C++ online documentation. To continue, you only need to understand that ADO's object model definition has now been imported into the `BeckwithATL` project and is now available for use in the `PromoteProspect()` and `PromoteStudent()` methods.

5. Return to the implementation of `CPromote::PromoteProspect()` located in `Promote.cpp`. You are now ready to implement these methods.

6. Declare two COM smart pointers to ADO `Connection` objects. You need two `Connection` objects because promoting a prospect involves two separate databases. Add the following code to declare the pointers:

   ```
   _ConnectionPtr pConnection = NULL;
   _ConnectionPtr pConnection2 = NULL;
   ```

   `ConnectionPtr` is a smart pointer declared in the `Msado15.tlh` file.

7. Add a `try..catch` block handler to `PromoteProspect()` to catch any COM or database errors that occur during execution. Add the following code:

   ```
   try
   {
   }
   catch (...)
   {
   }
   ```

   Most of the code added in the next steps goes inside the `try` block.

8. Add the following code to instantiate the `Connection` object and invoke its `Open()` method to open the connection:

   ```
   pConnection = new _ConnectionPtr(__uuidof(Connection));
   pConnection->Open(_bstr_t("BeckwithAD"), _bstr_t("sa"),
       _bstr_t(""));
   ```

   The first line of code allocates an instance of ADO's `Connection` object and assigns the first `Connection` pointer to it. The second line of code uses the pointer to the newly created `Connection` object to invoke its `Open()` method. `Open()` accepts three string parameters:

   ➤ ODBC data source name (DSN)

   ➤ Database user name

   ➤ Database user name's password

> **Note** The call to `Open()` in the preceding code uses the new type `bstr_t`, which is a C++ class wrapper for COM BSTRS. Class `bstr_t` is defined in the Visual C++ COM support header file `Comdef.h`.

9. Add the following code to execute a query against the database. This query retrieves information from the Admissions database for the student being promoted.

```
_RecordsetPtr pResults = pConnection->Execute(
  _bstr_t("select * from prospect where prospectid = '"
  + _bstr_t(bstrProspectID) + _bstr_t("'")), NULL,
  adCmdText);
```

This single line of code invokes the Connection object's Execute() method, which takes three parameters:

➤ CommandText—the SQL command to perform on the database. In this case a SQL SELECT is built using the PromoteProspect() input parameter bstrProspectID.

➤ RecordsAffected—a pointer to a long that receives the count of records returned in the Result set. The preceding code passes NULL, indicating that the count is unimportant.

➤ Options—an ADO enumeration that tells the Connection object how to interpret the string passed as the first parameter to Execute(). adCmdText is defined in Msado15.tlh and tells Connection that the query is a textual SQL command.

The return value of Execute() is a pointer to an ADO Recordset object that Execute() automatically creates. The preceding code assigns the pointer to the local smart pointer pResults. All information about the desired prospect has now been read from the Admissions database.

10. Add the following line of code to delete the prospect's record from the Prospect table:

```
pConnection->Execute(
  _bstr_t("delete from prospect where prospectid = '"
+ _bstr_t(bstrProspectID) + _bstr_t("'")), NULL, adCmdText);
```

This code also invokes Execute() for a SQL DELETE, even though no Result set is returned. The next step is to create the second connection to the Business Office database to write the information read from the Admissions database.

11. Add the following code to create and open a second Connection object:

```
pConnection2 = new _ConnectionPtr(__uuidof(Connection));
pConnection2->Open(_bstr_t("BeckwithBO"), _bstr_t("sa"),
  _bstr_t(""));
```

12. Add the following code to prepare and execute a SQL INSERT statement. This code uses the Recordset object obtained in step 9.

```
_bstr_t strInsert("insert Student (StudentID, FirstName, "
    "LastName, Address, City, StateOrProvince, PostalCode, "
    "Country, PhoneNumber, EmailAddress, GraduationYear) "
    "values (");
for(int i = 0; i < 10; i++)
{
    if (i) strInsert += ", ";
    _variant_t var((long)i);
    FieldPtr pField = pResults->GetFields()->GetItem(var);
    if (pField->GetType() >= adChar &&
        pField->GetType() <= adLongVarWChar)
    {
        strInsert += "'";
    }
    strInsert += (_bstr_t)(pResults->GetFields()->
        GetItem(var)->GetValue());
    if (pField->GetType() >= adChar && pField->GetType() <= adLongVarWChar)
        strInsert += "'";
}
// fill in graduation year (only field not read from Prospect table)
SYSTEMTIME st;
GetSystemTime(&st);
char szBuff[10];
wsprintf(szBuff, "%d", st.wYear + 4);  // assume only 4 years needed!
strInsert += ", ";
strInsert += szBuff;
strInsert += ")";
pConnection2->Execute(strInsert, NULL, adCmdText);
```

This code declares the first half of the SQL INSERT statement and assigns it to the variable strInsert. The for loop iterates each field of the Recordset object, extracts its value, and appends the value to strInsert. The only field defined in the Student table that is not defined in the Prospect table is the GraduationYear field. The call to the Win32 API method GetSystemTime()calculates a value for GraduationYear that is four years ahead of the current year. Finally, the Execute() method on the second connection object invokes the INSERT statement.

13. Add the following code to check the value of the parameter bForceFail, which is the second parameter of PromoteProspect(). If bForceFail is TRUE, force a rollback of all the preceding database code by invoking SetAbort() on the context object pointer:

```
if (bForceFail)
{
  pConnection->Close();
  pConnection2->Close();
  m_spObjectContext->SetAbort();
  return S_OK;
}
```

The preceding code closes both connections and then forces a rollback on both databases. The rollback occurs when SetAbort() is called and PromoteProspect() returns to the caller.

> **Note** The code associated with `bForceFail` and `SetAbort()` demonstrates the power of MTS-provided, component-based transactions. By calling `SetAbort()` in this situation, a DELETE in one database is rolled back and an INSERT in another database is rolled back, restoring both databases to their state prior to the invocation of Promote's `PromoteProspect()` method.

14. Add the following code for normal execution—that is, when no errors occur and `bForceFail` is not set to TRUE:

```
pConnection->Close();
pConnection2->Close();
m_spObjectContext->SetComplete();
```

This code closes the open `Connection` object and invokes `SetComplete()` on the context object to inform MTS that all operations are successful and to commit the current transaction.

15. Add the following code to the `catch` block to handle cases in which a database or COM error occurs. In these cases an exception is thrown, and the code contained within the `catch` block is executed.

```
catch (...)
{
  if (pConnection) pConnection->Close();
  if (pConnection2) pConnection2->Close();
  if (m_spObjectContext) m_spObjectContext->SetAbort();
}
```

This code simply closes the connections and aborts the transaction via the context object's `SetAbort()` method.

Listing 12.2 contains the entire implementation of `CPromote::PromoteProspect()`, along with comments explaining each step.

Listing 12.2. *The implementation of* Promote's PromoteProspect() *method.*

```
STDMETHODIMP CPromote::PromoteProspect(BSTR bstrProspectID,
  VARIANT_BOOL bForceFail)
{
  _ConnectionPtr pConnection = NULL;
  _ConnectionPtr pConnection2 = NULL;
  try
  {
  // STEP 1: Read information from Admissions database
  // create ADO connection object
  pConnection = new _ConnectionPtr(__uuidof(Connection));
  // open connection
  pConnection->Open(_bstr_t("BeckwithAD"), _bstr_t("sa"),
    _bstr_t(""));
  // read information from Admissions database
  _RecordsetPtr pResults = pConnection->Execute(
```

continues

Listing 12.2. *continued*

```
      _bstr_t("select * from prospect where prospectid = '"
      + _bstr_t(bstrProspectID) + _bstr_t("'")), NULL,
      adCmdText);
    // delete this record from Admissions database
    pConnection->Execute(
      _bstr_t("delete from prospect where prospectid = '"
      + _bstr_t(bstrProspectID) + _bstr_t("'")), NULL,
      adCmdText);
    // STEP 2: Write information into Business Office
    //        database
    // create ADO connection object
    pConnection2 = new _ConnectionPtr(__uuidof(Connection));
    // open connection
    pConnection2->Open(_bstr_t("BeckwithBO"), _bstr_t("sa"),
      _bstr_t(""));
    // prepare SQL statement to insert new record
    _bstr_t strInsert(
      "insert Student (StudentID, FirstName, "
      "LastName, Address, City, StateOrProvince, "
      "PostalCode, Country, PhoneNumber, EmailAddress, "
      "GraduationYear) values (");
    for(int i = 0; i < 10; i++)
    {
      if (i) strInsert += ", ";
      _variant_t var((long)i);
      FieldPtr pField =
        pResults->GetFields()->GetItem(var);
      if (pField->GetType() >= adChar &&
        pField->GetType() <= adLongVarWChar)
      {
        strInsert += "'";
      }
      strInsert += (_bstr_t)
        (pResults->GetFields()->GetItem(var)->GetValue());
      if (pField->GetType() >= adChar && pField->GetType()
        <= adLongVarWChar)
      {
        strInsert += "'";
      }
    }
    // fill in graduation year
    // (only field not read from Prospect table)
    SYSTEMTIME st;
    GetSystemTime(&st);
    char szBuff[10];
    // assume only 4 years needed!
    wsprintf(szBuff, "%d", st.wYear + 4);
    strInsert += ", ";
    strInsert += szBuff;
    strInsert += ")";
    pConnection2->Execute(strInsert, NULL, adCmdText);
    if (bForceFail)
    {
      pConnection->Close();
      pConnection2->Close();
      m_spObjectContext->SetAbort();
      return S_OK;
    }
    // close everything up
```

```
    pConnection->Close();
    pConnection2->Close();
    m_spObjectContext->SetComplete();
    }
    catch (...)
    {
    if (pConnection) pConnection->Close();
    if (pConnection2) pConnection2->Close();
    if (m_spObjectContext) m_spObjectContext->SetAbort();
    }
    return S_OK;
}
```

Implementing Promote's PromoteStudent() Method

The implementation of the `PromoteStudent()` method is almost identical to the implementation of the `PromoteProspect()` method. Follow these steps to implement `PromoteStudent()`:

1. Open the file `PromoteStudent.txt` from the companion CD-ROM. This file is in the folder `Beckwith\BeckwithATL\Import`.

2. Copy the implementation of `PromoteStudent()` from `PromoteStudent.txt` to the Clipboard.

3. Open the empty implementation of `PromoteStudent()` in the project's `Promote.cpp` file and replace it with the contents of the Clipboard.

4. Rebuild the project and fix any syntax errors.

> **Note** The only differences between the implementation of `PromoteProspect()` and `PromoteStudent()` are the databases and the tables they use.

Task Testing the ATL Component

Just as with MTS components created in other languages, the simplest way to test the functionality of `Promote` is to install it under MTS and create a simple Visual Basic application that uses the component. Follow these steps to test the `Promote` component:

1. Start SQL Server's ISQL/w application, either as a standalone or via the SQL Enterprise Manager.

2. Execute the following SQL query against the Admissions database:

   ```
   SELECT * FROM Prospect WHERE LastName="Gray"
   ```

   This query should return approximately 50 records of prospects whose last names are `Gray`. Jot down the `ProspectID` values of at least two of these records (for example, `116929657` for Tracey Gray and `116929803` for Joanne Gray).

3. Make sure your `BeckwithATL` project builds without errors and successfully registers itself with the system. If you prefer, copy the pre-built `BeckwithATL.dll` file from the CD ROM's `Beckwith\BeckwithATL` folder to your local hard drive and register it with `RegSvr32.exe`.

4. Double-click Transaction Server Explorer.

5. Open the `Beckwith` package you created in Chapter 8, "Installing Components," and install the `Promote` component into that package. For details on installing components, refer to Chapter 8. When installing `Promote`, remember that the in-process server that contains it is called `BeckwithATL.dll`, not `Promote.dll`.

6. Modify the transaction properties of the newly added `Promote` component to specify that it requires a transaction. To do so, highlight the component in Transaction Server Explorer and choose File | Properties. When the properties sheet dialog appears, click the Transaction tab and enable the Requires a Transaction radio button (see Figure 12.9). Click OK to commit the property change.

Figure 12.9.

Requiring a transaction for the Promote component.

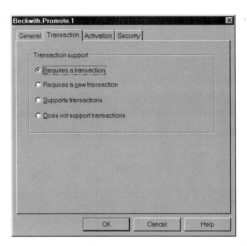

7. Double-click Visual Basic and create a new Standard EXE.

8. Add a reference to the `BeckwithATL` server by choosing **P**roject | Refere**n**ce from the main menu. When the References dialog appears, find the Beckwith ATL 1.0 Type Library item in the Available References list box and click the box to the left of the label.

9. Add a push button to the application's main form. This step creates a button with the default name of `Command1`.

10. Double-click `Command1` to open the code editor. Visual Basic creates a skeleton handler for the Click event of the `Command1` button. Inside this declaration, add the following code:

```
' Create instance of Promote
Dim objPromoter As New Promote
```

```
' Successfully promote Tracey Gray.
' This will move her from Admissions to Business Office.
objPromoter.PromoteProspect "116929657", False

' Force the failure of promoting Joanne Gray.
' This will keep her in the Admissions database.
objPromoter.PromoteProspect "116929803", True
MsgBox "All done!"
```

11. Start the project and click the form's push button. If everything runs successfully, the All done! message box appears.

12. Verify the correct execution of PromoteProspect() by returning to SQL Server's ISQL/w application. Perform the following query on the Admissions database:

```
SELECT * FROM Prospect WHERE ProspectID = "116929657"
OR ProspectID = "116929803"
```

If PromoteProspect() works correctly, this query returns one record only—Joanne Gray's record. This output is correct because the call to promote Joanne Gray's record was forced to fail by passing in True for its second parameter.

13. Verify that Tracy Gray's record moved successfully to the Business Office database by executing the following query on the Business Office database:

```
SELECT * FROM Student WHERE StudentID = "116929657"
OR StudentID = "116929803"
```

Again, this query should return a single record—this time Tracey Gray.

Troubleshooting Possible Problems

If an error occurs during the execution of PromoteProspect(), consider the following solutions:

➤ Make sure the ODBC DSN have been set up correctly. Refer to Appendix C for the correct DSN setup.

➤ Make sure the Promote component is instantiated correctly when you click the form's button. Check for proper instantiation by clicking the button and checking the component's icon in Transaction Server Explorer. The Beckwith.Promote.1 icon in the list view portion of Transaction Server Explorer should spin, indicating that the component is currently instantiated and under MTS control. If it isn't, remove the icon from the package and reinstall the component.

➤ Make sure ADO is properly installed. ADO comes with several samples. Try running one of the samples to see whether ADO is installed correctly.

➤ Verify that MTS itself is running correctly. Follow the steps in the "Verifying Correct Installation" task in Chapter 6, "Installing Microsoft Transaction Server."

Workshop Wrap-Up

This chapter shows you how to use Visual C++ and the ActiveX Template Library to build the transactional Promote component. You created an empty BeckwithATL project and added the MTS-compliant Promote component using the ATL Object Wizard. You also took advantage of Visual C++'s new COM compiler support to add ActiveX Data Objects database access support to the project. Finally, you implemented and tested code to perform a cross-database transaction that you can force to fail—showing off the power of MTS-hosted component transactions.

Next Steps

➤ To learn how to write components in Java, continue to Chapter 13, "Implementing Components in Java Using Visual J++."

➤ To write a robust client application to use the components you built in the previous chapter, along with the Promote component build in this chapter, proceed to Chapter 14, "Creating Windows Clients Using Visual Basic."

➤ To learn more about Active Server Pages, the product that installed ADO, skip to Chapter 16, "Building Dynamic Web Sites Using Active Server Pages."

CHAPTER 13

Implementing Components in Java Using Visual J++

Tasks in This Chapter

➤ *Creating Simple Objects in Java*

➤ *Using the ActiveX Component Wizard for Java*

➤ *Making COM Objects MTS–Friendly*

➤ *Retrieving Data from Databases*

➤ *Implementing Component Transactions*

➤ *Sharing State Between Components*

➤ *Testing the Java Component*

One of the newest languages in which to implement Microsoft Transaction Server (MTS) components is Java. With Microsoft's recent release of Visual J++ 1.1 as part of Visual Studio 97, creating COM objects in Java has never been simpler. Visual J++ 1.1 includes the ActiveX Wizard for Java, which makes creating a Java COM object as easy as creating simple Java classes.

This chapter describes the tasks necessary to implement MTS components written in Java. It assumes that you have either a working knowledge of Java or a basic understanding of Java with a solid C++ background. The tasks in this chapter focus on building new Java classes and converting existing ones into COM objects and placing those objects under MTS control.

Preparation Deciding Whether to Use Visual J++

You can implement MTS components in any traditional language that is capable of creating COM objects. You can write components in Basic, C and C++, Pascal, and even COBOL. Java is the latest addition to that list.

Why would you decide to use Java when other more popular choices are available for client/server development? The short answer is that Java is simple, yet powerful. Visual Basic developers searching for a true object-oriented language can easily migrate to Java. C++ developers who are looking for a simpler language in which to create COM objects can master the Java language in a matter of weeks, or even days.

Enter Java—simpler than C++ but more object-oriented than Visual Basic. Java enables developers to focus more on the business semantics of the components they are creating and less on the component's infrastructure. In contrast, when implementing COM objects in a language like C++, developers must consider several issues that simply do not exist in the Java scenario. For example, a C++ developer needs to be acutely aware of an object's reference count. In Java, however, the caller is not responsible for an object's reference count. Instead, the Java Virtual Machine automatically takes care of many COM-specific details.

Another advantage to using Java for MTS components is that Java syntax is similar to C++ syntax. Any developer who understands the basics of C++ can pick up Java quickly. Even if you don't have a C++ background, the simplicity of the language makes it easy to master.

One disadvantage of creating components in Java is that although several Java compilers are on the market, Visual J++ is currently the only product that supports this endeavor and thus ties you to Microsoft's implementation of Java. Additionally, only Microsoft's implementation of the Java Virtual Machine executes Java-based COM objects. Consequently, MTS components written in Java run only on Windows platforms (which isn't really a significant restriction because MTS runs only under Windows NT).

Task Creating Simple Objects in Java

The complete set of business objects used with the Beckwith College sample database are written in Visual Basic. Chapter 2, "Laying the Foundation: Client/Server Architectures," provides an overview of the object model used for the Beckwith sample database. In this chapter you build the Student component as a Java MTS component.

The Student component is built from the Java class JStudent. You need the latest version of Visual J++, version 1.1, as the compiler for this component. Version 1.1 also includes the ActiveX Wizard for Java, which automates the steps required for creating Java COM objects.

> **Note** The retail version of Microsoft Visual J++ 1.1 is not compatible with Sun's Java Development Kit (JDK) 1.1. The version numbers are the same, but Visual J++ was too far along in its development cycle to incorporate features that were not completely defined in the JDK. Microsoft has issued a Web-based release that upgrades the Visual J++ 1.1 compiler to fully support JDK 1.1. The compiler upgrade is part of the Java SDK 2.0 download. To download this SDK, visit the Visual J++ Web site:
>
> `www.microsoft.com/visualj`

Creating an Empty Java Project

The process of creating any component begins with an empty project. Follow these steps to create a new project to contain the JStudent Java class.

1. Start Visual J++ 1.1 and choose **F**ile | **N**ew to open the New dialog (see Figure 13.1).

Figure 13.1.

The Visual Studio 97 New dialog.

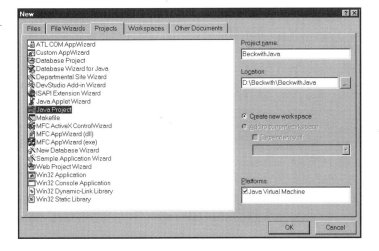

If no project is currently open in the Visual Studio development environment, the dialog appears with the Projects tab active, as shown in Figure 13.1. If an existing project is open, the Files tab is active by default; in this case, click the Projects tab.

> **Note** Your New dialog might not be identical to the one in Figure 13.1. The dialog pictured in Figure 13.1 shows other Visual Studio 97 tools (Visual C++ and Visual InterDev) installed with Visual J++. If you purchased only Visual J++ 1.1, only projects relating to Java appear.

2. Select the Java Project item by clicking its icon or label.

3. Type **BeckwithJava** in the Project Name edit box. As you type, Visual Studio mirrors characters in the Location edit box with a suggested folder for the new project.

   If the suggested location is unsatisfactory, change it before proceeding.

Adding Classes to the Project

The next step is to add classes to the project because in Java all code is contained within classes. To add new classes to a Java project, use one of these methods:

➤ Create a new .java source file and declare a new class within the file by typing its full declaration.

➤ Use Visual Studio's new Visual Editing feature, which automates the process of creating new classes.

The following steps show you how to create the `JStudent` class and add it to the project.

1. Choose **I**nsert | **N**ew Class from the main menu to display the Create New Class dialog (see Figure 13.2).

Figure 13.2.

The Create New Class dialog.

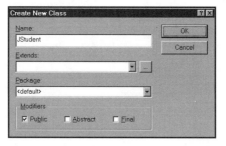

2. Provide the following information in the Create New Class dialog: the name of the new class, its superclass, the package that contains the new class, and three class modifiers: `Public`, `Abstract`, and `Final`. You can use all but one of the defaults for

the JStudent class; the exception is the Public modifier. This class is exposed to MTS as a component, so you must check the Public check box. This step adds the JStudent sample class.

> **Note** The process of adding an object to the project creates a new .java file with the same name as the object. For example, the JStudent object is declared in a file called JStudent.java, and this file is added to the current project. Also Java is extremely case sensitive. The case of the .java filename must match exactly the case of the Java class name.

3. Choose **B**uild | **R**ebuild All to compile the project. If all works well, the compiler should report zero errors and warnings; your display should now resemble Figure 13.3.

> **Note** You should not have any errors at this stage because the JStudent generated class has no methods or properties. If your project has errors, your installation of Visual J++ may be corrupt.

Figure 13.3.

A successful compile of the sample project.

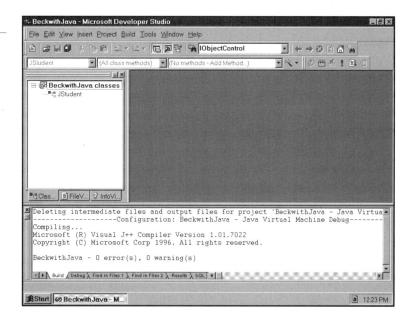

Defining Object Properties and Methods

The objects in the Beckwith database system have a common set of methods that other clients can invoke. Each object has four methods: Create(), Read(), Update(), and Delete(). Table 13.1 describes each function.

Table 13.1. *Standard object data manipulation functions.*

Method	Description
Create	Executes a SQL INSERT statement to create a new row in a table to store an object's attributes.
Read	Executes a SQL SELECT statement to read an object's attributes from the database.
Update	Executes a SQL UPDATE statement to modify an existing object's attributes.
Delete	Executes a SQL DELETE statement to remove an object's attributes from the database.

Listing 13.1 declares the JStudent class and its definitions of Create(), Read(), Update(), and Delete() methods. For details on the implementation of these methods, open the JStudent.java file from the Beckwith\JavaComponents folder on the companion CD-ROM.

Listing 13.1. *Declaring JStudent's data manipulation methods.*

```
public class JStudent
{
    public void Create(String strStudentID, String strFirstName,
        String strLastName, String strAddress, String strCity,
        String strStateOrProvince, String strPostalCode,
        String strCountry, String strPhoneNumber,
        String strEmailAddress, String strGraduationYear)
    {
    }
    public void Read(String strStudentID, String[] strFirstName,
        String[] strLastName, String[] strAddress,
        String[] strCity, String[] strStateOrProvince,
        String[] strPostalCode, String[] strCountry,
        String[] strPhoneNumber, String[] strEmailAddress,
        String[] strGraduationYear)
    {
    }
    public void Update(String strStudentID, String strFirstName,
        String strLastName, String strAddress, String strCity,
        String strStateOrProvince, String strPostalCode,
        String strCountry, String strPhoneNumber,
        String strEmailAddress, String strGraduationYear)
    {
    }
    public void Delete(String strStudentID)
    {
    }
}
```

You add methods to Java classes by typing the method declarations directly into the .java files or by using Visual Studio's Visual Editing feature. The following steps show you how to add the four JStudent methods.

1. Right-click the JStudent class in the ClassView Workspace dialog. Choose Add Method from the context menu to open the Add Method dialog shown in Figure 13.4.

Figure 13.4.

The Add Method dialog.

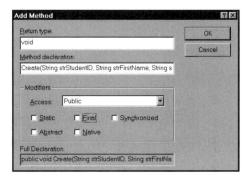

2. Fill in the Add Method dialog with the information shown in Listing 13.1 for the Create() method. Make sure to set a return type of void and make the method Public. Figure 13.4 shows what the dialog looks like with the Create() method information filled in.

3. Repeat step 2 for the remaining three methods: Read(), Update(), and Delete(). As a short cut, open the JStudent.java file from the Beckwith\JavaComponents folder on the CD-ROM; copy and paste the declarations of all the JStudent methods into the local JStudent.java file.

4. Recompile the project by choosing **B**uild | **R**ebuild All from the main menu. Fix any syntax errors that result from declaring JStudent's methods.

After adding all the data manipulation methods to the JStudent Java class, the definition of the component is complete. Although the class is declared as public, it is not very useful until it has been exposed to the system as a COM object.

Task Using the ActiveX Component Wizard for Java

The ActiveX Component Wizard for Java interprets compiled Java classes and automatically generates the necessary COM plumbing to turn plain Java classes into full-fledged COM objects. Rather than work directly with Java source files, the ActiveX Component Wizard for Java parses .class files. These .class files are the compiled output of .java files, so before invoking the ActiveX Wizard for Java, make sure you have completely rebuilt your project without errors.

Converting Java Classes into COM Objects

1. Open the JStudent.java source file in the DevStudio editor. The ActiveX Component Wizard for Java works on one Java class at a time, instead of on the entire project, so you need to open the source file of the class you want to turn into a COM object invoking the wizard.

2. Open the ActiveX Component Wizard for Java from the Tools menu. Figure 13.5 shows the initial screen when you invoke the ActiveX Component Wizard for Java on the JStudent source file.

Figure 13.5.

The ActiveX Component Wizard for Java dialog.

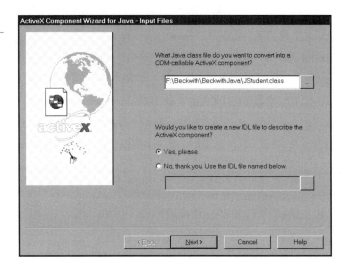

The first page of the wizard prompts you for the Java class file to convert into a COM object. The wizard fills in this edit control with a default based on the source file open in the editor before invoking the Wizard, in this case JStudent. The wizard also asks whether you want to generate a new IDL file for the converted Java class. Because JStudent is being converted for the first time, a new IDL file is necessary. You use an existing IDL file for subsequent invocations of this wizard on this class.

3. Accept the wizard defaults and click Next to continue.

Figure 13.6 shows the second page of the ActiveX Component Wizard for Java. On this page you specify whether you want a new COM class identifier (CLSID) for your object and whether to register the object as an ActiveX component when the wizard closes.

4. Select Yes, please to create a new CLSID. Select Yes, please to register the object. The only time to answer No, thank you to these questions is for subsequent invocations of the wizard on Java classes that are already converted but have different interfaces since the last time you ran the wizard. Click Next to continue.

The final page of the ActiveX Component Wizard for Java asks you to select an interface (Dispinterface or Dual Interface) and whether you want to convert the IDL file into a type library file (see Figure 13.7).

Figure 13.6.

The second page of the ActiveX Component Wizard for Java.

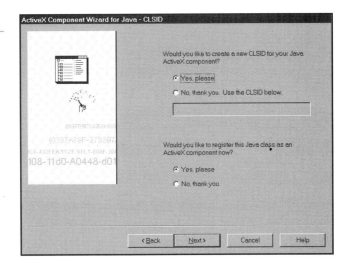

> **Note**   A *Dispinterface* is an IDispatch-based interface and is supported by almost every COM client including Visual Basic, Visual J++, and Visual C++. A *dual interface* supports an IDispatch-based interface as well as a virtual function table (v-table) custom interface. The custom interface offers improved performance over the Dispinterface, but fewer containers can take advantage of this type of interface.

5. Convert the generated IDL file into a type library. COM clients use the type library .tlb file to determine the methods and properties exposed by your Java classes at compile time. Without a type library, clients have to query an object for its properties and methods at runtime, resulting in degraded performance.

6. Select the Dual Interface and Yes, please options to create a dual interface for the JStudent component and to create a type library file. Click Next to continue.

Figure 13.7.

The final dialog page of the ActiveX Component Wizard for Java.

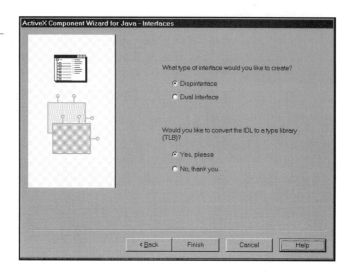

Modifying Class Definitions

After the ActiveX Component Wizard for Java converts the Java class into a COM object, one final step remains to complete the conversion process. You now need to modify the declaration of the Java class with some COM plumbing code to make the class a full-fledged COM object. The ActiveX Component Wizard for Java cannot insert this additional code automatically, so you must add it manually. The wizard displays this code in a dialog after it completes all automated conversion steps (see Figure 13.8).

Figure 13.8.

The Additional Steps dialog of the ActiveX Component Wizard for Java.

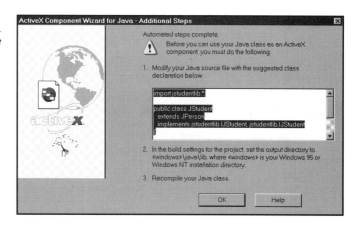

To modify the JStudent class declaration, follow these steps:

1. Copy the text displayed in the edit box to the clipboard; then click OK to close the dialog.

2. Return to the source code of the JStudent class and replace the first two lines of the class declaration with the text copied to the clipboard. Listing 13.2 shows the declaration of the JStudent object before modification, and Listing 13.3 shows the declaration after pasting the code from the clipboard.

Listing 13.2. *JStudent's class declaration prior to modification.*

```
public class JStudent
{
```

Listing 13.3. *JStudent's class declaration after modification.*

```
import jstudentlib.*;

public class JStudent
  implements jstudentlib.IJStudent, jstudentlib.IJStudent
{
  private static final String CLSID =
    "7fad5690-b9ce-11d0-ba76-00400520f095";
```

Packaging Java COM Objects

MTS requires all its components to be built as ActiveX dynamic link libraries (DLLs). Visual J++ compiles only to .class files—it knows nothing about DLLs. To translate .class files into ActiveX DLLs, you must use the Exegen.exe command-line tool that ships with MTS. Exegen is located in the Tools folder under the main MTS installation folder. Follow these steps to convert JStudent into an ActiveX DLL.

1. Add custom attributes used by Exegen to the IDL files for each Java COM object. These attributes provide information to Exegen so that it can create the standalone ActiveX DLL that MTS requires. Add these attributes to the JStudent component by modifying its IDL file to look like the one in Listing 13.4. Add all the lines of code in Listing 13.4 that end with the comment //EXEGEN.

Listing 13.4. *Modified IDL to support EXEGEN.*

```
#include <MtxAttr.h>  //EXEGEN
#include <JavaAttr.h>  //EXEGEN

[
  uuid(0ddc3e51-b9d0-11d0-ba76-00400520f095),
  helpstring("JStudentLib Type Library"),
  version(1.0)
]
library JStudentLib
{
  importlib("stdole32.tlb");

  [
    object,
```

continues

Listing 13.4. *continued*

```
        uuid(0ddc3e50-b9d0-11d0-ba76-00400520f095),
        dual,
        pointer_default(unique),
        helpstring("IJStudent Interface")
    ]
    interface IJStudent : IDispatch
    {
        [ helpstring("Create Method") ]
        HRESULT Create([in] BSTR p1, [in] BSTR p2, [in] BSTR p3,
            [in] BSTR p4, [in] BSTR p5, [in] BSTR p6, [in] BSTR p7,
            [in] BSTR p8, [in] BSTR p9, [in] BSTR p10,
            [in] BSTR p11);

        // remaining methods go here
    }


    [
        uuid(ff947fa0-b9ce-11d0-9fed-00400522ad68),
        helpstring("CJStudent Object"),
        JAVACLASS("BeckwithJava.JStudent"),      //EXEGEN
        PROGID("BeckwithJava.CJStudent.VJ"),     //EXEGEN
        TRANSACTION_REQUIRED                     //EXEGEN
    ]
    coclass CJStudent
    {
        [default] interface IJStudent;
    };

};
```

The #include directives at the top of the file simply define custom property macros that are used for the attributes of the CJStudent co-class declaration at the bottom of the listing. Following are the macros that Exegen needs for an ActiveX DLL used by MTS:

➤ The JAVACLASS macro specifies the package and class names that provide implementation for the COM object.

➤ The PROGID macro (optional) specifies the programmatic ID of the COM object. COM clients use the programmatic ID to instantiate the COM object without having to know the object's CLSID.

➤ The TRANSACTION_REQUIRED macro tells MTS to execute this component within the context of a transaction. You can also use three other macros in place of TRANSACTION_REQUIRED. Table 13.2 lists all four macros.

Table 13.2. *Transactional custom attribute macros.*

Name	Description
TRANSACTION_REQUIRED	The component must run within the context of a transaction. MTS begins a new transaction if one is not currently running.
TRANSACTION_SUPPORTED	The component supports transactions that need not be started prior to invoking methods on this component.
TRANSACTION_NOT_SUPPORTED	The component does not participate in component transactions.
TRANSACTION_REQUIRES_NEW	A new transaction must be started before using this component.

2. Make the necessary changes to the JStudent IDL file and rerun the ActiveX Component Wizard for Java to create an updated type library (.tlb) file. Exegen uses the compiled .class file, as well as the .tlb file, to create the standalone ActiveX DLL.

3. Run the Exegen tool with the following command to create the ActiveX DLL version of JStudent:

```
exegen /d /out:JStudent.dll JStudentlib.tlb JStudent.class
```

The parameters are as follows:

➤ /d tells Exegen to create an ActiveX DLL.

➤ /out specifies the name of created DLL.

➤ JStudentlib.tlb is the type library generated from the IDL file by the ActiveX Wizard for Java.

➤ JStudent.class is the compiled JStudent java class that Exegen binds to the created ActiveX DLL.

After you run Exegen, you're ready to use the Java class with any COM client that supports ActiveX DLLs. The next step is to embellish the JStudent class to support MTS features. Supporting these features enables components to be MTS–friendly.

Task Making COM Objects MTS–Friendly

The JStudent class you created at the beginning of the chapter is now a full-fledged COM object. COM-compliant clients, such as Visual Basic applications, can create and manipulate the object. You can place the JStudent object under MTS control as currently defined. However, you have not yet added MTS–specific logic in the Java code to use important MTS features, such as transactions and object pooling.

Implementing the IObjectControl Interface

To enable MTS to recycle Java components through the object-pooling mechanism, each component must expose and implement the IObjectControl COM interface. IObjectControl defines three methods: CanBePooled(), Activate(), and Deactivate(). Perform the following steps to declare and implement IObjectControl in the JStudent component:

1. Add the line import com.ms.mtx.*; to the beginning of the JStudent.java source file. This statement exposes the definition of MTS classes and interfaces, including IObjectControl.

2. Extend the implements section of the JStudent declaration by adding a reference to IObjectControl. After modification, the declaration of JStudent looks like this:

   ```
   public class JStudent

       implements jstudentlib.IJStudent, IObjectControl
   ```

3. Define and implement IObjectControl's three methods: CanBePooled(), Activate(), and Deactivate(). These methods have the following syntax:

   ➤ public boolean CanBePooled()

   ➤ public void Activate()

   ➤ public void Deactivate()

   MTS calls CanBePooled() to determine whether the component supports object pooling. True informs MTS that JStudent participates in object pooling; false tells MTS that the component does not support object pooling.

   MTS calls Activate() whenever JStudent is being activated. Because JStudent participates in object pooling, it may have to know when MTS begins to use the object to service a client request.

   MTS calls Deactivate() just prior to releasing a component and recycling it back to the object pool for future use.

4. Compare your version of the preceding modifications with Listing 13.5 and resolve any discrepancies.

Listing 13.5. *JStudent implementing IObjectControl.*

```
import com.ms.mtx.*;
import jstudentlib.*;

public class JStudent
    implements jstudentlib.IJStudent, IObjectControl
{
```

```
private static final String CLSID =
   "7fad5690-b9ce-11d0-ba76-00400520f095";

// IObjectControl methods
public boolean CanBePooled()
{
   return true;
}

public void Activate()
{
}

public void Deactivate()
{
}
```

Accessing an Object's Context through the `GetObjectContext()` Function

As mentioned in Chapter 10, "Understanding Microsoft Transaction Server Components," every object running under MTS has a companion context object that MTS creates automatically when you create the object. The context object enables a component to communicate with MTS. The primary reasons a component communicates with its context are to commit or abort transactions and to dynamically check security information related to the object's client.

To retrieve a handle to an object's context object, simply call the static method `GetObjectContext()` of the MTx class. The following line of code retrieves a reference to an object's context object:

```
IObjectContext oc = MTx.GetObjectContext();
```

MTx is a class defined in the `com.ms.mtx` package, so make sure to import `com.ms.mtx` at the beginning of each Java source file that uses its methods. MTx has only static methods and no constructor, so Java code can never directly instantiate an MTx object.

> **Caution**   You cannot call `GetObjectContext()` from everywhere inside a Java class. Don't call `GetObjectContext()` from a class's constructor or finalizer, as the call returns `null`. Additionally, if a component is not installed under MTS control, `GetObjectContext()` returns `null` wherever it is called, so make sure to check its value before dereferencing it.

Task Retrieving Data from Databases

The JStudent component now exists as a MTS component and exposes four data access methods—Create(), Read(), Update(), and Delete(). This task puts some database code behind those methods so that JStudent can do something useful by adding business-specific logic. For the Beckwith College sample, the JStudent component uses JDBC as its database access mechanism.

Using JDBC to Retrieve Data

JDBC is a set of Java classes used to access a variety of databases. Similar to Microsoft's open database connectivity (ODBC) API for Windows, JDBC provides a single interface for database systems from multiple vendors. The recent release of the Sun JDK 1.1 completed the JDBC specification, but few native database drivers for JDBC currently exist.

> **Caution** As of the time of this writing, MTS 2.0 did not fully support the Java SDK 1.1. Full support is likely to be added when Microsoft updates the Virtual Machine. Check the latest MTS service packs for updates. In the interim, the Account.VJ sample that ships with MTS contains the necessary JDBC-ODBC bridge files to complete the tasks in this chapter. Check the sample's sql folder for the necessary files.

The JStudent Java component uses a JDBC-ODBC bridge for database access. The bridge enables Java components to execute SQL queries against any database that has an ODBC driver. Given that ODBC has been available for several years, numerous drivers exist for practically all database systems. Java components using the JDBC-ODBC bridge take advantage of MTS's connection-pooling mechanism. Connection pooling is discussed in detail in Chapter 2.

> **Note** For more information about JDBC, check out Sun's Java Web site at java.sun.com.

The JStudent Read() method takes as an input parameter strStudentID, which dynamically creates and executes a SQL SELECT statement. The SELECT is expected to return a single row because StudentID is a primary key on the Beckwith Student table. The columns of the returned row are assigned to several Read() output parameters. The following steps illustrate how to use JDBC to implement the JStudent's Read() method. See Listing 13.6 for the full implementation of Read().

1. Create the following skeleton try-catch block to handle JDBC exceptions:

```
try
{
    // JDBC code goes here
}
catch (SQLException ex)
{
}
catch (java.lang.Exception ex)
{
}
```

When using an ODBC-JDBC bridge, you must force the Virtual Machine to load the bridge by using the static method forName() of the Java system class Class. The bridge is part of the CDriver class, which is contained in the com.ms.sql package.

2. Insert the following line of code inside the try block to load the bridge:

```
Class.forName("com.ms.sql.CDriver")
```

3. Request a Connection object from the JDBC Driver Manager to connect to the database server. The JStudent object reads from the Student table, which is part of the Business Office database. Insert the following code to create a connection to the Student table:

```
Connection con = DriverManager.getConnection
➥("JDBC:ODBC:dsn=BeckwithBO;database=BusinessOffice;", "sa", "");
```

4. Create a Statement object. A Statement object accepts a SQL string and returns a result set. The following code creates a Statement object:

```
Statement stmt = con.createStatement();
```

5. Build the query string and execute the query. The following code illustrates this process:

```
String strQuery = "SELECT FirstName, LastName, Address, City,
➥StateOrProvince, PostalCode, Country, PhoneNumber,
➥EmailAddress, GraduationYear FROM Student WHERE StudentID = '"
➥+ strStudentID + "'";
ResultSet rs = stmt.executeQuery(strQuery);
```

When a result set is first created, it does not by default point to the first row of returned data. Therefore, after performing the query and creating the ResultSet object, you need to advance the internal row pointer.

6. Call the ResultSet's next() method.

```
rs.next();
```

The result set now points at the desired data, so assign it to the Read() method's output parameters.

7. Add the following code:

```
strFirstName[0] = rs.getString(1);
strLastName[0] =  rs.getString(2);
strAddress[0] = rs.getString(3);
strCity[0] = rs.getString(4);
strStateOrProvince[0] =  rs.getString(5);
strPostalCode[0] = rs.getString(6);
strCountry[0] = rs.getString(7);
strPhoneNumber[0] = rs.getString(8);
strEmailAddress[0] = rs.getString(9);
strGraduationYear[0] = rs.getString(10);
```

8. Close all JDBC-related objects by invoking `Close()` on each of them. This step enables the objects to release any memory or other resources previously allocated. Add the following code:

```
// close up
        rs.close();
        stmt.close();
        con.close();
```

9. Recompile the project and fix any errors.

Listing 13.6 shows the implementation of `Read()` that performs database access via JDBC. Other than simply catching exceptions, no real error handling is yet in place. The following task adds full error-handling support and completes the implementation of `Read()`'s.

Listing 13.6. *JStudent's `Read()` method.*

```
import java.sql.*;
import com.ms.sql.*;

public class JStudent
   implements jstudentlib.IJStudent, IObjectControl
{
   public void Read(String strStudentID, String[] strFirstName,
      String[] strLastName, String[] strAddress,
      String[] strCity, String[] strStateOrProvince,
      String[] strPostalCode, String[] strCountry,
      String[] strPhoneNumber, String[] strEmailAddress,
      String[] strGraduationYear)
   {
      try
      {
         // force loading of JDBC-ODBC bridge
         Class.forName("com.ms.sql.CDriver");

         // create connection to database
         Connection con = DriverManager.getConnection(
            "JDBC:ODBC:dsn=BeckwithBO;" +
            "database=BusinessOffice;",
            "sa", "");

         // create query statement
         Statement stmt = con.createStatement();
```

```
        // perform query
        String strQuery = "SELECT FirstName, LastName, " +
            "Address, City, StateOrProvince, " +
            "PostalCode, Country, PhoneNumber, " +
            "EmailAddress, GraduationYear FROM Student " +
            "WHERE StudentID = '" + strStudentID + "'";
        ResultSet rs = stmt.executeQuery(strQuery);
        rs.next();

        // set output parameters
        strFirstName[0] = rs.getString(1);
        strLastName[0] =  rs.getString(2);
        strAddress[0] = rs.getString(3);
        strCity[0] = rs.getString(4);
        strStateOrProvince[0] =  rs.getString(5);
        strPostalCode[0] = rs.getString(6);
        strCountry[0] = rs.getString(7);
        strPhoneNumber[0] = rs.getString(8);
        strEmailAddress[0] = rs.getString(9);
        strGraduationYear[0] = rs.getString(10);

        // close up
        rs.close();
        stmt.close();
        con.close();
    }
    catch (SQLException ex)
    {
    }
    catch (java.lang.Exception ex)
    {
    }
  }
}
```

Other Data Access Mechanisms

JDBC is not the only mechanism by which to access databases from Java. Because Visual J++ allows Java components to act as COM clients, you can also use data access mechanisms that expose a COM interface. Examples of these data access mechanisms include Data Access Objects (DAO), Remote Data Objects (RDO), and Active Data Objects (ADO). RDO is the primary data access mechanism for the Beckwith objects written in Java (see Chapter 11, "Implementing Components in Visual Basic"). ADO is used for the C++ objects that are implemented in Chapter 12, "Implementing Components in Visual C++ Using the Active Template Library."

Task Implementing Component Transactions

The final task to complete the JStudent Read() method, outlines the steps necessary to implement transactions within JStudent. The basics of component transactions are described in Chapter 10. This task shows how to use an object's context to commit or abort transactions.

1. Declare a Boolean variable `bSuccess` prior to the `Read()` method's `try` block and set its initial value to `false`.

```
boolean bSuccess = false;
try
{
```

2. Close each JDBC object. At the end of the `try` block, set `bSuccess` equal to `true`. If this line of code is executed, all processing went well and no exceptions were thrown. If an exception is thrown, program execution skips to the `catch` blocks and `bSuccess` is never set to `true`.

```
    rs.close();
    stmt.close();
    con.close();

    bSuccess = true;
}
```

3. Evaluate the value of `bSuccess` from inside the `finally` block and call `SetComplete()` or `SetAbort()` based on its result. `SetComplete()` and `SetAbort()` are called on the object's context object, which is retrieved by a call to `GetObjectContext()`. The following code illustrates this process:

```
finally
{
    if (bSuccess)
    {
        MTx.GetObjectContext().SetComplete();
    }
    else
    {
        MTx.GetObjectContext().SetAbort();
    }
}
```

Listing 13.7 shows the complete listing of `Read()`, but without the JDBC code. This task completes the `JStudent` `Read()` method.

Listing 13.7. *Enabling* `JStudent` *for component transactions.*

```
public void Read(String strStudentID, String[] strFirstName, ...
{
    boolean bSuccess = false;
    try
    {
        // JDBC data access removed for brevity
        bSuccess = true;
    }
    catch (SQLException ex)
    {
    }
T       catch (java.lang.Exception ex)
    {
    }
    finally
    {
```

```
        if (bSuccess)
        {
            MTx.GetObjectContext().SetComplete();
        }
        else
        {
            MTx.GetObjectContext().SetAbort();
        }
    }
}
```

Task Sharing State Between Components

Instances of Java components can communicate with other objects through MTS's Shared Property Manager. The Shared Property Manager is discussed in detail in Chapter 10. To implement shared properties in Java, components use the ISharedPropertyGroupManager, ISharedPropertyGroup, and ISharedProperty interfaces contained in the com.ms.mtx package.

The following steps implement a counter in JStudent's Delete() method. Every time Delete() is called, this counter is incremented and its value is returned to the caller.

> **Note** Calls to the Shared Property Manager interface functions require in/out parameters. The first step is to modify the Delete() method to declare and initialize these parameters. Details of these parameters can be found in Chapter 10.

1. Add this code to the beginning of Delete() to declare and initialize the in/out parameters:

```
// declare and initialize in/out parameters
int[] nIsolationMode = new int[1];
int[] nReleaseMode = new int[1];
boolean[] bAlreadyExists = new boolean[1];
nIsolationMode[0] = ISharedPropertyGroupManager.LOCKMODE_SETGET;
nReleaseMode[0] = ISharedPropertyGroupManager.RELEASEMODE_PROCESS;
```

All access to the Shared Property Manager must go through the SharedPropertyGroupManager object. You must explicitly create this object before you can use it.

2. Add the following code to create the SharedPropertyGroupManager object:

```
// get reference to main property group manager object
ISharedPropertyGroupManager grpManager =
    new SharedPropertyGroupManager();
```

This code actually performs two actions. First, it creates the SharedPropertyGroupManager object. Second, it assigns the variable grpManager to the object's ISharedPropertyGroupManager interface.

Multiple property groups exist within the SharedPropertyGroupManager object.

3. Add the following code to select a specific group labeled JStudentDelete:

```
// get reference to a specific property group
ISharedPropertyGroup grp =
   grpManager.CreatePropertyGroup(
   "JStudentDelete", // group name
   nIsolationMode,
   nReleaseMode,
   bAlreadyExists);
```

4. Declare the CreatePropertyGroup() method in the ISharedPropertyGroupManager interface. The method creates a new property group named JStudentDelete if it doesn't already exist. If it does, a reference to the existing group is returned and assigned to the variable grp.

   A property group contains multiple properties. The CreateProperty() method of the ISharedPropertyGroup interface enables you to select or create a single property.

5. Add the following code to retrieve the DeleteCounter property:

```
// get reference to a specific property
ISharedProperty prop = grp.CreateProperty(
   "DeleteCounter", // property name
   bAlreadyExists);
```

   You can use the getValue() and putValue() methods of the ISharedProperty interface to manipulate the value stored by the property. These methods represent a property's value with the Variant class.

6. Add the following code to increment the DeleteCounter property by 1:

```
// increment this property
Variant vnResult = prop.getValue();
vnResult.putInt(vnResult.getInt() + 1);
prop.putValue(vnResult);
```

Listing 13.8 shows JStudent's Delete() method with all the code necessary to increment a shared counter. The actual code that performs a SQL DELETE has been removed for brevity. To see the complete implementation of Delete(), refer to the JStudent.java file in the companion CD-ROM Beckwith\JavaComponents folder.

Listing 13.8. *Using shared properties from Java components.*

```
public void Delete(String strStudentID, int[] nDeleteCount)
{
   // declare and initialize in/out parameters
   int[] nIsolationMode = new int[1];
   int[] nReleaseMode = new int[1];
   boolean[] bAlreadyExists = new boolean[1];
   nIsolationMode[0] =
      ISharedPropertyGroupManager.LOCKMODE_SETGET;
   nReleaseMode[0] =
      ISharedPropertyGroupManager.RELEASEMODE_PROCESS;
```

```
// get reference to main property group manager object
ISharedPropertyGroupManager grpManager =
   new SharedPropertyGroupManager();

// get reference to a specific property group
ISharedPropertyGroup grp =
   grpManager.CreatePropertyGroup(
   "JStudentDelete", // group name
   nIsolationMode,
   nReleaseMode,
   bAlreadyExists);

// get reference to a specific property
ISharedProperty prop = grp.CreateProperty(
   "DeleteCounter", // property name
   bAlreadyExists);

// increment this property
Variant vnResult = prop.getValue();
vnResult.putInt(vnResult.getInt() + 1);
prop.putValue(vnResult);

// return this value to the caller
nDeleteCount[0] = vnResult.getInt();
}
```

Implementing Programmatic Security

Another function of a component's context object is to implement programmatic security. In Java, components invoke the `IsCallerInRole()` method from the call to `MTx.GetObjectContext()` to check the role of its caller.

The following call adds a security check to the `JStudent` object's `Delete()` method. The purpose is to prevent a student with limited access from deleting records from the Beckwith Business Office database. Modify the `Jstudent` object's `Delete()` method by adding the following call to `IsCallerInRole()`:

```
public void Delete(String strStudentID, int[] nDeleteCount)
{
   if (MTx.GetObjectContext().IsSecurityEnabled() &&
      MTx.GetObjectContext().IsCallerInRole("Students"))
   {
      return; // Student's not allowed to delete!
   }
   // remaining code goes here
}
```

This code determines whether security is enabled for this component. If `true`, the code checks to see which role the user of this component is executing within. If the user is a member of the Students role, execution of `Delete()` returns immediately without deleting anything, because a student isn't allowed to delete.

Task Testing the Java Component

The simplest way to test a Java component is to install it into a package in Transaction Server Explorer and create a simple Visual Basic application to drive the component. The following steps show you how:

1. Make sure you have an up-to-date JStudent.dll. If you don't, copy the one from the Beckwith\JavaComponents folder on the companion CD-ROM or rebuild your own.

2. Click the Transaction Server Explorer icon.

3. Create a new package and give it the name JavaTest.

4. Install the JStudent.dll component into the newly created package.

5. Start Visual Basic and create a new Standard EXE project.

6. Create a reference to JStudent.dll by choosing the **P**roject | Refere**n**ces from the main menu. In the Available Reference list, select the JStudentLib Type Library.

7. Add a single push button to the project's main form.

8. Add the following code to the button's Click event:

```
Private Sub Command1_Click()

    Dim s1 As String
    Dim s2 As String
    Dim s3 As String
    Dim s4 As String
    Dim s5 As String
    Dim s6 As String
    Dim s7 As String
    Dim s8 As String
    Dim s9 As String
    Dim s10 As String

    Dim objStudent As New CJStudent
    objStudent.Read "320669203", s1, s2, s3, s4, s5, s6, _
        s7, s8, s9, s10

    MsgBox s1 & " " & s2

End Sub
```

9. Run the project and click the form's button. If everything worked as expected, a message box should display the name Kevin Bishop. If it doesn't, here are some possible solutions:

   ➤ Check to make sure the database is working correctly. Use the Microsoft SQL Enterprise Manager to perform a query on the BusinessOffice Student table.

   ➤ Verify that ODBC is set up correctly. A data source name (DSN) labeled BeckwithBO should be set up and point to the correct server and database.

➤ Make sure you have installed JDBC or the MTS-supplied JDBC-ODBC bridge correctly.

➤ Check to see that the JStudent object is being instantiated correctly by looking at the component icon in Transaction Server Explorer. When you run the test driver and click its button, the component icon should start spinning. If the icon doesn't spin, then the object is not being instantiated. Double-check the JStudent.java source file. Try rebuilding the JStudent.dll from scratch.

➤ Verify that Transaction Server itself is working correctly. Try running the sample Bank demo application that ships with MTS. The Bank demo can use a Java component. Try running the Bank demo using the Java component. If that fails, either MTS or the Java Virtual Machine installation is corrupt. Try reinstalling both.

Workshop Wrap-Up

In this chapter you used Java to implement the Beckwith JStudent MTS component. You learned how to create a Java project in Visual Studio, how to add Java classes to that project, and how to build that class into an ActiveX DLL. You added database access code to JStudent by using a JDBC-ODBC bridge and made the component MTS–friendly by implementing the IObjectControl interface. You also accessed additional features of MTS by working with the Shared Property Manager and implementing programmatic security. Finally, you installed the component in Transaction Server Explorer and tested it with a simple Visual Basic client application.

Next Steps

➤ Java components that have been created and packaged as ActiveX DLLs can be installed in the MTS environment through Transaction Server Explorer. Chapter 8, "Installing Components," explains this procedure.

➤ Java components that have been installed in the MTS environment are ready for client applications to use. Chapter 14, "Creating Windows Clients Using Visual Basic," and Chapter 15, "Setting Up Remote Windows Clients Using DCOM," explain how to create and set up Visual Basic applications to invoke MTS components via DCOM.

➤ For Internet or intranet applications, Part V, "Integrating Microsoft Transaction Server and the Internet," explains how to use MTS components, such as the JStudent component from Active Server Pages (ASP).

PART IV

Creating Microsoft Transaction Server Client Applications

CHAPTER 14

Creating Windows Clients Using Visual Basic

Tasks in This Chapter

- ➤ *Exploring the Beckwith College Database System*
- ➤ *Completing the Beckwith College Database System Application*
- ➤ *Building the Client as a Standalone Application*

Creating and installing Microsoft Transaction Server (MTS) compliant COM components is only half the struggle of creating a client/server application. The other half is constructing client applications that present a user interface to those components. The chapters in Part II, "Installing and Using Microsoft Transaction Server," taught you how to install components, and the chapters in Part III, "Microsoft Transaction Server Components," showed you how to create MTS friendly components. In Part IV, "Creating Microsoft Transaction Server Client Applications," you learn how to create the front end to the Beckwith College sample database and distribute it to client computers using Microsoft's Distributed COM (DCOM) protocol.

This chapter presents the tasks necessary to complete a client application written in Visual Basic. The Beckwith College Database System (BCDS) application enables the students of Beckwith College to do the following:

> ➤ Check their last semester grades

> ➤ Add or drop courses to the current semester schedule

> ➤ Get detailed information about a particular course

> ➤ Make electronic payments to the business office

Preparation Ensuring Correct Component and Database Setup

Before proceeding with the tasks in this chapter, you need to

> ➤ Make sure that the computer on which you develop the front-end application is the same computer running MTS. You can remove this limitation by following the tasks in Chapter 15, "Setting Up Remote Windows Clients Using DCOM."

> ➤ Make sure that MTS is installed correctly. Refer to Chapter 6, "Installing Microsoft Transaction Server," for details on ensuring that MTS is running properly.

> ➤ Make sure that SQL Server is set up and running correctly.

> ➤ Make sure you have installed the Beckwith College sample databases from the companion CD-ROM. See Appendix B, "Sample Database Schema and Entity-Relationship Diagram," for details on installing the database.

> **Note** SQL Server and the Beckwith College sample databases do not need to be installed on the same machine as MTS and the sample application you are about to build. If the databases are located on another machine, make sure your network and ODBC connections to the remote computer are operational.

➤ Verify that the Beckwith ODBC system data source names (DSNs) are set up correctly. You can use the Microsoft ODBC Administrator to make any corrections. Table 14.1 lists each DSN and the Beckwith database to which it should point.

Table 14.1. *Beckwith ODBC system DSNs.*

Data Source Name	Database
`BeckwithAD`	`Admissions`—Maintains demographic information on prospective students
`BeckwithAR`	`AlumniRelations`—Maintains demographic information on Beckwith's alumni
`BeckwithBO`	`BusinessOffice`—Maintains demographic information on enrolled students and their account balances
`BeckwithHR`	`HumanResources`—Maintains demographic information on the college's employees and professors
`BeckwithRG`	`Registrar`—Maintains students grades and current enrollment

➤ Check Transaction Server Explorer to make sure that the Visual Basic components you developed in Chapter 11, "Implementing Components in Visual Basic," are all installed inside a package named `Beckwith`. Also make sure that each component's transactional property is set to Requires a Transaction.

If you didn't build the Visual Basic components yourself, you can copy them from the CD-ROM. The server for these components is `Beckwith.dll` and is located in the `Beckwith\VB Components` folder. Copy this file to your local hard drive and then install the components from this copied file. For details on installing components, see Chapter 8, "Installing Components."

Task Exploring the Beckwith College Database System

The rest of this chapter builds one function of the BCDS: add or drop courses to current semester schedule. As you build this one feature, you work through all the steps necessary for creating a client application that uses Transaction Server components. The remaining features offer no new information; they are part of the sample code on the companion CD-ROM.

Before completing the construction of BCDS, follow these steps to copy the Visual Basic application to your local hard drive and run it:

1. Copy the folder `Beckwith\VB Client Apps\BCDS` and its subfolder `Import` from the companion CD-ROM to your local hard drive.

2. Start Visual Basic and load the `bcds.vbp` project file from the BCDS folder on your local hard drive.

   The BCDS project needs a reference to the VB components you developed in Chapter 11.

3. Choose **P**roject | Refere**n**ces to display the References dialog (see Figure 14.1) so that you can create or verify the reference to the Beckwith components.

Figure 14.1.

The References dialog.

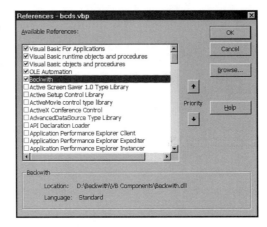

4. Make sure a reference to the `Beckwith` server is selected in the Available References list box. If not, click the check box to the left of the `Beckwith` label to select it.

> **Caution** When it is first displayed, the Available References list box may contain the following entry: MISSING: Beckwith. If so, uncheck this entry and close the References dialog by clicking OK. Bring up the References dialog a second time and check the `Beckwith` list entry. This situation occurs when your client application can't locate a specific version of the components it references. By reapplying the reference, you update your project to use the latest version of the components.

> **Caution** You may have more than one `Beckwith` entry in your Available References list box. This situation is likely because as you develop this server on your computer it may be registered multiple times from different folders. Each unique location of a registered `Beckwith.dll` results in a separate entry in the list box. Make sure you select the `Beckwith` entry that corresponds to the server you installed under MTS control. You can verify each entry's location by clicking it and noting the `Location` string at the bottom of the References dialog.

5. Start the BCDS application by choosing **R**un | **S**tart from the main menu. This step opens the Beckwith College Database System login dialog (see Figure 14.2).

Figure 14.2.

The Beckwith College Database System login dialog.

This dialog collects a student's Social Security number and a unique password to gain access to the system (PIN). The Student ID combo box on this form lists the names of several students who are part of the sample database. You can use any student ID from the combo box or type in your own, provided it identifies a valid student in the Student table of the BusinessOffice database.

6. Accept the default student ID and PIN (for simplicity) by clicking the Login button to proceed. After a brief pause, the BCDS Main Menu dialog should appear (see Figure 14.3).

7. Clicking the Login button is important because it invokes code that for the first time attempts to instantiate one of the MTS-controlled components: Student.

If you receive a Visual Basic error instead of the BCDS Main Menu dialog, then double-check that you have satisfied all of the provisions of the Preparation section at the beginning of this chapter. If the problem persists, jump to Chapter 22, "Troubleshooting the Complete Solution," to try to solve the problem.

Note The error message Invalid Student ID! Please try again. means that the Student ID you entered does not exist in the Student table of the BusinessOffice database. Perform a query on this table to obtain a valid Student ID.

The student's name is displayed in a text string at the top of the BCDS Main Menu dialog. This name was fetched from the database by invoking the Student component's Read() method and passing it the student ID retrieved from the login dialog. The Student component executes a transaction that performs a SQL SELECT on the Student table, returning the data stored in all columns to the caller.

Figure 14.3.

The BCDS Main Menu dialog.

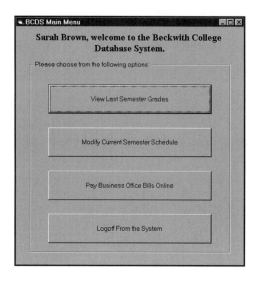

8. Select any of the following options from the main menu:

   ➤ View last semester grades

   ➤ Modify current semester schedule

   ➤ Pay Business Office bills online

   ➤ Log off from the system

   In the current state of the project, all but the Modify Current Semester Schedule choices are operational. You want to view last semester grades, so click the corresponding button. After some processing, the Last Semester Grades dialog opens (see Figure 14.4).

Figure 14.4.

The BCDS Last Semester Grades dialog.

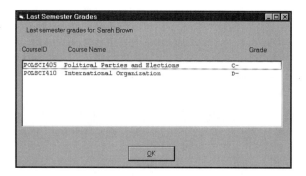

The Last Semester Grades dialog uses the MTS-controlled `Grade` component to query for the current student's last semester grades. You retrieve this information by invoking the `Grade` component's `QueryByStudent()` method. The returned information is added to the list box on the dialog.

9. Click OK to dismiss the Last Semester Grades dialog and return to the main menu.

10. Click the Pay Business Office Bills Online button to display the Business Office Account dialog (see Figure 14.5).

Figure 14.5.

The BCDS Business Office Account dialog.

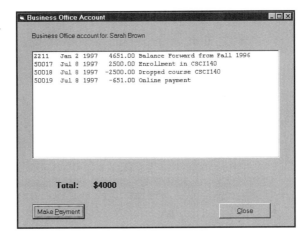

This dialog uses the `Transaction` component to post new transactions against the student's account and to query for all existing transactions. The `Transaction` component exposes two methods to accomplish these tasks: `PostTransaction()` and `Query()`.

9. Post a payment to the current student's account by clicking the Make Payment button. The application displays an input dialog where you can enter a dollar amount to credit to the account. For example, enter the value $50 and click OK to record a transaction against the current student's account for $50.

10. Click Close to return to the BCDS main menu when you are finished.

11. Click the Log off from the System button to close the BCDS system and return to the Visual Basic development environment.

Task Completing the Beckwith College Database System Application

The tasks in this section show you how to complete the implementation of the BCDS client application. What remains is to provide implementation for the Modify Current Semester Schedule button from the BCDS Main Menu dialog (refer to Figure 14.3). You need to follow these general steps to complete the implementation:

1. Import a new form to display the student's current schedule.

2. Add code to populate the form using the `Course` and `Enrollment` components.

3. Hook the new form into the main menu dialog.

4. Test the results.

Task Designing the Student Schedule Dialog

The following steps import and code the new student schedule dialog in the BCDS project.

> You can skip the steps of writing the code for the new dialog by adding the
> frmSchedule2.frm file from the Import folder of the BCDS project folder to your project.
> After inserting into your project, move on to the task "Hooking the New Form to the
> BCDS Main Menu.",

1. Import the new student schedule form to your Visual Basic project by choosing **P**roject | Add **F**orm from the main menu. Select the Existing tab and navigate to the Import folder contained by the BCDS project folder (see Figure 14.6). Double-click the frmSchedule.frm file to import it.

Figure 14.6.

The Add Form dialog with the Existing tab displayed.

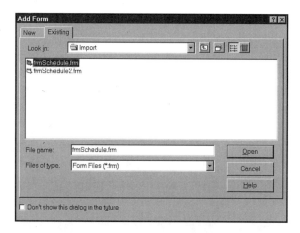

2. Double-click the frmSchedule icon from the Project Explorer window to display the dialog. It should look like the dialog in Figure 14.7.

3. Choose **F**ile | Sa**v**e Project from the main menu to save the project.

Figure 14.7.

The newly imported BCDS Student Schedule dialog in design mode.

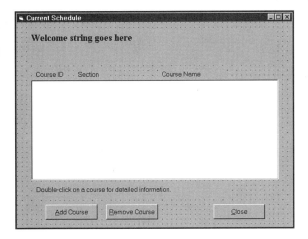

Task Using MTS-Controlled Components to Populate the New Dialog

Follow these tasks to put code behind the newly imported dialog to display the student's current schedule:

1. Make sure the new form is open. Choose <u>V</u>iew | <u>C</u>ode to open the code editor for the form.

2. Add an empty `Form_Load()` subroutine to the editor. Add the following code to the implementation of `Form_Load()`:

   ```
   lblWelcome = "Current schedule for: " & g_strStudentName
   LoadList
   ```

   The first line updates the welcome static text string at the top of the form with the current student's name. The second line invokes a private subroutine that you define and implement next.

3. Declare and implement the method `LoadList()`. Listing 14.1 contains a complete implementation for this method.

Listing 14.1. *The implementation of* `LoadList()`*.*

```
Private Sub LoadList()
    ' clear listbox of any previous information
    lstSchedule.Clear

    ' declare variant arrays to receive schedule information
    Dim rgCourseIDs As Variant
    Dim rgSections As Variant
    Dim rgCourseNames As Variant
```

continues

Listing 14.1. *continued*

```
' get list of classes student is enrolled in
Dim obj1 As New Enrollment
obj1.QueryByStudent g_strStudentID, rgCourseIDs, _
    rgSections, rgCourseNames
Set obj1 = Nothing

' populate the listbox by iterating the array
For i = 0 To UBound(rgCourseIDs) - 1
    lstSchedule.AddItem rgCourseIDs(i) & "     " & _
        rgSections(i) & "     " & rgCourseNames(i)
Next i
End Sub
```

LoadList() is a simple method that performs the following three functions:

➤ Clear the display list box on the form

➤ Retrieve schedule information by using the Enrollment component

➤ Populate the list box with schedule information

The important point with LoadList() is its use of the Enrollment component. As you can see from the code in Listing 14.1, you don't have to do anything special to use this component. An instance of Enrollment is created, one of its methods is invoked, and then the instance is released. The results of invoking its QueryByStudent() method are captured in the output parameters: rgCourseIDs, rgSections, and rgCourseNames.

Behind the scenes the Enrollment object is performing a database query under the supervision of the MTS runtime environment. When your VB application attempts to instantiate an instance of Enrollment, MTS acknowledges the request and creates an instance in one of its server processes. Then it passes back to the VB client a reference to the component instance.

When QueryByStudent() is invoked, MTS sets up a transaction context for the component. (When the component was installed, its transactional property was set to Requires a Transaction.) QueryByStudent() then does its work and either commits the transaction with a call to SetComplete() or aborts the transaction with a call to SetAbort().

4. Add code to handle the click event of the Add button on the schedule form. The Add button is responsible for adding a new course to the current student's schedule. Listing 14.2 contains a complete implementation for this button's click event.

Listing 14.2. *The implementation of btnAdd_Click().*

```
Private Sub btnAdd_Click()
    ' This method enrolls the student in a new course and
    ' charges their business office account the price of
    ' the course.  It utilizes the Enrollment and Course
    ' components developed in Chapter 11.
```

```
' reset globals
g_strCourseID = ""
g_nSection = 0

' retrieve desired course and section from user
frmPickCourse.Show vbModal, Me
frmPickSection.Show vbModal, Me

' if they have chosen successfully...
If Len(g_strCourseID) > 0 And g_nSection > 0 Then

    ' enroll the student in the new class
    Dim obj1 As New Enrollment
    obj1.EnrollStudent g_strStudentID, g_strCourseID, _
      g_nSection
    Set obj1 = Nothing

    ' get cost of this course and inform user
    Dim rgPropNames As Variant
    Dim rgPropValues As Variant
    Dim colPropBag As New Collection

    Dim obj2 As New Course
    obj2.Read g_strCourseID, rgPropNames, rgPropValues
    Set obj2 = Nothing
    PropBagToCol rgPropNames, rgPropValues, colPropBag

    MsgBox "You are now enrolled in course: " _
        & g_strCourseID & Chr$(13) & Chr$(13) & _
        "Your business office account has been charged: $" _
        & colPropBag("Cost"), , _
        "Beckwith College Database System"
End If

' refresh list of enrolled classes
LoadList
End Sub
```

The code in Listing 14.2 performs the following tasks:

➤ Displays two dialogs sequentially to prompt the user for the desired course and section (the day and time of the course). Although not shown in the code, these dialogs set the global variable `g_strCourseID` and `g_nSection` with the user's choices.

➤ Creates an `Enrollment` object and invokes its `EnrollStudent()` method. This method uses the cross-database transaction capabilities of MTS to modify the Registrar database to enroll the student in the class, as well as to debit his or her account in the BusinessOffice database for the cost of the course.

➤ Retrieves the cost of the course from the database by creating a `Course` object and invoking its `Read()` method. The success of the enrollment and the cost of the course is then communicated to the user via a message box.

5. Add code to handle the click event of the Remove button. The Remove button removes an existing course from the current student's schedule. Listing 14.3 shows the implementation of this method.

Listing 14.3. *The implementation of btnRemove_Click().*

```
Private Sub btnRemove_Click()
   g_strCourseID = Left(lstSchedule.Text, _
      InStr(1, lstSchedule.Text, " ") - 1)
   g_nSection = Mid(lstSchedule.Text, 14, 1)

   Dim obj1 As New Enrollment
   obj1.DropStudent g_strStudentID, g_strCourseID, g_nSection
   Set obj1 = Nothing

   ' get cost of this course and inform user
   Dim rgPropNames As Variant
   Dim rgPropValues As Variant
   Dim colPropBag As New Collection

   Dim obj2 As New Course
   obj2.Read g_strCourseID, rgPropNames, rgPropValues
   Set obj2 = Nothing
   PropBagToCol rgPropNames, rgPropValues, colPropBag

   MsgBox "You are dropped from course: " & g_strCourseID _
      & Chr$(13) & Chr$(13) & _
      "Your business office account is credited: $" _
      & colPropBag("Cost") _
      , , "Beckwith College Database System"

   ' refresh class list
   LoadList
End Sub
```

The only difference between the implementation of btnRemove_Click() and btnAdd_Click() is that the Enrollment component's DropStudent() method is invoked instead of the EnrollStudent() method.

6. Add a simple handler for the click event of the Close button. Add the following code to this handler:

```
Private Sub btnClose_Click()
    Unload Me
End Sub
```

7. Add a handler for the double-click event of the lstSchedule list box control. The double-click event is responsible for displaying a modal dialog that shows the user detailed information about the selected course. Listing 14.4 shows the implementation for this event method.

Listing 14.4. *The implementation of lstSchedule_DblClick().*

```
Private Sub lstSchedule_DblClick()
   ' display detailed information about the class
   g_strCourseID = Left(lstSchedule.Text, InStr(1, _
      lstSchedule.Text, " ") - 1)
   g_nSection = Mid(lstSchedule.Text, 14, 1)

   frmSection.Show vbModal, Me
End Sub
```

This code simply extracts the course ID and section number for the currently selected item in the list box and displays the detailed information dialog.

Task Hooking the New Form to the BCDS Main Menu

The final step to completing the BCDS application is to connect the Main Menu dialog to the newly added Student Schedule dialog. Follow these steps:

1. Open the code editor for the `frmMainMenu` form.

2. Replace the current implementation of the `btnSchedule_Click()` method with the following code:

```
Private Sub btnSchedule_Click()
    Me.Visible = False

    frmSchedule.Show vbModal, Me
    Me.Visible = True
End Sub
```

3. Choose File | Save Project to save the project.

Task Testing the Completed Application

Follow these steps to test the dialog you added to the BCDS project:

1. Choose Run | Start to start the application.

2. Click the Login button on the Login dialog to advance to the Main Menu dialog (refer to Figure 14.2).

3. Click the Modify Current Semester Schedule button on the main menu. After some processing, the Current Schedule dialog you just added should be displayed (see Figure 14.8).

Figure 14.8.

The newly added Current Schedule dialog.

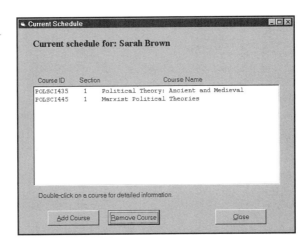

4. Click the Add Course button to display the Search for a Course dialog. In the edit box, type the string intro and then click the Search button. A list of all courses with the string **intro** in their names appears in the list box (see Figure 14.9).

Figure 14.9.

The Search for a Course dialog.

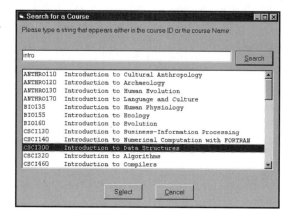

5. Select any course from the list box and click the Select button. After some processing, the Select a Section dialog appears (see Figure 14.10).

Figure 14.10.

The Select a Section dialog.

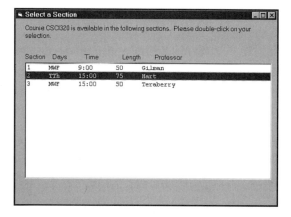

6. Select one of the sections from the list box and double-click it. After some processing, a message box informs you of the new course and its cost. Click OK to dismiss the message box. Notice that the new course has been added to the student's schedule.

7. Double-click the new class in the Current Schedule dialog list box. The Course Detail dialog should be displayed (see Figure 14.11). Dismiss the Course Detail dialog by clicking its OK button.

Figure 14.11.

The Course Detail dialog.

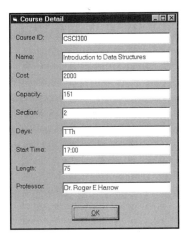

8. Test the Remove Course button by selecting any course from the schedule and clicking the button. A message box should now tell you that the class has been dropped and that your Business Office account has been credited for the cost of the class. To verify this information, close the Current Schedule dialog and return to the Main Menu dialog. Click the `Pay Business Office Bills Online` button to display the Business Office Account dialog. You should see transactions listed that show the enrollment and dropping of the class used in the previous steps (see Figure 14.12).

Figure 14.12.

The Business Office Account dialog with transactions as a result of enrolling and dropping classes.

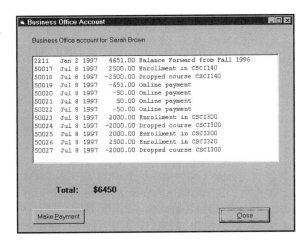

9. Close the BCDS application by clicking the Log Off from the System button on the Main Menu dialog.

Task Building the Client as a Standalone Application

The previous section used the Visual Basic development environment to modify and run the BCDS application. Unfortunately, this environment, which is great for development, is not practical when you are ready to deploy the application to the final end users. Asking end users to install Visual Basic on their machines and to run it each time they want to use your application obviously does not make sense.

Given that, the simplest way to distribute Visual Basic client applications is as standalone executables. If you already know how to create and distribute an executable from a VB project, then you can skip the steps in this section because Transaction Server imposes no changes to the way executables are built.

Follow these steps to create a standalone executable for the completed and tested BCDS project:

1. Choose <u>F</u>ile | Ma<u>k</u>e bcds.exe to display the Make Project dialog.
2. Navigate to the project's main folder, BCDS, and make sure the File name edit box contains the string bcds.exe.

> **Note** A bcds.exe file may already appear in the BCDS folder. Feel free to overwrite this file.

3. Click the Make Project dialog's OK button. Visual Basic compiles the project into the standalone bcds.exe application.
4. Test the executable by locating it with the Windows Explorer (or some other means) and opening it. You should see the Beckwith College Database System login dialog (refer to Figure 14.2).

Redistributing the Executable Created with Visual Basic

After you create the bcds.exe executable file, you can distribute it to other computers that do not have Visual Basic installed on them. However, you need one additional DLL file to accompany the executable file: Msvbvm50.dll. This DLL is the Visual Basic runtime DLL and contains a significant amount of Visual Basic code that your application relies on because it is written in Visual Basic.

You can find Msvbvm50.dll in the Winnt\System32 folder of your development computer on which Visual Basic is installed. The best approach is to copy this DLL to the System32 folder of your target computers, although you can place it in the same folder as your executable if you prefer.

Workshop Wrap-Up

In this chapter you completed the implementation of a client application written in Visual Basic. You saw how the application invokes the services of many of the components you wrote in Chapter 11 and installed under MTS control. After reading this chapter, you should realize that no MTS-specific code goes into a client application; that is, you simply create and invoke the services of components. The components themselves, along with MTS, take care of the data access and transactional details.

Next Steps

➤ Although you created a comprehensive client application in the chapter, in the current configuration it has to be run on the same machine in which MTS is running. It is not practical to install MTS on every client machine, so turn to Chapter 15 to see how to setup a client machine not running MTS to execute the sample developed in this chapter. In other words, you communicate with MTS on another machine through DCOM.

➤ To write client applications that don't use Visual Basic, check out Part V, "Integrating Microsoft Transaction Server and the Internet," to find out how to write Web-based client applications that use MTS components.

➤ If you had trouble getting the sample client application to work properly on you machine, use Chapter 22 to troubleshoot your problems.

CHAPTER 15

Setting Up Remote Windows Clients Using DCOM

Tasks in This Chapter

➤ *Exporting Packages*

➤ *Running the Client-Configuration Executable on Client Machines*

➤ *Uninstalling a Remote Configuration on a Client Machine*

➤ *Manually Registering Components on a Client Machine*

➤ *Manually Registering Components on a Client Machine Without Using* Clireg32.exe

➤ *Using the OLE/COM Object Viewer*

In Chapter 14, "Creating Windows Clients Using Visual Basic," you create a client application in Visual Basic that invokes Microsoft Transaction Server (MTS)–controlled COM components. However, the application suffers from one significant drawback: It has to run on the same machine that is running MTS. This chapter shows you how to break that dependency.

In this chapter you learn how to deploy the application from Chapter 14 on a machine that is not running MTS. You can achieve this feat by using Microsoft's Distributed COM (DCOM).

Preparation Understanding DCOM

At its simplest DCOM is merely an extension of the COM runtime environment. Whereas COM is limited to interprocess communication between binary components on the same machine, DCOM provides communication between components running on different machines. DCOM's responsibility is to handle all network communication between the component running on one machine and its client running on another.

One of the primary benefits of DCOM is that its handling of network communication is transparent to both the caller of the component and the component itself. The calling application thinks it is talking to a component running on the same machine, or even running in the same process. The same goes for the component—it doesn't know or care where its caller is executing.

Consider an example taken from the client application you developed in Chapter 14. The code in Listing 15.1 creates an instance of the Enrollment component, invokes its EnrollStudent() method, and then destroys the object.

Listing 15.1. *Visual Basic code that uses a COM component.*

```
' enroll the student in the new class
Dim obj1 As New Enrollment
obj1.EnrollStudent g_strStudentID, g_strCourseID, g_nSection
Set obj1 = Nothing
```

Recall that Enrollment is a COM component contained in the in-process server Beckwith.dll. If you don't install this server under MTS control, the code and data for the Enrollment component load and execute in the same operating system process as the client application (see Figure 15.1).

Figure 15.1.

An in-process component runs in the same process as its client.

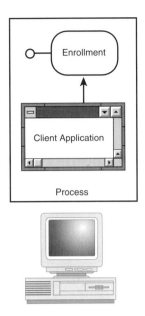

If you place `Enrollment` under MTS control, by default it loads and executes in an MTS-hosted server process. Provided the client runs on the same machine as MTS (as it did in Chapter 14), COM is sufficient to provide the communication between the client and `Enrollment`. COM is responsible for interprocess communication on the same machine (see Figure 15.2).

Figure 15.2.

An MTS-hosted component requires two processes.

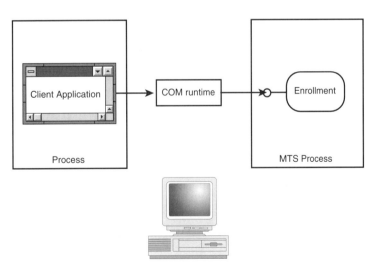

You use DCOM when the client and component run on separate computers connected by a network (see Figure 15.3). This configuration occurs when you have a single MTS server computer and many clients. Because MTS hosts the components, they load and execute on the single server machine. As each application creates an instance of your component, DCOM instantiates the component on the server, instead of on the client's computer.

Figure 15.3.

DCOM coordinates remote components between networked computers.

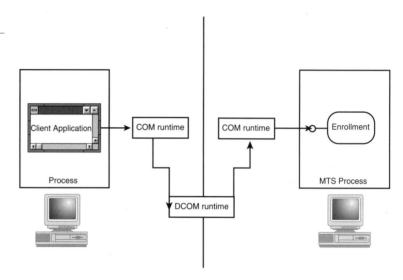

Transparent Remote Activation

The client code in Listing 15.1 is the same regardless of where the Enrollment component is loaded and running. If Enrollment is in the same process as the client or on the
same computer, COM takes care of the communication. If Enrollment is running on a
separate computer, DCOM transparently coordinates between the COM runtimes on
each machine.

DCOM uses proxy and stub objects to provide transparent remote activation and
invocation. A *proxy object* is a component that looks like the actual component (in this
case Enrollment) that gets loaded in the process of the client. A *stub* is the opposite of a
proxy. A stub runs in the process of the component and behaves like the client (see
Figure 15.4).

The transparency is achieved because the proxy exposes the same properties and
methods as the component it represents. To the client, the proxy is the component.
The stub responds to requests from the client and conveys them to the component. To
the component, the stub is its client.

Figure 15.4.

DCOM's use of proxies and stubs.

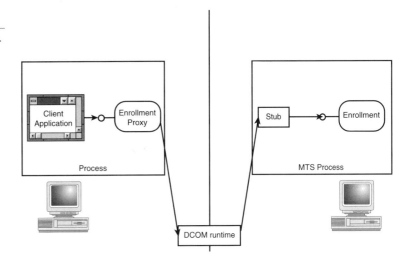

> **Note**   In addition to DCOM, COM also uses proxies and stubs to communicate between an object and its client when each runs in a separate process. Proxies and stubs are not necessary when the component runs in the same process as the client application.

When the client code in Listing 15.1 is executed, the following sequence of events occurs:

1. The client attempts to create an instance of `Enrollment`.

2. COM checks the Registry to see where `Enrollment` should be instantiated. If the component will run on a remote computer, COM delegates to DCOM.

3. DCOM communicates to the server computer to check its Registry for the component's server and checks the user's security permissions.

4. DCOM creates both the `Enrollment` object on the server and a stub to receive requests.

5. DCOM creates a proxy object in the Visual Basic client process for the `Enrollment` object. DCOM also returns (to the VB client) a reference to the proxy.

6. The VB client invokes the `EnrollStudent()` method. Although VB thinks it is invoking this method on the actual object, it really makes the call on the proxy.

7. The proxy packages the parameters passed to `EnrollStudent()` to prepare for network transit.

8. DCOM transmits the parameter package from the client to the server.

9. DCOM gives the parameter package to the stub.

10. The stub unpacks the parameters and invokes the `EnrollStudent()` method on the actual `Enrollment` object.
11. The component returns (to the stub) the results of the method call.
12. The stub packages the results and hands them to DCOM.
13. DCOM transmits the results.
14. The proxy receives the results from DCOM.
15. The proxy unpacks the results and returns them to the VB client.

Because this process goes through several steps just to invoke a single method on a remote component, you need to minimize the number of method calls you make on components that do not run locally. Invoking a method on a remote object is an order of magnitude slower than invoking a method on a local object.

> **Tip**   The relative slowness of invoking a method on a remote object is another good reason to write *stateless* objects instead of *stateful* ones. In a stateless object, you typically get all the information you need in a single method call, whereas a property-based, stateful object usually requires significantly more method calls to retrieve the same information.

Protocol Independence

DCOM defines a standard that sits on top of any standard networking protocol. Therefore, provided one machine can see another on the network and both computers can run DCOM, everything should work fine. DCOM runs on top of popular network protocols such as

➤ UDP
➤ TCP/IP
➤ IPX/SPX
➤ HTTP (Windows NT Service Pack 4)
➤ NetBIOS

Location Independence

Another key advantage to DCOM is that it can work between different computer makes and operating systems. If DCOM has been implemented for the machines on both sides of a communication, neither the component nor the client care which operating system is executing the other.

For example, a client written in Visual Basic running under Windows NT can instantiate and invoke methods on a component running on a Macintosh computer. Because of DCOM's transparent remote activation, the Macintosh component looks like a Windows NT component to the client because of the proxy. To the component, the client looks like a Macintosh client because of the stub.

DCOM is either currently or soon will be supported on the following platforms:

- ➤ Windows NT version 4.0+
- ➤ Windows 95+
- ➤ Apple Macintosh
- ➤ Sun Solaris
- ➤ AIX
- ➤ MVS
- ➤ SCO UnixWare
- ➤ Linux

Installing DCOM on Windows 95 Computers

DCOM is a built-in service of the Windows NT 4.0+ operating system. DCOM is also supported on Windows 95 machines, but you must first install DCOM on the system. DCOM will be part of future versions of Windows 95.

You can retrieve the DCOM for Windows 95 Setup program from the Microsoft Web site. One of the several links to the download area is
`http://www.microsoft.com/oledev`.

To install DCOM support on Windows 95 computers, you should download the following files from the Microsoft Web site:

- ➤ `Dcom95.exe`—The core DCOM system files Setup program
- ➤ `Dcm95cfg.exe`—The DCOM configuration Setup program

Both programs are straightforward and require little user interaction during installation. Simply run each program, starting with `Dcom95.exe`, on each installation of Windows 95 in which you want DCOM support.

Task Exporting Packages

To run a MTS client application that instantiates remote components, you need to register information about those components in the client's Registry. The client machine's COM uses the Registry information to determine that components instantiated by the application should run on a remote machine.

The information stored in the client machine's Registry includes the following:

➤ The components' CLSIDs

➤ Remote machine name for each component

➤ References to type library information of each component and its methods

You can use either of two methods to register this information on each client computer:

➤ Create a client installation executable with Transaction Server Explorer

➤ Manually copy registry files from your component development environment and register them on the client computers

The steps for the manual process are discussed later in this chapter.

The simplest way to configure client computers to invoke remote components through DCOM is to use Transaction Server Explorer to export the packages that contain your components. When you export a package, MTS creates a standalone executable that you run on each client workstation. This executable contains all component information necessary for DCOM including CLSIDs, type information, and remote connection information.

Follow these steps to export the sample Beckwith package and create the client installation executable:

1. Open Transaction Server Explorer through the Microsoft Management Console (MMC).

2. Make sure you have a Beckwith package installed and that it contains all the components defined in Beckwith.dll. If you don't, see Chapter 8, "Installing Components," for instructions on installing the sample Beckwith components.

3. Select the Beckwith package from the Transaction Server Explorer hierarchy.

4. Choose Action | Export Package from the toolbar to display the Export Package dialog (see Figure 15.5).

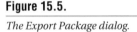

Figure 15.5.

The Export Package dialog.

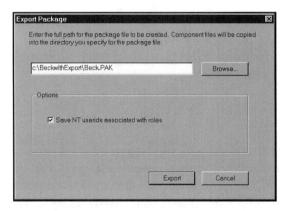

5. Supply the full path to a temporary folder on your local hard drive in the edit box. If you enter a folder name that does not yet exist, MTS creates it. In addition to the folder, you must also supply a filename for the resulting exported package file. This filename also serves as the name of the client-configuration executable.

   For this example type the string `c:\BeckwithExport\Beck` in the edit box.

> **Caution** A bug in some versions of MTS prevents you from creating the client-configuration utility if the temporary folder name you provide in the edit box contains any spaces. The workaround to this bug is to make sure the pathname you provide has no spaces.

> **Tip** You do not have to provide a file extension to the full pathname you provide. MTS automatically appends a .pak file extension for you.

6. Click Export to export the package and create the client-configuration executable. If all is successful, MTS displays a message box declaring: The package was successfully exported.

> **Note** If you export a package more than once to the same folder, MTS asks whether you want to overwrite the original exported files.

7. Use the Windows NT Explorer to navigate to the temporary folder you provided in step 5 (see Figure 15.6). There you should find two files and a folder:

   ➤ `Beck.pak`
   ➤ `Beckwith.dll`
   ➤ `clients` folder

`Beck.pak` and `Beckwith.dll` are export files that you can take to another MTS computer and then import. For the purposes of configuring client computers, you do not need to do anything with these files.

The `clients` folder should contain a file named `Beck.exe`. This file is the client-configuration executable that you use in the next task to configure a client workstation to run remote components with DCOM.

Figure 15.6.

Transaction Server Explorer created files and folders as a result of exporting a package.

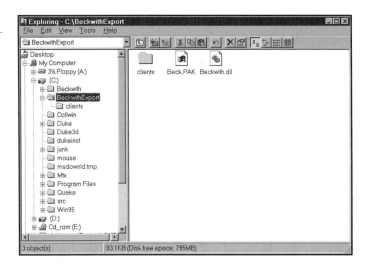

Task Running the Client-Configuration Executable on Client Machines

Follow these tasks to configure a client computer to invoke the Beckwith components on the remote MTS computer:

> **Caution** Do not complete the steps in this task on the same computer that you used to create the client-configuration application. (DCOM is unnecessary in this situation.) You should use a computer other than the one from which you exported the Beckwith package for this task!

> **Note** You can safely follow these steps and run the client-configuration application on a separate machine that also has MTS installed—even if the Beckwith package is installed on the second machine. The net effect is that clients running on the second machine invoke components on the remote computer, oblivious to the fact that MTS is installed locally.

1. Copy the Beck.exe file from the clients folder to each client computer you want to access your MTS computer. This executable file is the only one you need—all dependencies are packaged into the file.

2. Run the Beck.exe executable on the client computer. You may briefly see a progress-indicator dialog as Beck.exe unpacks itself and configures the client's Registry. (This processing occurs fairly quickly.)

Note Running the client-configuration utility displays a scanty user interface (a message box at most). In a production environment the executable is usually part of a larger setup application. The setup application spawns the client-configuration utility at an appropriate time to configure the Registry for remote-component instantiation.

Tip For absolutely no user interface during installation, append a /q (for "quiet" mode) to the command line when you run the client-configuration utility; for example, Beck.exe /q.

The client computer is now ready to run the Beckwith College Database System client application.

3. Follow the steps in Chapter 14 to copy the project or its built executable to the client machine and run it.

Tip You can verify that the Beckwith components are indeed creating themselves on the remote server by starting Transaction Server Explorer and selecting the Components folder under the Beckwith package. Run the BCDS client application from the client computer and watch the component icons in Transaction Server Explorer spin as they activate. You can also use the Transaction Statistics window of MTS to see the execution of transactions as you use the remote-client application.

Task Uninstalling a Remote Configuration on a Client Machine

In addition to easy manipulation of client Registry settings, the client-configuration utility provides a simple mechanism for uninstalling the configuration from the machine. Follow these steps to uninstall the Beckwith package setup you performed in the previous task:

1. Open the Windows Control Panel by choosing Start | **S**ettings | **C**ontrol Panel from the Windows taskbar.

2. Double-click the Add/Remove Programs icon to open the Add/Remove Programs Properties dialog (see Figure 15.7).

Figure 15.7.

The Add/Remove Programs Properties dialog.

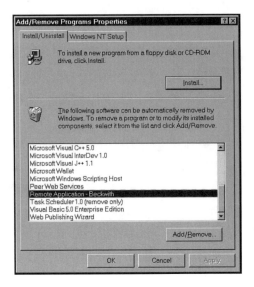

3. Locate Remote Application - Beckwith in the list box. The client-configuration utility created this entry.

> **Note** All remote installations on the computer start with the prefix Remote Application -.

4. Click Add/Remove to remove the remote configuration settings from the client computer.

Task Manually Registering Components on a Client Machine

If you prefer not to use the client-configuration installation utility that Transaction Server Explorer generates automatically, or if for some reason it doesn't meet your needs, you can manually configure the Registry of each client computer to create the components remotely.

> **Tip** Unless absolutely necessary, you should always use the configuration utility. MTS packages all dependencies into the single executable file and performs all Registry alterations automatically. Manually configuring clients is a much more complex task.

Follow these steps to manually configure a client computer to run the BCDS client application against a remote MTS installation:

1. Open Visual Basic and open the `Beckwith.vbp` file from the `Beckwith\VB Components` folder on your local hard drive. If you don't have this project installed on your computer, follow the instructions in Chapter 11, "Implementing Components in Visual Basic," to install this sample project.

2. Display the Project Properties dialog by choosing **P**roject | Beckwith Prop**e**rties from the main menu and selecting the Component property page (see Figure 15.8).

Figure 15.8.

The Project Properties dialog with the Component tab selected.

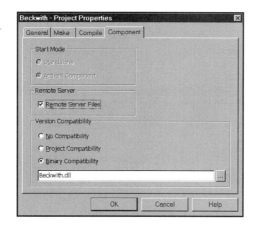

3. Examine the Remote Server Files check box and make sure the Binary Compatibility radio button is selected.

   By checking the Remote Server Files check box, the next time you compile the `Beckwith.dll` server, Visual Basic creates two new files:

   ➤ `Beckwith.vbr` is a Visual Basic registration file that modifies the Registry on the client workstation.

   ➤ `Beckwith.tlb` is a type library file that defines all the components and their interfaces in the `Beckwith.dll` server.

4. Rebuild the `Beckwith.dll` server by choosing **F**ile | Ma**k**e `Beckwith.dll` from the main menu; build the server into a temporary folder.

5. Use the Windows NT Explorer to navigate to the temporary folder and locate the produced `Beckwith.vbr` and `Beckwith.tlb` files. Copy these files to a folder on the client computer.

6. Locate the command-line utility `Clireg32.exe` that ships with Visual Basic. This utility normally resides in the `DevStudio\VB\Clisvr` folder if you accepted default directories on your installation of Visual Basic. Copy `Clireg32.exe` to the same folder on the client computer.

7. Copy the client application `Bcds.exe` to the client computer—it need not be the same folder as the others.

8. Use the `Clireg32.exe` utility on the client computer to merge the information from the `Beckwith.vbr` file into the client's Registry and register the `Beckwith.tlb` type library. Use the following command:

```
Clireg32 Beckwith.vbr -s {Server} -t Beckwith.tlb -d -a 4 -q
```

Replace the `{Server}` token with the computer name of the server running the Beckwith MTS components. Use the following command-line switches:

➤ `-t` specifies the type library to register.

➤ `-d` specifies to use DCOM as the protocol.

➤ `-a 4` specifies the security authentication level. This value can range from `0` to `6`.

➤ `-q` suppresses the display of dialogs during registration.

9. Run the `Bcds.exe` client application. If everything is configured correctly, the application should run just as it did at the end of the previous task. This time, however, you manually replicated the steps performed by the client-configuration utility.

> **Note**   The preceding task assumes you are using a Visual Basic– produced COM server. Other languages may not produce .vbr files, but all COM development environments should allow the production of .tlb type library files. You cannot use the `Clireg32.exe` tool in environments that do not produce .vbr files. The next section describes another way to modify the Registry.

Task Manually Registering Components on a Client Machine Without Using `Clireg32.exe`

As an alternative means of registering components on a client computer without using the `Clireg32.exe` tool, follow these steps:

1. Copy the component's in-proc server to a new folder on the client computer.

2. Locate the `Regsvr32.exe` utility that ships as part of Visual C++ 5.0 and Visual Studio 97. `Regsvr32.exe` normally resides in the Visual Studio `DevStudio\SharedIDE\bin` folder. Copy `Regsvr32.exe` to the client computer.

3. Use `Regsvr32.exe` to register the component DLL locally on the client computer. For example:

```
regsvr32 Beckwith.dll
```

4. Run the Windows Registry editor, `Regedit.exe` (see Figure 15.9) and make sure the following Registry keys are set:

```
HKEY_LOCAL_MACHINE\SOFTWARE\Microsoft\Ole\EnableDCOM = "Y"
HKEY_LOCAL_MACHINE\SOFTWARE\Microsoft\Ole\
    LegacySecureReferences = "N"
HKEY_LOCAL_MACHINE\SOFTWARE\Microsoft\Ole\
    LegacyImpersonationLevel = 2
HKEY_LOCAL_MACHINE\SOFTWARE\Microsoft\Ole\
    LegacyAuthenticationLevel = 4
```

These registry settings enable DCOM on the client computer and establish proper DCOM settings for MTS components.

Figure 15.9.

The Registry Editor.

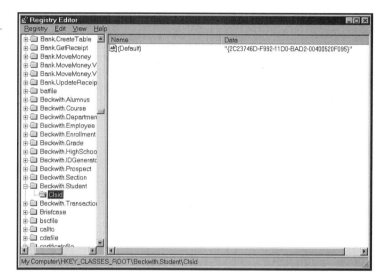

Tip

For more details on using `Regedit.exe`, see Chapter 19, "Performing Server Administration and Configuration."

Note

You can use the `Dcomcnfg.exe` tool to also change these settings. However, `Dcomcnfg.exe` is a user-interface-only tool that cannot be scripted from an installation program.

5. Determine the COM CLSID for every component in the server you registered in step 3. One of the easiest ways to do so is to use `Regedit.exe` to search the Registry for each component's programmatic ID (ProgID) string. Choose **E**dit | **F**ind and **E**dit | Find Ne**x**t from the main menu to search the Registry.

6. Locate the subkey associated with each CLSID determined in step 5 under the `HKEY_CLASSES_ROOT\AppID` parent key. For example, if the Beckwith `Student` component's CLSID is `2C23746D-F992-11D0-BAD2-00400520F095`, you would look for the key:

   `HKEY_CLASSES_ROOT\AppID\{2C23746D-F992-11D0-BAD2-00400520F095}`

7. Add the following value under each one of the keys. (Replace the string `"Server"` with the name of the server that contains MTS and on which the components are to be instantiated.)

   `RemoteServerName = "Server"`

> **Tip**
>
> Another useful tool, `Oleview.exe`, also provides a user interface to modify these Registry values. `Oleview.exe` is explored in more detail in the following section.

You can now run your application on the client machine with remote objects running under MTS control on a server machine.

Task   Using the OLE/COM Object Viewer

Manually digging through the internals of the Windows Registry just to configure the remote instantiation of COM components is not the simplest of tasks. However, Visual C++ ships with the OLE/COM Object Viewer tool, `Oleview.exe`, which provides a more user-friendly interface on top of the Registry for manipulating COM component settings, as well as many other COM- and OLE-related settings.

If Visual C++ is not installed on your machine, you can download the OLE/COM Object Viewer from Microsoft's Web site at `http://www.microsoft.com/oledev`.

Follow these steps to explore the OLE/COM Object Viewer:

1. Open the `Oleview.exe` executable. This file usually resides in the Visual C++ folder `DevStudio\VC\bin`. Opening this executable displays the main OLE/COM Object Viewer window (see Figure 15.10). When you perform this task, make sure to run the viewer on a computer on which the `Beckwith.dll` server is installed.

   The OLE/COM Object Viewer application has two display modes:

   ➤ *Novice* mode sorts the hierarchy tree view based on OLE-centric types.

   ➤ *Expert* mode sorts the hierarchy tree view based on COM constructs such as components, application IDs, type libraries, and interfaces. For MTS components, use Expert mode.

   To toggle between Expert and Novice mode, choose **V**iew | **E**xpert Mode from the main menu.

Figure 15.10.

The OLE/COM Object Viewer main window.

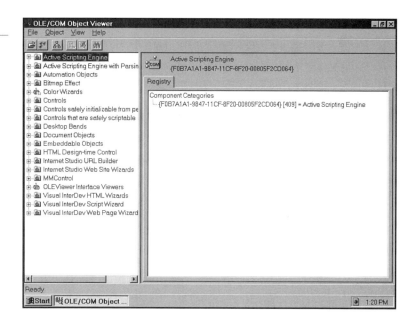

2. Select Expert mode.

In Expert mode, the hierarchy tree view of the OLE/COM Object Viewer contains the following root container items:

> ➤ Object Classes—Contains information on every single COM component registered on that computer.

> ➤ Application IDs—Lists all COM objects that are associated with an application ID. The list is sorted by AppID so this is a useful way to look up objects by AppID and determine their associated CLSID.

> ➤ Type Libraries—Enumerates all type libraries registered with the system.

> ➤ Interfaces—Contains a list of all interfaces defined on the system along with type information about each interface.

3. Locate the `Beckwith.Alumnus` ProgID item contained by the Application IDs icon in the tree control. Click the `Beckwith.Alumnus` icon to select it and display detailed information on the right side of the viewer window (see Figure 15.11).

The `Alumnus` component registered in this machine has the following CLSID: `2c237473-F992-11D0-BAD2-00400520F095`.

4. Expand the All Objects container item (under the Object Classes root object) to display a list of all COM components registered with the system.

5. Click the icon associated with `Beckwith.Alumnus` (under the All Objects container item) to reveal detailed Registry information about that component (see Figure 15.12).

Figure 15.11.

The OLE/COM Object Viewer with information associated with an AppID displayed.

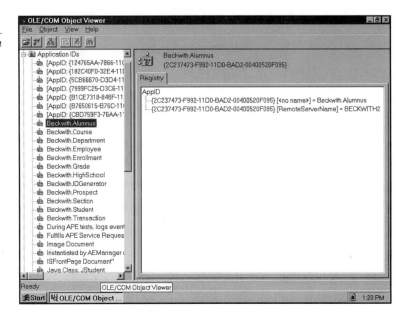

Figure 15.12.

The OLE/COM Object Viewer with detailed information of the Beckwith.Alumnus *component.*

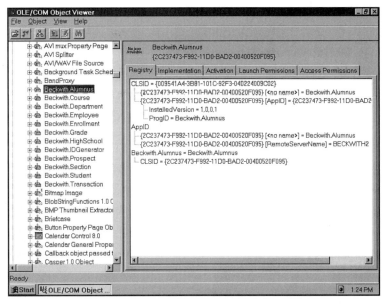

Note The components listed under the All Objects item are typically identified by their ProgIDs. Components that do not have ProgIDs are listed simply by their CLSIDs. If you can't find your component by its ProgID, check for its CLSID instead.

When you select a component from the hierarchy tree control, the right side of the OLE/COM Object Viewer contains a property sheet with five property pages:

➤ Registry—Details all Registry information known about the component.

➤ Implementation—Enables you to make changes to the component's Registry information—for example, changing the path to the component's server (see Figure 15.13).

Figure 15.13.

The OLE/COM Object Viewer displaying a component's Implementation tab.

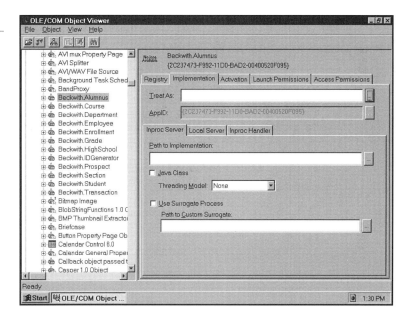

➤ Activation—Enables you to specify a remote machine name if this component is to be instantiated elsewhere. This tab is important when you are setting up a client machine to invoke MTS components remotely (see Figure 15.14).

➤ Launch Permissions—Enables you to specify who has permission to launch the component.

➤ Access Permissions—Enables you to specify who has permission to access the component.

Figure 15.14.

The OLE/COM Object Viewer displaying a component's Activation tab.

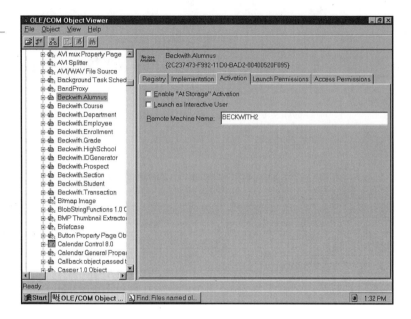

Another important feature of the OLE/COM Object Viewer is that it can create an instance of any of the components listed in the tree view. This feature, which is especially important with remote components, enables you to test the setup of DCOM connectivity without having to run your client application.

Follow these steps to create an instance of the `Beckwith.Alumnus` component:

1. Select the `Beckwith.Alumnus` component in the tree view and right-click its item to display its context menu.

2. Choose Create Instance from the context menu.

   OLE/COM Object Viewer attempts to create an instance of the component. If the component is set for remote instantiation, OLE/COM Object Viewer attempts to create the instance on the remote computer. If creation is successful, the tree control expands to show the interfaces exposed by the component (see Figure 15.15).

> **Note**   When the OLE/COM Object Viewer creates a component instance, its label in the tree view hierarchy appears in a bold font.

> **Tip**   If you use OLE/COM Object Viewer to create an instance of a component under MTS control, you can see the component's icon spinning in the Transaction Server Explorer window when the component is created. Watching the icon is a convenient way to ensure that MTS and the component's client are set up correctly.

Figure 15.15.

The OLE/COM Object Viewer displaying a component's interfaces after it is instantiated.

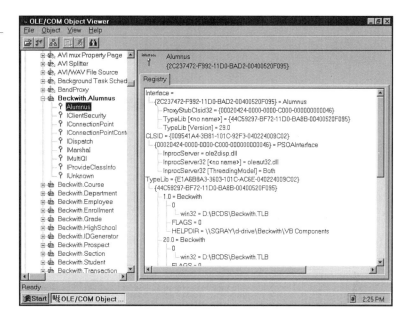

To get more information about a particular interface, double-click its icon contained by the component.

3. Double-click the Alumnus interface item in the tree control to display the Default Interface Viewer dialog (see Figure 15.16).

Figure 15.16.

The Default Interface Viewer.

The Default Interface Viewer dialog displays only the interface name and its globally unique identifier (GUID).

4. Click the View Type Info button to open the ITypeInfo Viewer dialog (see Figure 15.17), which displays information about interfaces using the Interface Definition Language (IDL). This type description of the selected interface is just like the IDL code used in Chapter 12, "Implementing Components in Visual C++ Using the Active Template Library," and Chapter 13, "Implementing Components in Java Using Visual J++," when you created components in C++ and Java, respectively.

5. Close the ITypeInfo Viewer dialog and the Default Interface Viewer to return to the OLE/COM Object Viewer main window. Destroy the instance of Beckwith.Alumnus you created in step 2 by right-clicking the Beckwith.Alumnus label in the tree view and choosing Release Instance from the context menu.

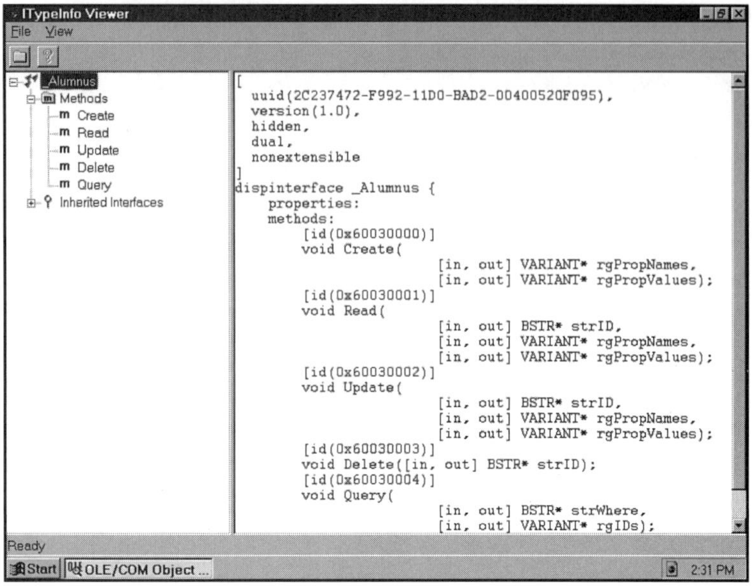

Figure 15.17.

The ITypeInfo Viewer dialog.

```
ITypeInfo Viewer
File  View

Alumnus                     [
  Methods                     uuid(2C237472-F992-11D0-BAD2-00400520F095),
    m Create                  version(1.0),
    m Read                    hidden,
    m Update                  dual,
    m Delete                  nonextensible
    m Query                 ]
  Inherited Interfaces      dispinterface _Alumnus {
                                properties:
                                methods:
                                    [id(0x60030000)]
                                    void Create(
                                                [in, out] VARIANT* rgPropNames,
                                                [in, out] VARIANT* rgPropValues);
                                    [id(0x60030001)]
                                    void Read(
                                                [in, out] BSTR* strID,
                                                [in, out] VARIANT* rgPropNames,
                                                [in, out] VARIANT* rgPropValues);
                                    [id(0x60030002)]
                                    void Update(
                                                [in, out] BSTR* strID,
                                                [in, out] VARIANT* rgPropNames,
                                                [in, out] VARIANT* rgPropValues);
                                    [id(0x60030003)]
                                    void Delete([in, out] BSTR* strID);
                                    [id(0x60030004)]
                                    void Query(
                                                [in, out] BSTR* strWhere,
                                                [in, out] VARIANT* rgIDs);

Ready
Start   OLE/COM Object ...                                          2:31 PM
```

Workshop Wrap-Up

This important chapter describes how to set up a client application on a computer that is not running MTS. DCOM can accomplish the remote instantiation of components without requiring any changes to client code. You learned how to use Transaction Server Explorer to create a client-configuration executable that automatically configures a client computer to invoke remote components. You also learned how to accomplish the same result manually, which is helpful when the client-configuration utility does not meet your needs. At the end of the chapter, you learned to use the OLE/COM Object Viewer for browsing and configuring a system's COM components.

Next Steps

➤ Another type of remote client, a Web browser, works well with MTS components. Continue to Chapter 16, "Building Dynamic Web Sites Using Active Server Pages," to learn how to create Web-based clients for MTS components.

➤ Many other Windows NT administration tools play an important role in the configuration of a client/server application. If you haven't used these tools before, or use them only infrequently, turn to Chapter 19 for tasks on completing the setup of a client/server system.

➤ If you're having problems with creating remote components with DCOM, turn to Chapter 22, "Troubleshooting the Complete Solution," for possible solutions.

PART V

Integrating Microsoft Transaction Server and the Internet

CHAPTER 16

Building Dynamic Web Sites Using Active Server Pages

Tasks in This Chapter

- ➤ *Using the Active Server Pages Intrinsic Objects*
- ➤ *Using the Active Server Pages Base Components*
- ➤ *Using the ActiveX Data Object Component*
- ➤ *Creating Database-Driven Web Applications with Microsoft Visual InterDev*

This chapter introduces Microsoft's product for generating interactive Web pages: Active Server Pages (ASP). You learn how to build a simple, Web-based front end to any ODBC-compliant database. To get the most from this chapter, you should have a working knowledge of HTML and proficiency in a high-level programming language. This chapter's tasks give you the tools you need to build Internet applications that use Microsoft Transaction Server (MTS) components.

The source code for the ASP pages in this chapter is in the `Beckwith\ASP` folder on the companion CD-ROM. To set up and configure your server, install the Beckwith sample application.

Preparation Understanding Internet Information Server

The explosive growth of the Internet has conceived a new client/server paradigm: the Web application. Web applications rely on the "thin client" approach, meaning that most of the server handles almost all the data processing, enabling clients to have a small memory and resource footprint. Typically, the term refers to applications that run within the constraints of a Web browser.

Organizations are looking to this new technology as an efficient way to distribute corporate information. Corporations are quickly moving to intranets as a method to provide employees with access to business information, corporate literature, training materials, and personnel records. Retail chains and merchandising outlets are looking to this technology as a way to increase sales while reducing costs.

Microsoft Internet Information Server (IIS) and ASP are two key technologies that can assist your company in developing a cohesive Internet plan. As a member of the Microsoft BackOffice line of products, IIS is the core component of Microsoft's Internet strategy. IIS is tightly integrated with Windows NT Server 4.0, sharing many common components, such as security and performance monitoring. Windows NT and IIS give your organization a high performance and robust way to deliver information across departments or around the world.

> **Note** The examples provided in this book require IIS version 3.0 or higher. Visit the Microsoft Internet Information Server Web site at
> `www.microsoft.com/iis`
> for details on downloading the free upgrade.

Early versions of Microsoft Windows NT Server version 4.0 shipped with Internet Information Server version 2.0. Microsoft has significantly enhanced the product and has provided a free upgrade to Windows NT Server version 4.0 users. You need this update to upgrade IIS 2.0 to version 3.0 and to use the examples in this book. For the tightest integration with MTS, you should install IIS 4.0.

Note For information on installing your Web server, refer to Chapter 5, "Configuring and Determining System Requirements."

The Internet Service Manager Snap-In for Microsoft Management Console (MMC) (Figure 16.1) provides a simple, easy-to-use graphical user interface to manage all Internet activities. You can configure World Wide Web, File Transfer Protocol (FTP), and Gopher services on the local server, or across the network.

Figure 16.1.

The IIS 4.0 Internet Service Manager Snap-In for MMC.

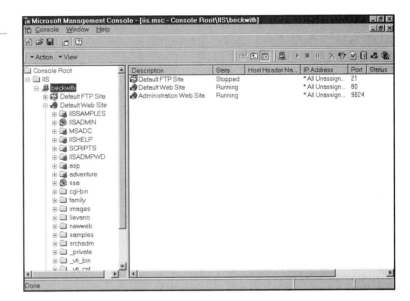

Tip To manage your Internet Information Server across the Internet, or from a Web browser, install the optional HTML Internet Service Manager. This program enables you to manage your server from any client—a useful feature if you frequently configure your Web server remotely.

ASP enables you to create interactive, high-performance Web applications that conform to the thin-client model described earlier. You can use ActiveX Scripting to develop scripts that execute on the Web server and return dynamic content to clients accessing your application. Because the ASP scripts return standard HTML that virtually any Web browser can interpret, supporting Microsoft Internet Explorer, Netscape Navigator, or most any other Web client becomes feasible.

Preparation Understanding Active Server Pages

ASP transforms static Web pages into full-featured interactive applications. ASP enables users of a corporate intranet that simply listed all employees to perform custom searches for any employee or update personal information. Developers can build sophisticated Web applications using ActiveX scripts and ActiveX server components.

ASP files are implemented as HTML pages with an `.asp` file extension. These special files house scripts that run on the server, perform a task, and return text that any HTML browser can display. The Web server processes the ASP files and removes the scripts before returning the files to the client.

> **Tip** You can obtain fully functional ASP sample applications to deploy in your intranet at
> `www.microsoft.com/intranet`.

You can use any editor that can save files to a standard ASCII format to create and edit a simple ASP page that displays the current date and time. This page is named `datetime.asp` and is installed in the `Beckwith\ASP` folder. Alternatively, you can create this script by following these steps:

1. Open the Windows Notepad editor.

2. Type the following HTML and VBScript:

   ```
   <HTML>
   <HEAD><TITLE>Date and Time</TITLE></HEAD>
   <BODY BGCOLOR="#FFFFFF">
   Today is: <% =Date %> <BR>
   The time is: <% =Time %> <BR>
   </BODY>
   </HTML>
   ```

3. Name the file `mydatetime.asp` and save it to the `Beckwith\ASP` folder.

4. Start Internet Explorer and type the URL

   ```
   COMPUTERNAME/Beckwith/ASP/mydatetime.asp
   ```

   to preview the page.

Your browser displays the following HTML output:

```
<HTML>
<HEAD><TITLE>Date and Time</TITLE></HEAD>
<BODY BGCOLOR="#FFFFFF">
Today is: 4/19/97 <BR>
The time is: 9:38:21 AM <BR>
</BODY>
</HTML>
```

The output is updated in your browser window every time you refresh the page. The scripts contained within the original ASP file are not visible to the client. This "script invisibility" guarantees browser compatibility and keeps your source code confidential.

Web Applications Before Active Server Pages

Web applications are not new to the Internet. Since the introduction of the first Web sites, programmers have been developing ways to make Web sites more dynamic. This task is inherently difficult, primarily because the underlying protocol used by Web browsers and servers is stateless.

Until now, the Common Gateway Interface (CGI) has been the standard way for Web servers to communicate with programs. The server starts a CGI program on behalf of a client request. Then the server passes the program any data submitted by the client, which could have been collected through an HTML form element. While the program executes, it performs a specialized task, such as accessing a database or conducting a Web site search, with the information received. When the program terminates, it returns its output to the Web server, which returns the information to the client. Needless to say, CGI is not noted for its efficiency or simplicity.

CGI programs are not closely integrated with the Web site's HTML pages. The programs, which can be written in almost any programming language, are most often scripts written in Perl or the operating system's shell scripting language (such as c-shell scripts or DOS batch files). Scripts are relatively easy to write and do not require compiling. However, this technique makes programs more difficult to maintain, enhance, and debug.

The ASP framework (see Figure 16.2) greatly simplifies the development of dynamic Web sites. ASP enables developers to continue using scripts to perform special tasks and generate HTML; however, the scripts are closely integrated with the HTML pages they serve. In addition, developers retain full access to all resources and functions provided by CGI and can create advanced object-oriented applications using ActiveX server components.

> **Note**   What about Microsoft's Internet Server Application Programming Interface (ISAPI)? Microsoft Internet Information Server (IIS) continues to support ISAPI as a lower level API. In fact, many IIS components, such as Secure Sockets Layer (SSL) and ASP, are implemented as ISAPI filters.

Server-Side State Management

Hypertext Transfer Protocol (HTTP) is the Internet protocol for communicating across Web servers and clients. HTTP is classified as a stateless protocol; that is, after the server delivers the requested data to the client, the connection is lost and the server retains no memory of the transaction.

Figure 16.2.

The ASP framework.

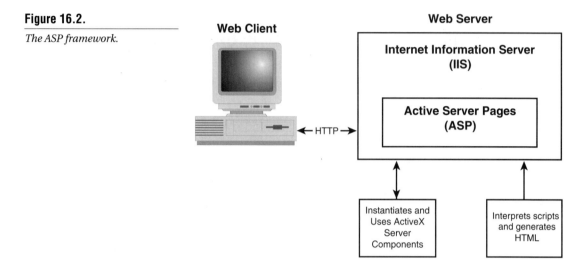

The following events occur during an HTTP connection:

1. The client requests a Uniform Resource Locator (URL).
2. The server specified in the URL acknowledges the request and sends a response to the client.
3. The connection terminates, and the server maintains no information on the transaction that just took place.

The statelessness of HTTP connections supports fast and efficient data transfers, and this architecture enables Web servers to handle hundreds of concurrent connections. However, this design makes creating Web applications a difficult task. Applications typically have "memory" or state on the user and data on which they perform work. HTTP does not have built-in support for this scheme; when the user leaves the current HTML page, the system issues another HTTP request and discards the current page.

Web servers require either CGI programs or application extensions to keep track of users or sessions. Many programmers have written workarounds to deal with statelessness. A common trick is to pass the data you want to preserve (such as the user name, or identifier) as an extension of the URL or as hidden HTML. The preferred method of managing sessions is to use "cookies." In this context *cookies* are tokens that uniquely identify a client. The information is transparent to the user, because it's usually included as part of the HTTP header. All major browsers support cookies, and they are the foundation of many state-management frameworks, including ASP.

The ASP framework extends the capabilities of cookies to allow for fully functional stateful Web-based applications. The framework provides this functionality while hiding the intricacies and complexities of dealing with cookies directly. The ASP built-in objects provide state-management functions, which are reviewed later in the chapter. All you need to know as a developer is that the process of controlling sessions is part of the framework.

Selecting an ActiveX Scripting Language

The ASP environment supports scripting through Component Object Model (COM) scripting engines; this product is not a scripting language. The framework includes built-in support for both Visual Basic Scripting Edition (VBScript) and JScript (Microsoft's implementation of Netscape's JavaScript). Scripting engines for other languages, such as Perl and REXX, are available from various vendors.

> **Tip** If you're considering using Perl in your ASP applications, check out ActiveState Tool Corp's PerlScript at `www.activestate.com`.

Active Server Pages enable developers to use multiple scripting languages within an application, or even within a single ASP page. You can specify the scripting language to use by explicitly declaring it in your `Begin Script` tag.

Sample VBScript code block:

```
<SCRIPT LANGUAGE=VBScript RUNAT=Server>
```

... VBScript code

```
</SCRIPT>
```

Sample JScript code block:

```
<SCRIPT LANGUAGE=JScript RUNAT=Server>
```

... JScript code

```
</SCRIPT>
```

Scripts are embedded inside HTML pages and are implemented within either the `<SCRIPT>` ... `</SCRIPT>` tags or the script directives (`<% ... %>`). The script directives are a simpler way to begin and end your scripts, although you cannot specify the scripting language when you use these tags; you must use the primary scripting language.

VBScript is the default primary scripting language for ASP. You can change the primary scripting language for individual pages or for your entire Web server.

> **Note** All ASP samples in this book use VBScript as their scripting engine. You will need to modify various ASP pages if you have changed the primary scripting language for your entire server.

> **Tip** Standardize on a single scripting language and use it consistently across your application.

VBScript has several advantages over JScript.

➤ VBScript has more features that support ActiveX server components.

➤ VBScript has better integration with ASP, including improved error reporting and handling.

➤ VBScript is a subset of Visual Basic, so Visual Basic developers can leverage their existing skills almost immediately.

ASP includes support for JScript primarily because of JavaScript's popularity as a Web client-side scripting language. Developers who have been writing client-side scripts, or using alternative Internet application frameworks such as Netscape LiveWire, can leverage their skills as well. If you are comfortable with the syntax of C/C++ or have used JavaScript in the past, you might want to consider JScript as your primary scripting language.

> **Note** Internet Explorer uses VBScript for client-side scripts that execute within the user's browser. These scripts typically perform data validation or other simple operations. Because you can download the scripts from potentially any source, the language syntax prevents them from using certain local resources, such as the local file system.
>
> In ASP files, VBScript enables file access (on the server) through an included COM component. However, server-side scripts have no user interface, so functions related to this subsystem are disabled. Invoking some functions (for example, **MsgBox** and **InputBox**) might cause an error.

You do not have to use your default scripting language for every page; you can use languages on a page-by-page basis.

Component-Based Internet Applications

ASP enables you to extend the functionality of scripts with ActiveX server components. These components, formerly known as OLE Automation servers, execute on your server as part of your Web application. You can use these components to design Web applications that are more robust, flexible, and maintainable than applications you design from scripts alone.

You can leverage ActiveX server components by reusing any of the hundreds of components commercially available and/or creating your own components. ASP installs a number of ActiveX server components that handle file and database access and display advertisements on a page.

You create instances of these components using the `Server.CreateObject` method. After you create the component, you can access its methods and properties. To create an instance of the ASP Browser Capability component:

1. Open the `sample.asp` file from the `Beckwith\ASP` folder.

2. Insert the following lines under the `'START SCRIPT` comment:

```
<% Set objBrowser = Server.CreateObject("MSWC.BrowserType") %>
<br>Browser: <%= objBrowser.browser %>
<br>Version: <%= objBrowser.version %>
```

3. Save the page in the `Beckwith\ASP` folder as `mybrowser.asp`.

4. Preview the page in your browser.

The statement **Set** `objBrowser = Server.CreateObject("MSWC.BrowserType")` creates an instance of the Browser Capability component. You can call methods and access properties associated with this component. When you execute this script, it returns the name and version of the client's browser.

To create ActiveX server components, you must use a programming language that supports writing Automation server components. You can make your components ASP-friendly by implementing the `OnStartPage` and `OnEndPage` methods. However, these methods are optional, and the framework is compatible with any Automation component. Part III, "Microsoft Transaction Server Components," covers component creation in detail.

> Note   ASP ActiveX server components and MTS components are similar in many respects. However, you must implement an MTS component as a DLL (in-process), whereas you can implement an ASP ActiveX server component as either a DLL (in-process) or an EXE (out-of-process). You should generally create a component as an in-process server to achieve better performance.

Understanding the Active Server Pages Configuration Files

An ASP application has one or more .asp files as well as a special configuration file named `global.asa`, which you can use to implement scripts and declare objects that have global scope. You can specify whether objects defined in this file are global to the entire application or to individual sessions. Applications can have only one global.asa file, which must be stored in the application's root directory.

For example, you create an AdRotator object having application scope with the following HTML statement:

```
<OBJECT RUNAT=Server SCOPE=Application ID=AdRot PROGID="MSWC.AdRotator">
</OBJECT>
```

The global.asa file is the only file that implements a number of special functions, which are referred to as *event handlers,* for particular application and session events. For example, Application_OnStart and Application_OnEnd are event handlers; they execute when the first user accesses the application and when the last user exits from it.

You can also implement event handlers that execute when a user first creates (and later destroys) a session. Session_OnStart and Session_OnEnd initialize settings that are unique to each user.

Task Using the Active Server Pages Intrinsic Objects

ASP's built-in objects enable developers to focus on writing the business logic of their applications, rather than the supporting infrastructure. ASP provides techniques for the following procedures:

➤ Managing the session and application state

➤ Accessing requests submitted by a client

➤ Returning responses to the client

The ASP object framework comprises the Application, Session, Request, Response, and Server objects. Each object serves a different purpose, from storing session properties to processing submitted forms. Collaboratively, the components enable developers to build Web applications without any of the complexities associated with CGI programming.

The following tasks use these objects in scripts. You learn the benefits of using these objects and the principles of using components in your ASP applications.

Using the Application and Session Objects

The Application and Session objects provide a mechanism to share information across an application. Neither object has many methods or properties, because the application developer generally defines them. These objects help developers solve one of the fundamental problems in developing Web applications: managing state. You learned the importance of retaining data across pages earlier in the chapter. The Application and Session objects make managing state an almost invisible process.

ASP uses the Application object to share data across all users of an application. The type of data shared can vary from simple properties to complex objects, such as an instance of the Scripting.Dictionary component to store a list of error descriptions. When multiple clients share properties defined in the Application object, they should use the Lock and Unlock methods to avoid overwrites to the same data member.

The following steps create a global variable to store —a simple data type—the current sales tax in an Application object:

1. Open the sample.asp file from the Beckwith\ASP folder.

2. Insert the following lines under the 'START SCRIPT comment:
   ```
   <% Application.Lock() %>
   <% Application("SalesTax") = 7 %>
   <% Application.Unlock() %>
   Sales Tax is <% =Application("SalesTax") %> %
   ```

3. Save the page in the Beckwith\ASP folder as mysalestax.asp.

4. Preview the page in your browser.

The Application object also enables you to share custom objects just as easily. For example, clients can share a single instance of the AdRotator object when you create it in the Application object:

```
<% Set Application("AdRot") = Server.CreateObject("MSWC.AdRotator") %>
```

You can refer to the SalesTax property in any script by referencing Application("SalesTax"). The preceding sample shows an alternative way of creating global Application objects (the first method described used the global.asa configuration file). Using the global.asa file and the <OBJECT> tag is the best method because the objects are easier to reference and in many cases offer better performance.

The behavior of the Session object is nearly the same as the behavior of the Application object except in the former shared data members and objects have only session scope. Only the client that owns the Session object can reference properties and objects declared in this object. For example, the Session object can store items in a user's shopping list or a user's display settings.

Using the Request and Response Objects

One of the most common methods of interacting with users of a Web site is by using HTML forms. For example, an electronic commerce application needs to obtain customer information, including the method of payment. The form shown in Figure 16.3 can perform this process.

With traditional CGI programming methods, processing this form is a painstaking process that usually requires the development of an external CGI script. ASP enables you to encapsulate all processing and presentation in the same ASP page. In this task you use the ASP Request object to process form data.

Figure 16.3.

HTML data entry form.

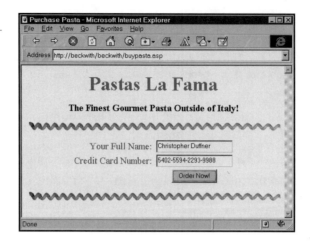

The `buypasta.asp` page requests and processes a customer information (see Figure 16.4). You can examine this file (located in the `Beckwith\ASP` folder) or develop your own by following these steps:

1. Create a new ASP page using Notepad or any other text editor.

2. Insert the following lines to process an HTML form with ASP:

```
<html>
<head><title>Purchase Pasta</title></head>
<body bgcolor="#FFFFFF">
<h1 align="center"><font color="#FF0000">Pastas La Fama</font></h1>
<h4 align="center">The Finest Gourmet Pasta Outside of Italy!</h4>
<p align="center"><img src="images/pastarl.gif" width="550"
    height="24">
<%
'
' Obtain name and credit card number from request object
'
strName   = Request.Form("name")
strCredit = Request.Form("creditcard")
'
' Verify the required data was entered
'
If Len(strName)=0 Or Len(strCredit)=0 Then
    '
    ' Display the form if elements are missing
    '
%>
<form action="buypasta.asp" method="POST" name="order">
    <div align="center"><center><table border="0">
        <tr>
            <td align="right"><font color="#FF0000">Your Full
            Name: </font></td>
            <td><input type="text" size="20" name="name"></td>
        </tr>
        <tr>
            <td align="right"><font color="#FF0000">Credit Card
            Number: </font></td>
            <td><input type="text" size="20" name="creditcard">
                    </td>
```

```
        </tr>
        <tr>
            <td align="right"> </td>
            <td align="center"><input type="submit" name="buy"
            value="Order Now!"></td>
        </tr>
    </table>
    </center></div>
</form>
<%
Else
    '
    ' Display a thank you message (and process order...)
    '
%>
<h3 align="center"><font color="#0000A0">
<% = strName %>, thank you for buying our delicious pasta!</font>
</h3>
<%
End If
%>
<p align="center"><img src="images/pastar1.gif" width="550"
height="24"></p>
</body>
</html>
```

3. Save the page in the `Beckwith\ASP` folder as `mybuypasta.asp`.

4. Preview the page in your browser.

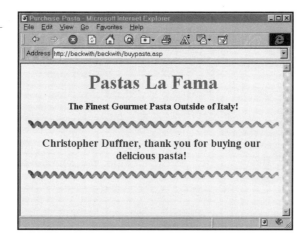

The `Request` object enables you to manage form input in an uncomplicated way. To obtain the values submitted by the user, reference the `Request` object's `Form` collection.

Form Processing in Active Server Pages

The first step to obtaining user information is to author a form in HTML. The following HTML snippet illustrates some key points of using forms with ASP:

```
<form action="buypasta.asp" method="POST" name="order">
```

The action keyword indicates the application or script to execute when submitting the form. In this case the script to execute is the page containing the form.

The method keyword indicates the HTTP method to use when submitting the form. You must use the POST method to submit form data to the ASP Request object.

The name parameter is simply the name of the form.

This sample posts the form data to the file that contains the form. Keeping the form data and the form file together is a powerful method for encapsulating the user interface and processing logic in a single page.

In addition to this method for processing forms, you may also process form elements:

From a static HTML page that posts values to an ASP page

From an ASP page that posts values to another ASP page

Using conventional methods of posting values to a CGI program

When the user submits his or her data by clicking Order Now!, the ASP page reloads and the Request.Form collection contains the user's information (unless he or she did not supply any values in the edit text fields). The following code validates the variables at the top of the page and selects an appropriate course of action.

```
<%
'
' Obtain name and credit card number from request object
'
strName   = Request.Form("name")
strCredit = Request.Form("creditcard")
'
' Verify the required data was entered
'
If Len(strName)=0 Or Len(strCredit)=0 Then
    '
    ' Display the form if elements are missing
    '
%>
```

To process the order, both parameters must contain data; otherwise, the form is displayed again.

The Request Object

The Request object provides some of the most useful and time-saving features of ASP. The Request object contains five collections: Form, QueryString, Cookies, ServerVariables, and ClientCertificates. (Refer to the ASP documentation for complete descriptions of the collections.)

The Response object returns data to the client. This object gives the developer full control over the HTTP connection, including the HTTP header and HTML. Although the

Response object is replete with functionality, the following examples use only the object's Write and Redirect methods. The Write method writes a specified string to the HTTP output. Redirect directs a client's request to an alternate URL.

The useragent.asp page displays the current browser. The script uses the Response.Write method to write data to the HTTP stream. Follow these steps to create the useragent.asp page:

1. Open the sample.asp file from the Beckwith\ASP folder.

2. Insert the following lines under the 'START SCRIPT comment:

```
<%
strAgent = Request("HTTP_USER_AGENT")
Response.Write(strAgent)
%>
```

3. Save the page in the Beckwith\ASP folder as myuseragent.asp.

4. Preview the page in your browser.

Using the Server Object

The Server object encapsulates methods and properties across applications. Only a few methods that serve as helper or utility functions are available. The Server method CreateObject becomes increasingly important as you build component-based Web sites that leverage MTS components.

Here's how to create an instance of a Beckwith College student (the Beckwith.Student component) in an ASP page:

1. Open the sample.asp file from the Beckwith\ASP folder.

2. Insert the following line under the 'START SCRIPT comment:

```
<% Set objStudent = Server.CreateObject("Beckwith.Student") %>
```

3. Save the page in the Beckwith\ASP folder as mystudent.asp.

4. Preview the page in your browser.

This sample generates output only if an error occurs during the object-creation process. Later chapters use this technique to create and use Beckwith application objects.

The Server object also contains methods for encoding strings using URL and HTML rules (URLEncode and HTMLEncode) and a method for mapping a specified virtual path into a physical path (MapPath). The MapPath method enables you to handle files that use the FileSystemObject component.

Task Using the Active Server Pages Base Components

Earlier in this chapter you used ActiveX server components to extend the ASP framework. ASP installs five base components that you can use to enhance your Web applications:

➤ ActiveX Data Objects (ADO) to access databases from your ASP scripts

➤ Advertisement Rotator to display collections of images in your pages

➤ Browser Capability to find out what browser the client is using

➤ Content Linking to automatically generate site maps of your Web site

➤ File System to access files located on your server

The Beckwith ASP application makes extensive use of the ASP intrinsic objects (which you learned about in the previous task). Portions of the application also use the File System, ADO, and Browser Capability components.

> **Tip** Visit the Microsoft Internet Information Server home page at
> `www.microsoft.com/iis`
> for updated versions of these components.

This chapter uses the ActiveX Data Objects (ADO) component to illustrate how to integrate MTS components into your Web site. Chapter 17, "Creating Interactive Web Applications Using Microsoft Transaction Server and Active Server Pages," explains how to use the Beckwith MTS components to access databases.

Accessing Files with VBScript

In the "Selecting an ActiveX Scripting Language" section of this chapter, you learned that many scripting languages such as VBScript and JavaScript lack direct file support. These two scripting languages were designed to give Web pages a small level of interactivity and programmability without the use of CGI programming. For security reasons, scripts running inside a browser would have limited access to the local machine's resources. Therefore, native support for the file system was not implemented in either language.

Now that scripts can execute on the server, this "sandbox" approach to the system's resources is no longer applicable. ASP gives developers a simple and efficient way to access files located on the server. The `FileSystemObject` and `TextStream` objects support full access to the server's file system. ASP enables you to process the contents of a file and display it as HTML, as shown in Figure 16.5.

Figure 16.5.

Viewing the contents of the
`fileio.txt` *file.*

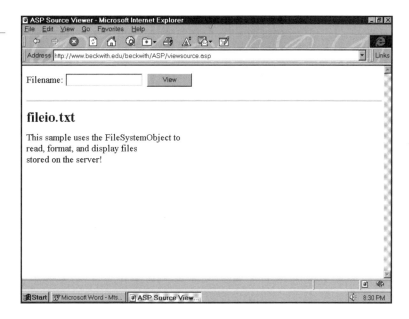

This task creates a simple ASP source viewer. Although its primary use is to view the source of ASP pages, the viewer displays the contents of any text file. The `viewesource.asp` file contains an ASP script that prompts the user for a filename and then writes the file's contents to the browser window.

1. Open the `sample.asp` file from the `Beckwith\ASP` folder.

2. Insert the following lines under the `'START SCRIPT` comment:

```
<form action="viewsource.asp" method="POST" name="viewer">
Filename: <input type="text" size="20" name="filename">
<input type="submit" name="view" value="View">
</form>
<HR>
<%
'
' Obtain filename from the form
'
strFilename = Request.Form("filename")
' Check the URL string for a filename
If Len(strFilename)=0 Then
    strFilename = Request.QueryString("filename")
End If
' Process file if a filename was provided by either method
If Len(strFilename)>0 Then
    ' Display the filename
    Response.Write("<H2>" & strFilename & "</H2>")
    ' Map the filename to a physical path
    strFilename = Server.MapPath(strFilename)
    ' Create the FileSystemObject
    Set objFile = Server.CreateObject("Scripting.FileSystemObject")
    ' Open as text file
    Set objStream = objFile.OpenTextFile(strFilename, 1)
    ' Read, format, and display each line
```

```
    While Not objStream.AtEndOfStream
        ' Read the next line
        strBuffer = objStream.ReadLine
        ' Apply HTML encoding to the buffer
        strBuffer = Server.HTMLEncode(strBuffer)
        ' Write the buffer
        Response.Write(strBuffer & "<BR>")
    Wend
  End If
%>
```

3. Save the page in the `Beckwith\ASP` folder as `myviewer.asp`.

4. Preview the page in your browser.

Managing files with the `FileSystemObject` component is much like using any other high-level language. The only distinction that you may have noticed was the call to the `Server.MapPath` method. As discussed earlier in the "Using the `Server` Object" section, this method maps virtual and relative paths to physical directories on the server. If you prefer using physical paths in your ASP scripts, you can avoid calling this method when opening files.

As an added feature, you can also specify the filename in the URL. Use the `QueryString` collection of the `Request` object to parse the URL for the filename. Here's the call:

```
strFilename = Request.QueryString("filename")
```

If provided, the contents of the specified file are displayed. This feature is helpful if you want to add links that display the source of a given file, without requiring any further input from the user. Try it out by using the following URL:

```
COMPUTERNAME/Beckwith/ASP/viewsource.asp?filename=viewsource.asp
```

Querying the Client Browser

You can determine the type and version of the client's browser from the Browser Capability component. This component also describes the client browser's capabilities to your scripts. In this task you learn to query clients for their capabilities and to leverage them when possible.

> **Caution** Early versions of MTS AdventureWorks sample application installed a nonworking version of the `browscap.dll` file. If you experience problems when using this component, reinstall ASP on your server.

The `browsercap.asp` page (see Figure 16.6) creates and queries the Browser Capability component. To create a page that uses this component, follow these steps:

1. Open the `sample.asp` file from the `Beckwith\ASP` folder.

2. Insert the following lines under the 'START SCRIPT comment:

```
<% Set objBrowser = Server.CreateObject("MSWC.BrowserType") %>
Browser: <%= objBrowser.browser %>
<br>
Version: <%= objBrowser.version %>
<br>
Frames:
<% If (objBrowser.frames = True) Then  %> Yes
<% Else  %> No
<% End If %>
<br>
Tables:
<% If (objBrowser.tables = True) Then  %> Yes
<% Else  %> No
<% End If %>
<br>
JScript:
<% If (objBrowser.javascript = True) Then  %> Yes
<% Else  %> No
<% End If %>
```

3. Save the page in the Beckwith\ASP folder as mybrowsercap.asp.

4. Preview the page in your browser.

As with any other object, you create an instance of this component by calling Server.CreateObject:

```
<% Set objBrowser = Server.CreateObject("MSWC.BrowserType") %>
```

After the object is created, you can query its properties to determine which features the client supports. For example, if you want to present a frames-enabled page to clients that support frames, query the Browser.Frames property. You could redirect requests from clients that do not support this feature to another page.

Caution This component uses the browscap.ini to store descriptions of the capabilities for supported browsers. The version of this file installed by ASP lacks definitions for some newer browsers, including Microsoft Internet Explorer 3.02. The missing definitions cause the component to report all properties as Unknown. The Beckwith\ASP folder of the CD-ROM has an updated version of this file.

Tip Visit the Microsoft IIS Web site at www.microsoft.com/iis for the latest information on this component, including the most current browscap.ini file.

You can use this component to help you leverage ActiveX-aware clients, such as Internet Explorer 3.*x*. By examining the object's ActiveX property, you can determine whether the client is capable of using ActiveX controls. If so, you can distribute certain processing tasks to the client via an ActiveX control; if not, you can just as easily process these tasks on the server. However, using the resources of client machines can significantly improve performance for busy Web sites.

Figure 16.6.

The Browser Capability component in action.

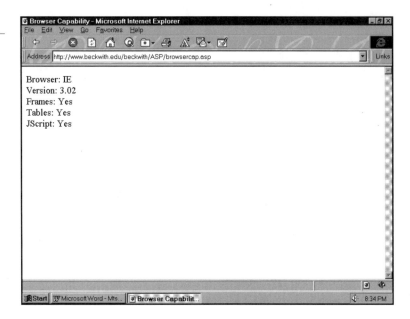

Tip You can also use the HTTP_USER_AGENT server variable directly to determine the type of browser. Use the Request object to return the HTTP_USER_AGENT server variable:
```
<% Agent = Request("HTTP_USER_AGENT") %>.
```

Task Using the ActiveX Data Object Component

Many organizations desperately need to distribute and publish their data efficiently. Web sites that enable access to corporate data, regardless of its source, are useful and appealing. With ASP and the ADO component, clients can access data from various providers.

ADO provides a simple and efficient way to access ODBC data sources (and many other types of data). In this section you use ADO objects to query the Beckwith Human Resources database. You can easily modify these examples to query any Beckwith database samples or any other ODBC-compliant data source.

> **Tip** Although ADO is installed as part of ASP, you can also use this component in your Visual Basic and Visual C++ applications.

This section touches on the many features of this high-performance data access mechanism. ADO technology is built on top of Microsoft's OLE DB data access framework, a product that is key to Microsoft's future. Visit the Microsoft ADO and OLE DB Web sites (at `www.microsoft.com/ado` and `www.microsoft.com/oledb`, respectively) for the latest details on this technology.

The ADO Object Model

ActiveX Data Objects was designed to be fast and easy to use. Figure 16.7 illustrates the ADO architecture, which contains objects for managing connections, SQL pass-through commands, result sets, and errors. For simplicity, the samples in this section rely on the `Connection` and `Recordset` objects only.

Figure 16.7.

The ADO object model.

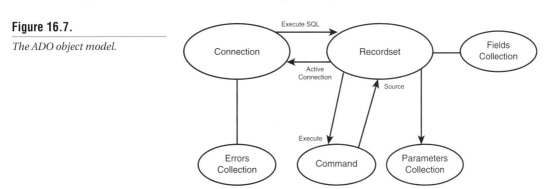

To create a `Connection` object using VBScript, use the `Server.CreateObject` method:

```
<% Set objDB = Server.CreateObject("ADODB.Connection") %>
```

You can create a `Recordset` object in a similar manner:

```
<% Set objRS = Server.CreateObject("ADODB.RecordSet") %>
```

The `Connection` object represents a connection to a database. As with many other data access models, you can open and close database connections and manage database transactions. The `Open` method establishes a connection to a data source. The `ConnectionString` property specifies a data source along with any required connection parameters. You can also specify these parameters as individual properties. In the examples that follow, the `Open` method is called with the full `ConnectionString` as its only parameter.

```
<% objDB.Open "dsn=BeckwithHR;uid=sa;pwd=" %>
```

The Connection object also supports an Execute method. As a parameter, this method accepts a SQL statement to perform. Unlike similar versions of this command found in database libraries you may have used, this method returns a Recordset object.

```
<% objRS = objDB.Execute("select * form department") %>
```

A Recordset object represents a collection of rows returned from a SQL command. This object supports operations for adding, deleting, and modifying individual rows, as well as for scrolling through the entire set of rows.

Connecting to Diverse Data Sources

A primary advantage of using ADO, as opposed to native database interfaces or even ODBC, is the capability to connect to a variety of data sources. Through OLE DB providers, you can establish ADO connections to ODBC-compliant databases and to Microsoft Office and BackOffice data stores, such as Excel and Exchange. If a provider is not specified when opening a connection, ADO assumes it is MSDASQL (Microsoft ODBC data provider for OLE DB). All examples in this book use the default ODBC data provider for their data access needs.

> **Note**   Unlike conventional client/server applications, Web applications should not allocate a database connection for an entire client session. The ADO and ODBC 3.0 connection pooling mechanisms facilitate the sharing and pooling of connections.
>
> When using ADO, you may notice slow response times on queries the first time a user connects to the database. After this initial overhead of allocating and pooling ODBC connections, response times improve significantly.

Retrieving and Displaying Recordsets

Most information available to users through Web applications is read-only. Using a database engine such as ADO greatly simplifies the development of these types of applications. In this section you implement a simple data access script with a rudimentary search engine that supports custom queries. In the section that follows, you examine a Web application with additional functionality, including the capability to add, modify, and delete records. Figure 16.8 illustrates a database query form.

This task creates an ASP page that connects to the HR database and processes user-defined queries. It uses the ADO component to establish a connection to the BeckwithHR ODBC data source, perform a query, and display the results.

The following hrdata.asp page listing enables users to perform these operations. The file is located in the /Beckwith/ASP folder. You can examine this file using Notepad, or you can create it by typing the following listing:

Figure 16.8.

The Beckwith HR database search form.

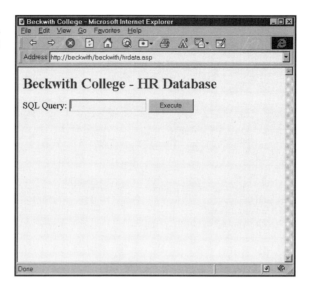

1. Open the `sample.asp` file from the `Beckwith\ASP` folder.

2. Insert the following lines under the `'START SCRIPT` comment:

```
<html>
<head><title>Beckwith College</title></head>
<body bgcolor="#FFFFFF">
<h2><font color="#0000A0">Beckwith College - HR Database</font></h2>
<%
' Always display SQL string form
%>
<form action="hrdata.asp" method="POST" name="query">
    <p>SQL Query: <input type="text" size="20" name="sql"><input
    type="submit" name="execute" value="Execute"></p>
</form>
<%
'
' Obtain the SQL statement
'
strSQL = Request.Form("sql")
'
' Verify the SQL was entered
'
If Len(strSQL)>0 Then
        '
        ' Perform the query
        '
        ' Create the connection object
        Set objDB = Server.CreateObject("ADODB.Connection")
        ' Open the connection
        objDB.Open "dsn=BeckwithHR;uid=sa;pwd="
        ' Issue the query
        Set objRS = objDB.Execute(strSQL)
        ' Redisplay the query entered
        Response.Write("<P><STRONG>Query: </STRONG>" & strSQL & "<P>")
        ' Display results in a table
        Response.Write("<TABLE BORDER=1><TR>")
```

```
' Write the column names
For i = 0 to (objRS.Fields.Count-1)
   Response.Write("<TD><B>" & objRS(i).Name & "</B></TD>")
Next
Response.Write("</TR>")
' Display result set
Do While Not objRS.EOF
   Response.Write("<TR>")
   For i = 0 to (objRS.Fields.Count-1)
        Response.Write("<TD VALIGN=TOP>" & objRS(i) & "</TD>")
   Next
   Response.Write("</TR>")
   objRS.MoveNext
Loop
' Close recordset and connection
objRS.Close
objDB.Close
Response.Write("</TABLE>")
End If
%>
</body>
</html>
```

3. Save the page in the `Beckwith\ASP` folder as `myhrdata.asp`.

4. Preview the page in your browser.

The HTML form "query" prompts the user to enter an SQL statement:

```
<form action="hrdata.asp" method="POST" name="query">
```

The Beckwith HR database contains two tables: `Employee` and `Department`. The example in Figure 16.9 shows the results of a query for all the rows in the `Department` table:

```
select * from department.
```

Figure 16.9.

The Beckwith HR database query results.

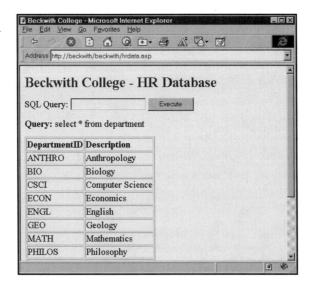

After the user enters a query and submits the form, the SQL statement is validated; if the statement is valid, the form is executed. The remaining VBScript code contained in the script processes the query and formats and displays the results.

To retrieve data from the BeckwithHR data source, you must create a connection object, open the connection, and execute the SQL statement. The following lines of code accomplish these functions:

```
' Create the connection object
Set objDB = Server.CreateObject("ADODB.Connection")
' Open the connection
objDB.Open "dsn=BeckwithHR;uid=sa;pwd="
' Issue the query
Set objRS = objDB.Execute(strSQL)
```

If the connection is successful, you can iterate through the returned Recordset object and format and display the rows accordingly. This sample displays the rows in an HTML table, a common way of formatting tabular data. The following code iterates through the Recordset object until it encounters the end-of-file marker (EOF). The objRS.Fields.Count property holds the total number of fields in the Recordset object. The value for a particular field in a record is returned by supplying to the Recordset object a zero-based index indicating the field to return. Processing continues for the next record in the set by calling objRS.MoveNext.

```
Do While Not objRS.EOF
    Response.Write("<TR>")
    For i = 0 to (objRS.Fields.Count-1)
        Response.Write("<TD VALIGN=TOP>" & objRS(i) & "</TD>")
    Next
    Response.Write("</TR>")
    objRS.MoveNext
Loop
```

Finally, you free all associated system resources by calling the appropriate Close methods:

```
' Close recordset and connection
objRS.Close
objDB.Close
```

Task Creating Database-Driven Web Applications with Microsoft Visual InterDev

Creating and managing sophisticated Web applications can be a very difficult task. As a Web site becomes more dynamic, the amount of scripts, components, static content, and graphics that it contains increases. Until now the tools available for building Web applications had been either simplistic or immature. Microsoft Visual InterDev enables you to build dynamic, data-driven Web applications in a robust, well-integrated development environment. As part of Visual Studio 97, the product is built on Microsoft's familiar Developer Studio environment. Users acquainted with either

Visual C++ or Visual J++ will appreciate the familiar surroundings. The focus of this book does not lend itself to a through evaluation of most InterDev features; however, in this section you learn how to quickly create data-driven Web applications using many of the built-in wizards.

> **Note** You must use Visual InterDev to recreate the examples in this section. You can create all other ASP samples in the book without Visual InterDev.

The database-access sample in the previous section built dynamic queries and presented read-only results. Although practical, this sample lacks most of the operations that make an application truly useful: manipulating the results. The following tasks create a fully functional database Web application that can browse employee records from the Beckwith HR database.

Creating the Web Site

To start the Web Project Wizard:

1. Choose File | New from the menu bar.
2. Click the Projects property page and select the Web Project Wizard item from the list control.
3. Name the project **Employee**, as shown in Figure 16.10, and click OK. If desired, you can modify the suggested directory before proceeding.

Figure 16.10.

Microsoft Developer Studio New dialog.

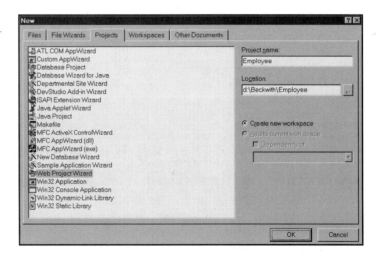

The first page of the Web Project Wizard, Figure 16.11, prompts you for the server you want to use to host your new Web site.

Figure 16.11.

The Web Project Wizard—Specify the server for your Web.

4. Type or select the machine name of your IIS server. Click Next to continue.

Figure 16.12.

The Web Project Wizard—Specify your Web.

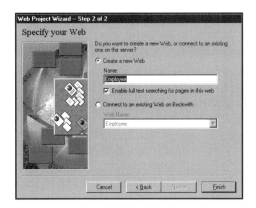

5. Accept the defaults for the remaining settings in page 2 of the wizard (see Figure 16.12) and click Finish. The wizard creates an empty Web application consisting of only the `global.asa` file.

Using the Data Form Wizard

To connect the application to the BeckwithHR data source, you use the Data Form Wizard. This powerful wizard helps you create a fully functional database Web application. It also generates the ASP script code required to navigate through record sets and perform the data manipulation operations. This task explains how to use the Data Form Wizard.

To start the Data Form Wizard:

1. Choose File | New from the menu bar.
2. Click the File Wizard property page and select Data Form Wizard.

3. Type **browser** in the filename edit text field because you are building an employee browser.

4. Accept the remaining defaults and click OK.

The Data Form Wizard opens after you complete the preceding task. The property pages that follow enable you to specify which data source to use and which operations your application will support. Respond to the Data Form Wizard property pages as follows:

1. Set up the database connection: Select New in the property page and then select the BeckwithHR data source from the Machine Data Sources tab.

2. Enter **Employee Browser** as the title of this form and click Next to continue.

3. Select the `Table` object type as the record source. Click Next to continue.

4. Select the Employee table in the Choose Fields for Your Form page. Click Next to go to the next page.

5. Accept the defaults in the Specify the Edit Options page to allow all record operations. Click Next.

6. Accept the defaults in the Select Viewing Options page. This option enables users to view data in either a list or form view. After completing this page, click Next.

   You can customize the look of your Web site by changing the theme in this property page.

7. Select any available theme and click Next.

8. Click Finish to complete the wizard.

The wizard adds three .asp files and the required database connection to your project:

➤ `BrowserAction.asp` contains the common VBScript code to select, insert, update, and delete rows from the record set.

➤ `BrowserForm.asp` displays a single record that the user can modify.

➤ `BrowserList.asp` displays scrollable lists of 10 read-only records. Any Web browser that supports tables can view the resulting application.

Running the Application

You can preview the complete application in your browser. Figure 16.13 shows the resulting application.

Figure 16.13.

The Employee Browser application in list view.

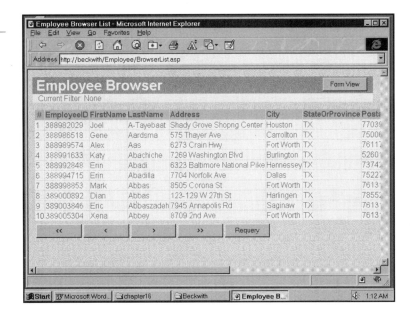

To execute the application:

1. Right-click the `BrowserList.asp` file and select Browse with.

2. Select any available browser from the Browse with dialog.

The Employee Browser list view displays employee records in a table. Through a scrollable record set, the application displays 10 employee records at any given time. Users can scroll forward or backward through the list of employees one page at a time or go directly to the first or last page. You specified the number of records to include in each page in the Data Form Wizard, and you can modify this setting by editing the `BrowserList.asp` file. Selecting an employee by clicking the assigned number or by clicking the Form View button displays the record in a form view.

The employee browser form view displays individual employee records and enables you to update and delete existing records or insert new ones (as shown in Figure 16.14). In addition having scrolling features similar to the list view (except in increments of 1, rather than 10), you can specify the filtering criteria to apply to the recordset by clicking the Filter button.

Visual InterDev brings the power and sophistication of conventional client/server development tools to the Internet and intranet. The product's use of the Developer Studio Integrated Development Environment (IDE) enables thousands of developers to leverage the skills they already possess.

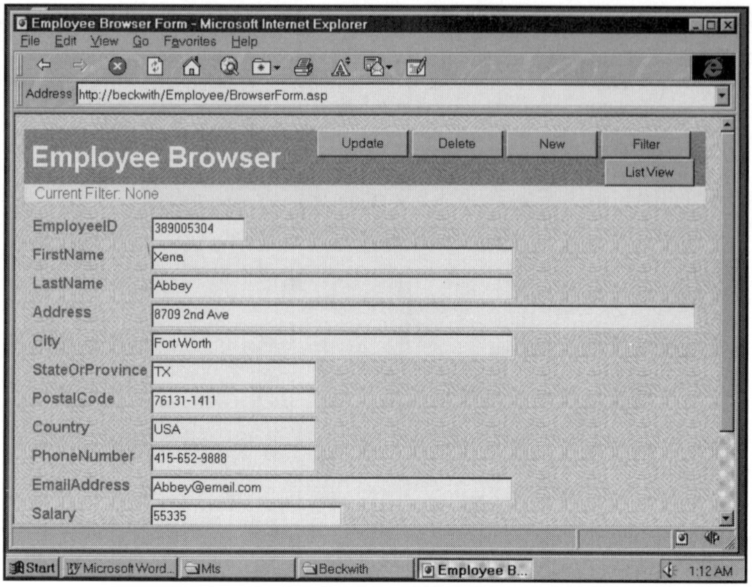

Figure 16.14.

The Employee Browser application in form view.

Workshop Wrap-Up

IIS coupled with ASP enables developers to build efficient, robust, and maintainable data-driven Web applications. The ASP framework simplifies the development of Web applications. This chapter explores the origin of Web applications and the benefits of using ASP to develop them. The many code samples show you how to quickly and easily build applications that are dynamic, interactive, and data-driven.

Next Steps

The following chapters discuss how to integrate MTS components with Active Server Pages.

➤ You review in detail the key aspects of integrating MTS components with ASP in Chapter 17.

➤ Chapter 17 also covers the importance of component-based Web application development and implements methods for shifting your business logic from ASP scripts to components.

➤ In Chapter 18, "Working with the Beckwith Online Sample Application," you install and configure the sample ASP application. Using components created in earlier chapters, you learn to build Web applications that leverage MTS-hosted components.

CHAPTER 17

Creating Interactive Web Applications Using Microsoft Transaction Server and Active Server Pages

Tasks in This Chapter

Internet/intranet applications are rapidly displacing the more traditional client/server applications that have dominated the desktop for many years. Microsoft Transaction Server (MTS) integrates seamlessly with this new breed of applications, enabling software developers to use MTS plumbing regardless of the application's target platform (for example, Visual Basic front end or Web browser).

In Part IV, "Creating Microsoft Transaction Server Client Applications," you learned how to create and deploy a full-featured client application written in Visual Basic that uses MTS components. In this chapter you examine the differences between Visual Basic–based and Web-based clients and build the foundation of the Beckwith Online sample application.

Preparation Examining the Role of Transaction Server in an Internet Application

The chapters in Part I, "Setting Up Shop," outlined the benefits of using MTS in your applications. These benefits apply whether you build applications using Visual C++, Delphi, Visual Basic, or Visual InterDev (and Active Server Pages).

Internet applications are usually referred to as *three-tier applications* simply because fulfilling a request typically spans three distinct processes:

➤ Client browser

➤ HTTP server

➤ Application (Active Server Pages [ASP] script, CGI, and so on)

Most Web applications that conform to this architecture are multitier in function, although they are not multitier in logic. Logically multitiered applications contain at least three logical tiers:

➤ Client tier—Presents the user interface of the application

➤ Middle tier(s)—Implements the business logic of the application

➤ Data tier—Manages the application's persistent data

In an Active Server Pages application, you can use MTS to control the components that ultimately generate HTML files. These components may implement business rules, manage the create/read/update/delete (CRUD) operations, or control the program flow of an application. Figure 17.1 illustrates the relationships among the many tiers of an application.

➤ Client browser—Web browsers are the targeted clients for most Internet/intranet applications. The browser presents the user interface of the application and can optionally perform tasks such as validating user data or reordering a query result set. Through ActiveX components, Microsoft's Active Desktop technology proposes to further use client resources by shifting some of the business processing to the client.

Figure 17.1.

Architecture of a MTS Internet application.

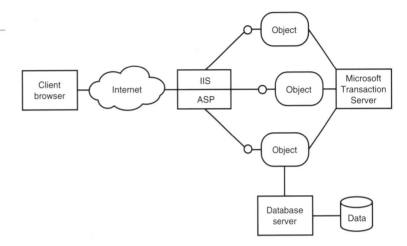

➤ IIS/ASP—Although other HTTP servers and application frameworks support MTS, nothing else is as tightly integrated with MTS. Through ActiveX scripting, developers can easily use MTS components within their ASP scripts.

➤ Microsoft Transaction Server—You can easily manage and employ application components by hosting them under MTS. These components implement the business rules and data access logic that make up the system. When loaded, these components are physically hosted under either a MTS server process or the IIS process space.

➤ Database server—Components that need to persist data rely on the data tier to store, protect, and manage this data.

Task Configuring and Validating Your System

Before proceeding with the tasks in this chapter, you need to perform the following steps:

1. Verify that MTS is installed correctly. Refer to Chapter 6, "Installing Microsoft Transaction Server," for details.

2. Verify that the Microsoft Distributed Transaction Coordinator (MS DTC) has been started. Refer to Chapter 7, "Using Transaction Server Explorer," for details.

3. Verify that SQL Server is set up and running correctly. Make sure you have installed the Beckwith College sample databases from the companion CD-ROM. See Appendix B, "Sample Database Schema and Entity-Relationship Diagram," for details.

4. Verify that the IIS World Wide Web Service is running (see Figure 17.2). Refer to Chapter 5, "Configuring and Determining System Requirements," for details.

Figure 17.2.

WWW service is running, as seen in Internet Service Manager.

> **Note** SQL Server and IIS do not need to be installed on the same machine as MTS. If the databases reside on another machine, make sure your network and ODBC connections to the remote computer are operational.

5. Verify that the Beckwith ODBC system data source names (DSNs) are set up correctly. Use the Microsoft ODBC Administrator to make corrections.

6. Check Transaction Server Explorer to make sure that the Visual Basic components you developed in Chapter 11, "Implementing Components in Visual Basic," are all installed inside a package named Beckwith. Also make sure that each component's transactional property is set to Requires a Transaction.

   If you didn't build the Visual Basic components yourself, you can copy them from the CD-ROM. The server for these components is Beckwith.dll and is located in the Beckwith\VB Components folder. Copy this file to your local hard drive and then install the components from the copied file. For details on installing components, see Chapter 8, "Installing Components."

7. If you're using IIS 3.0 and Transaction Server is running on the same machine, verify that each component's activation property allows instances of the component to be created in the creator's process (see Figure 17.3). Review Chapter 8 for details on setting this property.

Note
Both IIS 3.0 and IIS 4.0 allow MTS components to execute either in-process or out-of-process. The default configuration for IIS 3.0 uses only in-process components, thus forcing MTS components to be activated in the creator's process (as described). However, you can enable the use of out-of-process components by setting the `AllowOutOfProcCmpnts` Registry key to 1. You can find this key in the following Registry hive:

`HKEY_LOCAL_MACHINE\SYSTEM\CurrentControlSet\Services\W3SVC\ASP\Parameters`

This key enables MTS components to run in a MTS server process (rather than in the IIS process) when created from an ASP page.

Figure 17.3.

Component activation properties.

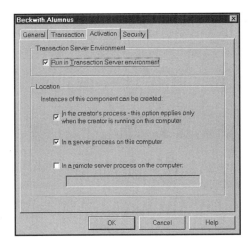

Task Invoking Microsoft Transaction Server Components in Active Server Pages

In Chapter 16, "Building Dynamic Web Sites Using Active Server Pages," you learned how to use ActiveX server components to extend the functionality of your ASP scripts. MTS components fall in the category of ActiveX server components; therefore, MTS components are easy to invoke in ASP applications.

The most common method of creating MTS objects within ASP is by calling the `Server.CreateObject` method from the ASP script. As discussed in Chapter 16, this method creates an instance of the specified server component by using the supplied ProgID.

> **Tip** Use the MTS components folder view to determine the ProgID assigned to a component. This approach is much more efficient than browsing the Windows NT system Registry or using the OLE-COM Object Viewer.

Objects created with `Server.CreateObject` have *page scope,* meaning they are automatically destroyed after the page completes processing. Because most MTS components are designed to be stateless, this behavior is preferred for object creation.

> **Note** You can use the `<OBJECT>` tag to create objects with session or application scope. However, all MTS component creation tasks and samples presented in this chapter use the `Server.CreateObject` method.

The `Beckwith.Course` component represents a unique course available at the university. You create instances of this component by using the `Server.CreateObject` method:

1. Open the `sample.asp` file from the `Beckwith\ASP` folder.
2. Insert the following line under the `'START SCRIPT` comment:

   ```
   <% Set course = Server.CreateObject("Beckwith.Course") %>
   ```

3. Save the page in the `Beckwith\ASP` folder as `mycourse.asp`.
4. Preview the page in your browser.

If successful, the script returns no output. Simply creating components is a valuable tool for debugging applications.

Task Driving Components Through Visual Basic Scripts

The components you create serve no purpose unless you use them. In this task you use Visual Basic Scripting edition to create ASP pages that create and use the Beckwith sample components.

Obtaining Information on a Beckwith Student

The `Beckwith.Student` component represents a Beckwith College student. Given a valid student identifier, this component retrieves the student's personal information. Although the data is stored in the Beckwith BusinessOffice database, the ASP script makes no reference to it. This underlying database can change without adversely affecting the client applications, which is one of the many advantages of multitier design.

In the following task you create a student object, call the `Read` method to load its attributes, and display the results:

1. Open the `sample.asp` file from the `Beckwith\ASP` folder.

2. Insert the lines in Listing 17.1 under the 'START SCRIPT comment:

Listing 17.1. *Creating, loading, and displaying a student.*

```
<%
' Create student object
Set objStudent = Server.CreateObject("Beckwith.Student")

' Set a student number
strStudentID = "320669203"

' Get student data
objStudent.Read CStr(strStudentID), rgPropNames, rgPropValues

' Display student properties
For i=0 to UBound(rgPropNames)-1
  Response.Write(rgPropNames(i) & ": " & rgPropValues(i) & _
    "<BR>")
Next
%>
```

3. Save the page in the `Beckwith\ASP` folder as `mystudent.asp`.

4. Preview the page in your browser.

When executed, this script creates and attempts to read the student identified by 320669203. The `rgPropNames` and `rgPropValues` variant arrays hold the column names and values, respectively. By iterating through these arrays you can display the student's attributes, as shown in Figure 17.4.

Figure 17.4.

Displaying a Student object.

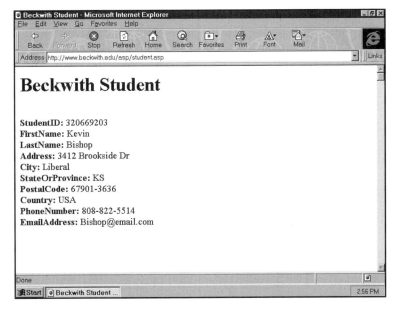

Updating the Beckwith Student

The Beckwith.Student component exposes a method to update a student's personal information. In the following task you build on the prior task to update the student's home address:

1. Open the student.asp file from the Beckwith\ASP folder.

2. Insert the lines in Listing 17.2 under the 'CONTINUE SCRIPT comment:

Listing 17.2. *Updating a student.*

```
<%
' Create an HTML horizontal separator
Response.Write("<hr>")

' Update the student's address
rgPropValues(3) = "6363 Springhouse Place"
rgPropValues(4) = "Bridgeville"
rgPropValues(5) = "PA"
rgPropValues(6) = "15017"

' Update the student information
objStudent.Update CStr(strStudentID), rgPropNames, rgPropValues

' Reload the student (to verify that it was changed)
objStudent.Read CStr(strStudentID), rgPropNames, rgPropValues

' Again, display student properties
For i=0 to UBound(rgPropNames)-1
    Response.Write(rgPropNames(i) & ": " & rgPropValues(i) & _
    "<BR>")
Next%>
```

3. Save the page in the Beckwith\ASP folder as mystudentupdate.asp.

4. Preview the page in your browser.

In addition to creating, reading, and displaying the specified student, this script updates address information. The rgPropValues array provides the update information, and a subsequent call to the Read method validates that the information was, in fact, changed (Figure 17.5).

Deleting the Beckwith Student

The Beckwith.Student component exposes a method to remove a student from the Beckwith BusinessOffice database. In the Beckwith sample application, a student may be deleted because

➤ The person is no longer a student and the account has been inactive.

➤ The student graduates and is "promoted" to an alumnus.

Figure 17.5.

Updating a Student object.

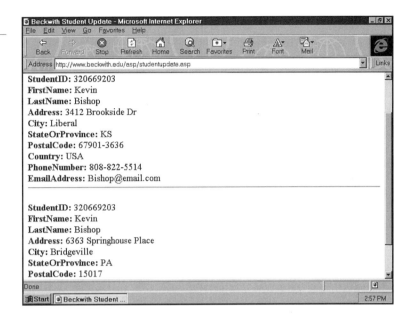

The following script deletes a student and verifies that the record no longer exists:

1. Open the `student.asp` file from the `Beckwith\ASP` folder.

2. Insert the lines in Listing 17.3 under the `'CONTINUE SCRIPT` comment:

Listing 17.3. *Deleting a student.*

```
<%
' Create an HTML horizontal separator
Response.Write("<hr>")

' Delete the student
objStudent.Delete CStr(strStudentID)

' Reload the student (to verify that it was deleted)
objStudent.Read CStr(strStudentID), rgPropNames, rgPropValues

' The rgPropValues array will not contain student information
If rgPropValues(0) <> strStudentID Then
  Response.Write("<H2>The student no longer exists!</H2>")
End If
%>
```

3. Save the page in the `Beckwith\ASP` folder as `mystudentdelete.asp`.

4. Preview the page in your browser.

When executed, this script attempts to delete the student identified by `320669203`. If the script is successful, it removes the row from the `student` table of the Beckwith BusinessOffice database (as seen in Figure 17.6).

Figure 17.6.

Deleting a Student object.

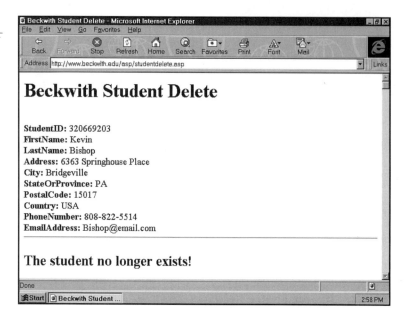

> **Tip**
> Perform the next task, "Creating a New Beckwith Student" to restore the deleted student. This step resets the tasks so that they will behave as expected the next time someone attempts to use them.

Creating a New Beckwith Student

You create new students by using the Create method of the Beckwith.Student. This method performs a SQL INSERT operation on the Student table of the Beckwith BusinessOffice database. The Create method uses the values in the rgPropValues property bag to populate the new student record.

> **Tip**
> To avoid confusion when returning to these tasks, re-create the sample student after completion of each task. Execute the included studentcreate.asp script from the Beckwith\ASP folder.

To re-create the sample student used in the previous tasks:

1. Open the sample.asp file from the Beckwith\ASP folder.
2. Insert the lines in Listing 17.4 under the 'START SCRIPT comment:

Listing 17.4. *Creating a Student object.*

```
<%
' Create student object
Set objStudent = Server.CreateObject("Beckwith.Student")

' Set a new student number
strStudentID = "320669203"

' Get student data (used only to populate the rgPropNames array)
objStudent.Read CStr(strStudentID), rgPropNames, rgPropValues

' Delete the student if it exists
If rgPropValues(0) = strStudentID Then
  objStudent.Delete Cstr(strStudentID)
End If

' Set the new student's information
rgPropValues(0) = CStr(strStudentID)
rgPropValues(1) = "Kevin"
rgPropValues(2) = "Bishop"
rgPropValues(3) = "3412 Brookside Dr"
rgPropValues(4) = "Liberal"
rgPropValues(5) = "KS"
rgPropValues(6) = "67901-3636"
rgPropValues(7) = "USA"
rgPropValues(8) = "808-822-5514"
rgPropValues(9) = "Bishop@email.com"
rgPropValues(10) = 2000

' Create the student (inserts into database)
objStudent.Create rgPropNames, rgPropValues

' Load the student (to verify that it was inserted)
objStudent.Read CStr(strStudentID), rgPropNames, rgPropValues

' Display student properties
For i=0 to UBound(rgPropNames)-1
  Response.Write(rgPropNames(i) & ": " & rgPropValues(i) & _
    "<BR>")
Next
%>
```

3. Save the page in the Beckwith\ASP folder as mystudentcreate.asp.

4. Preview the page in your browser.

When executed, the preceding script attempts to create the sample student identified by 320669203. If the script is successful, it inserts the row into the Student table of the Beckwith BusinessOffice database, as seen in Figure 17.7.

Note The initial call to Server.CreateObject("Beckwith.Student") creates an instance of the student object in memory—not a new student row in the database. The Student.Create method is responsible for inserting the new row.

Figure 17.7.

Creating a new Student *object.*

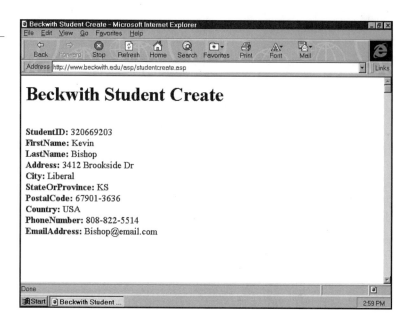

Task Creating Transactional Scripts

In Part III, "Microsoft Transaction Server Components," you created components that supported transactions. IIS 4.0 and MTS 2.0 extend this capability to your ASP scripts, allowing you to create scripts that run within a transaction. In this task you use the ASP ObjectContext intrinsic object to manage transactions within your scripts, and you write transactional event handlers to notify the user about the success or failure of a transaction.

> **Note** This feature is not supported in IIS 3.0 and MTS 1.x.

Declaring a Transactional Script

To declare a page as transactional, you must set the Transaction directive for the page. Table 17.1 lists the valid settings for the Transaction directive.

Table 17.1. *Transaction directive settings.*

Value	Description
Requires_New	Requires a new transaction to be started
Required	Starts a new transaction

Value	Description
Supported	Supports an existing transaction, but does not start a new transaction
Not_Supported	Does not start a transaction

To set the `Transaction` directive for a page, add the following line to your script:

```
<%@ Transaction = value %>
```

This directive must be the first line of the ASP page and must appear in every page that requires transactional support. You cannot declare transactional support globally for all pages within an application.

Handling Transaction Events

The event handlers listed in Table 17.2 notify the application of the outcome of the transaction. You can optionally provide implementations for these handlers to perform special operations, such as cleanup or URL redirection.

Table 17.2. *Transaction events.*

Event	Description
OnTransactionCommit	Triggered when any transaction participant calls `ObjectContext.SetComplete`
OnTransactionAbort	Triggered when any transaction participant calls `ObjectContext.SetAbort`

> **Note** Aborting a transaction does not roll back changes to any ASP session or application variables. Use the event handlers to manually reset these variables to their previous setting.

In this task you create a transactional script that uses the `Promoter` object.

1. Open the `sample.asp` file from the `Beckwith\ASP` folder.
2. Insert the following line at the top of the page:

   ```
   <%@ Transaction = Required %>
   ```

3. Insert the lines in Listing 17.5 under the `'START SCRIPT` comment:

Listing 17.5. *Managing transactions in an ASP script.*

```
<%
strProspectID = "100001780"

' Create promoter object
Set objPromoter = Server.CreateObject("Beckwith.Promote.1")

' Promote a prospect to a student
objPromoter.PromoteProspect CStr(strProspectID), True

' OnTransactionCommit() handler
Sub OnTransactionCommit()
 ' Output HTML or redirect to another page
 Response.Write "<HTML>"
 Response.Write "<BODY>"
 Response.Write "The student was successfully promoted."
 Response.Write "</BODY>"
 Response.Write "</HTML>"
end sub

' OnTransactionAbort() handler
Sub OnTransactionAbort()
 ' Output HTML or redirect to another page
 Response.Write "<HTML>"
 Response.Write "<BODY>"
 Response.Write "The student could not be promoted."
 Response.Write "</BODY>"
 Response.Write "</HTML>"
End sub
%>
```

4. Save the page in the `Beckwith\ASP` folder as `mytransaction.asp`.

5. Preview the page in your browser.

When executed, this script attempts to promote the prospect identified by `100001780`. If the script is successful, it moves the row into the `Student` table of the Beckwith `BusinessOffice` database and calls the `OnTransactionCommit` event (see Figure 17.8).

As detailed in Chapter 10, "Understanding Microsoft Transaction Server Components," the transaction fails when the second parameter to `Promote.PromoteProspect` is set to `False`. Force the transaction to fail by setting this parameter to `False` in Listing 17.5. Calling the `OnTransactionAbort` event enables the script to perform any special handling that results from an aborted transaction (see Figure 17.9).

Participating in a Transaction

In addition to receiving transaction notifications through the event handlers, a script can actively participate in a transaction by calling the `ObjectContext.SetComplete` and `ObjectContext.SetAbort` methods.

Figure 17.8.

Handling a completed transaction.

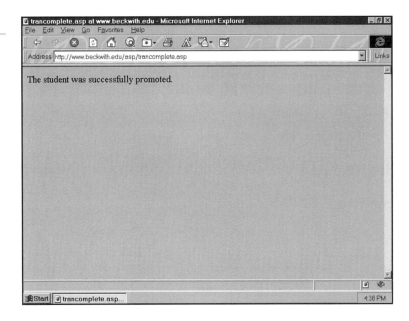

Figure 17.9.

Handling an aborted transaction.

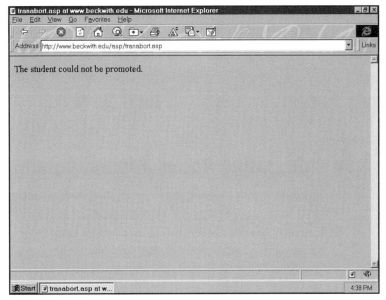

It's useful for scripts to provide input into the outcome of a transaction when they perform operations that persist or manipulate data. To complete a transaction, simply call `ObjectContext.SetComplete`, as shown in Listing 17.6

1. Open the `sample.asp` file from the `Beckwith\ASP` folder.

2. Insert the following line at the top of the page:

```
<%@ Transaction = Required %>
```

3. Insert the lines in Listing 17.6 under the 'START SCRIPT comment:

Listing 17.6. *Completing a transaction in an ASP script.*

```
<%
ObjectContext.SetComplete

' OnTransactionCommit() handler
Sub OnTransactionCommit()
 ' Output HTML or redirect to another page
 Response.Write "<HTML>"
 Response.Write "<BODY>"
 Response.Write "The student was successfully promoted."
 Response.Write "</BODY>"
 Response.Write "</HTML>"
end sub

' OnTransactionAbort() handler
Sub OnTransactionAbort()
 ' Output HTML or redirect to another page
 Response.Write "<HTML>"
 Response.Write "<BODY>"
 Response.Write "The student could not be promoted."
 Response.Write "</BODY>"
 Response.Write "</HTML>"
End sub
%>
```

4. Save the page in the Beckwith\ASP folder as mycomplete.asp.

5. Preview the page in your browser.

When executed, this script completes the transaction and triggers the OnTransactionCommit event.

Task Integrating Active Technologies

The Active platform encapsulates Microsoft's vision for the next generation of distributed computing. The Active Desktop and Active Server strategies encompass technologies used to create highly interactive Internet and intranet applications. Although still server driven, the ideal Active Desktop (client) application relies heavily on client-side scripting, ActiveX controls, and Dynamic HTML objects exposed through the Document Object Model.

On the server the Active platform uses the latest servers and ActiveX server components to host reliable, scalable, and efficient applications. These technologies include IIS, ASP, MTS, SQL Server, ActiveX Data Objects (ADO), and Remote Data Services (a service of ADO).

Tip Visit the Site Builder Active Platform Web site at

`www.microsoft.com/ activeplatform`

for the latest news on the Microsoft Active Platform.

Shifting Business Logic from Scripts to Components

This task demonstrates the key principles for integrating these technologies and creating robust applications that meet or exceed the promise of reliability, scalability, and performance.

You are probably already sold on the benefits of component-based application development. If you're not, (re)reading Chapter 4, "Getting Acquainted with COM," might change your mind. Building Internet/intranet applications is quite similar to building traditional client/server applications.

The client/server world generally accepts object-oriented analysis, design, and construction methods. Component-based architectures extend this paradigm. On the other hand, scripting languages, much like macro languages, have never been taken seriously as a means to build medium- or large-scale applications. Nevertheless, scripting (ActiveX scripting included) provides a quick and easy way to develop small applications. However, as the scope of the project increases, scripting approaches tend to break down and increase the complexity of the software architecture and the source code.

When developing ASP-based applications, review the following criteria to determine when to use components:

➤ Limitations of the scripting language

To make programming simple, or to improve security, most scripting languages include only enough capabilities to perform the most common or routine tasks. Understanding the limitations of the scripting language is the first step in determining when not to use scripting. For example, if your ASP application needs to access a Win32 API or to call a DLL function not exposed through COM, you are likely to need a component. Although you can program either case without components, the workarounds necessary to do so negate any possible benefit.

➤ Availability of third-party components

With the appearance of COM, Microsoft has created a market for third-party controls that extends far beyond the desktop. Initially, VBX controls inundated desktop applications; OCX/ActiveX controls followed. This component availability now extends to the server with ActiveX server components. Before scripting or building a business rule, particularly one that requires complex calculations or data access, check the component catalogs— your work may be easier than you expect.

➤ Ease of component creation

To become proficient in ASP application development, you must be a savvy Visual Basic (or JScript) programmer. Because of the intentional overlap between the Visual Basic and VBScript languages, VBScript developers can easily create components using Visual Basic. Many organizations will call on their Visual Basic developers to work on ASP projects, making the creation of these components that much easier.

➤ Encapsulation of your business logic

Scripts can include business logic encapsulated as subroutines for other scripts to use. However, scripts cannot implement truly object-oriented designs that simplify the interface to a business object by hiding unnecessary details from its clients.

➤ Abstraction of your business data

One of the greatest benefits of logical multitier architectures is the separation of the presentation, business, and data services of an application. Isolating the data access functions (the interface with data services) in the business services layer makes the system easier to maintain. In this case changes to the database affect only business services components, not the underlying client application. Reusing components whenever possible helps to minimize the total effect of a database change. However, when binding data access calls directly to the presentation services layer (in this case the ASP and HTML source code), changes to the database can be difficult to incorporate into the application.

For example, in Chapter 16 you learned how to create database-driven Web applications using Visual InterDev. Although the Data Access Wizard generated most of the source code for this application, the resulting files contained close to 2,000 lines of code. A simple, scaled-back version that only allows updates to the data was still more than 1,400 lines of code. The ASP/MTS version of this application, included as part of the Beckwith Online application, contains fewer than 150 lines. Although this count excludes the source for the components themselves, it clearly illustrates the benefits of component-based design. In the Beckwith Online sample, changing the database does not affect the ASP client.

➤ Maintainability of the application

When the line count soars to the thousands for simply manipulating a single table, you quickly learn about the hardships of wizard-generated source code. Although the Visual InterDev wizards can help you quickly prototype a concept, or build a small project, relying on them for critical tasks can produce unfavorable results.

➤ Distributing the processing for maximum performance

Because components can be distributed among many servers, you can improve performance by adding servers. MTS manages components with a single administrative tool (Transaction Server Explorer) even when multiple machines host the components.

➤ Improved reliability with better testing tools

Using mature tools to create components simplifies the debugging and testing of applications. Although ASP and Visual InterDev vastly improve previous technologies, these new tools offer very limited debugging support.

Using Visual Basic Scripts to Unite Components

An application is more than a collection of components. To use these components in your ASP application in any beneficial way, you must use ActiveX scripting (through VBScript or any other supported ActiveX scripting language). In fact, every ASP application needs at least one line of scripting code—components can't do it alone.

ActiveX scripting and COM components form partnerships that enable you to build reliable, robust, and scalable applications. In the ideal ASP application, components execute the business rules of the system and access databases, and scripts generate HTML based on results obtained from these components.

Workshop Wrap-Up

The tasks you completed in this chapter form the foundation of the Beckwith Online application. As Internet/intranet applications evolve, the techniques you examined in this chapter will become the norm for application development. These tasks demonstrate that you do not put MTS-specific code into a client application; instead, you simply create and invoke the services of components. As mentioned in earlier chapters, the components and MTS take care of the data access and transactional details.

Next Steps

➤ Now that you have examined the principles of integrating MTS with Active Server Pages, you're ready to explore the Beckwith Online sample application. Go on to Chapter 18, "Working with the Beckwith Online Sample Application."

➤ If you had difficulty getting the sample client application to work properly on you machine, read Chapter 22, "Troubleshooting the Complete Solution," for help.

CHAPTER 18

Working with the Beckwith Online Sample Application

Tasks in This Chapter

➤ *Configuring the Beckwith Online Application*

➤ *Understanding the Access Pages*

➤ *Building the Last Semester Grades Viewer*

➤ *Using the Beckwith Promoter Component*

➤ *Using the Update Employee Information Page*

The Beckwith Online sample application enables the university's students, faculty, and staff to gain access to the Beckwith database. Because the Beckwith database consists of a set of disconnected data stores (for example, multiple databases, possibly running on different servers), Beckwith Online uses the sample Microsoft Transaction Server (MTS) components you created in Part III, "Microsoft Transaction Server Components," to integrate the data sources into what appears as a single data store.

In this chapter you explore the Beckwith Online sample application and perform the tasks necessary to complete its functionality. The application supports two levels of access:

➤ Student

➤ Faculty and staff

A system user's role (student or staff) determines which tasks he or she can perform. The major functions of the system enable

➤ Students to check their grades from the previous semester

➤ Staff members to admit prospects into the university; that is, convert a prospect into a student

➤ Staff members to convert a student who graduates into an alumnus

➤ Employees of the university (faculty and staff) to update their personal information

The following tasks walk you through most of these features.

Preparation Understanding the Beckwith Online Sample Application

The Beckwith Online application uses many elements of the Microsoft Active Platform. On the server the application uses Internet Information Server (IIS), Active Server Pages (ASP), MTS, and SQL Server. However, because a primary goal of the application is to support both Microsoft and Netscape Web browsers, the application supports few advanced Active Desktop features. It also avoids the use of client-side VBScript, ActiveX controls, and Internet Explorer (or Navigator) specific tags.

Beckwith Online uses a subset of the components installed in the Beckwith package (see Figure 18.1). Using the techniques described in Chapter 17, "Creating Interactive Web Applications Using Microsoft Transaction Server and Active Server Pages," ASP scripts create these components as they are needed, and the results of their method calls are formatted as HTML. Generating simple HTML enables the application to support both major Web browsers.

Figure 18.1.

The Beckwith Online architecture.

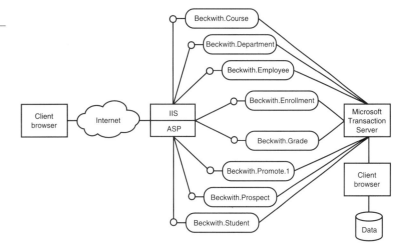

The home page of the application, shown in Figure 18.2, welcomes users to the system and enables them to log in to the appropriate area: student or staff.

Figure 18.2.

The Beckwith Online home page.

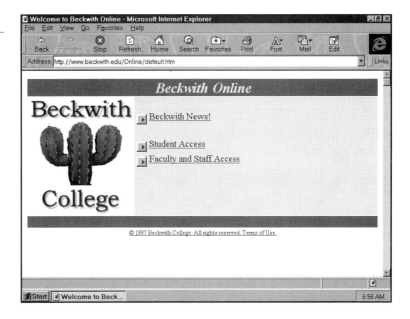

Note   To validate the correct installation of all components, refer to the "Configuring and Validating Your System" task in Chapter 17.

Task Configuring the Beckwith Online Application

This task works through the basics of installing and configuring the Beckwith Online application. For additional details on installing this sample, refer to Appendix C, "Beckwith Component Reference." The remaining tasks in this chapter require you to have installed the Beckwith Online sample application.

To begin exploring Beckwith Online, follow these steps to copy Active Server Pages (ASP) to your local server:

1. Copy the folder `Beckwith\Online` and its subfolder `images` from the book's companion CD-ROM to your local hard drive.

2. Verify that the `/Online` virtual directory is configured under IIS (see Figure 18.3). This directory should have both Read and Execute permissions.

Figure 18.3.

Configuring the Online Virtual Directory.

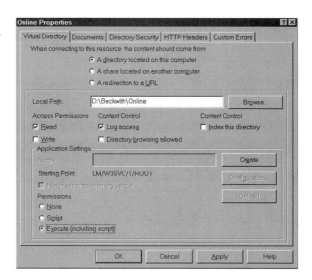

3. Check the default filename.

   The application expects `Default.htm` to be configured as the default file. If another filename is selected as the default (for example, `index.html`), change the name of the Beckwith Online `default.htm` file as required.

4. Start the Beckwith Online application by opening your browser and typing *COMPUTERNAME*/`Online` as the URL (refer to Figure 18.2).

Task Understanding the Access Pages

The Beckwith Online application supports two types of users: students and staff (faculty and staff). The system requires users to log in to determine their identify and classification. Both access pages are similar, so this section fully describes only the student access page.

The login and access pages were designed to complement the BCDS Visual Basic sample application. Related user interface objects, such as the student login process, behave similarly.

Caution The application might display the following error when the `Session` object no longer exists and you try to access a page that requires it:

The user account for the current session is no longer available.

Beckwith Online sets the `Response.Expires` property to 0 for pages that shouldn't be cached. You can also include the following tag inside the `<HEAD>` block of pages you don't want cached:

```
<meta http-equiv="pragma" content="no-cache">
```

These cache-prevention techniques are only recommendations from the application to a browser. Ultimately, the best solution is to refresh the page if the application seems to be behaving strangely.

Note The login pages are already filled with a default user identifier and PIN. Clicking the Clear button refreshes (but doesn't actually clear) the form's values.

The Beckwith Online Student Access Page

You can display the student access page by selecting the Student Access hyperlink from the main page. This page has two modes, depending on whether a user has logged in:

➤ Student Access login page (Figure 18.4)

➤ Student Access menu page (Figure 18.5)

The student login page collects a student's Social Security number and a unique password (PIN) to gain access to the system. The Student ID edit text field is prepopulated with a valid Student identifier. You can type in your own Student ID, provided it is a valid student found in the `Student` table of the `BusinessOffice` database. To log in to the system as the default student, click Login to accept the default student ID and PIN. After a brief pause the Student Access Menu appears (see Figure 18.5).

Figure 18.4.

Student Access login page.

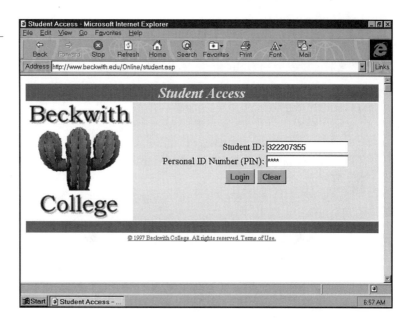

Figure 18.5.

Student Access menu page.

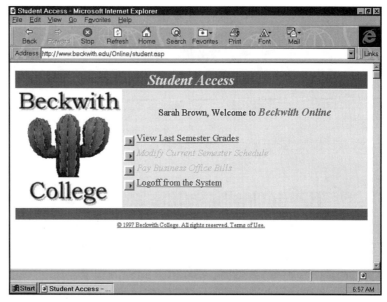

Just as in the Visual Basic sample application, clicking Login is important because it invokes code that attempts to instantiate a Beckwith.Student object.

> **Note** When entering a Student ID other than the default, you may receive the following message: Please specify a valid student ID and PIN! (Figure 18.6). This error usually indicates that the specified student does not exist in the `student` table of the BusinessOffice database. Perform a query on this table to obtain a valid Student ID.

Figure 18.6.

Student Access login page.

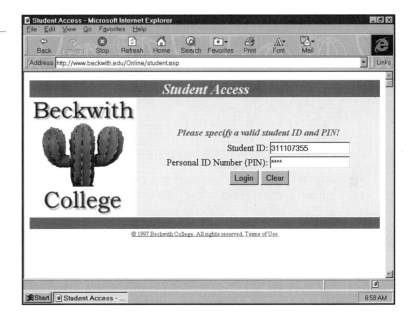

Data entry, form validation, object creation, and menu selections are all functions of the same ASP page. After you submit your Student ID and PIN, ASP executes the script in Listing 18.1.

Listing 18.1. *The implementation of* `student.asp`.

```
<%'
' Obtain student ID and PIN from request object
'
strStudentID = Request.Form("ID")
strPIN       = Request.Form("PIN")
blnInvalid   = False


' Verify the required data
'
If Len(strStudentID)>1 and Len(strPIN)>1 Then

    ' Declare property bag
```

continues

Listing 18.1. *continued*

```
Dim rgPropNames
Dim rgPropValues

'See if student is in database by trying to read its information
Set obj1 = Server.CreateObject("Beckwith.Student")
obj1.Read CStr(strStudentID), rgPropNames, rgPropValues

If rgPropValues(0) <> strStudentID Then
    blnInvalid = True
Else
    'store in global variable
    Session("StudentID") = strStudentID
    Session("StudentName") = rgPropValues(1) & " " & rgPropValues(2)
End If

End If
%>
```

If data was submitted by form, the script attempts to log in the specified student.

The call to `Server.CreateObject` creates a student object, and it is populated with the parameters specified in the call to the `Student.Read` method.

```
Set obj1 = Server.CreateObject("Beckwith.Student")
    obj1.Read CStr(strStudentID), rgPropNames, rgPropValues
```

If the student exists, the application saves the student identifier and the full name in the `Session` object. Saving the student identifier enables the ASP application to manage the session of the currently logged in user. By referencing this `Session` variable later, the application can determine the identity of the student.

```
Session("StudentID") = strStudentID
    Session("StudentName") = rgPropValues(1) & " " & rgPropValues(2)
```

If the student provides a valid identifier and PIN, the Student Access menu appears. This menu is simply a set of hyperlinks that enable students either to view their grades from the previous semester or to log off.

The Beckwith Online Staff Access Page

Like the Student Access page, the Faculty and Staff Access page has two modes, depending on whether a user has logged in:

> ➤ Faculty and Staff Access login page (Figure 18.7)
> ➤ Faculty and Staff Access menu page (Figure 18.8)

Figure 18.7.

Faculty and Staff Access login page.

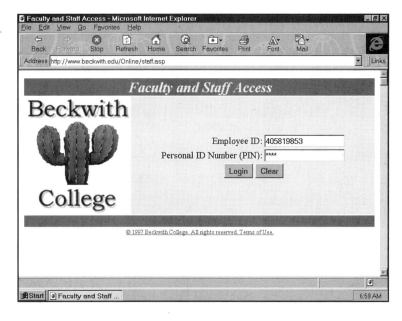

Figure 18.8.

Faculty and Staff Access menu page.

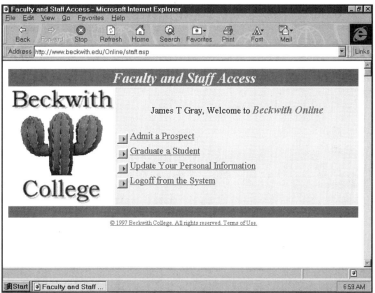

Unlike the Student Access menu, all the hyperlinks in the Faculty and Staff menu page are available to the university's staff.

Performing a System Logoff

When a student or staff member finishes using Beckwith Online, he or she should select the Logoff from the System hyperlink from the menu. Logging off prevents other users from accessing information or functions for which they might not have permissions.

The `logoff.asp` page (Figure 18.9) terminates the current session by calling the `Session.Abandon` method. This method destroys all variables contained in the `Session` object and releases their resources.

Figure 18.9.

Beckwith Online Logoff page.

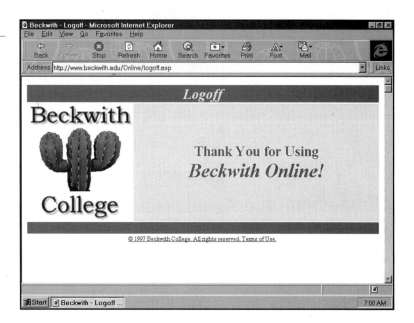

Task Building the Last Semester Grades Viewer

The `Beckwith.Grade` component obtains enrollment and grade information for a particular student. You can use this information to print end-of-semester grade reports to distribute to students, update financial aid records, and interactively inform students of their good (or poor) grades.

In this task you employ the `Beckwith.Grade` component to obtain grade information for a user and display the results. This underlying source code also creates the Beckwith Online Grade Viewer.

Obtaining the Grade Data with QueryByStudent

The QueryByStudent method of the Beckwith.Grade component uses a specified student identifier to retrieve a student's current enrollment information and grades. To create this sample script:

1. Open the sample.asp file from the Beckwith\ASP folder.

2. Insert the lines in Listing 18.2 under the 'START SCRIPT comment:

Listing 18.2. *Using QueryByStudent to obtain the grade data for a student.*

```
<%
' Create student object
Set objStudent = Server.CreateObject("Beckwith.Student")

' Set a student number
strStudentID = "320669203"

' Get student data
objStudent.Read CStr(strStudentID), rgPropNames, rgPropValues

Response.Write("<h1>Last Semester Grades</h1>")
Response.Write("<h2>" & rgPropValues(1) & " " & _
    rgPropValues(2) & "</h2>")

' declare variant arrays to receive grade information
Dim rgCourseIDs
Dim rgCourseNames
Dim rgGrades

'query for all grade records
set objGrade = Server.CreateObject("Beckwith.Grade")
objGrade.QueryByStudent CStr(strStudentID), rgCourseIDs,
    _
    rgCourseNames, rgGrades
```

If you create a student object and can call the Read method to load its attributes then you can display the student name in the HTML page.

The Beckwith.Grade component performs the work of retrieving and populating the property bags with enrollment and grade information. QueryByStudent populates the course IDs, course names, and grades into the appropriate property bag.

```
objGrade.QueryByStudent CStr(strStudentID), rgCourseIDs, rgCourseNames, rgGrades
```

Displaying the Query Results

After you execute QueryByStudent and populate the variant arrays, you can iterate through each one to display the results. To display the results from the call to QueryByStudent:

1. Complete the script with Listing 18.3.

Listing 18.3. *Displaying the query results.*

```
index = UBound(rgCourseIDs)

If index>0 Then
   For i = 0 To index
      Response.Write("<hr>" & rgCourseIDs(i) & " ")
      Response.Write(rgCourseNames(i) & " ")
      Response.Write(rgGrades(i))
   Next
Else
   Response.Write("You were not enrolled in any courses last semester.")
End If
%>
```

2. Save the page in the `Beckwith\ASP` folder as `mygradeview.asp`.

3. Preview the page in your browser.

The script displays the enrollment and grade information for the student whose identifier is `320669203`, as seen in Figure 18.10.

Figure 18.10.

Grade information screen.

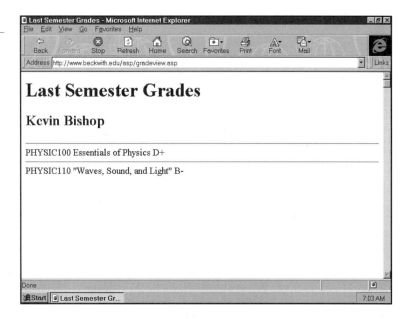

Using the Beckwith Online Grade Viewer

The Beckwith Online application extends the grade viewer to include an improved user interface (using an HTML table) and automatic retrieval of grades, based on the currently logged-in student's user ID (stored in the `Session` object).

You access this page (Figure 18.11) by choosing View Last Semester Grades from the Student Access menu.

Figure 18.11.

Beckwith Online—displaying last semester grades.

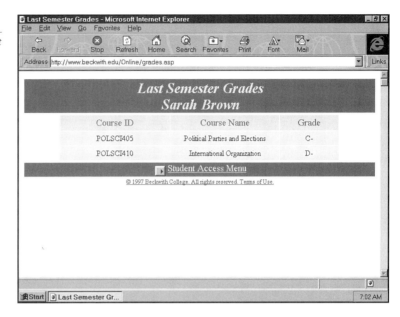

Task Using the Beckwith Promoter Component

In Chapter 12, "Implementing Components in Visual C++ Using the Active Template Library," you examined or built the Promote component. The role of the Promote object is to move records from one database to another. In this task you use this component to move a prospect record from the Admissions database to the BusinessOffice database after a prospect becomes a student. When a student graduates, the Promote component moves a student record from the BusinessOffice database to the AlumniRelations database.

The Promote component accomplishes these tasks by exposing two methods: PromoteProspect() and PromoteStudent().

Admitting a Prospect into the University

The Prospect table in the Admissions database contains names of high school students that have expressed interest in attending Beckwith College. When a prospect is admitted into the university (thus becoming a student), you must move (promote) this record to the Student table of the BusinessOffice database. The admit.asp page on the Beckwith Online application (shown in Figure 18.12) implements the user interface and scripts to promote a prospect.

Figure 18.12.

Beckwith Online—admitting a prospect.

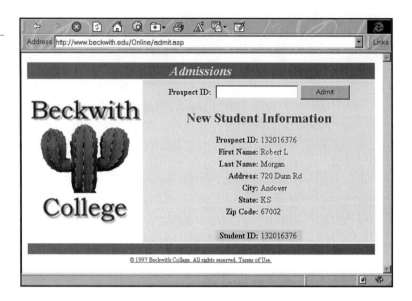

To create a simple ASP page that uses the `Promote` component to convert a prospect into a student:

1. Start the SQL Server ISQL/w utility to identify a valid prospect.

2. Select the Admissions database in the DB combo box.

3. Query the `Prospect` table for all prospects whose names begin with the letters *dema*. In the Query window, enter the following SQL:

   ```
   SELECT * FROM prospect WHERE lastname LIKE 'dema%'
   ```

4. Click Execute.

5. Write down a prospect identifier that appears in the Results window (see Figure 18.13). For this example you can use `110997509`.

> **Note** If you've performed this task before, the items in the output window may vary because some prospects may have already been promoted.

6. Close the ISQL/w application.

7. Open the `sample.asp` file from the `Beckwith\ASP` folder.

8. Add the code in Listing 18.4 under the `'START SCRIPT` comment:

Listing 18.4. *Promoting a prospect into a student.*

```
<%
strProspectID = "110997509"
Response.Write("Promoting Prospect ID: " & strProspectID)
Set objPromoter = Server.CreateObject("Beckwith.Promote.1")
objPromoter.PromoteProspect CStr(strProspectID), False
%>
```

Figure 18.13.

Using ISQL/w to verify that a prospect exists.

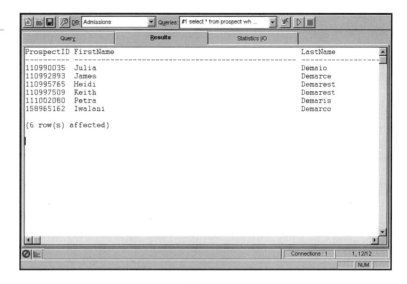

8. Save the page in the `Beckwith\ASP` folder as `mypromote.asp`.

9. Preview the page in your browser.

The `PromoteProspect` method performs all the work necessary to move the row from one database to another (see Figure 18.14). This method takes two parameters; the first is the identifier of the prospect to promote, and the second is the Boolean flag `bForceFail`. When set to `True`, the `bForceFail` parameter enables you to simulate a failed transaction. Because you do not want to force the transaction to fail, `False` is the second parameter.

Figure 18.14.

Promoting a prospect to a student.

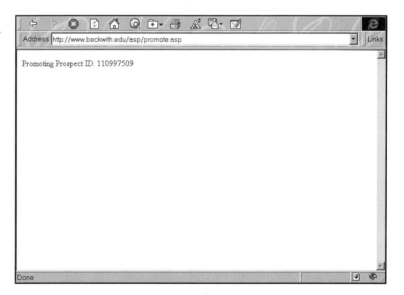

To verify that the prospect was indeed admitted into the university, and thus the associated row moved from one database to another, repeat steps 1 through 6. The prospect should no longer appear in the Results list. To validate that the application inserted the row into the Student table of the BusinessOffice database:

1. Start the SQL Server ISQL/w utility to identify a valid prospect.

2. Select the BusinessOffice database in the DB combo box.

3. Query the Student table for the promoted prospect. Enter the following SQL:

   ```
   SELECT * FROM student WHERE studentid='110997509'
   ```

4. Click Execute.

   The row appears in the Results window (see Figure 18.15).

Figure 18.15.

Using ISQL/w to verify the promotion.

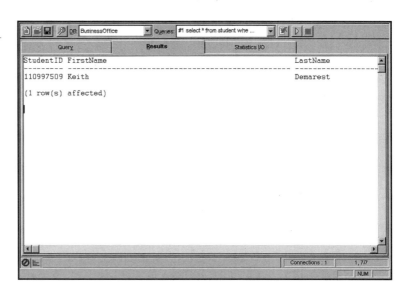

5. Close the ISQL/w application.

Promoting a Student to an Alumnus

The Student table in the BusinessOffice database contains names of students currently attending Beckwith College. When a student graduates from the university, you must move (promote) his or her record to the Alumnus table of the AlumniRelations database. The graduate.asp page on the Beckwith Online application (shown in Figure 18.16) implements the user interface and scripts to promote a prospect.

This page behaves like the admit.asp page except that it calls the PromoteStudent method, rather than the PromoteProspect method, of the Promote object.

Figure 18.16.

Promoting a student to an alumnus.

Task Using the Update Employee Information Page

University faculty and staff members can view or update their personal information by using the Update Personal Information page, shown in Figure 18.17. You access this page from the Faculty and Staff Access menu.

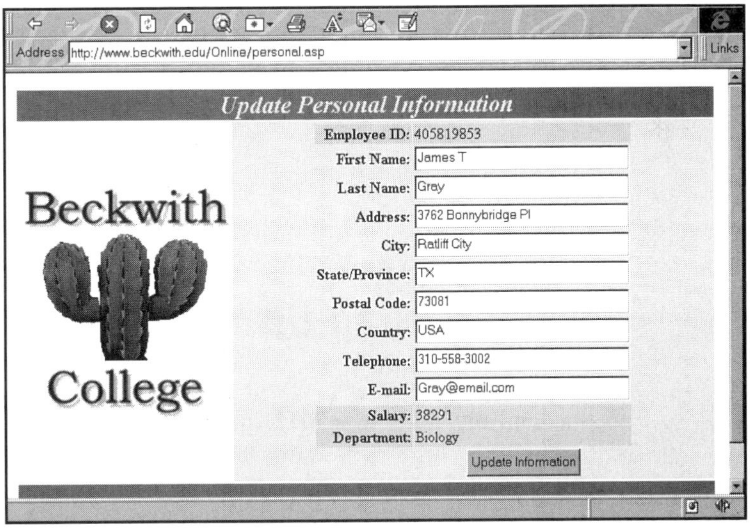

Figure 18.17.

Beckwith Online—Update Personal Information page.

The implementation for this page uses the employee identifier kept in the `Session` object to retrieve, display, and update the employee information. The code in Listing 18.5 implements the primary script.

Listing 18.5. *Implementation for* `personal.asp`.

```
<%'
' Obtain employeeID
'
strEmployeeID = Session("EmployeeID")

' Declare property bags
Dim rgPropNames
Dim rgPropValues
Dim rgDeptNames
Dim rgDeptValues

' Retrieve employee object
Set objEmployee = Server.CreateObject("Beckwith.Employee")
objEmployee.Read CStr(strEmployeeID), rgPropNames, rgPropValues

' Retrieve department object
Set objDept = Server.CreateObject("Beckwith.Department")
objDept.Read CStr(rgPropValues(11)), rgDeptNames, rgDeptValues

If Request.Form("submit") <> "" Then

    ' Update information
    rgPropValues(1) = Request.Form("firstname")
    rgPropValues(2) = Request.Form("lastname")
    rgPropValues(3) = Request.Form("address")
    rgPropValues(4) = Request.Form("city")
    rgPropValues(5) = Request.Form("state")
    rgPropValues(6) = Request.Form("zip")
    rgPropValues(7) = Request.Form("country")
    rgPropValues(8) = Request.Form("phone")
    rgPropValues(9) = Request.Form("email")

    objEmployee.Update CStr(EmployeeID), rgPropNames, rgPropValues

End If
```

Workshop Wrap-Up

In this chapter you created portions of the Beckwith Online application. You learned how to use ASP to integrate MTS components into your Internet/intranet applications. Although these samples used only a subset of the `Beckwith` components, the application touches on each major function the components expose.

Next Steps

➤ In Part VI, "Advanced Microsoft Transaction Server Administration," you learn how to manage multiple MTS servers, monitor and tune components, and troubleshoot your MTS applications. Refer to Chapter 21, "Monitoring and Tuning Components," for details on monitoring and optimizing the components.

➤ If you had difficulty getting the Beckwith Online application to work properly on you machine, refer to Chapter 22, "Troubleshooting the Complete Solution," for help.

PART VI

Advanced Microsoft Transaction Server Administration

CHAPTER 19

Performing Server Administration and Configuration

In addition to configuring and administering Microsoft Transaction Server (MTS), you must work with several other tools to complete the job of deploying a large-scale client/server system. This chapter focuses on the pertinent Windows NT tools and shows you how to use them in concert with Transaction Server Explorer.

This chapter also uncovers some handy MTS command-line utilities that you can use to administer your MTS configuration without having to start Transaction Server Explorer.

Preparation Familiarizing Yourself with the Windows NT Tools

This chapter focuses on the following Windows NT tools that complete the "big picture" of client/server system administration:

➤ Event Viewer—Browses events posted by the Windows NT system and critical system services like DTC.

➤ Performance Monitor—Gives vital, real-time statistics about various aspects of the system.

➤ Windows NT Diagnostics—Displays information about the current Windows NT installation.

MTS also provides the following useful command-line utilities that are explored later in the chapter:

➤ Mtxstop.exe—Shuts down all server processes on the current machine.

➤ Mtxrereg.exe—Refreshes all components registered on the current machine.

> **Tip** If you are already familiar with these Windows NT and MTS tools, skip to Chapter 20, "Managing Multiple Servers," to learn how to use MTS on more than one server.

Task Exploring the Event Viewer

The Event Viewer is a Windows NT application that lists all the system events that occur during the execution of the operating system. The Event Viewer also lists application-level events that occur. In fact, components and other applications that you construct can write custom events to the Event Viewer.

Because MTS components do not contain any user interface, you must write your components to take advantage of writing to the Event viewer. This approach helps you track down problems during the deployment and execution of your system.

Follow these steps to explore the main features of the Event Viewer:

1. Start the Event Viewer by choosing Start | **P**rograms | Administrative Tools | Event Viewer from the Windows taskbar (see Figure 19.1). If the Event Viewer menu option is missing, look for the Event Viewer application, Eventvwr.exe, on the hard drive on which Windows NT is installed. Eventvwr.exe is installed into your Windows NT's System32 folder by default.

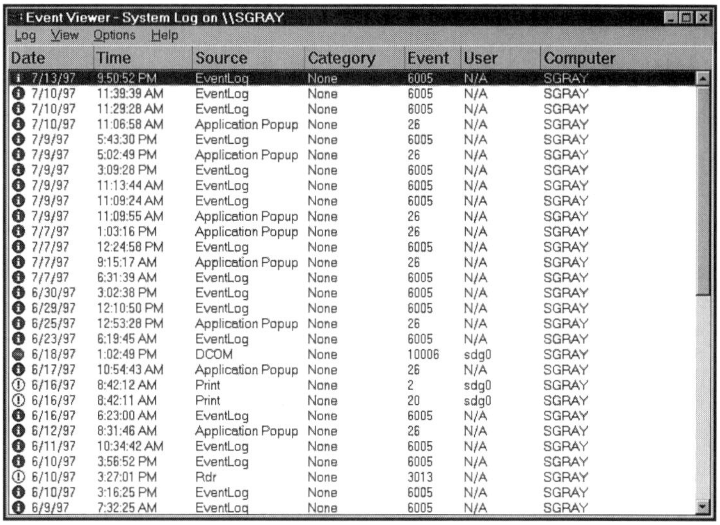

Figure 19.1.

The Windows NT Event Viewer.

2. Examine the events in the Event Viewer. The Event Viewer displays its events in a list control with multiple columns.

   ➤ Date—The date the event was posted.

   ➤ Time—The time the event was posted.

   ➤ Source—The source that posted the event. The source can be an application or other system code like services and device drivers.

   ➤ Category—A category for the event. Categories are defined by each source.

   ➤ Event—A unique event number. Event numbers are defined by the source.

   ➤ User—The identity of the current user when the event occurred.

   ➤ Computer—The name of the computer on which the event occurred.

   The Event Viewer shows three types of events:

   ➤ System—Windows NT events

   ➤ Security—Security-related events

   ➤ Application—Events posted by applications

> **Tip** The Event viewer displays one type of event at a time. Use the **L**og | S**y**stem, **L**og | Se**c**urity, and **L**og | **A**pplication menu options to switch among the three types of events.

3. Double-click an event in the list control to display the Event Detail dialog (see Figure 19.2). This log provides detailed information about an event in chronological order, either oldest to newest, or the other way around.

> **Tip** To switch the order in which the system displays the events, choose **V**iew | **N**ewest First and **V**iew | **O**ldest First from the main menu.

Figure 19.2.

The Event Detail dialog.

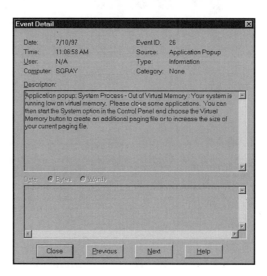

By default, the Event log displays all events for each type. However, if the log has many events, you might not be able to find exactly the ones you are looking for. In this case you can filter the events. For example, you can filter the System events for only those events whose source is EventLog.

4. Choose **V**iew | Fi**l**ter Event dialog from the main menu to display the Filter dialog (see Figure 19.3).

5. Select the Eventlog item in the Source combo box to filter only EventLog events. Click OK to commit the filter.

You can also point the Event Log to read the events of a remote computer.

6. Choose **L**og | **S**elect Computer from the main menu to open the Select Computer dialog, which displays all available computers (see Figure 19.4).

7. Select the remote computer you desire and then click OK.

Figure 19.3.

The Filter dialog.

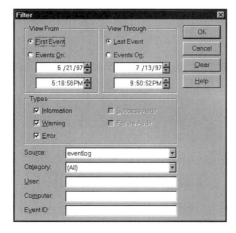

Figure 19.4.

The Select Computer dialog.

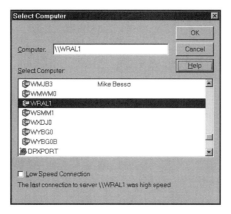

Tip Use the Low Speed Connection check box when the computer you are selecting is not directly connected to the LAN on which you are running, but instead is connected via a modem or other slow communications mechanism. This check box tells the Event Viewer to optimize the data it passes from the remote computer to your computer.

You can modify several additional Event Viewer settings with the Event Log Settings dialog (see Figure 19.5). For example, from the Event Log Settings dialog you can specify the maximum size for the log and how the Event Viewer should handle the overwriting of old events.

8. Choose **L**og | Log Se**t**tings from the main menu to open the Event Log Settings dialog.

Figure 19.5.

The Event Log Settings dialog.

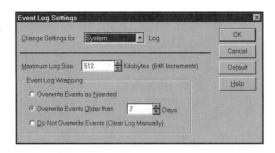

Task Using the Performance Monitor

The Performance Monitor enables you to track hundreds of indicators at regular intervals. This information enables you to analyze the performance of your running server. Although the Performance Monitor does not have MTS-specific indicators, you can track the Microsoft SQL Server indicators to make sure your database is functioning correctly.

Follow these steps to use the Windows NT Performance Monitor:

1. Choose Start | **P**rograms | Administrative Tools | Performance Monitor from the Windows taskbar to open the Performance Monitor main window (see Figure 19.6). The actual Performance Monitor executable is `Perfmon.exe`.

Figure 19.6.

The Performance Monitor.

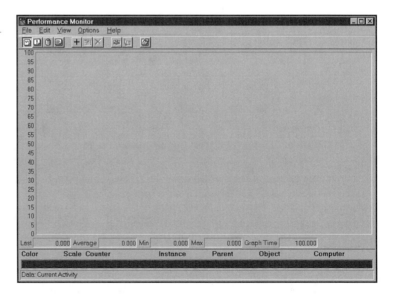

When the Performance Monitor starts, it performs no monitoring. You must add the counters you wish to monitor to the Performance Monitor.

2. Choose **E**dit | **A**dd To Chart from the main menu to display the Add to Chart dialog (see Figure 19.7).

Figure 19.7.

The Add to Chart dialog.

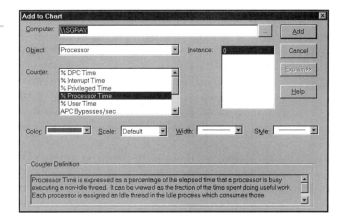

The hundreds of counters that the Performance Monitor can track are sorted based on objects. You can select which object to monitor from the Object combo box. Some examples of important objects are

➤ Processor

➤ Thread

➤ Memory

➤ Server

➤ System

When you select an object from the Object combo box, the Performance Monitor displays all available counters for that object in the Counter list box.

> **Tip** To see a detailed description of the counter currently highlighted in the Counter list box, click Explain on the Add to Chart dialog to open the **Counter Definition** edit box.

3. Select the `% Processor Time` counter of the `Processor` object to monitor the server processor's usage. Click Add to begin monitoring this counter. Click Done to return to the Performance Monitor's main window.

> **Tip** By default, the system monitors the counter on the computer from which you are running the Performance Monitor. However, you can monitor a remote computer by changing the value in the Computer edit box to the name of the appropriate computer.

When you return to the main window, notice that the Performance Monitor has begun to record and display the activity of the computer (see Figure 19.8). This chart is updated once per second and reflects the percentage of time that the CPU was not idle.

Figure 19.8.

The Performance Monitoring main window after you add a counter.

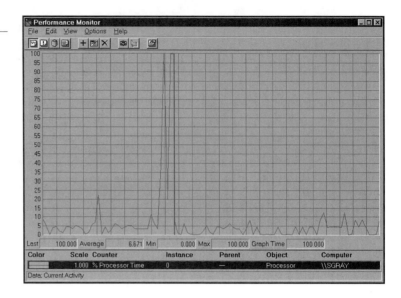

You can change the frequency of graph updates, as well as other chart properties.

4. Choose **O**ptions | **C**hart from the main menu to display the Chart Option dialog (see Figure 19.9).

Figure 19.9.

The Chart Options dialog.

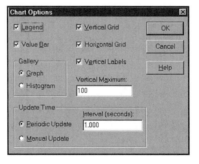

In the Chart Options dialog, you can customize the display of the chart, including the display of a legend, value bar, and vertical and horizontal grid lines. You can change the refresh rate of the chart by entering a new value in the Interval edit box.

5. Change the update interval to half a second by entering 0.5 in the Interval edit box. Click OK to commit your change and return to the Performance Monitor's main window.

You can monitor more than one counter at a time.

6. Choose **E**dit | **A**dd To Chart from the main menu to add a second counter.

This time, add the Available Bytes counter of the Memory object to the graph.

7. Click Add to add the counter and then click Done to return to the main window.

   The Performance Monitor tracks the second counter on the same graph but in a different color. The scale of the graph is adjusted to accommodate both counters.

8. Open a large application like Visual Studio 97 or any other application that requires a large amount of memory. Notice that as the application loads, the Available Bytes counter goes down.

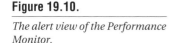 Other applications that run at the same time as the Performance Monitor may cover up the main Performance Monitor window, preventing you from seeing its graphs. To avoid this situation, choose **O**ptions I Always On To**p** from the main menu to force the Performance Monitor to always float above other windows.

   The Performance Monitor has an important feature known as Alerts. You can use Alerts to trigger the execution of custom applications when a counter reaches a given state. You can also use Alerts to send a network message to a specific computer when the Alert is triggered.

9. Choose **V**iew I **A**lert from the main menu to change the display of the Performance Monitor from the chart view to the alert view (see Figure 19.10).

Figure 19.10.

The alert view of the Performance Monitor.

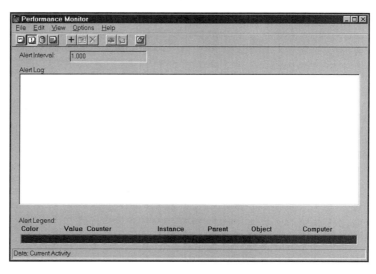

10. Choose **E**dit I **A**dd To Alert from the main menu to open the Add to Alert dialog (see Figure 19.11) and add a new alert.

    The Add to Alert dialog is very similar to the Add to Chart dialog except that the Alert If and Run Program on Alert fields have been added to the former. Use these fields to have the Performance Monitor open the Windows Notepad application if the % Processor Time field goes above 90.

Figure 19.11.

The Add to Alert dialog.

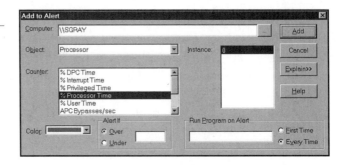

11. Type **90** in the Alert If edit box and type **Notepad.exe** in the Run Program on Alert edit box. Click the First Time radio button so that you don't get multiple instances of the Notepad.

12. Click Add and click Done to commit the Alert.

13. Perform a processor-intensive operation such as opening an application or switching to an already running application. This operation should force the **%** **Processor Time** counter above **90** and cause the Alert to be fired. The Performance Monitor updates its main window to display the alerts (see Figure 19.12) and opens an instance of Notepad.

Figure 19.12.

The alert view of the Performance Monitor after alerts have fired.

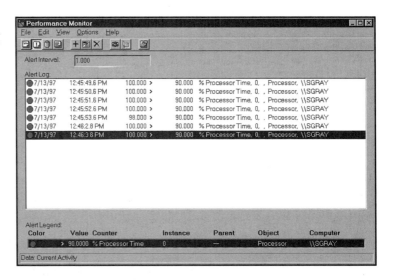

Task Using Windows NT Diagnostics

Another useful Windows NT utility to use when deploying client/server applications is Windows NT Diagnostics. This tool is useful for displaying many different types of information about a server's configuration, including:

➤ Version information

➤ CPU information

➤ Display adapter and driver information

➤ Drive information, including network and CD-ROM drives

➤ Memory information

➤ Services and their state

➤ Network information such as current user and domain

➤ Environment variable settings

➤ Resource information such as interrupts, I/O ports, DMA channels, memory, and device information

Follow these steps to use the Windows NT Diagnostics tool:

1. Choose Start | **P**rograms | Administrative Tools | Windows NT Diagnostics from the Windows taskbar to open the Windows NT Diagnostics main window (see Figure 19.13). The Windows NT Diagnostics executable is `winmsd.exe`.

Figure 19.13.

The Windows NT Diagnostics main window displaying the Version property page.

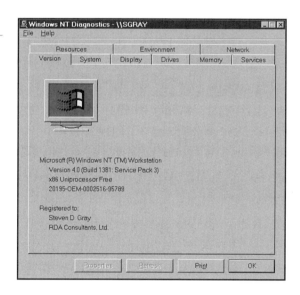

A property page on the main window represents each major diagnostic area.

2. Click the desired tab to view a property page.

Of primary importance for MTS-related setup are the Version, Memory, Services, and Network property pages.

3. Click the Version tab to display the Version property page (refer to Figure 19.13). This page shows which version of Windows NT you are running, including the latest service pack you have installed. Because MTS is so closely linked to the

operating system, you should run the latest service pack to reduce the number of problems your system might encounter.

4. Click the Memory tab to display the Memory property page (see Figure 19.14). You should run Windows NT Diagnostics during peak execution times of your client/server system to ensure that your server has enough memory to satisfy all requests.

Figure 19.14.

The Windows NT Diagnostics main window displaying the Memory property page.

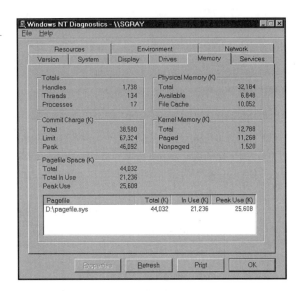

Tip To print a report of the Memory statistics displayed, or any of the other property pages, click the Print button at the bottom of the Windows NT Diagnostics main window.

5. Click the Services tab to display the Services property page (see Figure 19.15). The Services property page displays all the services defined for the system and whether each service is running or not. This page tells you whether services such as MSDTC and MSSQLServer are running.

   If either MSDTC or MSSQLServer are not running, check the Event log to see whether any entry suggests a reason that the services aren't running. To restart these services, use the system's Control Panel Services applet. See Chapter 22, "Troubleshooting the Complete Solution," for suggestions on resolving problems starting these services.

6. Click the Network tab to display the Network property page (see Figure 19.16). The Network property page displays useful network information including

   ➤ Domain

   ➤ Logged in users

➤ Access levels

➤ Transport information

➤ Various network settings

➤ Network statistics

To access transport, settings, and statistics information, click the Transports, Settings, and Statistics button located near the bottom of the property page.

Figure 19.15.

The Windows NT Diagnostics main window displaying the Services property page.

Figure 19.16.

The Windows NT Diagnostics main window displaying the Network property page.

Task Using Microsoft Transaction Server Command-Line Utilities

Two useful command-line utilities ship with MTS:

➤ `Mtxstop.exe` shuts down all server processes on the current machine.

➤ `Mtxrereg.exe` refreshes all components registered on the current machine.

`Mtxstop.exe` is equivalent to invoking Transaction Server Explorer's Action | **S**hutdown Server Processes from the Microsoft Management Console toolbar. The `Mtxrereg.exe` utility is the equivalent of invoking Transaction Server Explorer's Action | **R**efresh All Components.

These tools reside in the root MTS installation folder, usually `Mtx`.

Neither utility takes any command-line parameters. When you invoke `Mtxstop.exe`, it emits the following message to the console's output:

```
Mtxstop: Stopping all application server processes...
```

When you invoke `Mtxrereg.exe`, it emits the following to the console:

```
Mtxrereg: Refreshing all locally registered Mtx components...
          Done: All Mtx components were refreshed.
```

These utilities are useful additions to your component development environment. You can add them to your development environment as part of your component's build process to ensure that MTS always has refreshed references to your latest component builds.

Workshop Wrap-Up

This chapter shows you how to use three important Windows NT tools that aid in the administration of MTS client/server applications: the Event Viewer, the Performance Monitor, and the Windows NT Diagnostics. The chapter also covers two useful MTS command-line utilities: `Mtxstop.exe` and `Mtxrereg.exe`.

Next Steps

➤ To learn how to manage and coordinate components between multiple MTS computers, continue to Chapter 20, "Managing Multiple Servers."

➤ To learn more about monitoring and tuning MTS-controlled components, turn to Chapter 21, "Monitoring and Tuning Components."

➤ If you are encountering problems in the development and deployment of your MTS system, see Chapter 22 to help diagnose problems and their solutions.

CHAPTER 20

Managing Multiple Servers

Tasks in This Chapter

➤ *Adding New Servers to Transaction Server Explorer*

➤ *Configuring a Client Computer Using the Pull Method of Distribution*

➤ *Configuring a Client Computer Using the Push Method of Distribution*

One of the key advantages to a three-tier client/server application built with Microsoft Transaction Server (MTS) is that you can change configurations of each tier with minimal impact on the others. This feature enables administrators to quickly and easily reconfigure components of the architecture to reflect changes in business practices, product usage, and technology.

In the classic three-tier model, MTS runs on the computer in the middle tier between the user's client computer and the database server. MTS enables you to run multiple MTS machines in the middle tier. The primary benefit of multiple machines is to provide scalability for the system—as the number of simultaneous users increase, you can add more machines to the network to support the increased load.

MTS facilitates the administration of multiple servers running MTS via its Transaction Server Explorer. As briefly illustrated in Chapter 7, "Using Transaction Server Explorer," remote machines running MTS are added to the Explorer hierarchy and managed from a single server.

Preparation Distributing the Microsoft Transaction Server Load

Distributing components between MTS computers is a manual, albeit simple, process. Components are installed under a single MTS computer and then are either pushed to a destination computer or pulled by a destination computer from a source computer. The process of pushing or pulling components simply copies the component's type library and proxy/stub DLLs from one computer to another.

Figure 20.1 illustrates the scenario in which ComponentA is pushed from Server 1 to the destination computers Server 2 and Server 3. In a push scenario, Transaction Server Explorer on the source computer, Server 1, copies components to the destination computers.

Figure 20.2 illustrates the pull model of distribution. In this case ComponentA is pulled from Server 1 to Server 2. In the pull scenario, Transaction Server Explorer runs on the destination computer. The component's type library and other related files are copied from the source computer to the destination computer.

> **Note** Pushing and pulling components from one machine to another does not change the computer in which the objects are instantiated and run. A component always executes on the machine in which it was installed into an MTS package. Pushing and pulling components simply copies the information necessary for additional machines to access the component.

Figure 20.1.

The push model of distribution.

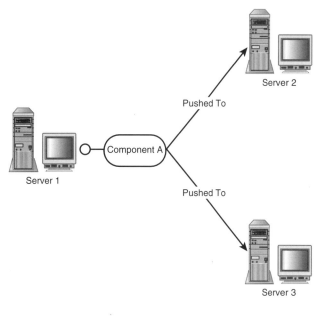

Figure 20.2.

The pull model of distribution.

> **Tip** To run a component on multiple servers, simply install it on each desired machine. As long as users of the components do not need to share information, this type of configuration should not cause a problem. The only issue in configuring client machines is to decide which machine to use to instantiate a component. For now, the developers and administrators of a system provide the configuration. Future versions of MTS and Windows NT will support dynamic load balancing. In dynamic load balancing client applications can point to a single server, but the component is instantiated on the least busy MTS server in the system without the client's knowledge.

Task Adding New Servers to Transaction Server Explorer

Whether you use the push model or the pull model of distribution, you need to create a link between the two computers participating in the connection. Follow these steps to create the link:

1. Start Transaction Server Explorer.

2. Confirm that the Computers folder in the Transaction Server Explorer tree hierarchy is highlighted by default (see Figure 20.3). If it isn't, click the Computers folder to highlight it.

Figure 20.3.

MTS with the Computers folder highlighted.

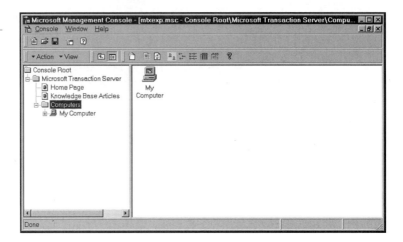

3. Choose Action | New from the Microsoft Management Console's (MMC) toolbar, or click the Create a New Object button, to display the Add Computer dialog (see Figure 20.4).

Figure 20.4.

The Add Computer dialog.

4. Type in the name of the computer to which you want to connect. If you are unsure of its name, click Browse to display the Select Computer dialog in which you can search for the desired computer (see Figure 20.5).

Caution The Add Computer dialog does not accept backslashes, so don't be tempted to use the Unified Naming Convention (UNC) path of the desired server (for example, \\ServerName). Simply omit the preceding backslashes.

Figure 20.5.

The Select Computer dialog.

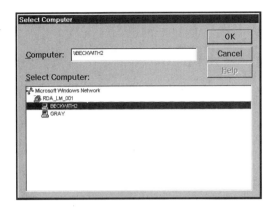

5. Click OK to add the second computer to the hierarchy. Figure 20.6 shows a second computer, beckwith2, added to the MTS hierarchy.

Figure 20.6.

Transaction Server Explorer hierarchy after adding a second computer.

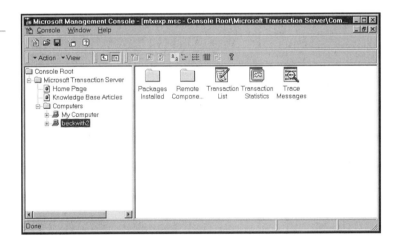

Task Configuring a Client Computer Using the Pull Method of Distribution

Follow these steps to pull a component from a source server, enabling the target computer to instantiate and use the remote component:

1. Start Transaction Server Explorer on the target computer.

2. Confirm that the source computer has been added to the Explorer hierarchy. If it hasn't, follow the steps outlined in the previous task.

3. Check to see whether security has been enabled on the source computer's System package. If so, make sure the user identity assigned to the target computer's System package is a member of the source computer's Reader or Administrator roles. This step is necessary because the System package on the destination server needs to call the source computer's System package to obtain configuration information.

   If the System package on the destination computer is set to Interactive User, make sure the user name you are currently logged in as on the target computer is a member of the source computer's Reader or Administrator roles. See the tasks in Chapter 9, "Configuring Component Security," on assigning users to roles.

4. Make sure a share has been established on the source computer that grants Read access to the user account you are currently logged in to on the destination computer. The components on the server must reside on folders contained under the server's share.

   If a share does not exist, use Windows NT Explorer on the server computer to create the share, making sure to grant at least Read access to the destination computer.

5. Select the Remote Components icon in the Transaction Server Explorer tree hierarchy contained by the My Computer icon (see Figure 20.7).

Figure 20.7.

Transaction Server Explorer hierarchy with the Remote Components icon selected.

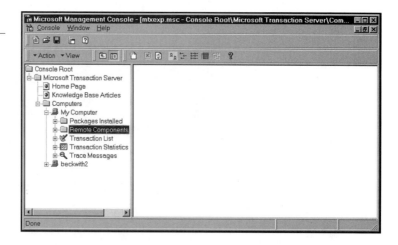

Caution   Make sure to select the Remote Components icon under the My Computer icon. Each computer in the Explorer hierarchy has its own Remote Components icon, and selecting one other than My Computer causes a push installation instead of the desired pull installation.

6. Choose Action | New from the toolbar, or click the Create a New Object button, to display the Remote Components dialog (see Figure 20.8).

Figure 20.8.

The Remote Components dialog.

7. Use the Remote computer combo box to select the computer from which you want to pull components.

8. Use the Package combo box to select the remote package from which you want to pull components.

9. Select the components you wish to pull from the Available components list box and click Add.

   Clicking Add transfers the selected components from the Available Components list box to the Components to Configure on My Computer list box (see Figure 20.9).

10. Click OK to close the Remote Components dialog and pull the components from the source server to the destination server. Transaction Server Explorer now contains icons for the pulled remote components (see Figure 20.10).

Completing step 10 enables you to pull components from one computer to another. Client applications on the destination machine can now create and invoke methods on the remote components. Remember that the remote components still run on the initial machine in which they were installed.

Figure 20.9.

Selecting some remote package components to configure on My Computer.

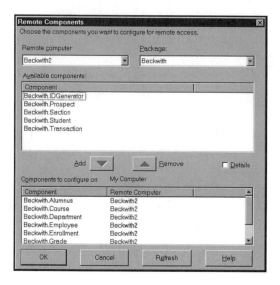

Figure 20.10.

Transaction Server Explorer hierarchy with the populated `Remote Components` *folder.*

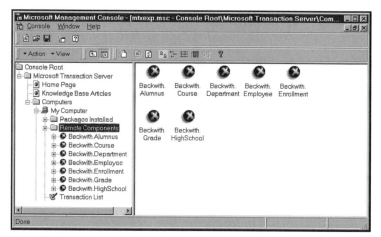

Task Configuring a Client Computer Using the Push Method of Distribution

Follow these steps to configure a target computer from a source computer using the push method of remote installation:

1. Start Transaction Server Explorer on the source computer.

2. Confirm that the target computer has been added to the Explorer hierarchy. If it hasn't, follow the steps outlined in the "Adding New Servers to Transaction Server Explorer" section of this chapter to add a new computer to Transaction Server Explorer.

3. Confirm that security has been enabled on the `System` package of the destination computer and that the account you are running under on the server computer is a member of the Administrator role on the target computer.

> **Caution** In this case being a member of the destination computer's Reader role is not sufficient. Although the Reader role is acceptable in the pull model of installation (because the destination computer only reads the server's information), in the push model the Administrator role needs read-write privileges (because the server needs to write to the destination computer).

4. If security is enabled on the server computer, confirm that the identity assigned to the destination's `System` package is a member of the server computer's Reader role.

5. Select the Remote Components icon within the destination computer's icon (see Figure 20.11).

Figure 20.11.

Transaction Server Explorer hierarchy with the Remote Components icon of the destination computer selected.

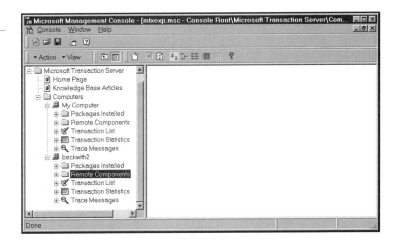

6. Choose Action | New from the toolbar, or click the Create a New Object button, to display the Remote Components dialog.

7. Use the Remote computer combo box to select the destination computer.

8. Use the Package combo box to select the package on the source server to push to the destination server.

9. Select the components to push in the Available components list box and click Add.

10. Click OK to push the components to the destination computer. Transaction Server Explorer now contains icons for the components pushed to the destination server (see Figure 20.12).

Figure 20.12.

Transaction Server Explorer hierarchy with the populated destination Remote Components folder.

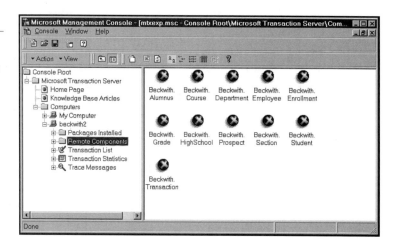

You have successfully pushed components from a source server to a destination server. You can now create and deploy applications on the destination computer that instantiate and invoke methods of components running on the source computer.

Workshop Wrap-Up

In this chapter you learned how to distribute components among MTS computers. Remote components enable applications on one computer to instantiate components on another computer and invoke its methods over the network. MTS supports two types of distribution—pushing and pulling. Pushing involves working at a source computer and copying component information to destination computers. Pulling requires working at each destination computer and copying component information from the source computer.

Next Steps

➤ For details on how to instantiate components remotely from computers that do not have MTS installed, return to Chapter 15, "Setting Up Remote Windows Clients Using DCOM."

➤ For more advanced MTS administration techniques, continue to Chapter 21, "Monitoring and Tuning Components," to learn how to best maintain a client/server system's deployment.

➤ If you encounter problems pushing or pulling remote components, refer to Chapter 22, "Troubleshooting the Complete Solution," for advice.

CHAPTER 21

Monitoring and Tuning Components

Tasks in This Chapter

System monitoring is a critical step in the deployment and maintenance of every application. Through Transaction Server Explorer, Microsoft Transaction Server (MTS) empowers administrators to monitor servers, components, and transactions and to trace messages. In this chapter you learn to configure MTS for monitoring and debugging. The following tasks build on the information in Chapter 7, "Using Transaction Server Explorer," by focusing on skills related to monitoring and tuning MTS components.

Task Optimizing the Server's Advanced Settings

The Advanced tab in the My Computer property sheet (Figure 21.1) contains most of the user-configurable settings for the selected MTS server. You can use the View section of the property page to adjust how frequently MTS should update the user interface objects and to determine the level of tracing you want to monitor in the trace messages view. This task optimizes these settings for improved monitoring, tuning, and debugging of components.

Figure 21.1.

My Computer — Advanced tab (default settings).

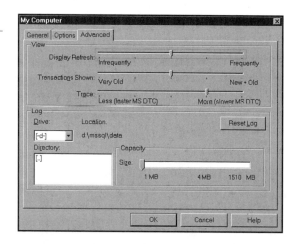

The view section contains three options:

➤ Display Refresh—Specifies the refresh rate used to update the transaction windows. This value ranges from 20 seconds (infrequently) to 1 second (frequently).

➤ Transactions Shown—Indicates the minimum age of the transactions displayed in the transaction windows. This value ranges from 5 minutes (Very Old) to 1 second (New + Old).

➤ Trace—Specifies the level of trace messages sent to the Trace Messages window. This value ranges from sending no trace information to sending all traces.

To optimize the advanced settings for component monitoring, tuning, and debugging, follow these steps:

1. Select the My Computer object from the hierarchy pane.
2. Choose Action | Prope**r**ties from the Microsoft Management Console (MMC) toolbar.
3. Click the Advanced tab on the property sheet (see Figure 21.2).
4. Click and hold the slider thumb for the desired option.
5. Slide thumb to the right-most setting.

Figure 21.2.

My Computer — Advanced tab (monitor settings).

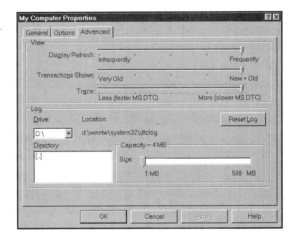

Caution Performance degrades if you run MTS with these settings. Reset these properties to their default settings after the application has been optimized or debugged.

Task Verifying the MS DTC State of MTS Servers

Most MTS applications use the services provided by the Microsoft Distributed Transaction Coordinator (MS DTC). Transaction Server Explorer enables an administrator to monitor and manage the state of this service.

This task determines the state of MS DTC in one or more servers. For additional information on the MS DTC service, consult the "Starting/Stopping the Distributed Transaction Coordinator (MS DTC)" task in Chapter 7.

Determining the MS DTC State Using the Server Icon

In the hierarchy or `Computers` folder views, Transaction Server Explorer reflects the current state of the MS DTC service by changing the color of the appropriate computer's icon. The monitor for the computer icon appears as follows:

➤ Dark green/gray indicates that MS DTC is stopped.

➤ Yellow indicates that MS DTC is starting.

➤ Green indicates that MS DTC is running.

To view the state of MS DTC for My Computer:

1. Click and expand the My Computer object in the hierarchy pane.
2. Verify the color of the My Computer icon in the hierarchy pane. Alternatively, you can verify the color of the My Computer icon in the `Computers` folder view.

Either pane can display the state of one or more servers. However, the `Computers` folder view also enables you to change the view. Like other Windows 95 style applications, Transaction Server Explorer supports large icon, small icon, list, and property view styles. In the following section you use the status view to determine the state of MS DTC.

Determining the MS DTC State Using the `Computers` Folder Status View

The `Computers` folder status view (see Figure 21.3) displays the current state of the MS DTC service for all configured servers. The list displays the name of each server and the state of the associated MS DTC service. Table 21.1 lists and describes the `Computers` folder status properties.

Table 21.1. *Computers folder status properties.*

Property	Description
Name	The computer name of the server
DTC	The current state of the DTC service: stopped, starting, or started

Figure 21.3.

Computers folder status view.

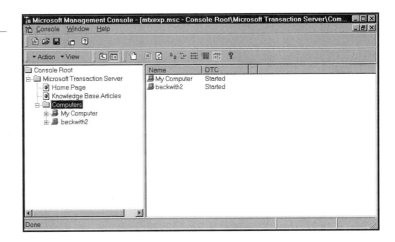

Here's how to view the state of MS DTC for My Computer:

1. Select the `Computers` folder in the hierarchy pane.
2. Choose View | Status view from the toolbar.

Task Refreshing Components Settings

The Windows NT system Registry contains configuration information about applications, components, and interfaces. MTS uses this information to build the runtime environment that hosts the installed packages and components.

Other applications may modify the Registry settings for a component. In such cases MTS components may no longer be properly registered in the Transaction Server Catalog, causing your MTS application to malfunction. For example, other applications can use `regsrv32.exe` to reregister a component; development environments such as Visual Basic may rewrite Registry entries after rebuilding a component.

You can use Transaction Server Explorer to update or refresh the settings for all MTS components. To refresh all the components installed in My Computer:

1. Click and expand the `Computers` folder object in the hierarchy pane.
2. Select the `My Computer` object in the hierarchy pane.

> **Note** You can refresh components installed on other servers by selecting the appropriate server, rather than selecting My Computer.

3. Choose Action | **R**efresh All Components.

Using the VB Add-In Option to Refresh Components

If you use Visual Basic 4.0 or 5.0 to develop MTS components, you can install the MTS VB Add-In option to automatically refresh your MTS components after rebuilding them. The VB Add-In is installed as part of the Development version of MTS. To install this feature, install MTS and select full installation. Check the optional VB Add-In option and complete the installation.

After you install the VB Add-In, it becomes part of the Visual Basic IDE. Components are automatically refreshed when they are compiled. You can use the Visual Basic Add-In Manager, shown in Figure 21.4, to enable or disable this or any other Add-In. To disable the MTxServer Add-In after it is installed:

1. Choose Add-Ins | Add-In Manager in the Visual Basic IDE.
2. Uncheck the MTxServer Registry Refresh option.
3. Click OK to close the dialog.

Figure 21.4.

Visual Basic Add-In Manager.

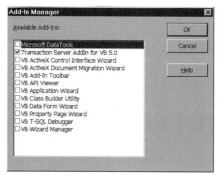

Task Shutting Down Server Processes

You can stop MTS processes to recapture system resources, reinitialize the state of an application, or debug components.

> **Tip** You can use the Windows NT Task Manager to view the number of active MTS processes. Start Task Manager and then click the Processes tab. The MTX.EXE images represent active MTS processes.

To shut down all server processes running in My Computer:

1. Click and expand the `Computers` folder object in the hierarchy pane.
2. Select the `My Computer` object in the hierarchy pane.

> **Tip** This option is available only if selection and focus are set to a computer object in either the hierarchy or view pane.

3. Choose Action | S**h**utdown Server Processes.

> **Caution** Shutting down server processes aborts all active transactions.

Task Monitoring Components

Transaction Server Explorer enables administrators to easily determine when components are being used. Components that are in use usually appear as animated MTS logos in Transaction Server Explorer.

> **Caution** Components spin only when hosted in a server process. When activated in the creator's process space, or in a remote server, the components do not spin.

To monitor the components contained in the Beckwith package:

1. Click and expand the `Computers` folder object in the hierarchy pane.
2. Click and expand the `My Computer` object in the hierarchy pane.
3. Click and expand the `Packages Installed` folder object in the hierarchy pane.
4. Click and expand the `Beckwith` package object in the hierarchy pane.
5. Select the `Components` folder under the `Beckwith` package.
6. Start the sample Beckwith Visual Basic application.

After completing the previous steps, the `Beckwith.Student` object begins to spin, which indicates that a client application is using the object (Figure 21.5). Closing the client application causes the icon to stop spinning.

> **Tip** You can test and validate the installation of new MTS applications by verifying that your components "spin" in Transaction Server Explorer when they are activated.

Figure 21.5.

Components large icon view.

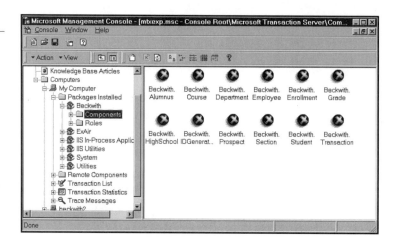

Checking the Status of a Component

You can use Transaction Server Explorer to monitor the status of the components in any package, as pictured in Figure 21.6. The component status view gives you continuously updated statistics on the usage of your components. Table 21.2 describes the information that this view contains.

Figure 21.6.

Component status view.

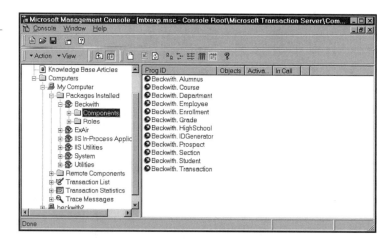

Table 21.2. *Component status properties.*

Property	Description
Prog ID	The programmatic identifier for the component
Objects	The total number of objects allocated
Activated	The total number of objects in use
In Call	The total number of objects that are currently processing a client request

To view the status of the Beckwith sample components in My Computer:

1. Click and expand the My Computer object in the hierarchy pane.
2. Click and expand the My Computer object in the hierarchy pane.
3. Click and expand the Packages Installed folder object in the hierarchy pane.
4. Click and expand the Beckwith package object in the hierarchy pane.
5. Select the Components folder under the Beckwith package.
6. Choose View | Status view from the toolbar.

Task Using the Transaction List to Monitor Active Transactions

As discussed in Chapter 7, the transaction list view displays the transactions that are occurring on components installed in the selected server. This task guides you through the process of monitoring and resolving transactions using the transaction list view.

Monitoring Active Transactions

To monitor the transactions in which the current server is participating:

1. Click and expand the My Computer object in the hierarchy pane.
2. Select the Transaction List object in the hierarchy pane.

 Although the View menu items are unavailable when the transaction list view is active, you can change the view mode with a context-sensitive menu.

The transaction list view (Figure 21.7) supports four view modes, outlined in Table 21.3.

Figure 21.7.

Transaction list view.

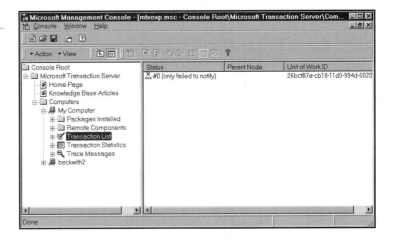

Table 21.3.   *Transaction list views.*

View Mode	Description
Large Icon	Displays the transactions using large icons
Small Icon	Displays the transactions using small icons
Details	Displays the transactions in a list and provides additional details
List	Displays the transactions in a list

To change the current view to provide details:

1. Right-click Transaction List view.
2. Choose Details from the View pop-up menu.

The details view lists transactions and their attributes: Status, Parent Node, and Unit of Work Identifier. Table 21.4 defines these attributes.

Table 21.4.   *Transaction attributes.*

Attribute	Description
Status	The current state of the transaction. This property is important when you are manually resolving transactions.
Parent Node	Displays the originator of the transaction (the server where the transaction began).
Unit of Work ID	A unique identifier assigned by MS DTC.

Resolving In Doubt or Only Failed Remain to Notify Transactions

Through the MS DTC service, MTS supports transactions across multiple servers. A two-phase commit protocol coordinates these transactions and guarantees that transactions spanning multiple servers are managed as a single, atomic unit; that is work is either committed on all servers or to none at all. Refer to Chapter 3, "Working with Database Transactions," for details on the two-phase commit protocol.

Applications that use multiple servers are at a higher risk for difficulties than those that operate on a single server. The inherent unreliability of computer hardware, networks, telephone connections, and system software can cause even the most dependable applications to fail. MTS supports recovery of these types of errors with a manual transaction-resolution mechanism.

The MS DTC service classifies transactions depending on their state. Table 21.5 lists the possible states a transaction may have. Transactions must be in either the In Doubt or Only Failed Remain to Notify state to be resolved manually.

Table 21.5. *Transaction states.*

State	Description
Aborted	The transaction has been aborted. Aborted transactions are removed from the transaction list view.
Aborting	The transaction is in the process of being aborted.
Active	The transaction is active.
Committed	The transaction has committed all its work. Committed transactions are removed from the transaction list view.
Forced Abort	The previously In Doubt transaction has been forced to abort.
Forced Commit	The previously In Doubt transaction has been forced to commit.
In Doubt	The transaction is prepared, and the coordinating MS DTC is not available.
Notifying Committed	The transaction is prepared, and MS DTC is notifying participants that the transaction has been committed.
Only Failed Remain to Notify	The transaction has been committed, and MS DTC has notified all participants except those that are currently inaccessible.
Prepared	The transaction participants have agreed to prepare the transaction.
Preparing	The transaction is preparing for commit. MS DTC is collecting responses from all participants.

With the current version of MS DTC and MTS, resolving transactions across multiple servers requires some investigative work. The following steps can help you determine what action to take when manually resolving transactions:

1. If the transaction list view contains transactions that are either in the In Doubt or Only Failed Remain to Notify states, you need to resolve them. You can use the Parent Node attribute to determine which server initiated the transaction. The Unit of Work ID is a unique number used to track transactions. You need this number to determine the relationships between transactions.

2. For In Doubt transactions, you must travel up the transaction hierarchy to find the immediate parent:

   ➤ Go to the Transaction Server hierarchy and select the computer named in the Parent Node column.

   ➤ Select the transaction list view for this server.

   ➤ If a transaction with the same Unit of Work ID exists on this server, verify its transaction state. If In Doubt, continue traveling up the transaction hierarchy. If Only Failed Remain to Notify, the transaction can safely be committed. The absence of a parent transaction indicates that the transaction was aborted, and in such case you should abort the transaction in any remaining server.

3. For Only Failed Remain to Notify transactions, you must work your way down the transaction hierarchy. This task can be quite difficult because MTS does not display all servers that are currently participating in a transaction.

   ➤ In such cases you must make note of the Unit of Work ID and then select each computer from the Transaction Server hierarchy.

   ➤ Select the transaction list view for each server.

   ➤ Locate and commit transactions with the same Unit of Work ID.

After you resolve transactions on the child servers, you must force the parent to forget the transaction. To manually resolve a transaction in My Computer:

1. Click and expand the My Computer object in the hierarchy pane.

2. Select the Transaction List object in the hierarchy pane.

3. Switch to the transaction list view and right-click the transaction that you must resolve manually.

4. Do one of the following:

   ➤ To commit the transaction, choose Resolve | Commit.

   ➤ To abort the transaction, choose Resolve | Abort.

   ➤ To forget the transaction, choose Resolve | Forget.

Task Using the Transaction Statistics Window to View Summary Statistics

The transaction statistics view (Figure 21.8) displays current and cumulative information on transactions serviced by MS DTC. The view also presents some performance and status information regarding MS DTC.

Figure 21.8.

The transaction statistics view.

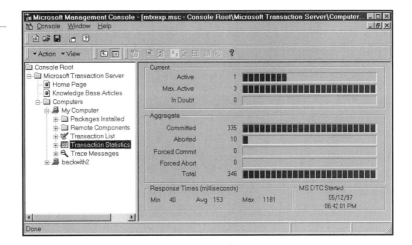

To view the statistics for the transactions in which the current server is participating:

1. Click and expand the My Computer object in the hierarchy pane.
2. Select the Transaction Statistics object in the hierarchy pane.

This view has four sections (see Table 21.6).

Table 21.6. *Transaction statistics groups.*

Group	Description
Current	Lists the current number of active transactions, the maximum number of allowable transactions, and the failed number of transactions due to communication problems with the transaction coordinator and the database server
Aggregate	Lists cumulative statistics on committed and aborted transactions
Response Times	Lists statistics on transaction performance
MS DTC Started	The date and time when MS DTC was last started

Note Restarting MS DTC resets the aggregate transaction statistics.

Task Using the Trace Messages Window to View MS DTC Messages

The MS DTC service logs messages during certain activities, such as starting and stopping. The volume of trace messages depends on the setting of the Trace object in the Advanced tab of My Computer property sheet. These messages are logged in the trace messages view, shown in Figure 21.9.

Figure 21.9.

The trace messages view.

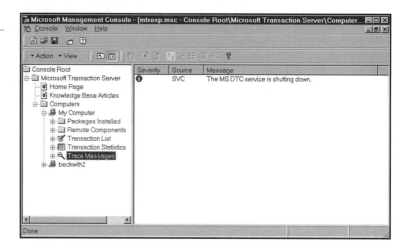

To view the MS DTC trace messages:

1. Click and expand the My Computer object in the hierarchy pane.
2. Select the Trace Messages object in the hierarchy pane.

The list displays any trace messages issued during the current MS DTC session, along with details regarding each message log. Table 21.7 describes the detailed information in each trace message.

Table 21.7. *Trace message properties.*

Property	Description
Severity	This attribute describes the severity level of the trace message. The messages can be informative, warnings, or errors.
Source	Trace messages may originate from three sources: SVC (MS DTC service), LOG (MS DTC log), or CM (network connection manager).
Message	The message text.

Workshop Wrap-Up

Component monitoring and tuning is a crucial phase in the deployment and maintenance of MTS applications. Transaction Server Explorer provides administrators with the tools necessary to accomplish this task. In this chapter you learned how to use Transaction Server Explorer to optimize your server for monitoring and debugging; to monitor servers, components, and transactions; and to determine the appropriate action to take when manually resolving a transaction.

Next Steps

➤ Monitoring components is a first step in managing a system that performs well with the minimum possible down time. But when problems occur, Chapter 22, "Troubleshooting the Complete Solution," can help you get your application back on track.

➤ To monitor other aspects of your system, refer to Chapter 19, "Performing Server Administration and Configuration."

➤ Using Explorer for all your monitoring needs can be cumbersome. In Chapter 24, "Scripting Transaction Server Explorer with Automation," you learn how to script Transaction Server Explorer to automate the monitoring tasks.

CHAPTER 22

Troubleshooting the Complete Solution

Even with Microsoft Transaction Server (MTS), developing a client/server application is a complex undertaking. During the development of the system, errors are going to occur, either as the result of bugs or as a result of improper setup of the many components that together form the entire system.

The tasks in this chapter show you how to verify the correct setup and operation of each player in the client/server architecture puzzle. The tasks begin at the database server end of the spectrum and work up the architecture, through the middle tier and finally to the client applications running on remote computers.

Some of the tasks presented in the chapter also appear elsewhere in this book. They are repeated here so that this chapter can serve as a complete guide for troubleshooting the entire system. This chapter uses the Beckwith College sample database to illustrate each troubleshooting task.

Task Verifying That Microsoft SQL Server Is Operating Correctly

The Beckwith College sample database stores its persistent data in several tables in multiple SQL Server databases. If MS SQL Server is not functioning correctly, the rest of the system cannot work.

Follow these steps to make sure that each Beckwith database is working correctly:

1. Open Microsoft SQL Enterprise Manager. You can use this tool to perform operations against any SQL Server installation you have permissions to access on your network.

2. Register the server computer running SQL Server with SQL Enterprise Manager. If the server computer is already registered, it appears in the Server Manager window under the SQL 6.5 icon (see Figure 22.1).

   If your server isn't registered, choose **S**erver | **R**egister Server from the main menu to display the Register Server dialog (see Figure 22.2). Use this dialog to register your database server with the Enterprise Manager.

   > **Tip**   If the Register Server dialog refuses to recognize and register your database server, then the operation of your network may be faulty. See the task, "Verifying That the Network Is Working Correctly," to troubleshoot.

3. Expand the database server's icon in the Server Manager tree control to reveal its Databases folder. Expand the Databases folder to reveal the database serviced by this server (see Figure 22.3). For the Beckwith sample database system, you should have the following databases:

> Admissions

> AlumniRelations

> BusinessOffice

> HumanResources

> Registrar

Figure 22.1.

Microsoft SQL Enterprise Manager with the NUPD registered server.

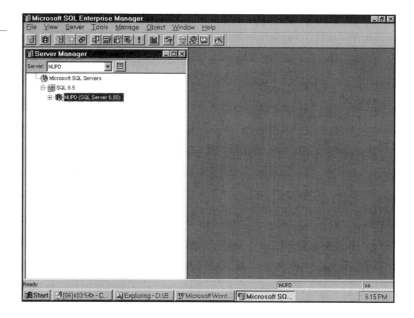

Figure 22.2.

The Register Server dialog.

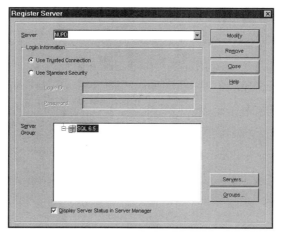

Figure 22.3.

The Beckwith databases revealed.

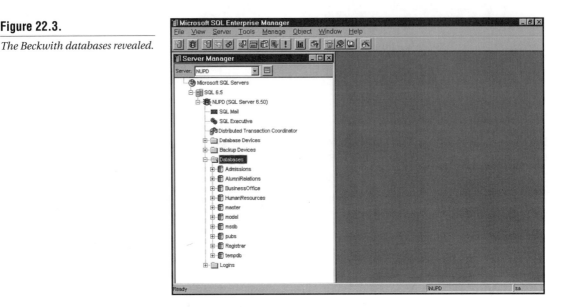

> **Tip** If you don't have these databases installed, refer to Appendix A, "Overview and Installation of the Beckwith College Sample Database," for instructions on installing and configuring the Beckwith sample databases.

4. Select the first Beckwith sample database, Admissions, by clicking its icon in the Server Manager tree control.

5. Choose **T**ools | SQL **Q**uery Tool from the main menu to display the Query window (see Figure 22.4). From this window you can issue SQL commands directly to the database.

6. Issue the following query and press Ctrl+E to make sure SQL Server is working correctly and the Admissions database is set up correctly:

```
SELECT * FROM PROSPECT WHERE LASTNAME="Gray"
```

If Microsoft SQL Server is working correctly, the SQL query returns a result set with approximately 50 records (see Figure 22.5).

> **Tip** You can repeat steps 4, 5, and 6 for the other Beckwith databases, but if SQL Server is working for one database, it is likely working for the others as well.

Figure 22.4.

Using the Query window to verify the Admissions database.

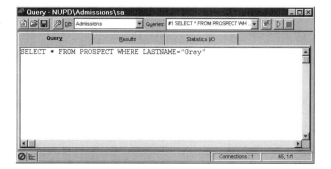

Figure 22.5.

Results of using the Query window to verify the Admissions database.

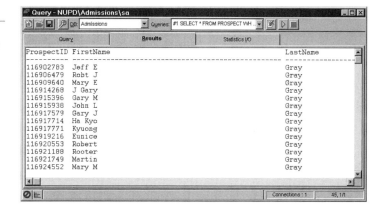

Task Verifying That the Network Is Working Correctly

If in the previous task the SQL Enterprise Manager refused to register your database server, then you probably have a network connectivity problem. If your network is TCP/IP, follow these suggestions to check your network.

1. Use the command-line tool `Ping` to determine whether your computer can see the other server. To use `Ping`, simply invoke it and pass the name of the remote server as the first parameter on the command line:

```
ping SGRAY
```

If `Ping` is successful, you should see output similar to

```
Pinging sgray.beckwith.com [137.114.203.135] with 32 bytes of data:
Reply from 137.114.203.135: bytes=32 time<10ms TTL=128
Reply from 137.114.203.135: bytes=32 time<10ms TTL=128
Reply from 137.114.203.135: bytes=32 time<10ms TTL=128
Reply from 137.114.203.135: bytes=32 time<10ms TTL=128
```

This output indicates that the client computer can communicate to the remote server computer.

Another way to test network connectivity is to try to create a Windows shortcut to the server.

2. Right-click an empty space of your Windows desktop to display a context menu. Choose Ne**w** | **S**hortcut from the context menu to display the Create Shortcut dialog (see Figure 22.6).

Figure 22.6.

The Create Shortcut dialog.

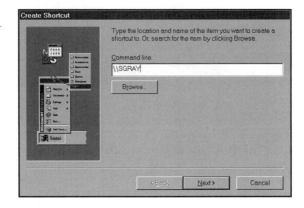

3. Go to the command-line edit box and type the UNC path of the server; for example:

    `\\SGRAY`

4. Click Next to have Windows attempt a connection to this server. If the test is successful, Windows displays the Select a Title for the Program dialog (see Figure 22.7). When this dialog is displayed, you can click either Finish or Cancel—the network is working.

Figure 22.7.

The Select a Title for the Program dialog.

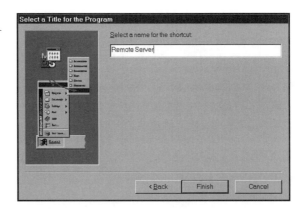

Task Verifying That ODBC Is Working Correctly

One of the biggest advantages of using ODBC in MTS client/server systems is that ODBC supports connection pooling. However, you must configure ODBC for each machine that executes components that communicate with the database.

Follow these tasks to ensure that ODBC is set up correctly:

1. Verify the correct configuration of the System Data Source Names (DSNs) in Table 22.1.

> **Tip** You should use System Data Source Names for MTS client/server systems. Do not use User Data Source Names.

Table 22.1. *Beckwith ODBC System DSNs.*

Data Source Name	Database
BeckwithAD	Admissions—Maintains demographic information on prospective students
BeckwithAR	AlumniRelations—Maintains demographic information on Beckwith's alumni
BeckwithBO	BusinessOffice—Maintains demographic information on enrolled students and their account balances
BeckwithHR	HumanResources—Maintains demographic information on the college's employees and professors
BeckwithRG	Registrar—Maintains students' grades and current enrollment

2. Open the MS Query tool that ships with Microsoft SQL Server. You can use this tool to verify that the DSNs are working correctly.

3. Choose **F**ile | **N**ew Query from the main menu to display the Select Data Source dialog (see Figure 22.8).

Figure 22.8.

The Select Data Source dialog.

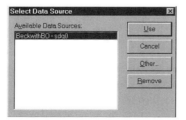

4. Click Other to display a list of data source names registered on the local computer. Select the BeckwithBO data source and click OK to add it to the Select Data Source dialog.

5. Click the Use button on the Select Data Source dialog to use the BeckwithBO data source.

6. Select the Student item in the Add Tables dialog (see Figure 22.9) and click Add. Then click Close.

Figure 22.9.

The Add Tables dialog.

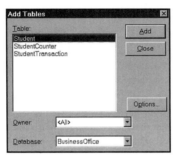

7. Double-click the * list item in the Student child window that is contained by the Query1 window.

If your ODBC connection is working properly, you should see the grid control on the bottom half of the Query1 window fill with data (see Figure 22.10).

Figure 22.10.

The results of a successful query through the ODBC DSN.

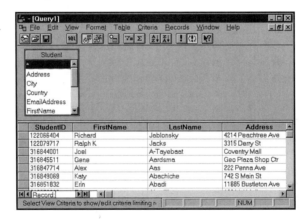

Task Verifying That MS Distributed Transaction Coordinator Is Running

Distributed Transaction Coordinator (DTC) runs as a Windows NT service on all machines that play a role in component transactions, for example, machines running SQL Server and MTS. For component transactions to work properly with SQL Server, you must make sure that DTC is running on each computer. Here are three ways to check the status of DTC and to start it.

The first method uses the Control Panel:

1. Open the Windows Control Panel and start the Services applet (see Figure 22.11).

Figure 22.11.

The Services applet.

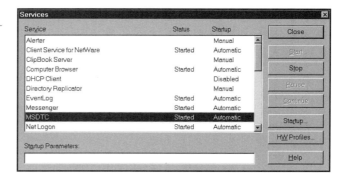

2. Locate the MSDTC list item and check its status attribute. If its status is not Started, click the MSDTC list item and click Start.

3. Repeat this step for every computer running MTS and Microsoft SQL Server.

You can also start and stop the DTC service from the SQL Enterprise Manager application that ships with SQL Server. Follow these steps to open the application and register each SQL Server computer with the Manager:

1. Locate the Distributed Transaction Coordinator icon contained by each server icon in the Server Manager tree control (see Figure 22.12).

2. Right-click this item to display its context menu. If the Start menu option on the context menu is disabled, then DTC is started on this computer.

Figure 22.12.

The Distributed Transaction Coordinator icon.

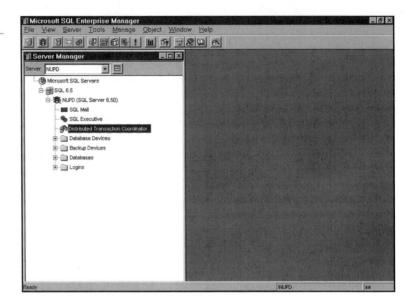

Finally you can use the Transaction Server Explorer to start and stop the DTC service on machines that are running Transaction Server. Follow these steps to open the Transaction Server Explorer and register each remote Transaction Server computer with the Explorer:

1. Right-click each computer icon in the tree view portion of the Transaction Server Explorer hierarchy to display its context menu.

2. Check the status of the first item of the context menu. If it is stop MSDTC, then DTC is successfully running on that computer. If it isn't, the first menu option is labeled start MSDTC and you should select it (see Figure 22.13).

Figure 22.13.

Starting MS DTC with the
Transaction Server Explorer.

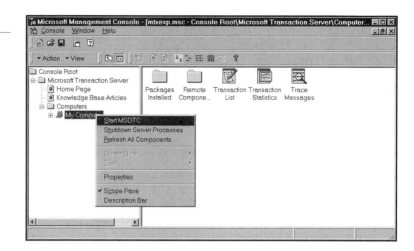

Task Verifying That Transaction Server Is Installed Correctly

After checking the database and ODBC, and verifying that DTC is running on all necessary machines, you need to check each installation of MTS to make sure it is operating correctly.

Follow these steps to verify the proper operation of MTS:

1. Execute the steps in the Chapter 6, "Installing Microsoft Transaction Server," task labeled "Verifying Correct Installation."

2. Open Transaction Server Explorer through the Microsoft Management Console (MMC) and install the `Beckwith.dll` server from the companion CD-ROM (see Figure 22.14). Copy this server from the `Beckwith\VB Components` folder to your local hard drive before installing.

3. Open the OLE/COM Object Viewer that ships with Visual C++ and locate the `Beckwith.Student` component. Expand the Object Classes tree item that contains the All Objects tree item. Expand the All Objects tree item to locate the `Beckwith.Student` icon (see Figure 22.15).

Figure 22.14.

Transaction Server Explorer after installing the Beckwith.dll components.

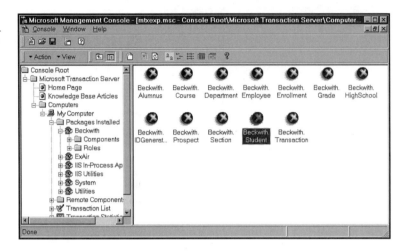

Figure 22.15.

The Beckwith.Student component in the OLE/COM Object Viewer tree hierarchy.

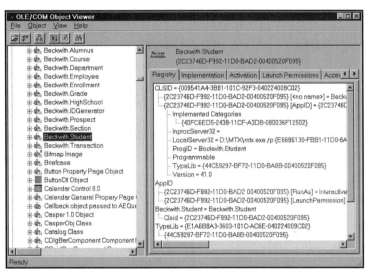

4. Right-click the Beckwith.Student component and choose Create Instance from the context menu. The OLE/COM Object Viewer now attempts to create an instance of the Beckwith.Student component. If no errors are reported, then the instance was created successfully.

5. Confirm that MTS is monitoring the component instance by returning to Transaction Server Explorer and selecting the Components folder contained by the Beckwith package icon in the hierarchy. In list view the Beckwith.Student component should be spinning, indicating that an instance of it has been created and is under MTS control.

> **Tip** If you have problems instantiating components under MTS control, you might consider uninstalling and then reinstalling MTS. See Chapter 6 for instructions on how to uninstall and reinstall MTS.

Task Restarting MTS Server Processes

Occasionally, code inside your components can corrupt the server processes hosted by MTS. Although MTS should immediately shut down any processes in which errors occur, for some reason this shutdown may not happen. To recover from these problems, perform either of the following procedures to destroy all MTS server processes:

➤ From the Transaction Server Explorer, click the My Computer icon and choose Action | S̲hutdown Server Processes from the toolbar to terminate all running MTS processes.

➤ From the Command Prompt, run the MTS command-line utility Mtxstop.exe. You can find this tool in the root MTS installation folder (usually Mtx).

Task Refreshing All Server Components

After you develop components, you place them under MTS control for the deployment of the system. However, as you're developing those components, you need to continually install and reinstall the components. If you don't, the information that MTS stores about components under its control becomes out of sync with the latest build of the components. To synchronize your components and MTS, you need to refresh MTS with the latest information about your components. Perform either of the following methods to refresh MTS:

➤ From Transaction Server Explorer, click the My Computer icon and choose Action | R̲efresh All Components from the toolbar. This step refreshes all components in all packages installed in MTS.

➤ From the Command Prompt, run the MTS command-line utility Mtxrereg.exe. You can find this tool in the root MTS installation folder (usually Mtx). Mtxrereg.exe stores up-to-date configuration information about components installed under MTS control.

Task Verifying That DCOM Is Set Up Correctly

The next troubleshooting routine checks the connectivity between client and server computers. This procedure shows that DCOM is correctly configured between the two computers.

Follow these steps to confirm that DCOM is set up properly:

1. Run the DCOM configuration utility `Dcomcnfg.exe`. It ships as part of Windows NT and resides in the Windows NT installation `System32` folder.

2. Select the Default Properties tab (see Figure 22.16).

3. Make sure the Enable Distributed COM on This Computer check box is checked.

4. Set the Default Authentication Level combo box to a level that is equal to or higher than the authentication level set on the packages installed in MTS.

5. Set the Default Impersonation Level combo box to Impersonate. MTS requires this setting. For more information on impersonation levels, click the Default Impersonation Level combo box and press F1.

   For more details on Authentication and Impersonation levels, see Chapter 9, "Configuring Component Security."

6. Click OK to close the `Dcomcnfg` utility and commit the security changes.

Figure 22.16.

The Default Properties tab of `Dcomcnfg.exe`.

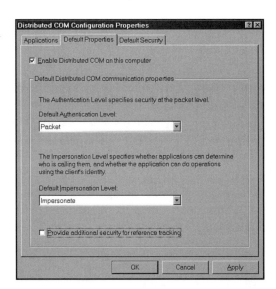

Task Verifying That DCOM Is Operating Correctly

The easiest way to determine if DCOM is working correctly between two computers is to run the client configuration utility created by MTS as a result of exporting a package. Follow these steps to export the `Beckwith` package and create and install a client configuration executable:

1. Open Transaction Server Explorer.

2. Select the `Beckwith` package from the Transaction Server Explorer hierarchy.

3. Choose Action | **E**xport Package from the main menu to display the Export Package dialog.

4. Provide the full path to a temporary folder on your local hard drive in the edit box. If you type in a folder name that does not yet exist, MTS creates it for you. In addition to the folder, you must also supply a filename for the resulting exported package file. This file name also serves as the name of the client configuration executable.

   For this example type the string `c:\BeckwithExport\Beck` in the edit box.

5. Click Export to export the package and create the client configuration executable. If all is successful, MTS displays the following message box: The package was successfully exported.

6. Use Windows NT Explorer to navigate to the temporary folder you provided in step # 4. There you should find two files and a folder:

   ➤ `Beck.pak`

   ➤ `Beckwith.dll`

   ➤ `clients` folder

7. Copy the `Beck.exe` to your client computer and run it.

8. Run the sample client application `Bcds.exe` on the client computer. If the application runs without errors, DCOM is operating correctly.

Task Deciphering Cryptic Error Messages

DCOM or other system errors that occur during the execution of the steps in the preceding tasks are likely to appear as simple message boxes with error codes. Here are some examples:

➤ `0x80070005`

➤ `0x8001010E`

➤ `0x80004005`

You might also see message boxes displaying the decimal equivalent of these hexadecimal numbers. However, these numbers by themselves are not very helpful.

Fortunately, the Error Lookup tool that ships with Visual C++ is very helpful in converting these error codes into more usable text strings. `Errlook.exe` resides in the `Bin` folder of your Visual C++ installation.

To use Error Lookup, click `Errlook.exe` to display its main window (see Figure 22.17).

Figure 22.17.

The main window of the Error Lookup applet.

To look up an error code, simply type the code into the Value edit box, complete with the 0x if the number is in hexadecimal, and click Look Up. Error Lookup displays any descriptive text about the error in question in the window's read-only box. This utility comes in very handy when you need to decipher obscure MTS and DCOM errors.

Workshop Wrap-Up

This chapter shows you how to troubleshoot the installation of a MTS-hosted client/ server system—from the database to the remote client using DCOM. Error Lookup is an important utility that can help you resolve cryptic system error codes.

Next Steps

➤ When the complete client/server system is finally working, go on to Part VII, "Working with the Software Development Kit," where you learn to control and monitor the behavior of MTS.

➤ For more details on the configuration of the Beckwith sample database, see Appendix A.

PART VII

Working with the Software Development Kit

CHAPTER 23

Installing and Exploring the Software Development Kit

Tasks in This Chapter

➤ *Obtaining and Installing the SDK*

➤ *Verifying SDK Installation with the Automation Sample*

To this point in the book, you have been using the built-in features and services of Microsoft Transaction Server (MTS) to develop component-based client/server systems. MTS provides plenty of default functionality to build highly scalable, robust architectures for distributed component-based applications. However, the default behavior of MTS may not always be sufficient for your needs.

To address this need, Microsoft has released the MTS Software Development Kit (SDK). The SDK enables you to extend the functionality of MTS by writing custom applications that interface directly with it.

This chapter shows you how to obtain the MTS SDK, install it on your system, and build and explore one of the samples that ships with it. The example is used with the sample Beckwith components built earlier in this book so make sure the components are installed before continuing (see Chapter 8, "Installing Components," for details).

Uses of the Software Development Kit

The SDK enables you to extend the functionality of MTS. It includes the following:

➤ The SDK exposes a set of Automation objects that give you programmatic control over Transaction Server Explorer. This feature is useful for automating common MTS tasks and for creating elaborate setup applications for your system.

➤ The SDK also includes the MTSSpy application, which enables you to listen in to the events that occur during the runtime execution of MTS. This application is especially helpful while you are debugging your system.

➤ The SDK enables you to write custom resource dispensers and resource managers. A *resource dispenser* is a service that manages unsaved data used between components. A *resource manager* is a service that manages the durable data used by components. *Durable* data is saved data that the resource manager guarantees to survive system failures. MTS comes with two resource dispensers: the ODBC resource dispenser and the Shared Property Manager. The resource managers that MTS uses include SQL Server 6.5 and Microsoft's ODBC driver for Oracle databases.

Task Obtaining and Installing the SDK

Before exploring what is in the SDK, you have to get a copy of it. The SDK does not currently ship with MTS. Instead, you must download a copy of it from the Web at www.microsoft.com/support/transaction.

> **Tip** Coincidentally, you can also check to see whether any service packs for MTS
> are available at the same Web address:
> `www.microsoft.com/support/transaction`.
> Service packs update the binaries of MTS to fix any known bugs. See Chapter 6,
> "Installing Microsoft Transaction Server," for details on installing MTS service packs.

The most recent version of the MTS SDK, version 2.0, is downloadable as a self-extracting setup file. Download this file to your computer.

Before installing the SDK, make sure you have a valid installation of MTS on your machine. The SDK searches for the installation and automatically installs itself in a subfolder labeled Sdk under the root folder of the MTS installation. If you do not have MTS installed, follow the tasks in Chapter 6 to install it.

1. Double-click the icon for the self-extracting executable from Windows NT Explorer.

   The first message box tells you that the SDK will be extracted to a temporary folder on your computer and that you must run the setup program placed in the temporary folder to continue the installation of the SDK. This two-step installation allows you to read the `readme` file that accompanies the SDK before installing the SDK.

2. Click Yes in the message box to extract the SDK setup files to a temporary directory.

   The Microsoft Transaction Server SDK dialog prompts you to enter a temporary folder name (see Figure 23.1).

3. Type the name of a temporary folder in the edit box or click Browse to select the folder from a list of all folders on the system. Click OK to accept your directory choice.

Figure 23.1.

Specify a temporary folder in the Microsoft Transaction Server SDK dialog.

> **Tip** You may enter the pathname of a folder that does not exist; the setup program
> confirms the creation of the new folder.

4. Wait while the setup program copies the necessary installation files to the temporary folder and then silently quits. When the file copy dialog disappears, you can continue.

5. Start Windows NT Explorer and navigate to the temporary folder you specified in step 3.

Note You may have to refresh Windows NT Explorer if you create a new temporary folder for the installation. To refresh Explorer, choose View | Refresh from the main menu or press F5.

The temporary folder contains a `readme.doc` file and another self-extracting executable.

6. Open and read the `readme.doc` file and decide whether you want to continue installing the SDK.

7. Continue the SDK installation. Start the second self-extracting executable by double-clicking its icon in the temporary folder from Windows NT Explorer.

The SDK setup program displays a dialog confirming your decision to install the SDK.

8. Click Yes to continue. The setup program begins to copy the files necessary to install the SDK.

9. Follow the prompts to close or terminate various applications and system components before continuing. These components include

- The Control Panel
- The MSDTC service
- Transaction Server Explorer
- All `MTX.EXE` processes running in the system

Caution Although not specifically mentioned in the message box, if the computer on which you are currently installing the SDK also has Microsoft SQL Server running, you should stop this service when you stop the MSDTC service.

To stop the services, use the Services applet from the Control Panel. After you stop the MSDTC and MSSQLServer services, close the Services applet and close the Control Panel.

To kill any `MTX.EXE` processes that may be running in the system, open the Windows NT Task Manager application. You can start the Task Manager by right-clicking an empty spot on the Windows NT taskbar and choosing Task Manager from the context menu. When the Task Manager is running, make sure the

Process tab is selected. If you find any MTX.EXE processes in the list, right-click the list item and choose End Process from the context menu (see Figure 23.2).

Figure 23.2.

Terminating any MTX.EXE *processes with Task Manager.*

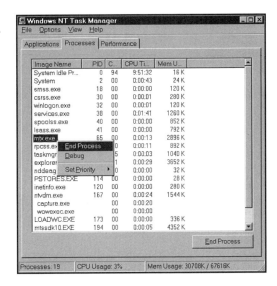

10. Click OK when all the requested applications and services have been stopped.

    After you click OK, the SDK setup program copies the remainder of its files from the temporary folder to the MTS main installation folder. The SDK setup program displays a final message box when the copy process is complete.

> **Tip** After the installation of the SDK is complete, you can delete the temporary folder and the files it contains. The SDK setup program does not do this for you automatically.

What's in the SDK?

The MTS SDK contains several binaries that enhance and extend MTS, similar to a service pack. In addition, examples are installed that demonstrate how to

➤ Script Transaction Server Explorer using Automation

➤ Create an Event Sink application that logs and responds to MTS events

➤ Build a resource dispenser

➤ Build a resource manager

See Chapter 24, "Scripting Transaction Server Explorer with Automation," for a complete discussion of scripting the Transaction Server Explorer with Automation, but the details of implementing resource dispensers and resource managers are beyond the scope of this book.

Task Verifying SDK Installation with the Automation Sample

The SDK installs Automation server components that enable external client applications to script Transaction Server Explorer. Any application capable of driving Automation servers can now automate all the tasks you perform manually in Transaction Server Explorer.

The SDK comes with three sample applications that use Automation to drive Explorer: Explore, Install, and Tasks.

➤ Explore provides an alternative user interface for examining the configuration of MTS with its packages, roles, and components.

➤ Install creates a package in Explorer and installs components into it.

➤ Tasks shows you how to code various Transaction Server Explorer tasks with Visual Basic version 5.0.

Explore and Tasks are written in Visual Basic, and the Install is written in both Visual Basic and Visual C++. Because of the simplicity of Install and Tasks, the remainder of this task focuses on Explore.

Follow these steps to build and run the Explore sample with the sample `Beckwith` package:

1. Use Windows NT Explorer to navigate to the `\Mtx\Sdk\Admin\Demo\Vb5\explore` folder. (If you installed MTS to a folder other than the default, your path will be slightly differently.)

2. Double-click the `explore.vbp` file to start Visual Basic version 5.0 and load the Explore application. The Explore application is ready to run.

3. Choose **R**un | **S**tart from the Visual Basic main menu. The MTS Admin SDK Sample dialog should appear (see Figure 23.3).

   From this main dialog you can read the current configuration of MTS and make changes to it.

> **Caution** The changes you make with this sample Automation application affect the current setup of MTS. Because the user interface of this demo is less robust than Transaction Server Explorer, exercise caution in any changes you make to avoid corrupting your MTS setup.

Figure 23.3

The main dialog of the Explore sample Automation client.

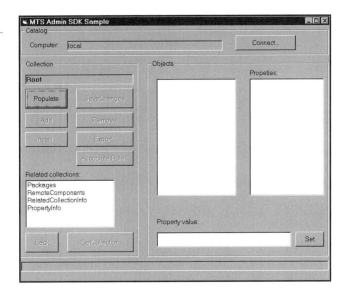

4. Select Packages in the Related Collections list box. This item enables the GetCollection button. Click GetCollection to populate the form with the currently defined packages installed in MTS (see Figure 23.4).

Figure 23.4.

The main dialog of the Explore sample Automation client populated with the Packages *collection.*

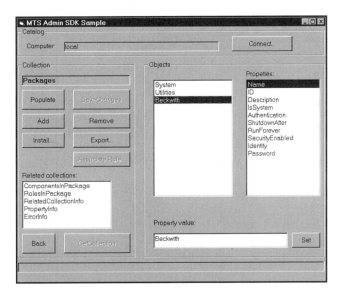

5. Select Beckwith in the Objects list box and select ComponentsInPackage from the Related Collections list box. Once again, click GetCollection to retrieve a list of all components installed in the Beckwith package (see Figure 23.5).

Figure 23.5.

The main form of the Explore *sample Automation client populated with the components of the* Beckwith *package.*

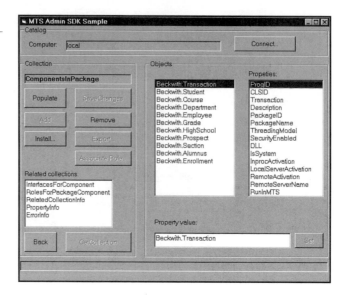

6. Browse the properties of any component by clicking the items in the Properties list box. As you select each property, its current value is displayed in the Property Value edit box.

7. Modify the Description property of any Beckwith component by clicking the Description property and typing **New description** in the Property Value edit box. Click Set to commit the change to the property (see Figure 23.6).

Figure 23.6.

Changing the property of a component with the Explore *sample Automation client.*

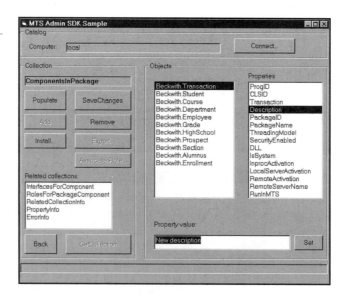

8. Click Save Changes to commit the changed property to the MTS configuration.

9. Explore the remaining options of the Explore sample to see which other functions of MTS can be scripted. For example:

➤ Managing remote servers with the Connect button

➤ Installing components into packages with the Install button

➤ Exporting packages with the Export button

➤ Associating roles with components and their interfaces with the Associate Role button

Workshop Wrap-Up

This chapter explains how to acquire and install the MTS SDK. It describes the features of the SDK and shows you how to test its installation by examining the Explore Automation client application written in Visual Basic.

Next Steps

➤ To build a custom Automation client, continue to Chapter 24.

➤ To spy on MTS at runtime, skip to Chapter 25, "Exploring the Software Development Kit's MTSSpy Application."

CHAPTER 24

Scripting Transaction Server Explorer with Automation

Tasks in This Chapter

➤ *Creating a Visual Basic Application That Uses MTS Scriptable Objects*

➤ *Deleting Packages*

➤ *Creating New Packages and Installing Components*

➤ *Scripting Component Transactions*

➤ *Scripting the Creation of Roles*

➤ *Completing the Scripting Application*

If you are reading this book from beginning to end, most of the tasks you have learned to perform with Microsoft Transaction Server (MTS) use Transaction Server Explorer. So far all your Transaction Server Explorer tasks have been manual—you've clicked and dragged components, packages, and role icons to configure your system. Although manual actions are great for initial development, you don't want to keep repeating the same actions as you develop a system.

The MTS Software Development Kit (SDK) provides a set of Automation-scriptable objects that you can use to programmatically perform the tasks you did manually in the previous chapters. For example, with Automation-scriptable objects you can automate regression testing, deploy packages as a product, and simplify administration:

> ➤ Automating regression testing—Testers of a client/server system can create scripts that create packages, install components, and configure security. Scripts that run unattended enable testers to create tests that are easy to execute and run over and over without intervention.

> ➤ Deploying packages as products—Microsoft intends for MTS to create a market for developers to create their own MTS components and deliver these components through a package to other software developers, who can incorporate the components into other client/server applications. An example of a prebuilt package is a specialized business calculation engine to compute sales taxes or interest payments. The developer of the engine can create an installation script that automatically installs the package under MTS.

> ➤ Simplifying administration—Transaction Server Explorer may not be an appropriate user interface to configure the system for some client/server applications. MTS scriptable objects enable developers to create entirely unique GUI applications, which offer Transaction Server Explorer's functionality but are fine-tuned to meet the specific requirements of the client/server system.

Preparation Understanding the Microsoft Transaction Server Scriptable Object Model

The MTS scriptable objects are installed to your system when you install the SDK (see Chapter 23, "Installing and Exploring the Software Development Kit"). Version 1.0 of the SDK exposes seven scriptable objects to your Automation clients. Table 24.1 lists each object and a gives a general description of its functionality.

Table 24.1. *MTS installation components.*

Object	Description
Catalog	Serves as the starting point to gain access to all other scriptable objects.
CatalogCollection	Contains a list of `CatalogObjects`. Use this object to add, delete, and modify MTS objects.
CatalogObject	Represents a MTS object. Examples of MTS objects are `Packages`, `Components`, and `Roles`.
ComponentUtil	Installs or imports a component into a package; a utility class.
PackageUtil	Imports or exports a package.
RemoteComponentUtil	Installs components from remote MTS computers to the local computer.
RoleAssociationUtil	Associates a role to a component or a component's interface; a utility object.

You can use the catalog objects (`Catalog`, `CatalogCollection`, and `CatalogObject`) to completely configure MTS programmatically. The catalog objects are fairly generic—you can create and delete objects, iterate through a list of objects, and retrieve and set the properties of objects.

The utility objects (`ComponentUtil`, `PackageUtil`, `RemoteComponentUtil`, and `RoleAssociationUtil`) perform very specific tasks, such as installing components, using specific methods from each component. For example, to install a component, invoke the `ComponentUtil`'s `InstallComponent()` method as follows:

```
objComponentUtil.InstallComponent "MyComponent.dll", "", ""
```

Task Creating a Visual Basic Application That Uses MTS Scriptable Objects

The tasks in this chapter collectively build the Beckwith sample installation program. This setup application installs the prebuilt `Beckwith.dll` component server under MTS control and then sets component transaction and security attributes. MTS scriptable objects handle all the work.

Follow these steps to create a new Visual Basic version 5.0 application and prepare it for manipulating MTS packages:

1. Start Visual Basic and create a new Standard EXE project.

2. Change the project's name from `Project1` to `BWSetup`.

3. Add two buttons to `Form1`, set their captions to Install and Uninstall, and set their names to `btnInstall` and `cmdUninstall` (see Figure 24.1).

Figure 24.1.

A new VB project with two buttons on its main form.

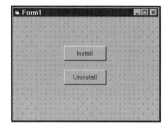

Before adding any code to use MTS scriptable objects, you should add a reference to the scriptable object's DLL.

4. Choose Project | References from the main menu. When the References dialog appears, locate and check the MTS 1.0 Admin Type Library list item (see Figure 24.2). If this item is not in the list, verify that the SDK installation is correct (see Chapter 23).

Figure 24.2.

Add a reference to the MTS scriptable objects through the Project References dialog.

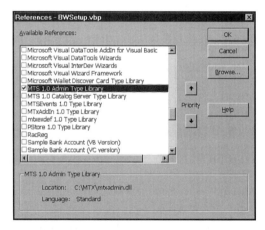

> **Note** The `BWSetup` example in this chapter uses *early binding*, which is accomplished by setting a project reference to the Admin type library. Alternatively, you can use *late binding* by omitting the project reference and declaring all variables as type `Object`. The scripting samples that ship with the MTS SDK 1.0 use the late-binding approach.

Task Deleting Packages

The first step in installing the Beckwith components into MTS is to remove any existing package named `Beckwith`. This step ensures that the setup program installs a fresh copy of all components. Follow these steps to add a `DeleteExistingPackage()` method to the `BWSetup` project:

1. Switch to the code editor that corresponds to `Form1`.

2. Declare a new global variable named `objCatalog` of type `Catalog` as follows:

```
Dim objCatalog As New Catalog
```

   `objCatalog` is the primary entry point for manipulating MTS.

3. Add a new, private subroutine named `DeleteExistingPackage()`:

```
Private Sub DeleteExistingPackage()
End Sub
```

4. Dimension a reference named `colPackages` of type `CatalogCollection` above the declaration of `DeleteExistingPackage()`. `colPackages` holds a collection of packages currently installed in MTS. The dimension of `colPackages` looks like:

```
Dim colPackages As CatalogCollection
```

5. Add the following lines of code inside the declaration of `DeleteExistingPackage()`:

```
Set colPackages = objCatalog.GetCollection("Packages")
colPackages.Populate
```

   The first line sets the `colPackages` reference to the collection of packages defined in the current MTS configuration. However, `colPackages` is empty until you make the call to `Populate()` to retrieve the current list of packages.

6. Add code that enumerates each package, looking for any packages with the name `Beckwith`. If found, that package is deleted. The following code accomplishes this task:

```
Dim nCount As Long
nCount = colPackages.Count
For i = nCount - 1 To 0 Step -1
   If colPackages.Item(i).Value("Name") = "Beckwith" Then
      colPackages.Remove (i)
   End If
Next
```

   The code declares a local variable, `nCount`, and sets it to the number of packages in the collection. Then the code enumerates the collection, looking for packages labeled `Beckwith`. If the code finds a match, it is deleted by a call to the `Remove()` method.

> **Note** The `For` loop in the preceding code works backward so that only one pass through the collection deletes all packages named `Beckwith`.

Before any changes made to a collection are permanent, you must commit the changes by invoking the `CatalogCollection`'s `SaveChanges()` method.

7. Add this final line of code to the definition of `DeleteExistingPackage()`:

```
colPackages.SaveChanges
```

Listing 24.1 shows the entire definition of `DeleteExistingPackage()` and comments:

Listing 24.1. *The `DeleteExistingPackage()` method.*

```
Dim objCatalog As New Catalog
Dim colPackages As CatalogCollection
Private Sub DeleteExistingPackage()
    ' retrieve reference to Packages collection
    Set colPackages = objCatalog.GetCollection("Packages")

    ' populate the collection with current values
    colPackages.Populate

    ' iterate packages, looking for and deleting any named Beckwith
    ' loop goes backward so only one pass needed through collection
    Dim nCount As Long
    nCount = colPackages.Count
    For i = nCount - 1 To 0 Step -1
        If colPackages.Item(i).Value("Name") = "Beckwith" Then
            colPackages.Remove (i)
        End If
    Next

    ' commit changes
    colPackages.SaveChanges
End Sub
```

`DeleteExistingPackage()` makes heavy use of the `CatalogCollection` object, one of the seven scriptable objects the MTS SDK exposes. Table 24.2 details the methods and properties that `CatalogCollection` exposes:

Table 24.2. *The methods and properties of `CatalogCollection`.*

Method/Property	Description
Add	Adds a new object to the collection.
AddEnabled	Determines whether new objects can be added to the collection. Certain types of collections do not permit the addition of new objects.
Count	Returns the number of objects contained by the collection.
DataStoreMajorVersion	Returns the major version number of the MTS data store. (Use `DataStoreMajorVersion` to determine which version of MTS you are scripting.)

Method/Property	Description
DataStoreMinorVersion	Returns the minor version number of the MTS data store.
GetCollection	Retrieves a reference to a specific collection. GetCollection() accepts a single string parameter—the type of collection to retrieve. Some examples are: Packages, ComponentsInPackage, and RemoteComponents.
GetUtilInterface	Retrieves a reference to the utility interface of the collection. Utility interfaces perform specific actions (for example, installing a component).
Item	Returns a specific item in the collection. The returned reference is of type CatalogObject. Item takes a single Long parameter, which is the zero-based index of the desired object.
Name	Returns the name of the type of collection—that is, the string passed as a parameter to GetCollection().
Populate	Loads the collection object with the latest information from the MTS data store.
Remove	Deletes an object from the collection. The object is not permanently removed until SaveChanges is called.
RemoveEnabled	Determines whether objects can be removed from the collection. RemoveEnabled returns False if the collection is read-only.
SaveChanges	Commits changes made to the collection to the MTS catalog.

Task Creating New Packages and Installing Components

When you delete an existing Beckwith package, you must create a new package. Follow these steps to create a new package:

1. Add the following declarations to the top of the source file:

```
Dim objBeckwithPackage As CatalogObject
Dim colComponents As CatalogCollection
Dim strInstallPath As String
```

objBeckwithPackage is set to the newly created Beckwith package after it is created. colComponents is used as the mechanism to install components, and strInstallPath is a string that is set with the path to the Beckwith.dll to install.

2. Add a new private subroutine, which takes no parameters, to the CreateNewBeckwithPackage() project.

3. Add code to create the new package inside the declaration of CreateNewBeckwithPackage(). Packages are added to MTS via the Packages collection object. Recall that a reference to this collection was retrieved and held in the definition of DeleteExistingPackage(). colPackages is a global variable that is a reference to the Packages collection. The following code creates a new Beckwith package:

```
Set objBeckwithPackage = colPackages.Add
objBeckwithPackage.Value("Name") = "Beckwith"
```

The call to the colPackages Add() method creates the new package. The default name of a newly created package is New Package, so the second line of code assigns the Name property of the newly created package to Beckwith.

Name is only one of many properties that a package object contains. Table 24.3 describes all the properties available for a package object.

Security is enabled by default for newly created packages.

4. Disable security on the Beckwith package with the following code:

```
objBeckwithPackage.Value("SecurityEnabled") = "N"
```

In addition to creating an empty package, CreateNewBeckwithPackage() also installs the components contained by the Beckwith.dll file. To install components, you must acquire a reference to the ComponentsInPackage collection. The colComponents variable was dimensioned for this purpose.

"ComponentInPackage" is a subcollection and is obtained through the GetCollection() method from the colPackages object. Recall that colPackages is a collection of all packages in the system. MTS scripting obtains all collections either from the root Catalog object or by invoking GetCollection() from already retrieved collections.

5. Add the following code to CreateNewBeckwithPackage() to obtain a reference to the "ComponentInPackage" collection:

```
Set colComponents = colPackages.GetCollection( _
    "ComponentsInPackage", objBeckwithPackage.Value("ID"))
```

GetCollection() requires two parameters: a string identifying the type of desired collection and a key specifying the particular collection. In this case the key is the ID property of the newly created Beckwith package.

Before installing the components, you must call SaveChanges() on the Packages collection to commit the new Beckwith package to MTS.

6. Add the following line to call SaveChanges():

```
colPackages.SaveChanges
```

7. Use the `ComponentUtil` object to install the components. `ComponentUtil` is a special utility object that installs or imports components into a package. You can obtain a reference to a `ComponentUtil` object from a `"ComponentsInPackage"` collection, in this case `colComponents`. Add the following code:

```
Dim objComponentUtil As ComponentUtil
Set objComponentUtil = colComponents.GetUtilInterface
```

8. Invoke the `InstallComponent` method of the `ComponentUtil` object by adding the following code:

```
objComponentUtil.InstallComponent strInstallPath, "", ""
```

`InstallComponent()` takes three parameters: the path and filename of the DLL to install, the path and filename of a corresponding type library if not bound to the DLL, and the path and filename of a custom proxy-stub DLL to use with the component server if necessary. The preceding code passes empty strings for the final two parameters.

Table 24.4 lists the methods available on the `ComponentUtil` object:

9. Save all changes to the `BWSetup` project and run it to check for errors. At this point the application does nothing—it still needs code to invoke `DeleteExistingPackage()` and `CreateNewBeckwithPackage()`.

Table 24.3. *The properties of a package object.*

Property	Description
`Authentication`	Numeric property that describes the Remote Procedure Call (RPC) authentication level for method invocations (see Chapter 9, "Configuring Component Security").
`Description`	This property describes text associated with the package.
`ID`	Read-only property that is a globally unique identifier (GUID) of the package. The GUID is a 128-bit integer represented as a hexadecimal string.
`Identity`	Specifies the Windows NT user account under which this package's server process should execute. Use the special string `Interactive User` for the process to run under the currently logged in user. `Interactive User` is the default.
`IsSystem`	Identifies whether the package is a special MTS system package. Property returns `Y` if the package is a system package and `N` otherwise.

continues

Table 24.3. *continued*

Property	Description
Name	This property is the human-readable identifier of the package.
Password	Validates the password of the user the Identity property defines. This property is write-only and is necessary only if Identity is set to something other than Interactive User.
RunForever	Specifies that the server process running this package should run forever—overrides the ShutdownAfter property. Valid values for this property are Y and N.
SecurityEnabled	Sets and retrieves the status of security on the package. Valid values are Y and N, and the default is Y.
ShutdownAfter	Specifies the number of inactive minutes a MTS server process should wait before terminating itself. Each package in MTS runs in its own server process.

Table 24.4. *The methods of the ComponentUtil object.*

Method	Description
InstallComponent	Installs all components contained by a specified DLL.
ImportComponent	Imports an already-registered component. The component is specified by its CLSID string.
ImportComponentByName	Imports an already-registered component but specifies it by its programmatic identifier (ProgID) rather than CLSID.

Listing 24.2 shows the complete definition of CreateNewBeckwithPackage() and comments:

Listing 24.2. *The CreateNewBeckwithPackage() method.*

```
Private Sub CreateNewBeckwithPackage()
    ' create new package object
    Set objBeckwithPackage = colPackages.Add

    ' set package name
    objBeckwithPackage.Value("Name") = "Beckwith"

    ' set security off, default is on
    objBeckwithPackage.Value("SecurityEnabled") = "N"
```

```
' get ComponentsInPackage collection of newly created package
Set colComponents = colPackages.GetCollection("ComponentsInPackage",
  objBeckwithPackage.Value("ID"))

' commit changes prior to installing components
colPackages.SaveChanges

' get component utility object
Dim objComponentUtil As ComponentUtil
Set objComponentUtil = colComponents.GetUtilInterface

' install the components
objComponentUtil.InstallComponent strInstallPath, "", ""

End Sub
```

Task Scripting Component Transactions

One of the primary functions of Transaction Server Explorer is to enable component transactions for installed components within a package. You perform this task by selecting each component in Transaction Server Explorer and its Properties option. Although this process is easy enough for a few components, Transaction Server Explorer doesn't currently provide any way to set the transaction attributes of several components at once. For large-scale systems, manually adjusting the properties of each component is a time-consuming task.

Fortunately, you can use MTS scriptable objects to automate this task. Perform the following steps to the BWSetup application to set the transactional property of all components to Requires a Transaction:

1. Add a new, private subroutine called
   RequireTransactionForBeckwithComponents()to the BWSetup application. This method takes no parameters.
2. Guarantee that the "ComponentsInPackage" collection, colComponents, is populated with current information from the MTS catalog. Add the following code to RequireTransactionForBeckwithComponents() to accomplish this:

   ```
   colComponents.Populate
   ```

   Recall that colComponents was set in the CreateNewBeckwithPackage() method.
3. Add the following code to iterate each component in the package and modify its Transaction attribute:

   ```
   Dim objComponent As CatalogObject
   For Each objComponent In colComponents
     objComponent.Value("Transaction") = "Required"
   Next
   ```

Note that colComponents is of type CatalogCollection, which can be treated as a Visual Basic Collection object. Therefore, you can use the Visual Basic language construct **For Each** to iterate all objects in the collection.

Transaction is only one of several properties that you can set and retrieve on component objects. Table 24.5 lists all properties associated with component objects.

4. Commit the changes by calling SaveChanges() on the colComponents collection. Add this last line:

```
colComponents.SaveChanges
```

5. Save all changes and build the BWSetup project to check for errors.

Table 24.5.   *The properties of a component object.*

Property	Description
CLSID	This read-only property is the 128-bit CLSID of the component.
Description	A textual description associated with the component.
DLL	This read-only property is the path and filename of the component's DLL.
InprocActivation	Specifies whether the component should run in the process of the component's creator, rather than in a MTS server process. Valid values are Y and N.
IsSystem	This read-only property is set to Y if the component is a MTS system component and to N otherwise.
LocalServerActivation	Specifies whether the component should be run in a MTS server process. The default is Y.
ProgID	This read-only property is the programmatic identifier of the component.
PackageID	This read-only property is the ID of the package that contains the component.
PackageName	This read-only property is the name of the package that contains the component.
RemoteActivation	Enables a component to run in another MTS server process on another machine. Valid values are Y and N.
RemoteServerName	If RemoteActivation is set to Y, this property specifies the machine name on which the component should be instantiated.

`RunInMTS`	This property defaults to Y to indicate that the component should be placed under MTS control. Set the property to N to prevent MTS control of the component.
`SecurityEnabled`	Set to Y if security is checked when methods on the component are invoked; N otherwise.
`Transaction`	Modifies the transactional property of the component. Valid values are `Required`, `Requires New`, `Not Supported`, and `Supported`. The default is `Not Supported`.

Listing 24.3 shows the complete definition of
`RequireTransactionForBeckwithComponents()`, along with added comments.

Listing 24.3. *The* `RequireTransactionForBeckwithComponents()` *method.*

```
Private Sub RequireTransactionsForBeckwithComponents()
    ' make sure components collection is populated
    colComponents.Populate

    Dim objComponent As CatalogObject

    ' change each component's Transaction attribute
    For Each objComponent In colComponents
        objComponent.Value("Transaction") = "Required"
    Next

    colComponents.SaveChanges
End Sub
```

Task Scripting the Creation of Roles

Add the following code to the BWSetup program to create the Roles needed for the
Beckwith College sample database system:

1. Add a new, private subroutine to the `CreateBeckwithRoles()` project.

2. Retrieve a reference to the `RolesInPackage` collection by adding the following code:
   ```
   Dim colRoles As CatalogCollection
   Set colRoles = colPackages.GetCollection(_
       "RolesInPackage", objBeckwithPackage.Value("ID"))
   ```

3. Add the six Roles necessary for the `Beckwith` package with the following code:
   ```
   Dim objRole As CatalogObject

   Set objRole = colRoles.Add
   objRole.Value("Name") = "Administrators"
   Set objRole = colRoles.Add
   objRole.Value("Name") = "Data Entry Clerks"
   Set objRole = colRoles.Add
   objRole.Value("Name") = "Managers"
   ```

```
Set objRole = colRoles.Add
objRole.Value("Name") = "Processors"
Set objRole = colRoles.Add
objRole.Value("Name") = "Professors"
Set objRole = colRoles.Add
objRole.Value("Name") = "Students"
```

A `Role` object exposes the properties listed in Table 24.6.

4. Commit the changes made to the `"RolesInPackage"` collection by invoking the `SaveChanges()` method on the `colRoles` object. Add this last line of code to `CreateBeckwithRoles()`:

```
colRoles.SaveChanges
```

5. Save all changes to the `BWSetup` project.

Table 24.6. *The properties of a* `role` *object.*

Property	Description
Description	A textual description of the role.
ID	This read-only property is the automatically generated 128-bit identifier (GUID) for the role.
Name	This property is the name label for the role.

Listing 24.4 shows the complete definition of `CreateBeckwithRoles()`, along with added comments.

Listing 24.4. *The* `CreateBeckwithRoles()` *method.*

```
Private Sub CreateBeckwithRoles()
    Dim colRoles As CatalogCollection
    Set colRoles = colPackages.GetCollection("RolesInPackage", _
        objBeckwithPackage.Value("ID"))

    Dim objRole As CatalogObject

    Set objRole = colRoles.Add
    objRole.Value("Name") = "Administrators"
    Set objRole = colRoles.Add
    objRole.Value("Name") = "Data Entry Clerks"
    Set objRole = colRoles.Add
    objRole.Value("Name") = "Managers"
    Set objRole = colRoles.Add
    objRole.Value("Name") = "Processors"
    Set objRole = colRoles.Add
    objRole.Value("Name") = "Professors"
    Set objRole = colRoles.Add
    objRole.Value("Name") = "Students"

    colRoles.SaveChanges
End Sub
```

Task Completing the Scripting Application

A few steps remain for completing the BWSetup application. You need to add code to handle the events fired when the user clicks Install and Uninstall on the main form. In addition, you want to add drag-and-drop support so that you can drop the Beckwith.dll on a compiled EXE version of BWSetup and automatically perform an installation.

Follow these steps to complete BWSetup:

1. Add a handler for the Click event of the Install button by adding the following code:

```
On Error GoTo failure

DeleteExistingPackage
CreateNewBeckwithPackage
RequireTransactionsForBeckwithComponents
CreateBeckwithRoles

MsgBox "Installation successful!"

Exit Sub

failure:

MsgBox "Installation failed with error code: " & Err.Number
```

This code invokes all the methods you created in the tasks earlier in this chapter. It puts some simple error handling in place in case a method fails.

2. Add a handler for the Click event of the Uninstall button by adding the following code:

```
On Error GoTo failure

DeleteExistingPackage

MsgBox "Uninstallation successful!"

Exit Sub

failure:

MsgBox "Uninstallation failed with error code: " & Err.Number
```

This code is similar to the code in the Click event of the Install button except that the Uninstall code invokes only the DeleteExistingPackage() method.

The final step is to add code to fill the strInstallPath variable dimensioned at the beginning of the chapter. The call to the InstallComponent() method of the ComponentUtil object uses strInstallPath.

3. Add a `Form_Load()` method to your project and add the following code to fill the `strInstallPath`:

```
Private Sub Form_Load()
    If Command() <> "" Then
        ' assume drag and drop
        strInstallPath = Command()
        btnInstall_Click
        Unload Me
    Else
        ' assume current working directory
        strInstallPath = "Beckwith.dll"
    End If
End Sub
```

When `BWSetup.exe` starts, the preceding code determines whether you passed a filename through the command line. For example, you supply a filename to `BWSetup.exe` if you perform a drag-and-drop operation or if you deliberately pass the pathname of the `Beckwith.dll` file on the command line when invoking the executable.

If a filename appears on the command line, the code calls the `cmdInstall_Click()` method, which automatically performs the installation. The application then automatically terminates.

If no filename is passed on the command line, `strInstallPath` is set simply to "`Beckwith.dll`", which makes the assumption that this DLL is in the current working directory or can be found by the system, given the current path search directories.

4. Save the project and run it. Click Uninstall and make sure you see the Uninstallation successful! message box. If you don't see this message, make sure you have correctly installed the MTS SDK (see Chapter 23) and that MTS is running properly.

5. Start Transaction Server Explorer and verify that no `Beckwith` package exists. Exit Transaction Server Explorer.

6. Copy the `Beckwith.dll` file from the `Beckwith\VB Components` folder on the companion CD-ROM to the folder in which the `BWSetup` project exists.

7. Return to the `BWSetup` application and click Install. You should see the Installation successful! message box. If the message doesn't appear, make sure that you copied the `Beckwith.dll` file properly from the CD-ROM.

8. Start Transaction Server Explorer and verify that a `Beckwith` package, complete with roles and components, exists. Verify that each component has been set to require a transaction.

9. (Optional) Compile the `BWSetup` project into an executable by choosing File | Make `BWSetup.exe` from the menu. Use Windows Explorer to drag and drop a copy of `Beckwith.dll` onto `BWSetup.exe`. You should see the Installation Successful! message box, but the main form should not be displayed.

Workshop Wrap-Up

The setup application for the Beckwith sample database system uses the scriptable objects that MTS exposes when you install its SDK. The sample uses both the catalog and utility scriptable objects to create and delete packages, to install components, and to set up roles.

Next Steps

➤ The setup program you built in this chapter is fairly primitive. You can expand its functionality to use more of the services MTS scriptable objects provide. Specifically, you could add the capability to export and import entire packages, modify more package and component properties, associate roles with components and component interfaces, and add users to those roles.

CHAPTER 25

Exploring the Software Development Kit's MTSSpy Application

Tasks in This Chapter

- ➤ *Building the MTSSpy Sample Application*
- ➤ *Preparing MTSSpy for Execution*
- ➤ *Running MTSSpy*

MTSSpy is a sample application that ships with the Transaction Server SDK. MTSSpy is like other spy programs, Visual C++'s Spy++, for example, which monitor the state of a running application and report significant events to the user. MTSSpy monitors packages as they run under MTS control and reports events to the user in a list control. MTSSpy is a great diagnostic tool to use if you are having problems with your components running under MTS control.

MTSSpy is a sample application; it includes the complete source code, which you can modify to meet your exact requirements. In fact, you must build MTSSpy before you can use it. This chapter shows you how to build, install, and use MTSSpy.

Task Building the MTSSpy Sample Application

Follow these steps to build the MTSSpy sample application:

1. Make sure you have installed the Transaction Server SDK. The MTS root installation folder (usually Mtx) should contain an Sdk folder. If the Sdk folder is missing, follow the tasks in Chapter 23, "Installing and Exploring the Software Development Kit," to download and install the SDK before continuing with this chapter.

2. Start Visual C++. (MTSSpy is an Active Template Library [ATL] C++ project.)

3. Open the MtsSpy\mtsspy.dsw Developer Studio workspace file in the Sdk folder.

4. Perform a full build on the project by choosing **B**uild | **R**ebuild All from the main menu. If you installed the SDK correctly, the project should build with no warnings and no errors (see Figure 25.1).

Figure 25.1.

A successful build of the MTSSpy project.

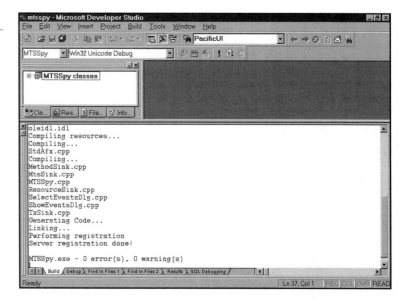

> **Caution** Do not attempt to run the MTSSpy application at this point. Complete the next task before executing the application.

Task Preparing MTSSpy for Execution

Before running the MTSSpy application to spy on MTS, perform the following setup tasks:

Set the following Registry key:

```
\HKEY_LOCAL_MACHINE\Software\Microsoft\
  Transaction Server\Extender\(Default) =
  "{6F9E4BD0-7970-11D0-B16C-00AA00BA3258}"
```

Setting this key enables MTS to fire events to event listeners like MTSSpy. Use the Windows tool Regedit.exe to modify this Registry key (see Figure 25.2).

> **Caution** Enabling events causes a performance hit in the execution of the MTS runtime environment. Make sure to clear this Registry key when you are finished spying on MTS packages.

Figure 25.2.

Using Regedit.exe *to enable MTS events.*

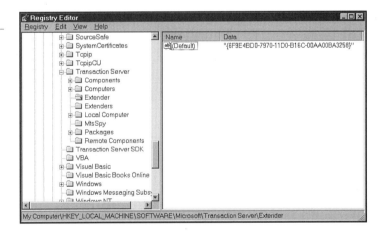

MTSSpy spies only on events of packages that are currently running. Unless a client application has requested a component instance from an MTS package, the only running package is the special System package.

Before running MTSSpy you need to force Transaction Server to "spin up" the Beckwith package so that you can spy on events that occur to components in that package.

Creating an instance of a Beckwith component causes the creation of a system process for the Beckwith package.

One of the simplest ways to create a component instance is to use the OLE/COM Object Viewer tool that ships with Visual C++. Follow these steps:

1. Start the OLE/COM Object Viewer application and locate the Beckwith.Student object in its tree view hierarchy (see Figure 25.3).

Figure 25.3.

The Beckwith.Student object in the OLE/COM Object Viewer tree view hierarchy.

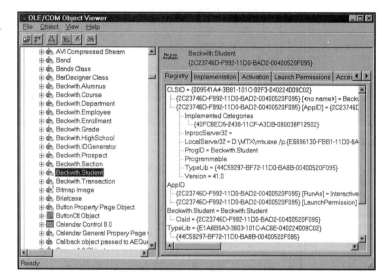

> **Tip** For more details on using the OLE/COM Object Viewer, see Chapter 15, "Setting Up Remote Windows Clients Using DCOM."

2. Create an instance of Beckwith.Student by right-clicking the tree item to display its context menu. Choose Create Instance from the context menu. The tree view of Beckwith.Student should expand to show the interfaces exposed by the component (see Figure 25.4)

3. Verify that indeed the Beckwith.Student component is instantiated under MTS control by starting Transaction Server Explorer. Select the Components folder of the Beckwith package. The icon for the Beckwith.Student component should be spinning (see Figure 25.5). This step proves that MTS has created a system process for the Beckwith package.

Figure 25.4.

The instantiated
`Beckwith.Student` *object in the*
OLE/COM Object Viewer tree
view hierarchy with the object's
interfaces exposed.

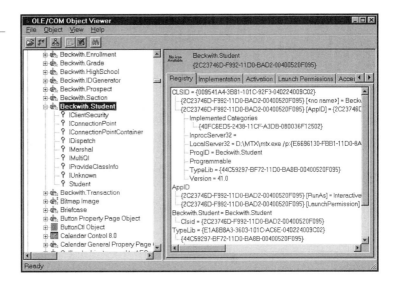

> **Note**　You do not necessarily need to keep the OLE/COM Object Viewer or an instance of `Beckwith.Student` running while you use MTSSpy. If you close either one, thereby destroying the instance of `Beckwith.Student`, MTS keeps the server process for Beckwith running.

> **Caution**　MTS shuts down a server process that remains inactive for a certain period of time (three minutes by default). For safety, leave the instance of `Beckwith.Student` running.

Figure 25.5.

The `Beckwith.Student` *compo-*
nent icon spins in Transaction
Server Explorer when the
component is instantiated.

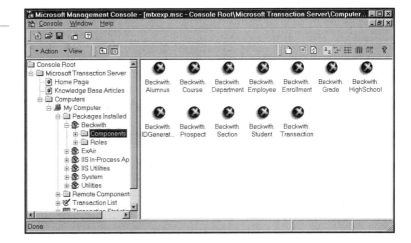

Task Running MTSSpy

Now that you have built MTSSpy, configured MTS for firing events, and created a server process for the Beckwith package, you can execute and explore the functionality of MTSSpy.

Follow these steps to execute and explore MTSSpy:

1. Return to Visual C++ and choose **B**uild | E**x**ecute MTSSpy.exe from the main menu to display the MTSSpy main window (see Figure 25.6).

Figure 25.6.

The MTSSpy main window.

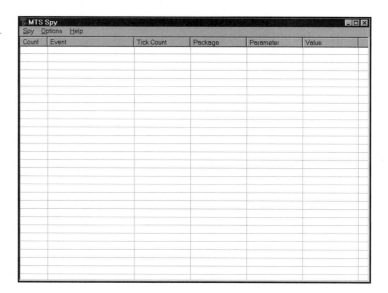

The main window of MTSSpy is a list control with six columns. These columns provide the following information:

➤ Count—A zero-based incremental counter assigned to each event

➤ Event—The name of the event that occurred

➤ Tick Count—The tick count of the system clock when the event occurred

➤ Package—The package from which the event occurred

➤ Parameter—The name of a parameter passed to the event handler

➤ Value—The value associated with the parameter passed to the event handler

You are now ready to begin spying on the Beckwith package.

2. Choose **S**py | **S**elect Packages from the main menu to display the Select Events dialog (see Figure 25.7).

Figure 25.7.

The Select Events dialog.

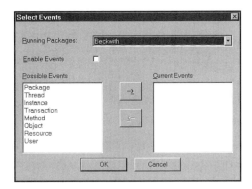

3. Make sure that the Beckwith package is selected as the Running Package (the MTS package you want to spy on).

4. Check the Enable Events check box to enable spying of events on this package.

5. Highlight all the items in the Possible Events list box and move them to the Current Events list box by clicking the arrow that points to the Current Events list box (see Figure 25.8).

Figure 25.8.

Enabling events for the Beckwith package and selecting all events to spy on.

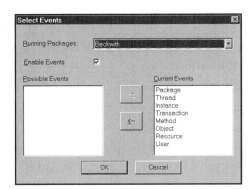

6. Click OK to begin spying on the Beckwith package.

7. Locate the Beckwith College Database System client application, Bcds.exe, and run it. Figure 25.9 shows the Beckwith College login dialog.

8. Click the Login button at the bottom of the BCDS login dialog. This button creates an instance of Beckwith.Student and invokes its Read() method. When the Main Menu dialog appears, click Logoff from the System to close the BCDS application.

9. Return to the MTSSpy main window. It now displays information about several events that occurred when you ran the BCDS sample application (see Figure 25.10).

Figure 25.9.

The login dialog for the Beckwith College Database System.

Figure 25.10.

The MTSSpy main window with captured events.

Note Your list of events may not be exactly like the one shown in Figure 25.10. For this example the `Student` component's `Read()` method was forced to abort its transaction to illustrate the usefulness of MTSSpy in troubleshooting component problems.

MTSSpy enables you to see the course of events for the lifetime of the
`Beckwith.Student` component. For example, in the following sequence of events,
the firing of the `OnTransactionAbort` event indicates that something is wrong. In the
previous event, `OnMethodCall`, one of the parameters sent by the event is `CLSID`,
which identifies the COM component whose method was invoked. This `CLSID`
resolves to `Beckwith.Student`, so you know the problem is with `Beckwith.Student` and
that you need to fix it.

➤ `OnCreateInstance`—Creates an instance of a component

➤ `OnTransactionStart`—Creates a transaction context for the component

➤ `OnMethodCall`—Invokes a component's method

➤ `OnTransactionAbort`—Aborts the transaction because processing in the
component's method failed

➤ `OnDone`—Indicates the component can be deactivated

➤ `OnMethodReturn`— Indicates that the method call returned to the caller

➤ `OnReleaseInstance`—Indicates that the component instance is released

10. Save the results of spying on a package by choosing **S**py | Save To **F**ile from the
main menu and providing a filename for the saved log.

MTSSpy saves its logs in tab-delimited format, making them easy to import into
spreadsheet programs such as Microsoft Excel.

Events Captured by MTSSpy

Table 25.1 contains a list of the events captured by MTSSpy.

Table 25.1. *Events captured by MTSSpy.*

Group	Event	Description
Instance	`OnCreateInstance`	Fired when a component instance is created
	`OnReleaseInstance`	Fired when a component instance is released
Method	`OnInstanceException`	Fired when an exception occurs during the processing of a component method
	`OnMethodCall`	Fired when a component method is invoked
	`OnMethodReturn`	Fired when a component method call returns

continues

Table 25.1. *continued*

Group	Event	Description
Object	OnActivate	Fired when a component is activated
	OnDeactivate	Fired when a component is deactivated
	OnDisableCommit	Fired when DisableCommit() is invoked
	OnDone	Fired when a component is available for deactivation
	OnEnableCommit	Fired when EnableCommit() is invoked
Package	OnPackageShutdown	Fired when a package's server process is terminated
Resource	OnResourceAllocate	Fired when a resource is allocated from the resource pool
	OnResourceCreate	Fired when a new resource is created
	OnResourceDestroy	Fired when a resource is destroyed
	OnResourceRecycle	Fired when a resource is returned to the resource pool
Thread	OnThreadAssignToActivity	Fired when a thread is used for object creation
	OnThreadStart	Fired when a server process is created
	OnThreadTerminate	Fired when a server process is destroyed
	OnThreadUnassignFromActivity	Fired when a thread is released
Transaction	OnTransactionAbort	Fired when a transaction aborts
	OnTransactionPrepare	Fired when a transaction prepares to commit
	OnTransactionStart	Fired when a component that supports transactions is created
User	OnUserEvent	Fired when a custom user event occurs

Workshop Wrap-Up

In this chapter you learned how to build, install, and implement the Transaction Server SDK sample, MTSSpy. You used MTSSpy to spy on the Beckwith package and to track down the component causing a transaction to abort.

Next Steps

You are ready to implement a full-featured, robust, and flexible client/server application built on top of COM components and MTS.

Good luck and happy coding!

PART VIII

Appendixes

APPENDIX A

Overview and Installation of the Beckwith College Sample Database

This appendix describes the sample database on the companion CD-ROM and provides instructions for installing the database on a fresh installation of Microsoft SQL Server.

Beckwith College Databases Description

The database on this book's CD-ROM appears throughout the *Roger Jennings' Database Workshop* series. The fictional Beckwith College in Beckwith, Texas, uses this database model to manage its prospective students, its current students, its staff, its business transactions, and its alumni.

The database tables for the system are divided into five databases, each representing a functional area of the school:

➤ Admissions

➤ Alumni Relations

➤ Business Office

➤ Human Resources

➤ Registrar

Because Microsoft Transaction Server (MTS) can coordinate component transactions across databases, this book keeps the databases separate. However, other books in the series may combine all tables into a single database for simplicity.

Figure A.1 illustrates each table and the database to which it belongs.

Figure A.1.

The Beckwith databases and their tables.

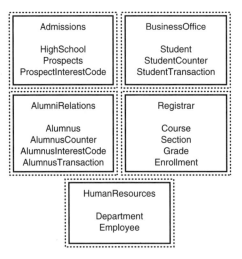

Installing the Sample Databases

Follow these steps to create and install the sample databases in SQL Server:

1. Create a device to hold the five databases. You need approximately 25 to 50MB allocated for the device, not including log space.

2. Create five databases:
   - ➤ Admissions
   - ➤ AlumniRelations
   - ➤ BusinessOffice
   - ➤ HumanResources
   - ➤ Registrar

   Give each database an equal portion of the device.

3. Run the corresponding Create SQL script with Microsoft ISQL/w on each database to create the tables in each database.

   For example, for Admissions run the CreateAdmissions.sql script found in the Beckwith\Database folder on the CD-ROM.

4. Mark each database as Select Into/Bulk Copy.

5. Run the LoadData.bat file from the Beckwith\Database folder, passing the name of your server as a single parameter. For example:

   `LoadData MyServer`

   This batch file uses the Bulk Copy Program (BCP) to fill the tables with data from the tab-delimited text files.

> **Note** For additional information and troubleshooting, see the Microsoft SQL Server Books Online for details on the Bulk Copy Program.

6. Run the corresponding CreateKeys SQL script on each database to create the primary keys for each table.

   For example, for AlumniRelations run the CreateAlumniRelationsKeys.sql script found in the Beckwith\Database folder on the CD-ROM.

7. Add any other indexes your application might need.

> **Note** To re-create the entire database system from scratch, review Appendix B, "Sample Database Schema and Entity-Relationship Diagram."

APPENDIX B

Sample Database Schema and Entity-Relationship Diagram

This appendix lists the details of the sample database schema and provides an entity-relationship diagram for handy reference.

Beckwith College Databases Schema

HighSchool		
HighSchoolID	char(6)	PK
Name	varchar(255)	
Contact	varchar(255)	
Address	varchar(255)	
City	varchar(50)	
StateOrProvince	varchar(20)	
PostalCode	varchar(20)	
Country	varchar(20)	
PhoneNumber	varchar(20)	

Prospect		
ProspectID	char(9)	PK
FirstName	varchar(50)	
LastName	varchar(50)	
Address	varchar(255)	
City	varchar(50)	
StateOrProvince	varchar(20)	
PostalCode	varchar(20)	
Country	varchar(20)	
PhoneNumber	varchar(20)	
EmailAddress	varchar(50)	
HighSchoolID	char(6)	FK – HighSchool
PrimaryInterestCode	char(4)	FK – ProspectInterestCode
SecondaryInterestCode	char(4)	FK – ProspectInterestCode

ProspectInterestCode		
InterestCode	char(4)	PK
Description	varchar(255)	

Alumnus		
AlumnusID	char(9)	PK
FirstName	varchar(50)	
LastName	varchar(50)	
Address	varchar(255)	
City	varchar(50)	
StateOrProvince	varchar(20)	
PostalCode	varchar(20)	
Country	varchar(20)	
PhoneNumber	varchar(20)	
EmailAddress	varchar(50)	
GraduationYear	char(4)	
PrimaryInterestCode	char(4)	FK – AlumnusInterestCode
SecondaryInterestCode	char(4)	FK – AlumnusInterestCode

AlumnusCounter		
CounterID	int	PK
NextTransactionID	int	

AlumnusInterestCode		
InterestCode	char(4)	PK
Description	varchar(255)	

AlumnusTransaction		
TransactionID	int	PK
AlumnusID	char(9)	FK – Alumnus
PostDate	datetime	
Amount	float	
Description	varchar(255)	

Student		
StudentID	char(9)	PK
FirstName	varchar(50)	
LastName	varchar(50)	

Student

Address	varchar(255)	
City	varchar(50)	
StateOrProvince	varchar(20)	
PostalCode	varchar(20)	
Country	varchar(20)	
PhoneNumber	varchar(20)	
EmailAddress	varchar(50)	
GraduationYear	char(4)	

StudentCounter

CounterID	int	PK
NextTransactionID	int	

StudentTransaction

TransactionID	int	PK
StudentID	char(9)	FK – Student
PostDate	datetime	
Amount	float	
Description	varchar(255)	

Department

DepartmentID	char(9)	PK
Description	varchar(255)	

Employee

EmployeeID	char(9)	PK
FirstName	varchar(50)	
LastName	varchar(50)	
Address	varchar(255)	
City	varchar(50)	
StateOrProvince	varchar(20)	

Employee

PostalCode	varchar(20)	
Country	varchar(20)	
PhoneNumber	varchar(20)	
EmailAddress	varchar(50)	
Salary	float	
DepartmentID	char(9)	FK – Department

Course

CourseID	char(9)	PK
Name	varchar(100)	
Cost	float	
Capacity	int	

Section

CourseID	char(9)	PK
Section	int	PK
Days	char(3)	
StartTime	char(5)	
Length	int	
ProfessorID	char(9)	

Grade

StudentID	char(9)	PK
CourseID	char(9)	PK
Grade	char(2)	

Enrollment

CourseID	char(9)	PK
Section	int	PK
StudentID	char(9)	PK

Beckwith Sample Database Entity-Relationship Diagram

Although the Beckwith database system is divided into five distinct physical databases, the contained tables operate as a single logical unit. The entity-relationship diagram in Figure B.1 illustrates the relationships across databases and tables.

Figure B.1.

Beckwith database system entity-relationship diagram.

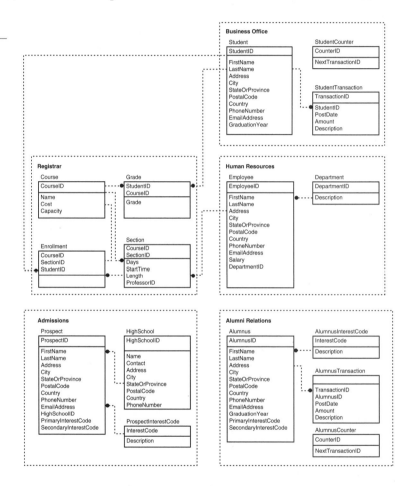

APPENDIX C

Beckwith Component Reference

This appendix lists each Beckwith component built in Part III, "Microsoft Transaction Server Components," and provides the Visual Basic syntax for each component's methods.

Alumnus

Sub Create(rgPropNames **As Variant**, rgPropValues **As Variant**)

➤ `rgPropNames`—Array of table column names

➤ `rgPropValues`—Array of values for each element in `rgPropNames`

Sub Delete(strID **As String**)

➤ `strID`—Identifier of object to remove from database

Sub Query(strWhere **As String**, rgIDs **As Variant**)

➤ `strWhere`—SQL WHERE clause for query

➤ `rgIDs`—Receives array of object identifiers that match WHERE clause

Sub Read(strID **As String**, rgPropNames **As Variant**, rgPropValues **As Variant**)

➤ `strID`—Identifier of object to read from database

➤ `rgPropNames`—Array of table column names

➤ `rgPropValues`—Array of values for each element in `rgPropNames`

Sub Update(strID **As String**, rgPropNames **As Variant**, rgPropValues **As Variant**)

➤ `strID`—Identifier of object to update in database

➤ `rgPropNames`—Array of table column names

➤ `rgPropValues`—Array of values for each element in `rgPropNames`

Course

Sub Create(rgPropNames **As Variant**, rgPropValues **As Variant**)

➤ `rgPropNames`—Array of table column names

➤ `rgPropValues`—Array of values for each element in `rgPropNames`

Sub Delete(strID **As String**)

➤ `strID`—Identifier of object to remove from database

Sub Query(strWhere **As String**, rgIDs **As Variant**)

➤ `strWhere`—SQL WHERE clause for query

➤ `rgIDs`—Receives array of object identifiers that match WHERE clause

Sub Read(strID **As String**, rgPropNames **As Variant**, rgPropValues **As Variant**)

➤ `strID`—Identifier of object to read from database

➤ `rgPropNames`—Array of table column names

➤ `rgPropValues`—Array of values for each element in `rgPropNames`

Sub Update(strID **As String**, rgPropNames **As Variant**, rgPropValues **As Variant**)

➤ `strID`—Identifier of object to update in database

➤ `rgPropNames`—Array of table column names

➤ `rgPropValues`—Array of values for each element in `rgPropNames`

Department

Sub Create(rgPropNames **As Variant**, rgPropValues **As Variant**)

➤ `rgPropNames`—Array of table column names

➤ `rgPropValues`—Array of values for each element in `rgPropNames`

Sub Delete(strID **As String**)

➤ `strID`—Identifier of object to remove from database

Sub Query(strWhere **As String**, rgIDs **As Variant**)

➤ `strWhere`—SQL WHERE clause for query

➤ `rgIDs`—Receives array of object identifiers that match WHERE clause

Sub Read(strID **As String**, rgPropNames **As Variant**, rgPropValues **As Variant**)

➤ `strID`—Identifier of object to read from database

➤ `rgPropNames`—Array of table column names

➤ `rgPropValues`—Array of values for each element in `rgPropNames`

Sub Update(strID **As String**, rgPropNames **As Variant**, rgPropValues **As Variant**)

➤ `strID`—Identifier of object to update in database

➤ `rgPropNames`—Array of table column names

➤ `rgPropValues`—Array of values for each element in `rgPropNames`

Employee

Sub Create(rgPropNames **As Variant**, rgPropValues **As Variant**)

➤ `rgPropNames`—Array of table column names

➤ `rgPropValues`—Array of values for each element in `rgPropNames`

Sub Delete(strID **As String**)

➤ strID—Identifier of object to remove from database

Sub Query(strWhere **As String**, rgIDs **As Variant**)

➤ strWhere—SQL WHERE clause for query

➤ rgIDs—Receives array of object identifiers that match WHERE clause

Sub Read(strID **As String**, rgPropNames **As Variant**, rgPropValues **As Variant**)

➤ strID—Identifier of object to read from database

➤ rgPropNames—Array of table column names

➤ rgPropValues—Array of values for each element in rgPropNames

Sub Update(strID **As String**, rgPropNames **As Variant**, rgPropValues **As Variant**)

➤ strID—Identifier of object to update in database

➤ rgPropNames—Array of table column names

➤ rgPropValues—Array of values for each element in rgPropNames

Enrollment

Sub DropStudent(strStudentID **As String**, strCourseID **As String**, nSection **As Long**)

➤ strStudentID—Identifier of student to drop from a course

➤ strCourseID—Identifier of course to drop

➤ nSection—Section of course to drop

Sub EnrollStudent(strStudentID **As String**, strCourseID **As String**, nSection **As Long**)

➤ strStudentID—Identifier of student to enroll in course

➤ strCourseID—Identifier of course to enroll in

➤ nSection—Section of course to enroll in

Sub QueryByStudent(strID **As String**, rgCourseIDs **As Variant**, rgSections **As Variant**, rgCourseNames **As Variant**)

➤ strID—Identifier of student to query for schedule

➤ rgCourseIDs—Receives array of course identifiers in which student is enrolled

➤ rgSections—Receives array of course sections in which student is enrolled

➤ rgCourseNames—Receives array of course names in which student is enrolled

Grade

Sub QueryByStudent(strID **As String**, rgCourseIDs **As Variant**, rgCourseNames **As Variant**, rgGrades **As Variant**)

- ➤ strID—Identifier of student to query for grades
- ➤ rgCourseIDs—Receives array of course identifiers for which student has grades
- ➤ rgCourseNames—Receives array of course names for which student has grades
- ➤ rgGrades—Receives array of student grades

HighSchool

Sub Create(rgPropNames **As Variant**, rgPropValues **As Variant**)

- ➤ rgPropNames—Array of table column names
- ➤ rgPropValues—Array of values for each element in rgPropNames

Sub Delete(strID **As String**)

- ➤ strID—Identifier of object to remove from database

Sub Query(strWhere **As String**, rgIDs **As Variant**)

- ➤ strWhere—SQL WHERE clause for query
- ➤ rgIDs—Receives array of object identifiers that match WHERE clause

Sub Read(strID **As String**, rgPropNames **As Variant**, rgPropValues **As Variant**)

- ➤ strID—Identifier of object to read from database
- ➤ rgPropNames—Array receives table column names
- ➤ rgPropValues—Array receives values for each element in rgPropNames

Sub Update(strID **As String**, rgPropNames **As Variant**, rgPropValues **As Variant**)

- ➤ strID—Identifier of object to update in database
- ➤ rgPropNames—Array of table column names
- ➤ rgPropValues—Array of values for each element in rgPropNames

IDGenerator

Function GetNextID() **As Long**

- ➤ Returns a unique integer used in transaction posting

Prospect

Sub Create(rgPropNames **As Variant**, rgPropValues **As Variant**)

➤ `rgPropNames`—Array of table column names

➤ `rgPropValues`—Array of values for each element in `rgPropNames`

Sub Delete(strID **As String**)

➤ `strID`—Identifier of object to remove from database

Sub Query(strWhere **As String**, rgIDs **As Variant**)

➤ `strWhere`—SQL WHERE clause for query

➤ `rgIDs`—Receives array of object identifiers that match WHERE clause

Sub Read(strID **As String**, rgPropNames **As Variant**, rgPropValues **As Variant**)

➤ `strID`—Identifier of object to read from database

➤ `rgPropNames`—Array of table column names

➤ `rgPropValues`—Array of values for each element in `rgPropNames`

Sub Update(strID **As String**, rgPropNames **As Variant**, rgPropValues **As Variant**)

➤ `strID`—Identifier of object to update in database

➤ `rgPropNames`—Array of table column names

➤ `rgPropValues`—Array of values for each element in `rgPropNames`

Section

Sub Query(strID **As String**, rgSections **As Variant**, rgDays **As Variant**, rgStartTimes **As Variant**, rgLengths **As Variant**, rgProfessorIDs **As Variant**)

➤ `strID`— Identifier of course for which to look up sections

➤ `rgSections`—Receives an array of section numbers

➤ `rgDays`—Receives an array of the days each section is offered

➤ `rgStartTimes`—Receives an array of section start times

➤ `rgLengths`—Receives an array of section lengths

➤ `rgProfessorIDs`—Receives an array of professor identifiers

Sub Read(strID **As String**, rgPropNames **As Variant**, rgPropValues **As Variant**)

➤ `strID`—Identifier of object to read from database

➤ `rgPropNames`—Array of table column names

➤ `rgPropValues`—Array of values for each element in `rgPropNames`

Student

Sub Create(rgPropNames **As Variant**, rgPropValues **As Variant**)

➤ `rgPropNames`—Array of table column names

➤ `rgPropValues`—Array of values for each element in `rgPropNames`

Sub Delete(strID **As String**)

➤ `strID`—Identifier of object to remove from database

Sub Query(strWhere **As String**, rgIDs **As Variant**)

➤ `strWhere`—SQL WHERE clause for query

➤ `rgIDs`—Receives array of object identifiers that match WHERE clause

Sub Read(strID **As String**, rgPropNames **As Variant**, rgPropValues **As Variant**)

➤ `strID`—Identifier of object to read from database

➤ `rgPropNames`—Array of table column names

➤ `rgPropValues`—Array of values for each element in `rgPropNames`

Sub Update(strID **As String**, rgPropNames **As Variant**, rgPropValues **As Variant**)

➤ `strID`—Identifier of object to update in database

➤ `rgPropNames`—Array of table column names

➤ `rgPropValues`—Array of values for each element in `rgPropNames`

Transaction

Sub PostTransaction(strTranType **As String**, strID **As String**, nAmount **As Double**, strDescription **As String**)

➤ `strTranType`—Either "Student" or "Alumnus"

➤ `strID`—Identifier of person's account to post to

➤ `nAmount`—Amount of transaction

➤ `strDescription`—Description of the transaction

Sub Query(strTranType **As String**, strID **As String**, rgTransactionIDs **As Variant**, rgPostDates **As Variant**, rgAmounts **As Variant**, rgDescriptions **As Variant**)

➤ `strTranType`—Either "Student" or "Alumnus"

➤ `strID`—Identifier of person to query for all transactions

➤ `rgTransactionIDs`—Receives array of transaction identifiers

➤ `rgPostDates`—Receives array of transaction post dates

➤ rgAmounts—Receives array of transaction amounts

➤ rgDescriptions—Receives array of transaction descriptions

Promote

Sub PromoteProspect(strProspectID **As String**, bForceFail **As Boolean**)

➤ strProspectID—Identifier of prospect to promote to a student

➤ bForceFail—True to force cross-database transaction abort

Sub PromoteStudent(strStudentID **As String**, bForceFail **As Boolean**)

➤ strProspectID—Identifier of student to promote to an alumnus

➤ bForceFail—True to force cross-database transaction abort

APPENDIX D

Useful Web Sites and Newsgroups

This appendix lists Microsoft Web sites and newgroups related to Microsoft Transaction Server (MTS) and other Microsoft BackOffice technologies.

Useful Web Sites

➤ www.microsoft.com/transaction—The main MTS Web page

➤ www.microsoft.com/support/transaction—The main MTS support page; contains pointers to the Knowledge Base for MTS and service packs

➤ backoffice.microsoft.com—Central Web site for all Microsoft BackOffice products

➤ www.microsoft.com/iis—The main Internet Information Server Web site

➤ www.microsoft.com/oledev—The OLE/COM development site

Transaction Server Newsgroups

The following public newsgroups are useful forums for posting MTS-related questions and answers. To access the newsgroups, set your news reader to the Microsoft newsgroup server at
msnews.microsoft.com.

➤ microsoft.public.microsofttransactionserver.programming

➤ microsoft.public.microsofttransactionserver.integration

➤ microsoft.public.microsofttransactionserver.administration-security

➤ microsoft.public.microsofttransactionserver.announcements

INDEX

out-process components, 343
output components, 16
overwriting
    data, preventing, 319
    events, 385
    files, 124
    MS DTC Registry, 71

P

package events, 476
Package Object property, 109
package objects, 457
Package Wizard, 88
PackageID property, 460
packages
    components, 141
        adding, 131-133
        deleting, 135
    creating, 118-120, 455-458
    deleting, 125, 453-455
    DLLs, 122
    empty, 118-120
    exporting, 135-136, 291-293
    identity, 140-142
    importing, 121-125
    MTSSpy, 472
    pre-built, 135-136
    properties, 109-110
        Activation, 126, 130
        Advanced, 126-129
        General, 125-127
        Identity, 126, 129
        Security, 125-127
    server processes, terminating, 476
    System, 111, 156
    Utilities, 111
    see also components
Packages Installed folder,
    108-109
Packages Installed property
    view, 110
PackageUtil installation
    component, 451
packaging Java COM objects,
    249-251
Packet authentication level,
    154

Packet Integrity authentication
    level, 154
Packet Privacy authentication
    level, 154
page scope, 344
Pakcage ID property, 110
PakcageName property, 460
parameters
    bForceFail, 373
    CommandText, 231
    False, 373
    in/out, 259
    MTSSpy, 472
    Options, 231
    RecordsAffected, 231
    True, 373
parent components (context
    objects), 176-177
Parent Nodetransaction
    attribute, 113, 414
Password method, 458
passwords
    PIN, 363
    storing, 165
paths, 323
performance, 407
    components, 169, 357
    drivers, 76
    IIS ISM, 73
    improving, 357
    three-tiered applications, 29
Performance Monitor, 382,
    386-390
Perl, 313, 315
PerlScript Web site, 315
permissions
    administrator, assigning,
        156-159
    System package, 156
Personal Web Server, *see* PWS
physical directories, 326
physical paths, 323
Ping utility, 425
platforms
    independence, 26
    support, 290
plus (+) sign, 98
pooling
    ADO connections, 330
    database connections, 12

objects, 12, 178, 252
ODBC connections, 330
resources, 12-13
threading, 12
Populate method, 455
porting applications, 30
POST method, 322
PostTransaction( ) method,
    209, 273
PowerBuilder, 5
pre-built packages, 135-136
Prepared transaction state, 415
preventing data overwrites, 319
printing reports, 392
procedure calls, 41
processes
    objects, 8, 19
    servers, 20, 476
processing HTML forms,
    320-322
processor performance, 387
ProgID (programmatic identi-
    fier), 49, 458
    assigning, 344
    edit box, 220
ProgID property, 412, 460
programmatic security, 15-16,
    145-146, 179, 209
Project menu commands
    Add Class Module, 193
    Add File, 194
    References, 192, 262, 270, 452
projects
    classes, 242-243
    compiling, 221
    creating, 241-242
    saving, 53
Promote component, 371-374
    ATL (testing), 235-237
    methods, adding, 221
    PromoteProspect( ) method,
        228-233
    PromoteStudent( ) method,
        235
Promote object
    PromoteProspect( ) method,
        221-223
    PromoteStudent( ) method,
        221-223

remote
access (imported compo-
nents), 134
activation (DCOM), 288
clients, 17-19
configuration (uninstalling),
295-296
IIS (managing), 311
servers, 48
Remote Components, 111
**Remote Components dialog
box, 401-403**
**Remote Data Objects (RDO),
257**
**remote procedure call (RPC),
169**
**RemoteActivation property,
460**
**RemoteComponentUtil
installation component, 451**
**RemoteServerName property,
460**
Remove method, 455
RemoveEnabled method, 455
rental threading, 183
reports, printing, 392
Request object, 319, 322, 326
Required value, 350
Requires New value, 350
**RequireTransactionForBeckwith
Components( ) method, 461**
**resetting aggregate transaction
statistics, 114**
Resolve menu commands, 416
resolving transactions, 414-416
resource dispensers, 440
resources
allocating, 476
creating, 476
destroying, 476
events, 476
managers, 440
pooling, 12-13
recycling, 476
see also database connections; threads
Response object, 322
**Response Times transaction
group, 114**

**Response Times transaction
statistics group, 417**
Response.Write method, 323
restarting
DTC, 417
MS DTC, 114
Retrieve( ) method, 170
retrieving
context objects, 253
data, 5, 227-228, 254-257, 333
returning
data, 322
method calls, 475
objects, 454
REXX, 315
**Role Membership Folder
property, 109**
Role Object property, 109
**RoleAssociationUtil installa-
tion component, 451**
roles
assigning
to components, 151-152
to domain users, 149-150
naming, 148
punctaation, 148
scripts, 461-462
security, 146-148
see also user groups; users
Roles Folder property, 109
**ROLLBACK TRANSACTION
statement, 38-39**
rollbacks, 232
components, 39
transactions, 38-39
rows, 330
**RPC (Remote Procedure Call),
169, 457**
Run Always property, 110
**Run command (Start menu),
133**
Run menu commands, 279
RunForever method, 458
RunInMTS property, 461
running
applications, 336-337
Beckwith College sample
application, 211-212
Beckwith components on
client computers, 294-295

components, 343
objects in processes, 8
PromoteProspect( ) method,
237
queries, 231
SQL SELECT statement, 254

S

SafeRef( ) method, 179
**Save Project command (File
menu), 53, 194, 279**
Save( ) method, 170
**SaveChanges( ) method,
454-457**
saving
MTSSpy results, 475
projects, 53
scalability
applications, 30
three-tiered applications, 29
schedules, 274
SCO UnixWare, 291
scripting languages, 315-316
scripts, 315, 324-326
business logic, 356
c-shell, 313
code, 18
components
combining, 357
transactions, 459-460
creating, 312-313, 350-351
date, 312-313
declaring, 350-351
directives, 315
event handlers, 463
HTML forms, 322
invisible, 313
limitations, 355
Notepad, 312-313
roles, 461-462
server-side, 316
time, 312-313
transactions, 18
**SDK (Software Development
Kit), 12, 97, 440, 450**
components, 443-444
files, 86
installing, 441-443
MTSSpy, 468-476
obtaining, 440

Windows NT 4 Server Unleashed, Professional Reference Edition

—Jason Garms

The Windows NT server has been gaining tremendous market share over Novell, and the new upgrade—which includes a Windows 95 interface—is sure to add momentum to its market drive. *Windows NT 4 Server Unleashed, Professional Reference Edition* meets the needs of that growing market. This book provides information on disk and file management, integrated networking, BackOffice integration, and TCP/IP protocols. The CD-ROM includes source code from the book and valuable utilities.

Price: $69.99 USA/$98.95 CAN *Accomplished–Expert*
ISBN: 0-672-31002-3 *1,776 pages*

Visual Basic 5 Developer's Guide

—Anthony T. Mann

Visual Basic 5 Developer's Guide takes the programmer with a basic knowledge of Visual Basic programming to a higher skill level. You learn how to exploit the newest features of Visual Basic, how to implement Visual Basic in a network setting and in conjunction with other technologies and software, and how to use expert programming techniques and strategies to create better applications. The book also contains a full section of real-world examples that you can incorporate into your applications. The CD-ROM contains the complete source code for all programs in the book.

Price: $49.99 USA/$70.95 CAN *Accomplished–Expert*
ISBN: 0-672-31048-1 *1,000 pages*

Visual C++ 5 Unleashed, Second Edition

—Viktor Toth

This book is perfect for advanced Visual C++ programmers. *Visual C++ 5 Unleashed, Second Edition* not only covers Visual C++ 5 and its capabilities but also teaches LAN programming, OLE, DLLs, OLE Automation, and I/O timers. The text also explains how to update old programs to the new version of Visual C++. The CD-ROM contains source code and illustrative programs from the book.

Price: $49.99 USA/$70.95 CAN *Accomplished–Expert*
ISBN: 0-672-31013-9 *1,000 pages*

Teach Yourself OLE DB and ADO in 21 Days

—John Fronckowiak

Teach Yourself OLE DB and ADO in 21 Days is a tutorial that guides you through the latest Microsoft server-side technologies and explains how to develop distributed Web-based database applications. Learn all about OLE DB and ActiveX Data Objects (ADO), utilize ADO and OLE DB for deploying distributed database applications, and discover how ADO and OLE DB work with new technologies such as ADC, Visual InterDev, Transaction Server, and Active Server Pages.

Price: $39.99 USA/$56.95 CAN *Beginning–Intermediate*
ISBN: 0-672-31083-X *688 pages*

Add to Your Sams Library Today with the Best Books for Programming, Operating Systems, and New Technologies

The easiest way to order is to pick up the phone and call

1-800-428-5331

between 9:00 a.m. and 5:00 p.m. EST.
For fastest service please have your credit card available.

ISBN	Quantity	Description of Item	Unit Cost	Total Cost
0-672-31002-3		Windows NT 4 Server Unleashed, PRE	$69.99	
0-672-31048-1		Visual Basic 5 Developer's Guide	$49.99	
0-672-31013-9		Visual C++ 5 Unleashed, 2E	$49.99	
0-672-31083-X		Teach Yourself OLE DB and ADO in 21 Days	$39.99	
		Shipping and Handling: See information below.		
		TOTAL		

Shipping and Handling: $4.00 for the first book, and $1.75 for each additional book. If you need to have it NOW, we can ship product to you in 24 hours for an additional charge of approximately $18.00, and you will receive your item overnight or in two days. For overseas shipping and handling, add $2.00 per book. Prices subject to change. Call for availability and pricing information on latest editions.

201 W. 103rd Street, Indianapolis, Indiana 46290

1-800-428-5331 — Orders   1-800-835-3202 — FAX   1-800-858-7674 — Customer Service

Book ISBN 0-672-31130-5

MACMILLAN COMPUTER PUBLISHING USA

A VIACOM COMPANY

Technical ---- Support:

If you need assistance with the information in this book or with a CD/Disk accompanying the book, please access the Knowledge Base on our Web site at **http://www.superlibrary.com/general/support**. Our most Frequently Asked Questions are answered there. If you do not find the answer to your questions on our Web site, you may contact Macmillan Technical Support **(317) 581-3833** or e-mail us at **support@mcp.com**.

WHAT'S ON THE CD-ROM

The companion CD-ROM contains the authors' source code and samples from the book.

Windows 3.1 and Windows NT 3.5.1 Installation Instructions

1. Insert the CD-ROM into your CD-ROM drive.
2. Choose File | Run from either File Manager or Program Manager.
3. Type *<drive>*\`SETUP.EXE` and press Enter. (*<drive>* corresponds to the drive letter of your CD-ROM. For example, if your CD-ROM is drive D:, type `D:\SETUP.EXE` and press Enter.)

Installation creates a program group named RJDW MTS, which contains icons to browse the CD-ROM.

Windows 95 and Windows NT 4.0 Installation Instructions

1. Insert the CD-ROM into your CD-ROM drive.
2. Double-click the My Computer icon from the Windows 95 desktop.
3. Double-click the icon representing your CD-ROM drive.
4. Double-click the `SETUP.EXE` icon to run the installation program.

Installation creates a program group named RJDW MTS, which contains icons to browse the CD-ROM.

> **Note** If Windows 95 is installed on your computer and the AutoPlay feature is enabled, the `SETUP.EXE` program starts automatically whenever you insert the CD-ROM into your CD-ROM drive.